WORCESTER TOWN RECORDS

1784–1800

Franklin P. Rice

HERITAGE BOOKS
2024

HERITAGE BOOKS
AN IMPRINT OF HERITAGE BOOKS, INC.

Books, CDs, and more—Worldwide

For our listing of thousands of titles see our website at
www.HeritageBooks.com

A Facsimile Reprint
Published 2024 by
HERITAGE BOOKS, INC.
Publishing Division
5810 Ruatan Street
Berwyn Heights, MD 20740

Originally published 1890
Worcester, Massachusetts

— Publisher's Notice —
In reprints such as this, it is often not possible to remove blemishes from the original. We feel the contents of this book warrant its reissue despite these blemishes and hope you will agree and read it with pleasure.

International Standard Book Number
Paperbound: 978-0-7884-1955-3

Preface.

After an interval of eight years, the publication of the Worcester Records is, with this volume, resumed.

The first essay in this enterprise was the printing in 1878 of the *Inscriptions from the Old Burial Grounds*, supplemented by a complete list of deaths in the town from 1717 to 1825. This publication was followed in 1879 and 1880 by the *Early Town Records of Worcester from 1722 to 1753*, in two volumes. In 1881 the *Records of the Proprietors from 1667 to 1788* appeared, with all the plans, some three hundred in number; and the next year the *Town Records from 1754 to 1783* were printed. At this stage, difficulties, chiefly financial, compelled a suspension of the undertaking for a time, to await circumstances more favorable for its continuance to completion.

In 1889, influenced by the laudable endeavors of the New England Historic Genealogical Society to induce the printing of town records, and the recommendations of the State Record Commissioner, The Worcester Society of Antiquity again considered the matter, and a Committee[*] was appointed to petition the City Government for an appropriation of money to aid the Society in the publication of the Town Records from 1784 to 1848. This Committee, after a careful estimate of the expense,

---

[*] Ellery B. Crane, Richard O'Flynn, Franklin P. Rice.

and with the assurance of support in certain sums from prominent citizens, felt justified in making a proposition to the City Council to continue the printing of the Records if the City would pay half the cost. There remained to be printed at that time to complete the history of the town organization, the Town Records from 1784 to 1848 and all the Births and Marriages to the year last named, and it was thought that the whole could be completed in five years. The plan set forth was, to undertake a certain portion each year, so that the small appropriation required would not embarrass the administration for the time being, as might be the case if the entire sum was voted at once. The proposition of the Committee was cordially met by the City Council, and, on petition, the sum of five hundred dollars was voted towards the cost of copying, editing, indexing, and printing, the Town Records from 1784 to 1800 inclusive, the City to receive one hundred copies when completed. The Society entered upon the work, and the result appears in the present volume.

The style and plan of the former volumes have been adhered to in the publication of this section. The peculiarities of the text are preserved so far as the possibilities of type will allow, and the proofs have been carefully compared with the original manuscript. A copious general index has been supplied.

RECORDS

Worcester Town Records.

At a Meeting of the Freeholders & Other Inhabitants of the Town of Worcester Qualified to Vote in Town affairs legally warned and assembled at the Publick Meeting house in Worcester on Monday the First day of March A, D, 1784 to act on the Several Articles mentioned in the Warrant for Said Meeting

Joseph Allen Esqr. Chosen Moderator

Capt Samuel Brooks Chosen Grand Juror For the year ensuing

Voted that this meeting be adjourned for half an hour then to meet at the Court house in this Town & the meeting Was accordingly adjourned——

Met according to the above adjournment at which Time and on the adjournment to the Second Day of the Same march the Following Town officers were Chosen & the Following Votes Passed–Viz——

Voted that their be Five Select men the Current year——

M^r. David Bigelow Colo Ebenezar Lovell Capt. Samuel Brooks Capt. Nathaniel Brooks Daniel Goulding Select men

Voted that the Select men be overseers of the Poor the Current year

Worcester Town Records, 1784.

Voted that the Select men be assessors the Current year

Daniel Goulding Town Clerk

Deacon Nathan Perry Town Treasurer

M^r. Samuel Jenison M^r. Josiah Perry Wardens

Joseph Allen Esqr. M^r. Isaiah Thomas M^r. Nathan Baldwin Committee of Correspondence & Safety

M^r. Nathan Hurd Sealer of Leather

M^r. James Macfarland M^r. Joseph Ball Tything Men

Leu^t. Samuel Bridge M^r. John Stanton Clerks of the market

M^r. Ignatius Goulding M^r. Josiah Flagg Fence Viewers

Field Drivers Mr Benjamin Whitney Jur. Capt. Joshua Whitney

M^r. Samuel Bridge Capt. David Moore Deer Reeves

M^r. Ignatius Goulding M^r. David Bigelow Surveyors of Bords & Shingles

Voted the Town Treasurer be Desired to hire money Sufficient to pay Josiah Pierce a Debt he has Sued the Town For—

M^r. Jonathan Grout M^r. Thomas Knight M^r. Daniel Heywood Leu^t. John Gleason Leu^t. Josiah Pierce M^r. Joseph Blaire M^r. Asa Moore Deacon Thomas Wheler M^r. Elijah Harrington M^r. Thadeas Chamberlain Mr James Barber M^r. Benjn Whitney Ju^r. Mr Asa Ward M^r. Daniel Beard Surveyors of Highway & Collectors of Highway Taxes

M^r. John Goodwin M^r. William Mahan M^r. Ephraim M^{c}farland Leu^t. Josiah Pierce M^r. Daniel Willington M^r. Nathan Patch M^r. Samuel Mower M^r. William Jones M^r. William Parker Ju^r M^r. Joseph Ball Hog Reeves

Leu^t. Samuel Bridge Capt. Samuel Brooks William Young Esqr. M^r. Jonathan Lovell Leut Phineas Jones Mr Elijah Harrington M^r. Nathan Patch M^r. James Macfarland M^r. Josiah Harrington Leu^t. John Gleason School Committee

Committee to Settle accompts with the Town Treasurer, Joseph Allen Esqr., Timothy Paine Esqr., & M^r. David Bigelow

Voted that M^r. Jacob Holms be annexed to the School Destrict Called the Midle Destrict

Voted that the Sum of one hundred pounds be granted Levied & assessed upon the Poles & Estates in this Town For the purpose of Supplying the Town with Schooling the Current year—

Voted that Eatch School Destrect do not Send to any Other but their owne

Voted to Choose a Committee to view the School Destrects None by the Names of Capt. Smiths & Leu^t. Perces & to take into Consideration the Petetion of Joseph Barber & others.[1] then Chose Colo Ebenezar Lovell William Young Esqr. & Capt. Samuel Brooks a Committee for Said Purpose & if they Report that it is best for them to make a Nother Destrect to Say where the School housen Shall Stand in Said Destrects

Voted that the Sum of two hundred pounds be granted Levied & assessed upon the Poles & Estates in this Town to be appropriated to keep the Publick & Town Roads in repair the Current year

Voted that the Inhabitants have Liberty of Working out their Highway Tax afore S^d. at the price of Six Shillings p^r. Day for a man & three Shillings p^r. Day a Yoke of Oxen & 1/6 for a Cart p^r. Day & that the price of a Plow p^r. Day be Left discretionary with the Surveyors

Voted that those that are deficient in Working out their highway Tax for the year 1783 be allowed to work them out on or before the Last day of June 1784 & those that have over worked be allowed towards their Tax the present year

Voted that the Swine go at Large the Current year they Being yoked & Ringed according to Law

Voted that the Select men be allowed their account being For Doctering Done to Kata Curtis & Cash paid for mendg the Bell £1-12 : 6.

---

[1] ARTICLE 11:—"To act if the Town See Cause upon the Petetion of Joseph Barber & Others praying the Town would take under consideration the disadvantages they labour under in regard to Schooling their Children & that the Petitioners may have liberty to expend their own money within their own Limits as by Said petition may appear."

Worcester Town Records, 1784.

Voted to Choose a Committee to Consider of a Number accompts excibited at this meeting against the Town they to make report at a Futer Time, then Chose Doct^r. Elijah Dix, Colo Eben^r. Lovell & M^r. John Stanton a Committee for Said purpose

Voted that the Select men be Desired to make enquirey in regard of Simon Glasco^s Support to now whether the Town is abliged to Support him or not & if need be to git Councel at the Cost of the Town

Voted to Choose a Committee to Collect the Tools mentioned in 15th article in the warrant[1] then Chose Colo Benjamin Flagg, Leu^t. Josiah Pierce, & Timothy Paine Esqr For Said purpose

Voted to Choose a Committee to meet at M^r. Saml. Browns Innholder in this Town on the Third Tuesday of this present march at Ten OClock in the morning & with them to Form into a County Convention agreeable to the Sixteenth Article in the Warrant for this meeting,[2] then Chose Colo Eben^r. Lovell, M^r. David Bigelow, & M^r. Robert Smith a Committee for Said purpose

Voted to Choose a Committee to Consider the Request of Daniel Goulding & John Stanton agreeable to the Twelvth article in the Warrant[3] & for them to make Report at the adjournment of this meeting then Chose Colo Benjamin Flagg, Deacon Nathan

---

[1] "A number of entrenching tools formerly provided by this Town for the Service of Government."

[2] ARTICLE 16:—"For the Town if they Should judge proper to Choose a Committee to meet at the house of Mr. Samuel Brown Innholder in this Town on the Third Tuesday of march next at tin OClock in the morning & with them to form into a County Convention & when So Formed to take into Consideration the Impost granted to Congress for Twenty Five years agreable to a Letter Sent by order of the Town of Sutton & a petetion signed by Ebenr. Lovell & Others Freeholders in this Town."

[3] ARTICLE 12:—"To See if the Town will Sell or lease to Daniel Goulding & John Stanton a piece of Land lying between the Pound & Capt. Palmer Gouldings Malt house of about one Acre for the purpose of erecting a Kiln & Other necessary works for carrying on the business of making Earthen ware & of erecting a Dwelling house thereon if the Said Goulding and Stanton Should think proper for their greater convenience" &c.

Perry, M^r. David Chadwick, Capt. Samuel Brooks, & Timothy Paine Esqr. For Said Committee.

Voted that the Committee Last Chosen take the Request of Samuel Flagg^s into Consideration & make Report at the adjournment Said Request being the thirteenth article in the Warrant[1] for this Meeting.

Voted that Leu^t. Joseph Barber be Collector of Taxes the Current year & that he giving Sufficient Bonds for the Faithfull performance of his Trust & that he be allowed three pence Farthing p^r Pound for Collecting.

Voted that the Select men fix the Weight of Bread agreeable to Law.

Voted that the Select mens Report relative to the monies arrising From the Sale of the Ministerial & School Lands be accepted

The Report is as Follows—Viz——

We the Select men of the Town of Worcester beg leave to report the following Accounts of the Monies arising from the Sale of Ministerial & School Lands, & also of the Sums of Money due on Account of the Sale of four new pews Lately made by order of the Town part of the amount of which is by a Vote appropriated to make good the Deficiency of the Ministerial money arising by Deprecation of the Remainder for Such as the Town May direct

In the hands of Capt. Palmer Goulding £ 46 - 13 - 4 Interest p^d. to No^v. 1 1783

	Stephen Dexter	33 - 6 - 8	Intr p^d. to No^v. 1 1782
Ministerial	John Taylor	42 - 3 - 4	Intr p^d. to No^v. 1 1782
Money	Ezekiel How	20 - 0 - 0	In p^d. to aug^t. 1 1780
So Called	Phineas Ward	22 - 15 - 0	In p^d. to No^v. 1 1783
	David Bigelow	35 - 16 - 8	In p^d. to No^v. 1 1783
	Nehemiah Hinds	50 - 0 - 0	In p^d. to Dec^m. 13 1783

In the hands of the Town   35 - 17-10   6 years In^t. Due.

---

[1] ARTICLE 13:—"To See if the Town will Lease or Sell to Samuel Flagg a piece of Common Land nearly opposite to Mr. John Nazros Store & between the meeting house and the Store of Samuel & Charles Chandler to consist of forty feet square for the purpose of erecting a Store thereon"

there was a bond originally given by Saml. McCracken & others for the Sum of £80. but by Said Bond being Shifted by former Select men & taken for the Same nominal Sum when money had depreceated, the amount thereof when renewed amounted only to the Sum of Eighteen pounds three Shillings & Sixpence (including intrest) which the Rev^d. M^r. Maccarty rec^d. as Intrest only on Said original Sum of Eighty pounds to June 12th. 1783 So that the principal Sum of the Bond is Entirely lost

School Land In the hands of David Baldwin £83 - 6 - 8 Intrest on which is due for three years ending March 29th. next as also one dollar due as Intrest on the preceeding year

and Likewise £8 - 4 - 4 in the hands of the Select men for the year 1780 not accounted for

Moneys arrising upon the Sale of four pews in the meeting House

Isaiah Thomas Bond Dated July 21st. 1783   £42 - 15 - 0
Elijah Dixes Bond the Same Date   39 - 5 - 0
Nathan Patch D^o. D^o.   33 - 5 - 0
Saml. Brown D^o. D^o.   39 - 5 - 0

Exclusive of the Charge of Building Said Pews

All which is humbly Submitted by us

M^r. Maccarty has rec^d. what Sums of Intrest have been Collected & which are appropriated to the Minister

Nathan Perry
Jos. Wheeler
Saml. Brown
David Bigelow
Jos. Allen

Select men of Worcester

Worcester Feb^{ry} 24th. 1784

Voted that this Meeting be adjourned to Tuesday the Ninth Day of this Present March at one OClock in the after noon then to meet at the Publick meeting house in this Town & the Meeting was adjourned accordingly

A True Entry   attest   Daniel Goulding Town Clerk

At a Legal Town Meeting Continued by adjournments From March the first Day A, D, 1784 to the Ninth Day of the Same March & then Met the Following Votes were passed–Viz—

Worcester Town Records, 1784.

Voted to accept the Report of the Committee Chose in Consequence of Daniel Goulding & John Stantons Request Said Request being the Twelvth article in the Warrant[1] for this Meeting, the Report is as Follows——

The Committee appointed upon the Petetion of John Stanton & Daniel Goulding Report that they have attended that Business and Viewed the Ground Petetioned for for the Purpose of Building thereon in order to Cary on the Pottery Business as mentioned in their Request——

Report that the Town dispose of the Following Piece of Land with the Consent of the Re^v. M^r. Maccarty to Said Stanton & Goulding Scituate between the Pound and Capt Gouldings Malt house being Part of the Ministerial Land, Bounded as follows Southerly upon the Common Land of the Towns where it measures Nine Rods and From the Pound where the Line of the Ministerial Land joyns on the Easterly Side of the pound to run North in a Line with the East End of the Pound Ten Rods then turning a Right angle & running Easterly Eleven Rods, parrellel with the South Bounds, then turning a Right angle & runing Southerly Parrellel with the west bounds till it comes to Capt Goulding^s Malt House & from thence by S^d. Malt house to the Common Land aforesaid—for the Sum of thirty Five pounds, that they give good Security to the acceptance of the Selectmen to pay S^d. Sum in one year with Intrest, & that the Intrest arising by S^d. Sum yearly & Every year during the Continuance of the Ministry of the Re^v. M^r. Maccarty be paid to him. and after that to be disposed of as the Town Shall order, and that S^d. Stanton & Goulding make & maintain the Fence round S^d. Land adjoyning the Other Parts of the ministerial Land the whole containing about Five Eighths of an Acre of Land, All which is humbly Submitted   Benj^a. Flagg p^r. Order

March 8th. 1784

Voted to Choose a Committee to give a Title to Daniel Goulding & John Stanton of a Piece of Land mentioned in the above

---

[1] See note, page 12.

Report & agreable to Said Report then Chose Timothy Paine, Joseph Allen Esq.rs & Colo Eben.r Lovell a Committee for Said Purpose——

Voted to accept the Report of the Committee in Regard of Cap.t Flagg.s Request,[1] the Report is as Follows——

The Committee appointed by the Town at their last Town meeting to Consider of the Request of Cap.t Sam.l Flagg Report that they have attended the Business and viewed the Ground Petitioned for for the purpose of Building a Store thereon and have alloted out a Piece of Land accordingly Forty feet in front & thirty three feet in rear upon the Easterly Side of a Direct Line from the North west Corner of the Front Porch of the meeting House to the South west Corner of M.r Clark Chandlers Store the South west Corner of S.d Plot So allotted out to be on S.d Line Just Eight Rods From the North west Corner of S.d Porch—That the Town Lease Said Plott of Land to S.d Flagg For the Term of Thirty years at the yearly Rent of Six pounds

all which is humbly Submitted
Worcester March 8th 1784   Benj.a Flagg p.r Order

Voted that the Select men of Worcester For the Time being be a Committee to give & Take Leases of the Piece of Land mentioned in the above Report and agreable to Said Report in behalf of the Town

Voted that if the Rent Should not be paid of the Land mentioned in the Last Report within Six month after it becomes Due then Said Land Shall go Back to the Town

Voted to accept and allow the Following Accounts Viz—

To Joseph Wheler Esq.r For Cash paid for Shirts for John Spence	£0 - 9 - 0
To Doct.r Thadeas Maccarty for Visits & Sundrys	1 - 12 - 6
To Henery Patch for Boarding & Nursing Mis.s Johnson & Dafters two weeks & paying the Doct.r by order of the Select men	2 - 0 - 0

---

[1] See note, page 13. The piece of ground above described is where the City Hall now stands.

To Robert Gray For Boarding Lydia Collins 17
   weeks at 6/0 p^r. week   5 - 2 - 0
To William Elder for Boarding John Spence 43
   Weeks ending the First Day of March 1784 at
   4/ p^r. week & Shirt Briches & Stockings for S^d.
   Spence   9 - 7 - 0
To James Quigley for Suporting Betty a Child
   of Nancy Brooks From march 1783 to march
   1784 being 52 weeks at 3/ p^r. Week   7 - 16 - 0
                                                       £ 26 - 6 - 6

Voted that the accounts allowed at this Meeting be assessed and Raised upon the Polls & Estates in this Town

Voted to allow M^r. John Nazro his accounts they to be Consolidated acording to the Time That the Other School Committee got Orders for their proportions of School money the year he was one of S^d. Committee his accounts is as Follows Viz 1779

Paper Mo

To paid M^r. Aron Hutchinson for keeping School
   4 weeks   £ 47 - 0 - 0
to paid Ephraim Mower for Boarding M^r. Hutch-
   inson   189 - 0 - 0
                                                       £ 236 - 0 - 0

Voted to accept the Report of the Committee Chose to enquire after a Number of entrenching Tools & that the Select men be Directted to Collect S^d. Tools & Depossett them with the Town Stock

the Said Report is as Follows, The Committee appointed to enquire after a Number of entrenching Tools formerly procured by the Town by order of Government Report that they have attended the Business and find that the original Number provided was, 1 Doz. Pick axes 1 Doz Narrow axes 2 Doz Iron Shod Shovels one of the Narrow axes is in the hands of W^m. Young Esqr. two Shod Shovells in the hands of L^t. Josiah Pierce—4 of

Said Shovels cannot be found and all the Remainder of Said Articles are in the Possession of M^r. Stephen Salsbury

     All which is humbly Submitted

Worcester March 8th. 1784   Benj^a. Flagg p^r Order

 Voted that this Meeting be adjourned to the First Monday in April Next at three OClock in the afternoon then to meet at this Place & the Meeting was adjourned accordingly

    A True Entry Attest

      Daniel Goulding Town Clerk

 At a meeting of the Freeholders & Other inhabitants of the Town of Worcester Qualified as the Constitution or frame of Government Directs in the Choice of a Governor Lieut Governor & Senators Legally warned a[nd] assembled at the publick meeting house in Said Town on monday the Fifth Day of April in the year of our Lord Seventeen hundred & Eighty Four—The following Persons were Voted for as Governor & had the Number of Votes expressed against their Respective Names

His Excellency John Hancock Esqr.	30	*Voted for*
Honble James Bowdwain Esqr.	12	*as*
Honble John Adams	2	*Governor*

 The Following Persons were Voted for as Lieut. Governor & had the Number of Votes expressed against their respective Names

Honble Thomas Cushing Esqr. 34 Honble James Warren Esqr. 2

 Then The following Persons were Voted for as Senators & Councellors and had the Number of Votes expressed against their respective Names—Viz—

Honble Moses Gill	40	Eben^r. Crafts Esqr.	1
Caleb Ammidown Esqr.	24	Rufus Putnam Esqr.	4
Isarel Nichols Esqr	26	Joseph Allen Esqr.	1
Seth Washburn Esqr.	31	Jona^n. Warner Esqr.	29
Saml. Baker Esqr.	16	Artimas Ward Esqr.	7

Worcester Town Records, 1784. 19

Honble John Sprague	10	Tim^o. Paine Esqr.	2
Honble Levi Lincoln	8	Saml. Curtis Esqr.	4

Voted that meeting be Dissolved & it was accordingly Dissolved
A True Entry
Attest Daniel Goulding Town Clerk

At a Town Meeting Continued by adjournments from march the First A, D, 1784 to April 5th Day & then Met the following Votes were passed Viz

Voted to Choose a School Committee man in the Room of Lieu^t. John Gleason he being out of Town Then Chose M^r. John Tatman a School Committee man in the Room of Said Gleason

Voted to Choose a highway Surveyor & a Collector of highway Taxes in the Room of Lieu^t. John Gleason he being out of Town, Then Chose Capt. Joshua Whitney a highway Surveyor & Collector of highway Taxes in the Room of Said Gleason

Voted to allow the Following accounts Viz

to Abel Heywood for Carrying Hannah Arnold to Grafton	£0 - 9 - 0
to Ditt^o. for Carrying Anna Packard to Holden	0 - 6 - 0
to Ditt^o. for keeping over Nnight Sarah Rider, Deborah Rebeckah & Philunder her Children & also Carrying them to Grafton	0 - 15 - 0
to Phineas Gleason for 2 Loads of Wood Delivered Simon Glasco	0 - 6 - 0
to Robert Gray for Boarding Lydia Collins one Week	0 - 6 - 0
	£2 - 2 - 0
Voted to abate Saml. Goddard a pole Tax in a Tax Committed to Daniel Goulding to Collect being	0 - 5 - 4
Voted to abate Benjamin Stowell a pole Tax in a Tax Committed to Daniel Goulding to Collect being	0 - 5 - 4

Voted that the Select men be a Committee to view the meeting house & See what repairs it is necessary to make to it & make report at the Next Meeting

Voted that the money Granted at this meeting be assessed & Raised on the Polls & Estates in this Town

Voted to accept the Report of a Committee Chose in Consequence of Joseph Barber & Others Petetioners, the Report is as Follows—Viz—

To the Inhabitants of the Town of Worcester in Town meeting assembled we the Subscribers a Committee appointed at the Annual meeting of Said Town of Worcester in march last in Consequence of a petetion of Joseph Barber and Others to view the School Destricts known by the Names of Capt. Smiths & Lieut. Pierces, Beg Leave to Report that we have attended Said Service and are of oppinion that the prayer of Said Petetion be granted —Viz that Jonathan Gleason, Thomas Stowell, Joseph Barber, Nathaniel Brooks, James Barber, Robert Smith, and Rufus Flagg, be considered as a destinct School Destrect and that the School house be Set upon the Road leading by Said inhabitants and as neer the Center of the way between Jonathan Gleasons Dwelling house & the Dwelling house of Rufus Flagg as may be which is humbly Submitted by Eben^r. Lovell ⎫
W^m. Young ⎬ *Committee*
Saml. Brooks ⎭

A True Entry   Attest   Daniel Goulding Town Clerk

[Articles in the Warrant for the March meeting not acted on :

"17th For the Town if they See cause to make enquiry upon what tenure those persons who Claim to hold the house erected on the ministerial land near the Country road hold the land on which Said building is erected

"18th For the Town to Take Such Steps as they may judge proper respecting 2 Cannon delivered to the Town of Glocester pursuant to a Recommendation of the then Council of this State"]

At a meeting of the Freeholders & Others Inhabitants of the Town of Worcester qualified to Vote for a Representative legally warned & assembled at the meeting house in Said Town on Friday the fourteenth day of May A, D, 1784 upon a motion made & Seconded & the question put whether the Town will Choose a Representative to represent this Town this Current year it passed in the affirmative—The Town then made Choice of Saml. Curtis Esqr. for their Representative—at the Same Time & place the Inhabitants qualified to vote in Town affairs being legally warned and assembled met & Chose Joseph Allen Esqr. Moderator & the following Votes passed Viz—

Voted the Sum of one hundred pounds levied & assessed upon the Poles & Estates of the Inhabitants of this Town for the Re^v. thaddeus Maccartys Salary for the Current year—

Voted that their be a Collection on the first Sabath of eatch month for the purpose of paying the Re^v. M^r. Maccartys Salary the Current year & that Eatch person paper & mark his money & be allowed the Same out of their Tax, begining the first Sabbath in July

on the fourth article in the warrant [1] a motion was made & Seconded & the Question put Voted that the Report of the Committee mentioned in Said Article be read & acted on paragraph by paragraph—the Report being read & passed agreable to the last Resolve & eatch & every paragraph being approved of it was moved & Seconded that the Same be Recorded in the Town Book & the original attested by the Town Clerk & Sent to the General Court of this Commonwealth as a Petition—the Report is as follows.

Commonwealth of Massachusetts   To the Honourable the Senate & House of Representatives of this Comonwealth

The Petition of the Town of Worcester Humbly Sheweth that although the good People of this Comonwealth have by the kind

---

[1] ARTICLE 4 :—"to hear the Report of the Committee Chose in march last for to meet in Convention & Vote thereon as the town Shall think proper"

hand of [the] Supreme Governor of the Universe been preserved through a long & an unnatural & Cruel war, & have by the Same protecting & over ruling hand arrived to a happy Issue and peace in our Borders : & although in addition to the above S^d blessing we are favoured with a good Constitution under which we Injoy a good form of Government : yet there are Certain matters of agreevence which this Commonwealth Labours under in general & this town as part of the Same, which we think may and ought to be redressed, of which we Shall mention to your Honoures the Following Viz

1^{ly} The giving into the hands of the honourable the Continential Congress the impost to be under their Sole controle we conceive to be a grievance, under our opinion ought to be Imediately Repealed not but that we are free & willing that an Impost on all Imported Articles ought & Should Imediately take place but the Revinue thereof ought to be paid into our State Treasurey and in a Constitutionaly way Drawn out by a warrant from the Governor of the commonwealth and if appropriated to Congriss or any other part thereof it ought to be Set to our own Credit that so we may Receive the Benefit of the Same which we conceive no State in the Union have any just Right to

2dly· Wee Conceive that the Expence of Days of Publick Rejoicing ought not to be paid out of the Publick Treasurey but ought to be paid by those who partake of the Same & not by the Comonwealth at Large

3dly· The making large grants to the Officers of the Continental Army or officeres of the Publick any more than a Honourable pay for their Services wee conceive a grievance & under our present Circumstances ought not to be & whenever any has been heretofore made they ought to be reconsidered for In our opinion the grants heretofore made cannot be more binding on the Good People of this Commonwealth than that of the Redemption of the Old Money which in our Opinion ought most earnestly to be urged by the General Court & that no further grants be made to Congress until the Other States in the Union Comply with the Redemption of S^d· money and that his Excellency the Governor be requisted not to sign any Warrant on the Treasurey for the Remainder of the four hundred thousand pounds which is now Assessed and paid or to be paid into the Treasury until a Redress is Obtained

$4^{thly.}$ That the Good People of this State are greatly oppressed & distressed for the want of a ballance of a Circulating medium, & that the Credit of the State greatly Suffers from no other motive than the Necessity of the people & by reason of the States holding the property of Individuals binds one part of the people So that the Other part makes their Necessity their Opportunity which much agrieves the good People of this State & we pray that ways & measures may be found out for Relief

Wee your humble Petitioners pray your Honours to take those matters into your wise Consideration & grant Such Relief as you in your wisdom may See Just & Reasonable as your Petitioners In duty Bound Shall ever Pray

Wee the Delligates duly & legally appointed & by our Respective Towns to meet in County Convention to consider of certain matters of agrievances which the good People of this comonwealth in general & this County in particular labour under are unanimously of the opinion that the aforegoing Petition be laid before the Several Towns in this County for their approbation & if by them approved of the Same be by their several Representatives to the General Court with particular Instructions to use their Influence to See that the Same be Immediately attended to

Ebenezer Davis P^r. Order

Worcester April ye 22th. 1784

Voted That the Select men be a Committee to Settle with M^r. John Waters for takeing care of the meeting house in Time past & that they agree with Some person or Persons to take Care of the meeting house & Ring the Bell

Voted that the Select men be a Committee to make necessary repairs to the meeting house in this Town & to New hang the Bell

Voted that the Sum of Fifteen pounds be Raised & assessed on the polls & Estates in this Town for the purpose of Repairing the meeting house & that the Select men be accountable for the Same — £15 - 0 - 0

Voted to allow to Edward Knight the Sum of Fifteen Shilling being for 5 Loads of Wood to Simon Glasco & that the Same be assessed — 0 - 15 - 0

Voted to abate a pole Tax to Joseph Sprague in Danl. Gouldings Tax he Bringing a Certificate certifying that his Son was not of age when the Tax was made — 0 - 5 - 4

Voted that the Select men be a Committee to Dispose of the Carriage belonging to the cannon in this Town & that they do the Same at Publick Sale

Voted that their be a Committee Chose to form instructions for our Representative & that they Lay them before the Town at the adjournment for their approbation, then Chose William Young Esqr. Capt. Joshua Whitney & M^r. Daniel Beard a Committee for Said Purpose

Voted that this meeting be adjourned to Friday the Twenty first day of this Instant may at four OClock in the afternoon then to meet at this place & the meeting was accordingly adjourned—

  A True Entry Attest Daniel Goulding Town Clerk

At a meeting of the Freeholders & Other Inhabitants of the Town of Worcester qualified to Vote in Town affairs begun & held at the publick meeting house in Said Town on Friday the fourteenth day of May A, D, 1784 & Continued by adjournment to Friday the Twenty first Day of the Same may at Four OClock P. M. & then met then the following Votes were passed—Viz—

Voted to take into consideration Nathan Johnsons Petition So far as to abate him his Town Taxes in M^r. Nathan Patches Taxes & for which he is now confined in Worcester Goal being the Sum of — £1 - 15 - 7

Voted that the Instructions formed by the Committee be read paragraph by paragraph & accepted as the Town may think proper then the Town Voted that the following part be accepted & Delivered as Instructions to our Representative

To Samuel Curtis Esqr. Sir having made Choice of you to Represent this Town in General Court the Current year not with Standing the Good opinion we have of your abilities and integrity we think proper to give you the following instructions

1^{stly} Whereas the Sea porte Towns by the General Court being held in Boston have great advantage of the Countrey Towns by takeing the advantage of a thin house to call in all their members to carry any motion that best Serves their intrest, you will therefore Use your best indeavours that the General Court be Removed into Some Town in the Countrey

2dly Whereas great uneasiness prevails amongst the good people of this Commonwealth Respecting our publick moneys we think it would tend to Quiete the minds of Said people to have an Exact account of the publick Debts annually published together with a particular account of the charge of Civel Goverment and a True account of all the money arising by Excise or otherwise So that we may know what becomes of our publick moneys and whether a proper use is made of the Same.

W^m. Young p^r Order

At a meeting of the Freeholders & Other Inhabitants of the Town of Worcester Qualified to Vote in Town affairs Legally warned and assembled at the publick meeting house in Said Town on monday the Twenty Eighth day of June A, D, 1784 the Following Votes were passed—Viz—

1st Joseph Allen Esqr. Chosen Moderator

2dly Voted that the Committee appointed in July Last to procure Some person or persons to preach upon Probation with a view of his being Setled as Colleague with the Rev[d]. M[r]. Maccarty continue the Service assigned them by the Vote aforesaid

3[dly] Voted that the Sum of Thirty Pounds be granted & assessed upon the Poles & Estates in this Town Towards Supplying the Pulpit with preaching or to Enable the Committee to do it

4[thly] Voted that the Selectmen be Desired & impowered at the expence of the Town to provide a Black Smiths anvel for Cato Walker & Lend it to him or Let him have it during their Pleasure

Voted that this meeting be adjourned to the Ninth Day of august Next at three OClock in the afternoon then to meet at this Place & the meeting was accordingly adjourned

    A True Entry   Attest   Daniel Goulding Town Clerk

At a meeting of the Freeholders & Other Inhabitants of the Town of Worcester Qualified to Vote in Town affairs begun and held at the Publick meeting house in Said Town on monday the Twenty Eighth day of June A, D, 1784 and Continued by adjournment to monday the Ninth day of august Following & then met

Voted that this Town hire a Grammar School master to keep School in this Town a greeable to Law the Remainder of the Present year

Voted that the School Committee Chose march Last to provide the Town with Schooling be the Committee to procure & hire a Grammar School Master to keep School in this Town the Remainder of the present year & that the School be keep in the Diferent School Quarters or Destrects according to their proportion of the other School money

Voted that the Sum of thirty Pounds be Raised and assessed on the Poles & Estates in this Town for the purpose of keeping a Grammar School in this Town the Remainder of the present year

Worcester Town Records, 1784.   27

Voted that the Committee Chosen to procure Some person to preach upon Probation Continue in office and that two be added to them then Chose Deacon Jacob Chamberlain & Deacon Nathan Perrey for Said purpose

Then Voted that this meeting be Dissolved & it was Dissolved accordingly

  A True Entry Attest Daniel Goulding Town Clerk

At a meeting of the Freeholders & Other Inhabitants of the Town of Worcester Qualified according to Law to Vote for Representatives Legally warned and assembled at the Publick meeting house on Wednesday the Twenty fifth day of august A, D, 1784 for the purpose of Voting for a County Register—then the following persons were Voted for as Register & had the Number of Votes expressed against their Respective Names— Viz

Timothy Paine	33	Luther Fisk	25	Daniel Goulding	19
Joseph Stone	14	Samuel Allen	5	John Nazro	4
Benjamen Reed	4	William Young	4	Benjamen Heywood	3
Samuel Brooks Ju^r	1	William Henshaw	1		

Voted the Selectmen be the Persons to Count & Sort the Votes

then Voted that this meeting be dissolved & it was accordingly Dissolved

  A True Entry Attest Daniel Goulding Town Clerk

At a meeting of the Inhabitants of the Town of Worcester Qualified to Vote for Representatives Legally warned and assembled at the Publick meeting house in Said Town on Monday the Twenty Second Day of November A, D, 1784 For the purpose of Voting for a County Register then the following persons were voted for and had the Number of Votes expressed against their Respective Names viz

Timothy Paine	36	Benj^a. Reed	13	Samuel Allen	4
Joseph Stone	24	Daniel Clap	7	Daniel Goulding	3
		Colo William Henshaw	1		

At a Meeting of the Freeholders & Other Inhabitants of the Town of Worcester Qualified to Vote in Town affairs Legally warned and assembled at the above mentioned Time & Place Passed the following Votes—viz—

Joseph Allen Esqr. Chosen Moderator

A Motion being made & Seconded & the Question put Whether the Town will hear any Candidates further or not and it passed in the affirmative

Voted that M^r. Haven be Desired to Preach for us another Day after the Time is out he has Engaged to Preach for us & Change with Some of the Neighbouring Ministers

Voted that their be a Day Set apart for fasting & Prayer in this Town for calling on the Divine for assistance for the re-establishment of the Gospel ministry in this Place   then voted that Thursday Senet be the Day Set apart for Said Purpose & that the three Deacons be a Committee to Desire Some of the Neighbouring Ministers to Preach with us on Said Day

Voted that this meeting be adjourned to monday the Twenty-Ninth Day of this Instant November at one OClock in the afternoon then to Meet at this Place & the Meeting was accordingly adjourned

  A True Entrey Attest Daniel Goulding Town Clerk

At a legal Town meeting continued by adjournment from the Twenty Second Day of November A, D, 1784 to the Twenty Ninth day of the Same month & then met the following Votes were passed viz—

Voted to reconsider the Vote passed Last monday in regard of hearing any Candidates Further

Worcester Town Records, 1784.   29

Voted that the Committee for Supplying the Pulpit be Desired to apply to M^r. Haven to preach four Sabbaths commencing the Sabbath after Next & to apply to M^r. Bancraft to preach the Next four Sabbaths after

Voted not to grant the Prayer of the Petition mentioned in the Fifth Article in the warrant for this Meeting [1]

Voted to Choose a Committee to view the Ministerial Land Laying near the meeting house in this Town and if they Should think it expedient for the Town to Sell any part of it to Lay out a Road & Building Lots & Draw a plan & Lay before the Town at the adjournment of this meeting then Chose Timothy Paine Esqr., Colo Ebenezar Lovell, Capt. Samuel Brooks, Capt. John Curtis and M^r. Robert Smith a Committee for Said Purpose and Voted that they Lay or Reserve a peace of Ground for a Burying Yard

Voted that Doct^r. Elijah Dix have Liberty to Build a Tomb in the Burying Yard under the Directions of the Selectmen

Voted to Choose a Committee to examine the accounts brought in against the Town at this meeting then Chose Timothy Paine Esqr. Colo Ebenezar Lovell & Capt. Samuel Brooks a Committee for Said Purpose

M^r. James Barber Chose a School Committee Man [2]

Voted that this meeting be adjourned to Monday the Thirteenth Day of December Next at one oClock in the afternoon then to meet at this Place and the Meeting was accordingly adjourned

    A True Entry   Attest   Daniel Goulding Town Clerk

At a Town meeting Legally warned and assembled at the

---

[1] ARTICLE 5 :—" For the Town to take into Consideration the Petition of Deacon Nathan Perry and Others in regard of having the Fore Seat Taken out on the Womens Side in order that Some aged women may have the previledge of Setting in Chairs in the Room of S^d. Seat "

[2] For Mr. Barber's School Quarter, so called.

publick meeting house in Said Town on Monday the Twenty Ninth day of November Seventeen hundred & Eighty four the following Votes were passed viz—

Joseph Allen Esqr. Chosen Moderator

Voted that the School Quarter in the Midle of the Town be Divided and that the Division Line be at the Barn of Daniel Heywoods

Voted that the Northern Division of the School Quarter in the Midle of the Town have Liberty to Erect a School house on the Towns land near the court house where the old School house Stands that the Same when Built be the property of those who Shall be at the Expence of Building Said house unless at any future Time the Inhabitants of Said Town Shall have occasion to use Said house for keeping a School therein that in Such case the Town to reimburse the Builders the value thereof

Voted that this meeting be dissolved & it was dissolved accordingly

  A True Entry Attest Daniel Goulding Town Clerk

At a Town meeting held by adjournment from the Twenty Ninth Day of November A, D, 1784 to the Thirteenth Day of December following & then Met then the Following Votes were passed, viz—

Voted to accept the Report of the Committee Chose to examine the accounts brought in against the Town which report is as follows—

The Committee appointed by the Town to examine the accounts of Sundrey Persons exhibited to the Town at their meeting on the Twenty Ninth of November 1784 Report that they have Exam^d the following accounts &c vizt.

No 1 Due to Willm. Macfarland for Mutton dd
   to Heps Bow[man]   £0 - 3 - 6

Worcester Town Records, 1784.

2 to Nath[n]l. Brooks for 70 [lb] Mutton dd
   Simon Glasco   0 - 17 - 6
3 to Sam[l]. Brown for Cash paid John Goodwin for mendg Bell   0 - 2 - 0
4 to Eben[r]. Wiswell for Sitting Glass &
   painting the Bell Fraim   1 - 18 - 11
5 to Mary Bigelow for Boarding Lydia Indian   6 - 18 - 0
6 to Ephraim Miller for two loads of wood
   dd Heps Bowman   0 - 5 - 0
7 to Sam[l]. Brooks for meat & meal dd
   Simon Glasco   6 - 1 - 9
8 to Thomas Knight for Sundreys dd Cato
   Walker   2 - 12 - 4
9 to Thomas Knight for Salt Pork dd
   Simon [Glasco] 3/9 & a Journey to
   Carry a Seighttation to the Select   1 - 1 - 9
   men of Framingham 18/
10 To Jedediah Heley for a Coffin for
   M[c].Neel 10/ for a Coffin for M[r].
   Maccarty, 12/ & one D°. for M[r].
   Weltch 10/ & 1 D° for Lydia Bo-   6 - 12 - 0
   man 10/ & making a Fraim Wheel
   & Block for the Bell 90/
11 to John Stowers for Time horse &
   Expenses after Bearers for the Funeral of the Re[v]. M[r]. Maccarty   1 - 0 - 0
12 to John Goodwin for work Done to
   the Bell   0 - 19 - 10
13 to Simeon Duncan for Diging a grave
   for M[c]Neal 8/ & Sundrey other
   graves & Work Done to the Herce 39/   2 - 7 - 0
14 to Sam[l]. & Stephen Salsbury to Sundreys dd Miss Betsey & Lucy Maccarty 70/4 & Glass for the Meeting
   house 36/6   4 - 16 - 10
15 to John Nazro for Sundreys dd at
   Re[v]. M[r]. Maccartys Funeral   11 4 - 6½

16	to Daniel Goulding for Sundreys for the Rev. Mr. Maccartys Funeral 14/3 for Sundreys for to Lay out Mr. Weltch 11/8 for a Rope for the Bell 14/	1 - 19 - 11
17	to Ebenr. Lovel Ephm. Miller & John Chamberlain for Defending agst. Judge Lincolns application to the Court for an abatement of Taxes	11 - 7 - 0
18	to Joseph Miller for Carrying Sundrey Persons out of Town	3 - 2 - 8
19	to Ebenr. Lovel Ephraim Miller & Phineas Jones for making Taxes & Valuation 7 Days Each 4/ pr Day	4 - 4 - 0
20	to Hepsebeth Bowman for Sundreys and attendance for her mother	2 - 7 - 3
21	to Edward Knight for 2 Loads of Wood dd Simon Glasco	0 - 12 - 0

£ 70 - 13 - 9½

which Accounts the Committee Submitt to the Town for their allowance   pr Timo Paine pr order

Voted that the Sum of three Shillings pr. week be allowed to Samuel Eaton for Supporting his mother from Sept. 1st. 1782 to the 1st of Sept. 1784

Voted that the Selectmen be Desired to make Enquirey whether or Not three Shillings a Week is not Sufficient for Samuel Eaton to have for the Support of his mother & make report at Some futer meeting

Voted that the money granted at this meeting be Levied & assessed on the Polls & Estates in this Town

Voted to Reconsider the Reconsidering Vote passed Last meeting

Voted to Choose three Persons in addition to the Committee for Supplying the Pulpit in the Room of three that have resigned this Day then Chose Capt. John Curtis, Deacon Thomas Wheler & Capt. Saml. Brooks for Said purpose

Voted that the Committee apply to some person or persons to Preach until the Time M[r]. Haven & M[r]. Bancraft come

Voted that the Committee request M[r]. Haven & M[r]. Bancraft to Preach agreeable to a Vote of this Town passed Last meeting

Voted that the thanks of the Town be given to three of the Gentlemen Committee for Supplying the Pulpit that have this day resigned viz—Joseph Allen, Joseph Wheler, & Timothy Paine Esq[rs].

The Committee appointed by the Town at their meeting held on y[e] 29th of No[v]. A, D, 1784 to take into Consideration that article relating to the Sale of the Ministerial Land are of opinion that it would be most for the advantage of the Town to sell the Same, and in order to Sell it for a greater Price the Committee humbly propose to the Town the following Method, Viz[t]. That that part of Said Land lying North of the Common be Divided by a Road to be laid out two Rods and a half wide through S[d] Lott beginning at the Town Street North of Chandlers Homestead and to run Easterly along the North Side of Said Homestead and in that course a Strait Line Untill it goes as far East as Land Lately Sold by the Town to Mess[rs]. Stanton & Goulding, then to turn and run by the Towns Land & Land of Said Stanton & Goulding out to the common. That the Land upon the Northerly Side of Said New proposed Road be divided into Six Lotts, the Lott Next to the Town Street to front on S[d] New Road Twelve Rods Each the other Lotts to have equal Fronts on S[d] Road of about Nine Rods, and all S[d] Lotts to extend as far as the North as the Ministerial Land Extends. That the Lands Lying South of Said New proposed Road be Divided into four Lotts fronting on the common Six Rods and an half the three Eastermost Lotts to be of equal wedth at Each End, the westermost Lott, its proposed Shall be reserved and not Sold, at Present and that the Land lying Northerly of Said Goulding & Stantons Land be reserved for a burying Place if the Town please, and in order to give the Town a general Idea of the above proposed method they have made a Plan of S[d] Lotts and marked out thereon S[d] new proposed Road and here with exhibitt y[e] Same

All which is humbly Submitted   Tim[o]. Paine p[r]. order

5

The above Report having been read is accepted & thereupon Voted that Timothy Paine Esqr., Capt. John Curtis, Joseph Allen Esqr., Colo Timothy Bigelow & Colo Eben^r. Lovell or the major part of them be a Committee to make Sale of part of the Ministerial Land So called, in this Town, agreeable to S^d. Report that they Sell the Same by publick auction for the most the Same will fetch after giving Seasonable Notice in the Worcester Gazette & make Execute & Deliver good & Sufficient deed or Deeds in Law to the purchaseer or purchasers, & take reasonable Security for the payment of the Sum or Sums for which they may Sell payable to the Town in one year from the Time of Sale with Lawfull Interest therefor

Voted that the Selectmen be Desired to use their Endeavours to get Some of the above accounts which ought to be paid by Some other Town or by Some Person or Persons

Voted that this Meeting be adjourned to monday the Twenty Seventh Day of this Instant December at one OClock in the afternoon then to meet at this Place & the meeting was accordingly adjourned

A True Entry Attest Daniel Goulding Town Clerk

At a Town meeting held on Monday the Twenty Second day of November A, D, 1784 and continued by adjournment From Time to Time to this Twenty Seventh Day of December & then Met then the following Votes were passed—viz—

Voted that the walls of the Present Pound be removed on the Ground between Capt. Gouldings & M^r. Stowells & that Capt. Samuel Brooks Capt. Nathaniel Brooks & Capt. John Curtis be a Committee to remove Said Pound in the Cheapest & Best way they can

Voted that the proprietors of the house w[h]ere M^r. Samuel Warden Lives have Liberty to move it of the ground in a Reasonable time after the Land is Sold

Worcester Town Records, 1785.

Voted that the proprietors of the new School house on the common have Liberty to move it after the Sale of the Land

Voted to allow the following accounts & that they be assessed on the Polls & Estates in this Town in the Next Town Tax—viz

To M^r. Daniel Waldo for Shugar dd Capt.
Brook for Cato Walkers use £0 - 4 - 6
To M^r. Solomon Bixbee for Plank for a Bridge   0 - 13 - 4
£0 - 17 - 10

Voted to allow the Quarter Sessions Liberty free from expence to git Rock of Mill Stone hill to Build a New Goal in this Town

Voted that the Selectmen be requested to Lay out the New proposed Road in the Ministerial Land

Voted that this meeting be dissolved & it was accordingly Dissolved

A True Entry   Attest   Daniel Goulding Town Clerk

I the Subscriber hereby Promise that I discharge & indemnify the Town of Worcester against any cost that has arrisen to this date in consequence of one Dinah Barbers being Brought into Town as one of Said Towns Poor

Worcester February 24th. 1785   James Barber

At a Meeting of the Freeholders & Other Inhabitants of the Town of Worcester Qualified to Vote in Town affairs Legally warned & assembled at the publick meeting house in Said Town on Tuesday the first Day of March in the year of our Lord Seventeen hundred & Eighty Five

Deacon Nathan Perry Chosen Moderator

It was Moved, that the Town agree to Settle M^r. Bancraft in the work of the Gospel Ministry, and Such other Person as may be agreable to and chosen Solely by those who are desierous of hearing furthar and the Settlement and Salaries of both to be at the Expence of the Town at Large, & the Question being put it passed in the Negative

It was then Moved, inasmuch as the Town by their Last vote have refused to Settle M^r. Bancraft as a Minister that the Town will consent that those persons who are Satisfied with M^r. Bancraft & Desirous of Settling him may form into a religious Society for that purpose, & the Question being put it passed in the Negative

Voted to Choose a Committee of three Persons to Take into consideration the Petetion of a Number of Inhabitants Living in the gore So called in regard of their being anexed to Worcester & to Run the Line where they think it is most Proper the Line Should be & make Report to the Town as Soon as may be Then Chose M^r. Daniel Beard, Capt. John Pierce & Colo Benjamin Flagg a Committee for Said Purpose

The Petition Mentioned in the Second Article in the Warrant for this Meeting [1]

To the Selectmen and the Committee for Supplying the Pulpit in the Town of Worcester

Gentlemen

For near two years before the Decease of the Rev^d. M^r. Maccarty it was cruel to have wished and unreasonable to have expected of him a Discharge of the Ministerial Duties of his office Such was his health & Such the Nature of his complaints at that Time as deprived us in a great measure of the Benefit of his Services this Parish was in a Degree vacant which rendered it necessary to think of Some Person Suitable for his

---

[1] ARTICLE 2:—"To hear the Petition of a Number of Inhabitants of this Town addressed to the Selectmen & Committee for Supplying the pulpit that Such measures may be adopted for the Settlement of a Minister in the Town of Worcester as may Seem most proper & fit & most conducive to the peace welfare & happiness of the Town "

Worcester Town Records, 1785. 37

assistant or his Successor—three years have almost elapsed and the Business is yet to Be done From the Scarcity of Preachers and the Difficulty of procureing them our Pulpit has been frequently unsupplyed and the Town Destitute of Publick worship—About eighteen Months Since the Town thought it expedient to Settle a Colleague with their then worthy Pastor and they then passed a Vote & chose a Committee for that Purpose. it then became the Duty of the Committee in particular as well as the Interest & Duty of the Town at Large to enquire after and communicate their Knowlidge of Such Caracters as would probably have Suited and given Satisfaction to the Town—the Committee we Trust have been faithfull if not it is to be hoped the Town have not been unfaithfull to themselves there has been Sufficient oppertunity in Point of Time and yet no one Person can be even mentioned in whom it is probable the Town would be united or so well united in the Person they have already heard —a former Committee reported Publickly that they had done their best and that they could hear of no Candidate whom there was any reason to Suppose would be so generally agreable as those they had procured recent Endeavors have confirmed the Report it is Time Something was done many Parishes must continue vacant the Number of Preachers not being half Sufficient to Supply them the Longer they are So the greater the Danger of Division religious contentions and party Strife

The Gentleman now with us is preaching under a third Invitation from the Town, to his Sentiments there have been but few objections in the Breast of any to his Character his Person or his abilities we know of none—perfect Unanimity is not to be expected to wait for it will be to wait forever—most people have had an opportunity to form their opinions their Preatcher has been Explisit & un Reserved the Subscribers are Satisfied with his Character his abilities and ministerial accomplishments and think it of Importance to themselves and the Town to have him Settled —Under these Circumstances they wish for Such Proceedings as may be fair equal & consistant with the Rights Sentiments & religious Liberties of all—they have on Principle and with Deliberation & Information made their Choice and consider the

Object of their Choice as a Person qualified to be of particular Benefit to Individuals and a Singular Blessing to the Town most devoutly hoping that the honest Difference in Sentiments among Proffessed Christians may not occasion a want of Charity or a Spirit of Bitterness———Therefore the Subscribers from the great Probability of M^r. Bancrafts being engaged else where do now beg the Selectmen & the Committee aforesaid to adopt Such measures for the Settlement of him as a minister in the Town of Worcester as may Seem to them most proper & fit and most conducive to the Peace welfare and Happiness of the Town

Worcester January 13th. 1785

Joseph Wheler, Saml. Curtis, Tim^o. Paine, Palmer Goulding, Benjamen Flagg, Saml. Bridge, John Goodwin, William Gates, Lemuel Rice, Nathan Patch, Samuel Brazier, Nathl. Paine, Ignatius Goulding, Thaddeus Maccarty, John Pierce, John Stowers, Jed^e. Healey, William Treadwell, John Mower, Micah Johnson, Charles Stearns, Benj^a. Andrews, Thos. Stowell, John Walker, Jos Miller, W^m. Jenison, Andrew Tufts, Simeon Duncan, David Chadick, Benj^a. Stowell, Abraham Lincoln, Samuel Mower, John Barnard, Corneleus Stowell, Joseph Allen, Ephriam Mower, Eli Chapen, John Smith, Phinehas Heywood, Levi Lincoln, Joel How, Saml. Allen, Isaiah Thomas, Thad^s. Chapen, Saml. Prentice, Nathan Heard, John Stanton, Saml. Flagg, Abel Stowell, Clark Chandler, Charles Chandler, Tim^o. Bigelow, Saml. Chandler, Edward Bangs,—

The Petition of a Number of Inhabitants Living in the Gore &c

Worcester February 4th. 1785—

Gentlemen   we the Subscribers Inhabitants of a Tract of Land commonly known by the Name of Worcester Gore—Earnestly Request you to Insert an Article in your Next warrant for calling a Town meeting To See if the Town of Worcester will Vote to receive us and our Estates as parte of Said Town that we may do Duty and Receive Town Previliges with them in full and as in Duty Bound we will ever Pray

To the Selectmen of the Town of Worcester

Hilyer Tanner, Isaac Willard, Phineas Flagg, Noah Harrington, John Willard, Elijah Newton, Thomas Rice, Benja Flagg, Stephen Hayward, James Hayward———

Voted that this meeting be dissolved & it was dissolved accordingly

  A True Entry Attest Daniel Goulding Town Clerk

At a Meeting of the Freeholders & Other Inhabitants of the Town of Worcester qualified to Vote in Town affairs Legally warned & assembled at the Publick Meeting house in Said Town on Monday the Seventh Day of March A, D, 1785 to act on the Several Articles mentioned in the foregoing Warrant

 M^r. David Bigelow was Chosen Moderator

 Deacon Nathan Perry Capt. Samuel Brooks M^r. John Chamberlain M^r. Jesse Taft M^r. Daniel Beard Selectmen Overseers of the Poor and assessors

 Daniel Goulding Town Clerk

 Deacon Nathan Perry Town Treasurer

 M^r. Asa Ward M^r. Ignatius Goulding Wardens

 M^r. Thomas Nickels Ju^r. M^r. Josiah Flagg Tythingmen

 M^r. Nathan Heard Sealer of Taned & Curryed Leather

 M^r. Samuel Chandler M^r. John Stowers Clerks of the Markit

 M^r. Ignatius Goulding M^r. Jonathan Flagg Fence Viewers

 Voted for a County Treasurer and the Votes were as follows John Chamberlain 6 Tim^o. Paine 10 Nathan Perry 29 Clarke Chandler 32

 M^r. John Smith Mr Jacob Holms Field Drivers

 M^r. Joseph Miller M^r. John Moore Deer Reves

 M^r. Ignatius Goulding M^r. David Bigelow Surveyors of Boards & Shingles &c

 Timothy Paine Esqr. Colo Saml. Flagg Capt. Benjn. Heywood Committee to Settle accounts With the Town Treasurer

Worcester Town Records, 1785.

Nathan Perry Chosen Grand Juror

Voted that M^r. William Trobridge be the Collector of Taxes the Current year he giving Sufficient Bonds for the faithfull performance of his Trust and that he be allowed four Pence on the Pound for Collecting

Then Chose M^r. William Trobridge & M^r. Abel Stowell Constables

Josiah Perry, David Chadwick Nathan Patch Joshua Whitney Joseph Kingsbury Moses Miller Stephen Dexter, William Taylor Jonathan Rice John Chamberlain William Bowles Samuel Whitney John Pierce Ruben Gray Surveyors of Highways & Collectors of Highway Taxes

John Stowers Simon Gates Amos Johnson William Brown Ju^r. David Willington Abraham Taylor John Elder Samuel Hambelton Samuel Griggs James Fisk Hog Reives

Doct^r. Elijah Dix John Smith Samuel Brooks Stephen Dexter Josiah Flagg Charles Stearns Jonathan Rice William Gates Joseph Blaire Benjamen Whitney Samuel Curtis Jonathan Gleason School Committee

Voted that the Sum of Two hundred Pounds be Raised Levied & assessed on the Polls & Estates in this Town for the purpose of keeping the Publick & Town Roads in repair the Current year

Voted that the Inhabitants have Liberty of Working out their Highway Tax aforesaid & be allowed the Same Price Labour was Set at the Last year

Voted that those that are Deficient in Working out their former highway Taxes be allowed Liberty to work them out on or before the Last day of June Next & those that have overworked be allowed towards their Tax the Present Year

Voted that the Sum of one hundred & fifty Pounds be Raised Levied and assessed on the Polls & Estates in this Town for the purpose of Supplying the Town with Schooling the Current year

Voted that Each School Destrict Send to No Other but their owne

on Timothy Paine Esq^rs. Request mentioned in the Eleventh

Article in the Warrant for this Meeting[1] Voted that the open Road Laid out in the year Seventeen hundred & Sixty Five to accomodate M^r. John Kelso be Discontinued & that the Same be 'a Bridle Road[2]

Voted that this Meeting be adjourned to Tuesday the Fifteenth Day of this Instant march at one OClock in the afternoon then to Meet at this Place & the meeting was adjourned accordingly

 A True Entry Attest Daniel Goulding Town Clerk

Met according to adjournment March 15th. 1785

Voted that the Swine go at Large the Current year being yoked & Ringed according to Law

Voted to allow to Jacob Hemenway Sixteen Shillings in hard money in addition to a grant of Twenty Shillings of Paper money made to him No^v. 18th 1778 for assisting in Removing Mary Hambelton & her Mother to Leicester & Bringing them home again   £0 - 16 - 0

Voted to allow to M^r. Jonathan Nash the Sum of 19/6 which Sum he was assessed in a Tax or Taxes Committed to M^r. Patch to Collect for his Brothers Pole when at the Same Time he was at Boston   £0 - 19 - 6

Voted that the accounts exhibited at this Time against the Town Lay until Some futer Time

Voted to accept of M^r. Jesse Taft as Collector of Taxes in the Room of M^r. James Trobridge

Voted that the Committee for Providing Metereals for Building

---

[1] ARTICLE 11 :—"To hear the Request of Timothy Paine Esqr. in regard of Discontinuing an open Road formerly Laid out to accomodate M^r. John Kelso & if the Town See cause to Vote to have Said Road be a Bridle way"

[2] See pages 117 and 120, *Worcester Town Records, 1753–1783*. (Volume IV., Collections of The Worcester Society of Antiquity.)

Worcester Town Records, 1785.

a New Goal in this Town have Liberty of getting Stone on Mill Stone Hill for Said purpose Free of expence

Voted that Joseph Wheeler Esqr. have Liberty to Build a Tomb in the Burying Yard in Such Place as the Selectmen Shall Direct

Voted to accept of a List of Persons Qualified to Serve as Jurors which List is as Follows viz

Benjamen Andrews	Benjamen Green	Moses Miller
Joel Wesson	Samuel Godard	Ephraim Miller
Timothy Bigelow	John Gleason	John Mower
Samuel Brooks	Jonathan Gleason	Samuel Mower
Samuel Bridge	Jonathan Grout	Ephraim Mower
Thadeas Bigelow	Ignatius Goulding	Joseph Miller
Joseph Blaire	Nathaniel Harrington	Thomas Nickels Ju^r.
James Barber	Elijah Harrington	John Nazro
Joseph Barber	Josiah Harrington	Jonathan Nash
Samuel Brooks Ju^r.	Silas Harrington	Timothy Paine
Nathan^l. Brooks	Joseph Hastings	Nathan Perry
Daniel Beard	Daniel Heywood	Josiah Perry
Joseph Ball	Abel Heywood	John Pierce
John Barnard	Jacob Holmes	Nathan Patch
Solomon Bixbee	Nathan Hurd	Amos Putnam
David Bigelow	Noah Harris	Lem^l Rice
Eben^r. Barber	Jedediah Heley	Stephen Salsbury
Samuel Braizer	Ezekiel How	Elisha Smith
William Bowles	Phineas Heywood	Robert Smith
William Gates	Benjamen Heywood	John Smith
Ruben Gray	Samuel Jenison	Benjn. Stowell
Daniel Goulding	William Jenison	Cornelas Stowell
Charles Chandler	Phineas Jones	Abel Stowell
Saml. Chandler	Micah Johnson	Thomas Stowell
Eli Chapen	Peter Johnson	John Stowers
David Chadwick	William Johnson	John Stanton
Samuel Curtis	Ruben Hambelton	Charles Stearns
Clark Chandler	Thomas Knight	John Tatman
Tyler Curtis	Josiah Knight	Isaiah Thomas

Worcester Town Records, 1785.

Jacob Chamberlain	Edward Knight	Willm. Trobridge
John Chamberlain	Willm. Knight	Willm. Taylor
Thadeas Chamberlain	Joseph Kingsbury	Jesse Taft
Thadeas Chapen	Thomas Lynds	John Taylor
Nathaniel Coolidge	Abraham Lincoln	Willm. Treadwell
Benjamen Childs	Ebenr. Lovell	Danl. Waldo
Stephen Dexter	Jonathan Lovell	Thomas Wheeler
Benjamen Flagg	Josiah Lyon	Amos Wheeler
Isaac Flagg	James M{c}farland	Asa Ward
Josiah Flagg	Asa Moore	Ebenr. Wiswell Ju{r}.
Jonathan Flagg	David Moore	Ebenr. Willington Ju{r}.
Elijah Flagg	Saml. Moore	Benjn. Whitney Ju{r}.
Samuel Flagg	John Moore	Nathan White
Palmer Goulding	John Moore 2d.	Samuel Whitney

Then Chose William Young Timothy Paine Esq{rs}. Colo Benjamen Flagg Mr. Asa Moore & Joseph Allen Esqr. a Committee to Select out one Quarter Part of the above List as they Shall Judge best Qualified to Serve at the Supreme Judicial Court Then Said Committee Laid the following List before the Town which they Voted Should be put in the Box For Jurors for the Supreme Judicial Court & the Remainder put into the Box to Serve on Petit Jury at the Courts of Common Pleas & General Sessions of the Peace——

Timothy Bigelow	Daniel Goulding	Nathan Perry
Samuel Brooks	Ezekiel How	Stephen Salsbury
Nathaniel Brooks	Benjn. Heywood	Benjn. Stowell
David Bigelow	Micah Johnson	Cornelas Stowell
Samuel Curtis	Ebenr. Lovell	Isaiah Thomas
Jacob Chamberlain	Asa Moore	Jesse Taft
John Chamberlain	David Moore	Daniel Waldo
Benjn. Flagg	John Mower	Thomas Wheeler
Saml. Flagg	John Nazro	Robert Smith
Palmer Goulding	Tim{o}. Paine	Daniel Beard
William Gates	John Pierce	William Bowles

Voted to accept of the Report of a Road Laid out by the Selectmen through the Ministerial Land So called Lying North of the Towns Common & that the Same be Recorded in the Town Book of Records which Report is as Follows—Viz—

To the Inhabitants of the Town of Worcester in the County of Worcester at their Annual March Meeting in ye year 1785

We the Subscribers Selectmen of the Town of Worcester afore Said agreeable to the Vote & Directions of Said Town have this Day Laid out a Town Road through the Ministerial Land So Called Lying north of the Towns Common near the Meeting house described as follows, Begining on the Town Street at the North west Corner of Chandlers Homestead So called and from thence extends E. 26. S. 53 Rods then Turns and runs S. 29. W. 18 Rods & one Quarter to S^d. Common the S^d. Road, to Lye Northerly of the first mentioned Line and Easterly of the Second Line and to be two Rods and an half wide—

All which is humbly Submitted to the Town for their acceptance

Worcester January 4th. 1785   David Bigelow
Eben^r. Lovell
Saml. Brooks
Nathl. Brooks
Daniel Goulding

} *Selectmen of Worcester*

Voted that this Meeting be adjourned to Monday the fourth Day of April Next at one OClock in the afternoon then to meet at this Place & the meeting was accordingly adjourned

    A True Entry   Attest   Daniel Goulding Town Clerk

At a Town Meeting Legally warned & assembled at the Publick Meeting house in Worcester on Monday the Seventh Day of March A, D, 1785 For the Purpose of Voting for a Register of Deeds for the County of Worcester then the Following Persons were Voted for & had the Number of Votes expressed against their Respective Names viz

Timothy Paine Twenty two

Benjamen Reed Thirty two

Daniel Clap four
Samuel Allen one
Voted then that this meeting be dissolved and it was dissolved accordingly

    A True Entry   Attest   Daniel Goulding Town Clerk

Annual March Meeting met according to adjournment April the Fourth Then Voted to accept the Report of the Selectmen in Regard of the Ministeral & School money and other Monies Due to the Town which Report is as Follows viz

We the Selectmen of the Town of Worcester beg Leave to report the following Accounts of the Monies Arising from the Sale of the Ministeral & School Lands also of the Sums of Money due on account of the Sale of four New Pews Lately made by order of the Town and also a peace of Land Leased to Capt. Samuel Flagg

  In the hands of Palmer Goulding
                £.46..13..4 Interest p^d. to No^v. 1st 1783
  Stephen Dexter   33..6..8 Interest p^d. to No^v. 1 1784
  John Taylor   42..3..4 In — p^d. to No^v. 1 1782
  Ezekiel How   20..0..0 In — four year Interest Due
  Phineas Ward   22..15..0 In — p^d. to No^v. 1 1784
  David Bigelow   35..16..8 In — p^d. to No^v. 1 1784
  Joseph Allen   51..1..1 In ————————
  In the hands of the Town
                35..17..10 In Due 7 years
  Stanton & Goulding 35..0..0 ————
  Pew Money   Isaiah Thomas 42..15..0
    Elijah Dix   39..5..0 In P^d. July 25th 1784
    Nathan Patch   33..5..0
    Samuel Brown 39..5..0 In P^d. July 25th 1784

School Money in the hands of David Baldwin £83..6..8 on which is Due three years Interest Next March 29th day and Likewise in the hands of the Selectmen for the year 1780 not accounted for Capt. Saml. Flagg^s. Lease Eaquil to Six pounds p^r. Year Due 9th. of March Next the Interest Money that we have received is in our hands.

All which is humbly Submitted by us

Worcester February 24th 1785   David Bigelow, Eben^r. Lovell, Saml. Brooks, Nathl. Brooks, Daniel Goulding } Selectmen of Worcester

Then Voted that the Selectmen pay the Interest money they have Rec^d. to the Town Treasurer

Then Voted that this Meeting be Dessolved & it was Dessolved accordingly

A True Entry   Attest   Daniel Goulding Town Clerk

At a Town Meeting Legally warned & assembled at the Publick Meeting house in Worcester on Monday the four Day of April A D, 1785 for the Purpose of Voting for Govenor Leu^t. Govenor & Senators the following Persons were Voted for & had the Number of Votes expressed against their Respective Names viz

Honble James Bowdoin   35
Honble Thomas Cushing   4   } as Govenor
Frances Dana Esqr.   33

Honble Thomas Cushing 62 as Leu^t. Govenor

Honble John Sprague   32
Hon Saml. Baker   34
Hon Jona Warner   13
Hon Moses Gill   33
Artimas Ward   17   } as Senators
Jonathan Grout Esqr.   6
Rufus Putnam   18
Tim^o. Paine   4
Seth Washburn   9

Levi Lincoln   4
Saml. Curtis   5   } as Senators
Israel Nickels   1
Abel Wilder   1

Worcester Town Records, 1785. 47

Then Voted that this Meeting be Dissolved & it was Dissolved accordingly

    Attest   Daniel Goulding Town Clerk

At a Meeting of the Inhabitants of the Town of Worcester Qualified to Vote for Representatives Legally warned & assembled at the Publick meeting house in Said Town on Monday the Ninth Day of May, A, D, 1785 upon a Motion being made & Seconded & the Question put whether the Town will Choose a Representative to represent this Town the Current year & it passed in the affirmative

The Town then made Choice of Samuel Curtis Esqr. for their Representative

At the Same Time & Place the Inhabitants Qualified to Vote in Town affairs Legally warned & assembled Passed the Following Votes

1st Chose Timothy Paine Esqr. Moderator

Voted to accept of the Report of the Committee appointed by the Town to ascertain the Bounds of Part of a Gore of Land lying between Worcester & Sutton & that the Inhabitants living thereon who are owners & proprietors of Said Land be annexed to this Town Said Report is as Follows—

Agreeable to a Vote of the Town of Worcester Holden on Tuesday the first day of March 1785 We the Subscribers being appointed a Committee to ascertain the Bounds of Part of a Gore of Land lying between Worcester & Sutton belonging to a Number of the inhabitants of Said Gore together with a few Small Pieces lying in Said Gore belonging to Some of the Inhabitants of S^d Town of Worcester—Have attended Said Service and report as follows viz Beginning at the Southeasterly Corner of the Town of Worcester thence running Southerly on a right line untill it comes to the Northeast Corner of the farm formerly belonging to Isaac Morse, Now in possession of Noah Harrington—thence running South 5 degrees west 87 perches on the Easterly Side of Said farm to a Stake & Stones on Sutton Town Line—From thence turning westerly on Said Line to a white Oak tree being the Southwest Corner of John Goddards Land & the Southeast Corner of Oliver Curtiss Land thence turning Northesterly on Ward Town Line untill it comes to Worcester Town Line including those who have been heretofore annexed to Said Town

Worcester March 1785   Daniel Baird ⎫
                                John Pierce ⎬ *Committee*
                                Benj^a. Flagg ⎭

Voted not to act on the third article in the warrant[1] for this meeting

Voted to Choose a Committee of three to Lease out the Ministerial Land lying East of Capt. Palmer Gouldings this Season to the heighest Bidder then Chose Tim^o. Paine Esqr. Capt. Samuel Brooks & Colo Tim^o. Bigelow a Committee for Said Purpose

The Committee Leased the Land to Capt. Goulding for the Present Season for the Sum of one Pound four Shillings

Voted that the Committee Chose to Lease the Ministerial Land Lying East of Capt. Palmer Goulding be a Committee to lay the Said Land out in lots & make Report to the Town whether it will be expedient to Sell it or not

Voted to allow the Following accounts viz—To David Bigelow, Eben^r. Lovell Samuel Brooks, Nathl. Brooks, & Daniel Goulding assessors for making three Valuations & a State & Town & a highway Tax & paper   £16..16..0

  to Willm. Bowles for making 4 Rods of Stone
    wall   0..12..0
  to Elijah Dix for Doctering Simon Glasco &
    medicen   2..6..4
  to James Quigley for Boarding Agnas Brooks ⎫
    from may 1st. 1784 to may 1st. 1785, 52 ⎬ 8..13..4
    weeks & 3/4 p^r Week   ⎭

---

[1] ARTICLE 3:—"To See if the Town have any objections against Several Towns being taken off the west part of this County agreeable to their Petition to the General Court"

Worcester Town Records, 1785. 49

to James Quigley for Boarding Elizabeth Brooks from the first of march 1784 to the first Day of march 1785, 52 weeks at 2/8 p^r.	6 .. 18 .. 8
to W^m. Trobridge for 100 Feet of Plank to Lay on the Bridge	0 .. 5 .. 0
to W^m. Trobridge for Conveying Molly Moore to Marlborough	1 .. 7 .. 0
to W^m. Elder for Boarding John Spence from march 1st. 1784 to march 1st. 1785, 52 weeks at 4/ p^r. Week & Some Cloathing for S^d Spenc	11 .. 5 .. 6
to Daniel Goulding for a pair of Shoes for John Spence	0 .. 8 .. 0
to John Goodwin for mending the Meeting house Bell	0 .. 4 .. 0

march 15th. 1784

to Joseph Wheeler for a Warrant & a Notification hearing and Judging upon the Cause of Sarah Paine & Coppying the Proceedings for the Town of Bolton	0 .. 9 .. 0

august

to Joseph Wheeler for a Warrant &c for Susanna Munna pauper from the Town of Boston	0 .. 12 .. 0

November 15th.

to Joseph Wheeler for a Warrant &c for Hannah Wait a pauper belonging to the Town of Framingham	0 .. 12 .. 0
to Ignatius Goulding for Timber for a fraim for the Bell	0 .. 13 .. 3
to Thadeas Chapen for 120 Feet of Plank	0 .. 14 .. 0
to Jedediah Heley for a Coffin for a Woman that Died at M^{rs}. Tracys	0 .. 9 .. 0
Voted to allow James M^{c}farland a Pole Tax in M^r. Joseph —— hands being	0 .. 19 .. 3
	£53 .. 4 .. 4

Voted to allow to Saml. Eaton the Sum 1/6 p^r. week in addition to what was allowed him for Supporting his mother the Last year this Sum is to be added to the £53.4.4

Voted that the above Sum of Fifty three Pounds four Shillings & four Pence be assessed & Raised on the Polls & Estates in this Town for the Purpose of Paying Said Accounts

Voted that the Selectmen be a Committee to git the Herse Repaired or a New one built at the expence of the Town

Voted that the Proprietors of the School house on the Towns Common have Liberty to move it to Some other Place on Said Common under the Direction of the Selectmen

Voted that the Sum of £1..7..3 be allowed to Saml. Flagg & J Stanton for Cloath & Buttons for John Spence Said Sum to be allowed out of the Rent of the Land Said Flaggs & Stantons Store Stands on

Then Voted that this Meeting be Dissolved & it was Dissolved accordingly

  A True Entry Attest Daniel Goulding Town Clerk

At a Publick Town meeting held at the Publick meeting house in Worcester on thursday the Twenty fifth day of August A, D, 1785 the Following Votes were passed viz

Deacon Nathan Perry Chosen Moderator

Voted that the Selectmen be a Committee to Confer with the proprietors of the Grammar School now Keeping in this Town to See if they can agree with them So the Town may be Exempt from paying a Fine for the future [1]

---

[1] ARTICLE 2:—"To See what the Town will do with Regard to a presentment for not keeping a grammar School also to See what the Town will do in Regard of keeping a Grammar School for the future"

Worcester Town Records, 1785.   51

On a Motion made & Seconded & the Question put to See if the Town would act on the Third Article in the Warrant for this meeting[1] & it passed in the Negative Number 57 against 50

Voted to accept the Report of the Committee Chose to view & Lay out the Ministerial Land Near Capt. Gouldings into Lots & Voted that they git the Same Surveyed & an accurate Plan taken with the Several allotments & that the Selectmen put an article in the Warrant for the Next meeting in order that the Land may be Sold—the Report is as Follows viz

The Committee appointed to Lease out the Ministerial Land lying in the middle of the Town Report that they Leased the Same out for the present Season to Capt. Palmer Goulding for the Sum of Twenty four Shillings which Sum is now due from Said Goulding to the Town

And the Same Committee further Report that according to the Desire of the Town they have viewed Said Land and find that in Case the Town is disposed to Sell the Same it may be divided into Lotts in the following manner /reserving Sufficient Ground for a Burying Place on the East Side of the Swale runing through Said Land/ in the first Place to Continue the Road Lately laid out through that part already Sold in the Same Course Easterly acros Said Swale untill it goes near the Brow of the Hill towards the Brook then to turn Southerly and runing until it meets with the Road Leading by Capt. Gouldings House about Eleven Rods west of Mill Brook So called which will leave one Lott between the Brook and S^d. proposed Road & the Lands Lying between Said Proposed Road & the Towns House in which Crosby Lives be divided into two Lotts, and to extend North as far as y^e. Said proposed Road that the Lands Lying North of Mes^s Stanton & Gouldings Pot House and South of S^d. Road be one Lott & to extend East So as to include that Part of the Swale adjoyning thereto—that the Land Lying East of M^r. Allens Lott & North of

---

[1] ARTICLE 3:—"To here the Petetion of Timothy Paine Esqr. & Twelve others Requesting to be Exempt from paying any Ministerial Taxes in the Town of Worcester with all those who have or Shall Joine them"

Said Proposed Road be another Lott to extend to the North Bounds of the Ministerial Land and on the East to Joyn the Land proposed to be Left for a Burying Place that another Lott may be Laid at the East End of the S^d. proposed Road to extend Easterly to ye Brook and to take in all the Lands Joyning up to the Last mentioned Lott lying west of the Brook except what Shall be reserved for the burying Place that the Lands lying East of the Brook be considered as one Lott that where the Town House Stands there be reserved five Rods in front & to extend North as far as the New proposed Road and what then remains will be only the Land joyning upon the Road Scituate between Said Goulding Malt House and the House where Crosby Lives and as the Committee by this Report only mean to give a general Idea of the Premises would propose further that in Case the Town agrees to Sell the Lands that an accurate Plan be taken of the whole with the Several allotments making Such alterations as may be found necessary upon a Survey

Worcester August 25th. 1785
All which is Humbly Submitted
Tim^o. Paine P^r. order

Voted that Levi Lincoln Tim^o. Paine & Joseph Allen Esq^{rs}. be a committee to appear at the Next Court in regard of a presentment for not keeping a Grammar School in this Town to See if they can git the Town excused from a Fine

Voted that the two Center School Quarter be Joined in one as they formerly were

On a Motion made & Seconded & the Question to See if the Town would grant a Sum of money agreeable to a petition mentioned in the Seventh Article in the warrant [1] for the purpose of Building School Houses in this Town & it passed in the Negative

Then after Some Consideration the Question was put again & it passed in the affirmative

---

[1] ARTICLE 7:—"To See if the Town will grant a Sum of money for the purpose of Building School houses according to a petetion of the Center Quarters"

Voted that the Prayer of the Petition of Tim°. Paine Joseph Allen & Levi Lincoln Esq^{rs}. Stiling themselves a Committee from the two Center School Quarters So called be & hereby is granted —and it is hereby voted that the Sum of Nine hundred Pounds be & hereby is Granted upon the Polls & Estates in this Town & that the Same be assessed & paid as in Said petetion is mentioned for the purposes therein Specified with the conditions & Limitations therein Set forth Provided any of the Inhabitants in this Town Shall at all Times have full Liberty to Send any Children to the Center School house & there be taught the languages without paying any other or greater expence for tuition than what their average proportion will amount to in common with the Inhabitants of the Center School Quarter & provided also the Inhabitants of the Center School quarter pay for the charge of assessing & collecting Such Sums as may be necessary for building their School house, & Save harmless the Town from presentments for not keeping a Grammar School for the term of one year Next Ensuing—

The Petition is as Follows viz

To the Freeholders & other Inhabitants of the Town of Worcester The petition of the Subscribers a Committee appointed by the two Center School Quarters So called in Said Town in their behalf humbly Sheweth—

That the School Quarters afore Said have been for a considerable Time destitute of convenient School houses—That agreeably to the usage & practice of the other School Quarters in Said Town the Center quarters have come to an agreement to build a commodious School house at their own cost & charge—that without the aid of the Town the monies necessary for So beneficial a purpose cannot be legally assessed or conveniently collected— your petetioners therefore in behalf of the Center Quarters aforesaid pray that the Town will assess Such a Sum of Money upon the Polls & Estates of this Town as the proportion thereof upon the Center School Quarters Shall amount to a Sum Sufficient for Building the School house afore Said & order that the Same be collected & paid as by law is provided in other Town assessments and that the Inhabitants of those other School Quarters which are already or may be provided with places for keeping a School Should be allowed & Discounted their rateable parts of the assessment afore Said, The cost & Charges attending the assessment & Collection aforeSaid to be borne & paid by the Center School Quarters afore Said—Or otherwise to afford Such aid to the petitioners as the Town in their wisdom Shall Seem meet

and as in Duty Bound will ever pray

> Tim°. Paine
> Jos Allen } Committee as afores^d.
> Levi Lincoln

The Petetion mentioned in the 3^d article in the Warrant[1]

To the Selectmen of Worcester in the County of Worcester

Gentlemen—The Subscribers a Committee appointed by the Society usually attending on the ministry of M^r. Aaron Bancroft in Worcester—Shew—

That whereas a Number of the Inhabitants of Said Town on the 13th. day of January 1785. Petitioned to the then Selectmen & the Committee for Supplying the pulpit in Said Town for the reasons in Said petitions mentioned praying that they would adopt Such measures for the Settlement of M^r. Aaron Bancroft as a Minister in the Town of Worcester as may Seem to them most proper & fit & most conducive to the peace welfare & happiness of the Town

That in consequence of Said petition the Selectmen were pleased to appoint & warn a meeting of the Freeholders & other Inhabitants of Said Town qualified to Vote in Town affairs to meet at the publick meeting house in Said Town on the First Day of March Last to consider & act upon S^d. petition

That at Said Meeting after Some debate upon Said Petetion a Motion was made & Seconded that the Town agree to Settle M^r. Bancroft in the work of the Gospel Ministry & Such Other Person

---

[1] "ARTICLE 3:—"To here the Petetion of Timothy Paine Esqr. & Twelve others Requesting to be Exempt from paying any Ministerial Taxes in the Town of Worcester with all those who have or Shall Joine them"

Worcester Town Records, 1785.

as may be agreeable to & chosen Solely by those who are desirous of hearing further and the Settlements & Salaries of both be at the expence of the Town at Large and the Question being put it passed in the Negative

It was then moved inasmuch as the Town by their last Vote have refused to Settle M^r. Bancroft as a minister that the Town will Consent that those persons who are Satisfied with M^r. Bancroft & desirous of settling him may form into a religious Society for that purpose, & the Question being put it passed in the negative—as by Said Votes on record may appear

Since which those persons Inhabitants of the S^d. Town who were Satisfied with M^r. Bancroft & desirous of his being their minister have formed themselves into a Society & have invited M^r. Bancroft to Settle with them in the Gospel Ministry which Invitation he has accepted & has been preaching to S^d. Society ever Since the 20th. day of march last at their expence & charge

That in order to prevent unnecessary law Suits & that peace & happiness in S^d. Town may continue & nothing Should happen to disturb that harmony that has hitherto Subsisted in civil affairs, & that not withstanding the separation already taken place we might all live together in Brotherly love & friendship—The Subscribers pray that a Town meeting may be forthwith notified to See if the Town will exempt the members that do or may belong to Said Society from being assessed to any Ministerial Taxes in Said Town the S^d. Society having made Voluntary provision for the Support of M^r. Bancroft agreeable to the Constitution and for the Town to take Such measures as they may think just & proper to secure to the Inhabitants of the Town at Large & members of each society in particular the full benefit of their respective assessments for Ministerial purposes for the future—

      Tim^o. Paine, Levi Lincoln, Palmer Goulding
      Jos: Wheeler, Cornelas Stowel, David Bigelow
      Nathan Patch, Saml. Bridge, John Barnard
      Joseph Allen, Isaiah Thomas, Micah Johnson
      Joel How,

Worcester June 27th 1785

Voted that the Petetion of Millicent Goulding be granted that the Selectmen give her liberty to live in the house belonging to the Town in which M^r. Crosby lives or provide Some other Place for her to live in—the Petition is as follows—

To the Selectmen of Worcester—Gentlemen I am in need Curcumstances destitute of an house or Home to Shelter me but thank god am in a good degree of health and by my industry am able at present to Support my Self if I had a Room provided for me—I am loath to put the Town to any expence for my Support & maintenance but necessity obliges me to request that you would lay my curcumstances before the Town at the next Town meeting and See if they will not give orders that I may be permitted to Live in the house belonging to the Town in which M^r. Crosby Lives or Such other Place may be provided for me for a Shelter as may Suit & you will oblige your Distresed Towns Woman

Worcester July 4th 1785   Mellicent Goulding

Then Voted that this meeting be Dessolved and it was dissolved accordingly

    A True Entry   Attest   Daniel Goulding Town Clerk

At a Legal Town Meeting held at the Publick Meeting house in Worcester on Monday the Seventh Day of November A, D, 1785 then the Following Votes were passed—Viz

1   Chose Deacon Nathan Perry Moderator

2^d it was then moved & Seconded to See if the Town would hear any Candidates Further and the motion was put & it passed in the affirmative

3dly Voted to Choose an addition to the Committee for Supplying the Pulpit, then Chose M^r. John Nazro, M^r. Daniel Waldo, M^r. Stephen Salsbury & Doct^r. Elijah Dix for Said addition

Voted that this Meeting be Desolved & it was Dissolved accordingly

    A True Entrey   Attest   Daniel Goulding Town Clerk

Worcester Town Records, 1785.

At a Meeting of the Freeholders & Other Inhabitants of the Town of Worcester legally warned & assembled at the publick meeting house in Said Town on Monday the Twenty Eighth day of November A, D, 1785 then the following Votes were passed—viz—

Deacon Nathan Perry Chosen Moderator

Voted to accept the Report of the Committee mentioned in the Second article in the warrant[1] which report is as Follows—

The account of Nathan Perry Town Treasurer with the Town of Worcester November 28th. 1785

The S^d. accountant chargeth himself with the Ballance of his account Settled with the Town 12th. may 1783 being at that Time

	£ 2335 .. 12 .. 0¾
also with a Tax committed to M^r. Daniel Goulding 2^d Sep^t 1783 being	345 .. 15 .. 4
also with a Tax committed to M^r. Joseph Barber 13 Jan. 1785	447 .. 16 .. 0
Interest money Rec^d. of the Selectmen due upon Bonds for money for which the Ministerial Lands were formerly Sold for	31 .. 14 .. 6
on an Execution in favour of y^e Town agst. Nathan Patch	284 .. 12 .. 5
orders on Jacob Severy Constable of Sutton for money due from the State Treasurer to the Town for Soldiers Wages	96 .. 1 .. 10
Cash Rec^d. of Capt. Sam$^{l!}$ Flagg for ground Rent for his Store	6 .. 0 .. 0
Rec^d. of Justice Hawes a fine for Swearing	0 .. 7 .. 0
Note of Hand due from Cyrus French	6 .. 0 .. 0
	£ 3353 .. 19 .. 1¾

and dischargeth himself by the Payment of the following Sums p^d. by orders from y^e Selectmen—viz—

---

[1] ARTICLE 2:—"to here the report of the Committee Choosen Last march to Settle with the Town Treasurer"

Pd. Josiah Pierce £185..11..7
  Pd. Sol Bixbee £2..8..1 £187..19.. 8
Pd. Whitney & Lovel £6
  Pd. Sam¹. Johnson 30/ 7..10.. 0
Pd. Wᵐ. Mᶜfarland 38/6
  Pd. Jonᵃ Philips 73/5½ 3..15..11½
Pd. Wᵐ. Elder £9..7 Pd. David Bigelow 60/ 12.. 7 ——
Pd. Ephraim Miller £9..4..5
  pd. John Chamberlain £9..19/6 19.. 3..11
Pd. Wᵐ. Forbes 30/
  pd. James Mᶜfarland £143..17 145.. 7.. 0
Pd. School Committees £53..6..7
  pd. School Grant £100 153.. 6.. 7
Pd. Sam¹. & Ruben Eaton 19/5
  Pd. Thoˢ. Clewes £13..17..2 14..16.. 7
Pd. David Stowel £12..6..2
  pd. Noah Gale £12..8 24..14.. 2
Pd. Asa Jones £13..2..2
  pd. Lydia Taylor £12..0..9 25.. 2..11
Pd. Sam¹. & Stephen Salsbury 7/2
  Pd. Israel Jenison £8..8..4½ 8..15.. 6½
Pd. John Barnard £51..1..7½
  pd. Sam¹. Goddard £21..16..5 72..18.. 0½
Pd. Sam¹. Eaton £15..12/
  pd. Wᵐ. Stearns £7..5..5 22..17.. 5
Pd. Nathan Perry 38/6
  pd. Elijᵃ. Dix £5..8..9 7.. 7.. 3
Pd. Ebenʳ. Lovel £9..4..5
  pd. John Gleason 59/2 12.. 3.. 7
Pd. Ebʳ. Willington Jʳ. 19/1½
  pd. John Fisk 24/8 2.. 3.. 9½
Pd. Daniel Harris Junʳ. £10..14/3
  David Bigelow £14.2 24..16.. 3
Pd. Levi Pierce £18
  pd. David Bigelow 25/0¼ 19.. 5.. 0¼
Pd. Levi Lincoln Esqʳ. 35/9
  pd. Daniel Bigelow £9..11 11.. 6.. 9

P^d. Daniel Bigelow adm^r. £9..11
  p^d. John Weltch 1/7   9..12..7
P^d. Nathan Perry 12/
  p^d. Eben^r. Lovel £37-13   38..5..0
P^d. Eph^r Mower 9/ p^d. John Gleason 47/6   2..16..6
P^d. W^m. Stearns 46/2½ Ditto 64/5¼   5..10..7¾
P^d. Nat Robbins £12 p^d. Saml. Whitney 84/   16..4..0
P^d. Re^v. Jos Davis 26/ p^d. Sundrey
  Soldiers for Guns &c 20.13.10¾   21..19..10¾
P^d. Danl. Bigelow for Dana £9.15/2
  p^d. W^m. Stearns 24/   10..19..2
P^d. James M^cfarland £56..5..7 from w ⎫ Leaves
  deduct 79/8 due from M^cfarland to the ⎬ 52..5..11
  Town ⎭
P^d. Joshua Whitney £9..6..4
  p^d. Jef Hemenway £13..5..10   22..12..2
P^d. Micah Johnson 66/6
  p^d. Charles Chandler £49..19..3½   53..5..9½
P^d. John Chamberlain £25..1..7
  p^d. Saml. Goddard £9   34..1..7
P^d. Joshua Whitney £8..13
  P^d. Levi Lincoln 15/6   9..8..6
P^d. John Waters 7/10
  p^d. David Stowell £16..2   23..12..0
P^d. John Goodwin 7/
  p^d. David McLeland 12..6..8   12..13..8
P^d. Abel Heywood 30/
  p^d. Ephraim Mower £7..10   9
P^d. Moses Miller 10..2..4
  p^d. Jede Healey 12/   10..14..4
P^d. Josiah Pierce £7..14..6
  p^d. Saml. Brooks 15/11   8..10..5
P^d. James Quigley 13..13..0
  p^d. Wheeler & Allen 22..18..2   36..11..2
P^d. Isaac Willard 6..17..6
  p^d. Willm. Stearns 15/   7..12..6

P^d. Danl. Bigelow for Dana £10..12/
   Tim^o. Paine &c 62/   13..14.. 0
P^d. John Goodwin 19/10
   p^d. Jacob Hemenway 24/   2.. 3..10
P^d. M^r. Maccarty^s. Exct^r. £100
   p^d. School Committees for 83 £100 200.. ———
P^d. Nathl. Robbins £46..3..6
   p^d. Nathan Perry £39..10/11 85..14.. 5
P^d. Re^v. M^r. Maccarty £142..5/5
  P^d. Jacob Davis for Beef 564..10/4 706..15.. 9
P^d. Willm. Young £3..6..3¾
   P^d. Jacob Davis an order £46 49.. 6.. 3¾

           2219.. 7.. 7
  Ballance due to ye Town   £ 1334..11.. 6¾
  Errors Excepted p^r Nathan Perry Town Tres^ur

Worcester No^v. 28 1785

The Committee appointed by the Town to Settle accounts with the Town Treasurer Report that they this day attended S^d. Service and Present the foregoing account which they find right cast & well Vouched by which it appears there is a Ballance due to the Town of £1334..11..6 which the S^d. Treasurer is further to Account for as also for the Sum £601..5..8 in New Emission money at one & Seven Eights for one due to the Town by an order drawn on M^r. Nathan Patch former Collector dated Fe^b. 18 1783—Also for a Sum uncertain drawn by the State Treasurer on Joseph Barber Collector for ye year 1784 in favour of the Town   all which is humbly Submitted
       P^r. Tim^o. Paine
       Saml. Flagg

Voted to accept the Report of the Committee Chose for the purpose of Selling the Ministerial Land So called & that they be discharged from S^d. Service paying the Ballance of the Earnest money to the Town agreeable to there Report & Voted that the Plan of S^d. Land be Recorded

The Committee appointed by the Town of Worcester in December 1784 to make Sale of the Ministerial Land so called lying in Worcester near the Meeting house Report their Doings as follows that they caused a Survey of the Nine Lotts ordered to be Sold to be taken by W^m. Young Esqr. that after duely notifying the Sale in the Worcester Gazette they exposed the Same for Sale at the House of L^t. Thomas Stowers^s. Innholder in Worcester afore s^d. on the fifteenth day of February A. D. 1785 at Public Auction and then & there Sold S^d. Lotts to the following Persons they Being the Highest Bidders vizt.

Persons Names	No. Lotts	Price
Daniel Goulding	7	£ 50 .. 0 .. 0
Willm. Young Esqr.	8	50 .. 0 .. 0
Levi Lincoln Esqr.	9	53 .. 0 .. 0
Joseph Allen Esqr.	6	36 .. 10 .. 0
Paul Gates	5	36 .. 10 .. 0
John Stanton	4	38 .. 0 .. 0
Simeon Duncan	3	41 .. 10 .. 0
Joseph Allen Esqr.	2	51 .. 0 .. 0
W^m. Treadwell	1	154 .. 0 .. 0
		£ 510 .. 10 .. 0

P^d. Down by the Several Purchasers to
pay Charges &c   13 .. 10 .. 0

                              Ballance   £ 497 .. 0 .. 0

they have Taken Bond of ye Several Purchisers to the Selectmen of ye Town Chosen for ye year 1784 & their Successors for ye Sums aforesaid Payable in one year with Interest as follows vizt

of Daniel Goulding Palmer Goulding &
    Ignatius Goulding   £ 48 .. 10 .. 0
of W^m. Young Peter Johnson & John Taylor   48 .. 10 .. 0
of Levi Lincoln Joseph Allen & Ignatius
    Goulding   51 .. 10 .. 0
of Paul Gates William Gates & William Mahan   35 .. 0 .. 0
of John Stanton Saml. Flagg & Clark Chandler 36 .. 10 .. 0

of Simeon Duncan Joseph Blair & Joseph Allen Esqr.	40..	
of Joseph Allen Levi Lincoln & Ignatius Goulding	84..10..0	
of W^m. Treadwell Nathan Patch & John Stowers	152..10..0	
	£ 497..0..0	

which Bonds your Committee now deliver to ye Town which Report together with the Survey & Plans of ye Several Lotts which Plan ought to be recorded on the Town Book — all which is humbly Submitted   Tim^o. Paine P^r. Order

Worcester Novr. 28th. 1785

Committee for the Sales of the Ministerial Land Sold 15th. Feb^b. 1785 to the Town of Worcester D^r.

To Cash Rec^d. of the Several Purchasers as Earnest to pay Expences &c	13..10..0	
Supra Credit		
to the first Committee there Time & Expence in viewing the S^d. Land & reporting thereon to ye Town 1 Day Each	£1..0..0	
Committee of Sales 1 Day Each Surveying & Lotting out the Lands at 4/	1..0..0	
Committee attending the Sale 3/ Each	0..15..0	
Expences P^d. at Stowers at ye Sale	0..16..8	
1 Day Each attending the Executing y^e Deeds & taking Bonds	1..0..0	
Writing Deeds	2..8..0	
P^d. M^r. Thomas advertising	2..8..0	
P^d. W^m. Young Surveying & Planing	0..6..0	
Writing & making Report	0..3..0	£9..16..8
due to the Town		£3..13..4

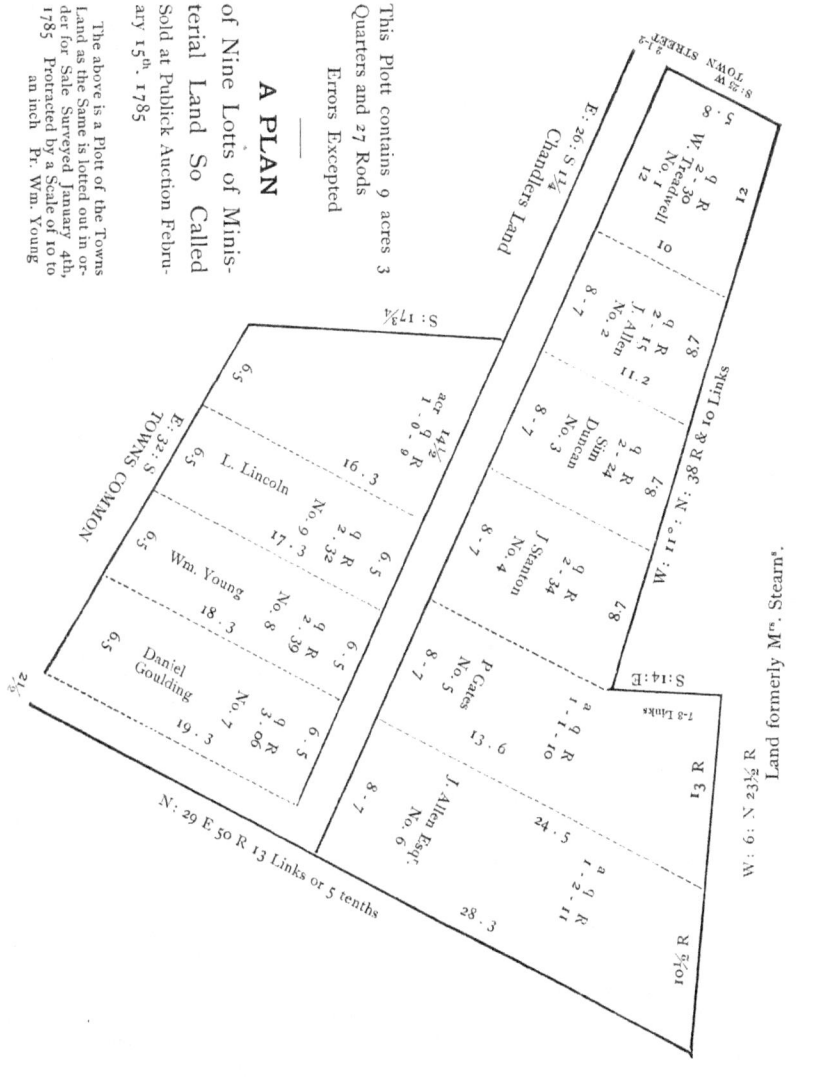

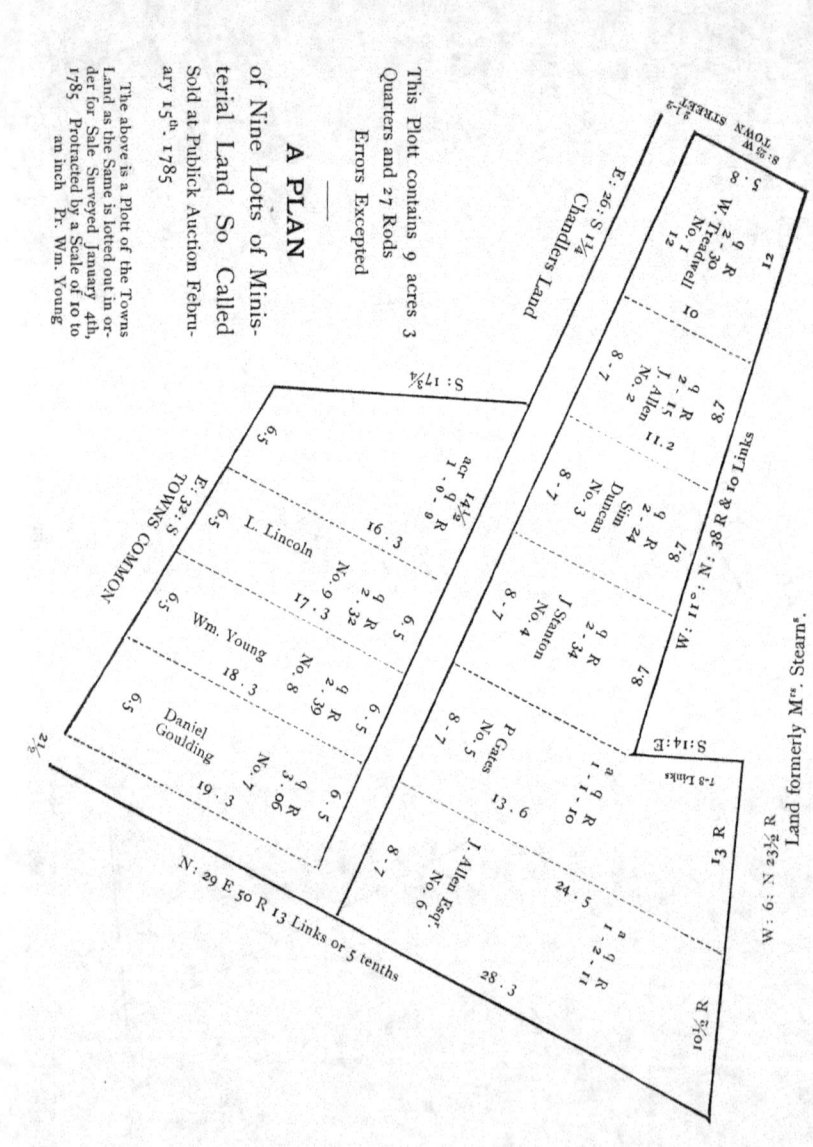

This Plott contains 9 acres 3 Quarters and 27 Rods Errors Excepted

A PLAN

of Nine Lotts of Ministerial Land So Called Sold at Publick Auction February 15th, 1785

The above is a Plott of the Towns Land as the Same is lotted out in order for Sale Surveyed January 4th, 1785 Protracted by a Scale of 10 to an inch Pr. Wm. Young

Voted to allow to Deacon Nathan Perry the Sum of £4..1..6 for moving the Pound & New Building the Same & that the Same be assessed on the Polls & Estates in this Town

Voted to Choose a Committee to examine the accounts brought in against the Town at this meeting & that they make report at the adjournment then Chose Tim°. Paine Esq'. M'. John Nazro & Deacon Nathan Perry a Committee for Said Purpose — then Esq'. Paine made an objection against Serving on Said Committee as their was account Relative to Ministerial Matters

Voted that M'. Patch be indemnifyed in not putting Uriah Ward in Goal until the adjournment of this meeting for his Taxes

Voted that John Chamberlain, & Ephraim Miller, be a Committee to examine M'. Patches Taxes to See how much the Ballance of Uriah Wards, Samuel Fullertons, William Croxford, Thomas Tracy & Cato Walkers Taxes are who have this day asked the Town to abate them

Voted that Cap'. Nathaniel Brooks Leu'. Pierce Cap'. Curtis & Thomas Eaton be a Committee to proportion the School money between the North School Quarters & that they do it according to the Last Valuation

Then Voted that this Meeting be adjourned to monday the Twelvth Day of December Next at one OClock in the afternoon then to meet at this Place & the meeting was accordingly adjourned

    A True Entry   Attest   Daniel Goulding Town Clerk

At a meeting of the Freeholders & Other Inhabitants of the Town of Worcester Qualified to Vote in Town affairs begun & held at the meeting house in Said Town on Monday the Twenty Eighth Day of December[1] A, D, 1785 and Continued by adjournment to Monday the Twelvth day of December following at one OClock P, M, & then met then the following votes were passed viz

---

[1] November.

Voted to allow the following accounts which the Committee have examined viz

to Thadˢ. Chapen Eʳ. to William Elder Decᵈ. for keeping John Spence from the first of March to the 29ᵗʰ Day of July 1785 21 Weeks & an half at 3 pʳ. Week	£3 .. 4 .. 6
To Willᵐ. Elder for keeping John Spence from the Death of his Grand father to yᵉ. 26ᵗʰ. Noᵛ. 1785 being 17 Weeks at 3/	2 .. 11
To Doctʳ. Nahum Willard his account for Boarding Sundrey Ministers as on file appears	23 .. 6
To Joshua Johnson his accᵗ. for keeping Sundrey Ministers Horses as on File	8 .. 4
to Capᵗ. Samuel Brooks for Sundreys Supplyes Simon Glasco	6 - 11 - 11½
To Mary Boyd for keeping Ritchard Moore a poor Child by order of the Selectmen 32 Weeks & five Days & for a pair of Shoes 3/ to the 28 of Noᵛ. 1785	3 - 8 - 6
To Abel Stowell for his Time & Expences in Carrying Jane MᶜKelhony & 5 Children to to Grafton by Authority	1 - 2 - 0
To Joseph Torry for a new Axeltree for the Bell & painting	1 - 10 -
To David Bigelow for Boarding Temperance Cummings &c	0 - 16 - 4
To David Bigelow for Serving a Citation on the Town of Bolton	0 - 6 - 8
To Danˡ. Heywood & John Mahan for Plank for Bridges Seventeen hundred & a half at 7/6 pʳ. hundred	6 - 11 - 3
To John White for Boarding & Washing Mʳ. Howard & Mʳ. Shuttlesworth as on File	7 - 13 -
To Edward Knight for Wood for Simon Glasco	3 - 3 -
To Samuel Eaton for Supporting his mother one Year ending Sepᵗ. 1 1785	11 - 14 -
To David Bigelow for his Services attending the Case of Hoyt against Shrewsbury	9 - 18 - 0
To Joseph Wheeler for his Services attending the Case of Hoyt against Shrewsbury & Cash advanced	0 - 14 - 8

66   *Worcester Town Records, 1785.*

To Nathan Perry for Iron found for ye Bell 6/1 & for his Time & Expences about the Bell 4 Days at 3/ – 12/	0 - 18 - 1
To Nathan Perry for 7 yards of Tow Cloath & making Shirts for John Spence	0 - 12 - 6
To Levi Lincoln attending on Hoyts affair advice &c at 4 Courts of Sessions and 8 Superior Courts at 15/	9 - 0 - 0
To Joseph Barber for Transporting John Rugels one of the poor from Worcester to Holden	0 - 6 - 0
To Clark Chandler his account being for Sundreys for Benony Grout 24/3½ & for Cash Paid for a Town Book of Records 42/	3 - 6 - 3½

Voted that the above accounts be paid out of moneys all Ready Taxed or assessed

Voted that Joseph Allen Esqr., Tim°. Paine Esqr., Doct^r. Elijah Dix & M^r. John Nazro, be a Committee to assist the Selectmen in making a Settlement with M^r. Nathan Patch Late Collector

The Report of the Committee Chose to examine M^r. Patches Taxes to See what of Sundrey Persons Taxes were

We your Committee Chosen for the purpose of Examining Into the Circumstances of Sundrey Persons who petition for abatement of their Taxes in M^r. Nathan Patches hands for to Collect Beg leave to report as Follows—viz—

M^r. Uriah Ward Stands taxed to a tax designed for M^r. James M^cfarland made in New emission Pole 16/ Real 20/ Personal 3/ in hard M   Total   £1 .. 11 .. 5
June   hard money to be p^d. in New Emission

			Real	36/3	2 .. 19 .. 1
Sep^t.	Town D°.	D°.	37/7	2 .. 1 .. 6
	State D°.		34/2	3 .. 3 .. 2
	Minister D°.		2/1	0 .. 3 .. 9½
	Town D°.		4/7	0 .. 8 .. 4
	Town D°.		18/4	1 .. 13 .. 11
	D°.			0 .. 19 .. 0
	D°.			0 .. 18 .. 10

Worcester Town Records, 1785.   67

Dº.	0 .. 3 .. 4¾
	£14 .. 2 .. 3¼
Paid to Mʳ. Patch	1 .. 7 .. 3
	12 .. 14 .. 10¼

Also Willᵐ. Croxford Stands Taxed
    £6 .. 13 .. 6¾
        Paid   2 .. 4 .. 0   Remains   4 .. 11 .. 6¾

Thomas Tracy Stands Dº.
    £4 .. 18 .. 0½
        Paid   0 .. 7 .. 5   Dº.   4 .. 10 .. 7½

Samuel Fullerton Dº.
    14 .. 4 .. 1¼
        Paid   1 .. 7 .. 7¼   Dº.   12 .. 16 .. 6

Cato Walker Dº. 5 .. 11 .. 1¼
        Paid   0 .. 11 .. 6   Dº.   4 .. 19 .. 7¼

as to the Cercumstances of the above named persons it appears to your Committee that they are not in a Capacity to pay at present but are willing to be obligated to pay it to the Town
    All which we humbly Submitt
            John Chamberlain }
            Ephraim Miller   } Committee

Voted to abate the Ballance of Uriah Wards, William Croxford, Thomas Tracys & Samuel Fullertons, Taxes in Mʳ. Patches hands to Collect they giving Security to the Town on Interest for the Same

Voted to abate or discharge Cato Walker the Ballance of his Taxes in Mʳ. Patches hands to Collect

Voted that the Ballance of the above Named Persons Taxes be allowed to Mʳ. Nathan Patch

Voted that this Meeting be Dessolved & the Meeting was accordingly dissolved

    A True Entry   Attest   Daniel Goulding Town Clerk

68   *Worcester Town Records, 1786.*

At a Meeting of the Freeholders & Other inhabitants of the Town of Worcester qualified to Vote in Town affairs duly called & assembled on the Thirtieth day of January A, D, 1786

Deacon Nathan Perry Chosen Moderator

Voted to Choose a Committee to Join a Committee of the Church to consider what measures is best to be taken with regard to the intended ordination of M^r. Bancroft—then Chose Capt. Saml. Brooks, Capt. Nathaniel Brooks, M^r. John Nazro, M^r. Daniel Baird, & M^r. Elijah Harrington a Committee for S^d. Purpose

Voted that this Meeting be dissolved & the Meeting was Dissolved accordingly [1]

    A True Entry   Attest   Daniel Goulding Town Clerk

At a meeting of the Freeholders & other Inhabitants of the Town of Worcester, Qualified to Vote in Town affairs, legally warned and assembled at the Publick Meeting house in Said Town on Monday the thirteenth Day of March, A, D, 1786 to act on Several Articles Contained in the foregoing Warrant

Deacon Nathan Perry Chosen Moderator

Deacon Nathan Perry, Capt. Samuel Brooks M^r. John Chamberlain M^r. Jesse Taft M^r. Daniel Baird, Selectmen assessors & Overseers of the Poor

Daniel Goulding Town Clerk

Deacon Nathan Perry Town Treasurer

William Parker Jonathan Osland Wardens

Josiah Perry John Barnard Tythingmen

Nathan Heard Sealer of Tanned & Curryed Leather

Clark Chandler Ephraime Mower Clerk of the market

---

[1] 3d ARTICLE:—"to See if the Town will vote to allow a certain Number of the inhabitants of Said Town Stileing themselves a Religious Society the use of the Meeting house on Wednesday the first day of February Next for the Purpose of Ordaining Mr. Aaron Bancroft agreeable to a petetion of Timothy Paine Esqr. and Others"

Jonathan Gates 2ᵈ. Samuel Mower Fence Viewers

John Stanton Thadeas Chamberlain Deer Reives

Samuel Chandler Thadeas Bigelow Field Drivers

Ignatius Goulding William Treadwell Surveyors of Boards & Shingles &c

Doctʳ. Elijah Dix Timᵒ. Paine Esqʳ. Capᵗ. Benjamen Heywood Committee to Settle accounts with the Town Treasurer

William Treadwell John Knower Constables

Voted that the Sum of two hundred pounds be Raised & assessed on the Polls & Estates in this Town for the purpose of keeping the publick Roads in this Town in repair the Current year & that the Price of Labour be Four Shillings pʳ. Day & that oxen Carts & Plows be in Proportion then Voted that those that have over Worked there Last years Tax be allowed the Same out of this years Tax & those that have not worked out there Last years Tax have Liberty to work out the Same

Noah Harris John Curtis Daniel Heywood Joshua Whitney Josiah Pierce Joseph Blaire John Mower Thomas Wheeler Benjamen Stowel Thomas Nickels Juʳ. Thomas Stowel Thomas Eaton William Trobridge Isaac Flagg Surveyors and Collectors of Highway Taxes

Voted to Choose one Collector of Publick Taxes the Current year Voted that Mʳ. Nathan Patch be Collector of Taxes for the Current year he giving Sufficient Bonds with Sureties to the Town to the acceptance of the Selectmen for the faithfull performance of his trust and that he be allowed two pence half penny on the pound for Collecting

Voted for Register of Deeds & there was 104 Votes for Colo Daniel Clap

Voted for a County Treasurer & the Following Persons were voted for & had the Number of Votes Expressed against ther Names

    Timothy Paine 48
    Nathan Perry 46
    Samuel Flagg 1

Doct^r. Elijah Dix Saml Brooks Stephen Dexter William Bowles John Pierce Noah Harris thomas Wheeler Thadeas Chamberlain Ebenezer Barber Gideon Smith Nathl. Brooks Committee to Supply the Town with Schooling the Current year

Andrew Tufts John Mahan Isaac Pratt Oliver Pierce Tyler Curtis Willm. Taylor Saml. Curtis Ju^r. Henery Patch Elijah Hawes Ruben Knight Hog Reives

Voted that the Sum of one hundred & fifty pounds be assessed on the Polls & Estates in this Town & Raised for the purpose of Supplying the Town with Schooling the Current year

Voted that Said money be proportioned according to the Tax Said money is Taxed in

Voted that the Committee Chose to Supply the Town with Schooling Proportion Said Money

Voted that the Swine being Yoked & Ringed according to Law go at Large the Current year

Voted to Choose a Committee of three Persons to Consider on the Request of Robert Smith in regard of his being annexed to the School Quarter Commonly Called Smiths Roe, & make report at the adjournment of this meeting then Chose Tim^o. Paine Esqr., Capt. John Curtis, & Leu^t. Josiah Pierce a Committee for Said purpose

Voted that Doct^r. John Green be annexed to the Center School Quarter agreeable to His Request mentioned in Twelvth Article in the Warrant with his proportion of School money

Voted that Doct^r. Elijah Dix, Joseph Allen Esqr., M^r. Daniel Waldo, Capt. Benjamen Heywood, & Capt. Samuel Flagg be a Committee to take the Request of Capt. Samuel Flagg & Others mentioned in the Tenth article in regard of the Towns Granting a Sum of Money to purchase a Fire Engine & make Report at the adjournment of this Meeting what the cost of one may be

Voted to accept the Report of a Road Laid out by the Selectmen agreeable to a Request of Capt. Samuel Flagg & Others through Nathan Patch^s. Land—which Report is as Follows viz— We the Subscribers by a Request of Samuel Flagg & Others to

Lay out a road through M^r. Nathan Patch^s. Land have attended Said Service & Laid a road as follows viz begining at the County [road] Leading from Worcester to Paxton near the Brow of Tackick hill So called at a Stake & Stones on the Easterly Side the S^d. Road thence runing Northerly on S^d. Easterly Side to a Small walnut marked thence to a Walnut thence to a Chestnut 3 Feet East of the Fence thence to a read Oak 3 Feet E Fence thence to a Chestnut Stub thence to a Small walnut thence to a walnut thence to a white oak thence to a Small white Pine thence to Holden Lines the Easterly Side of Said road Bounds as the Fence now Stands Said road Extending one road & a half wide Said Patch giving the Land for S^d. Road

Worcester February 25th. 1786
Nathan Perry
Saml. Brooks
John Chamberlain
} Selectmen of Worcester

Voted to accept the Report of a Road Laid out by the Selectmen agreeable to the Request of Ebenezer Wiswall Ju^r. Said report is as Follows—viz—

We the Subscribers by the Request of Ebenezer Wiswall Ju^r. to Lay out a Road to accomidate him have attended Said Service & Laid out a Road as Follows viz begining at the County Road Leading from Worcester to Springfield and Runing Southerly till it Comes parrilell to the South Side of Said Wiswalls House Said Road to be two Rods wide the Line between Said Wiswalls Land & the Land formerly owned by Zebediah Rice to be the Westerly Bounds of Said Road

Worcester Fe^{br}. 27th. 1786
Nathan Perry
Saml. Brooks
Daniel Baird
} Selectmen of Worcester

Voted that the Road through Patches Land & the Road to accommodate Eben^r. Wiswall be no Cost to the Town

Voted that this meeting be adjourned to Monday the Twentyeth Day of this Present Month of March at two OClock in the afternoon then to meet at this Place, & the Meeting Was accordingly adjourned

A True Entry   Attest   Daniel Goulding Town Clerk

Worcester Town Records, 1786.

At a Town Meeting held on Monday the Thirteenth Day of March, A, D, 1786 and continued by adjournment to monday the Twentyeth Day of the Same March & then Met then the Following Votes were passed viz—

Voted to Sell the Ministerial Land Lying East & Near Capt. Palmer Gouldings & that the Same be Sold at Publick Vendue to the highest Bider then Chose Tim^o. Paine Esqr. Capt. Samuel Brooks, Colo Tim^o. Bigelow, Joseph Wheeler Esqr. & Doct^r. Elijah Dix a Committee for Said purpose Voted that Said Committee or the major Part of them be impowered to give & execute good & Sufficient Deed or Deeds to the Purchaser or Purchasers & take Security for the payment of the Sum or Sums for which they may Sell Said Lands with Lawfull Interest payable to the Town then Voted that S^d. Committee git Said Land Surveyed & an accurate Plan Drawed & if the S^d. Committee on Survey find that it will be for the advantage to the Sale of Said Land to make any alteration in the Lots made in the Report by the Committee Chose Some Time Past that they make Such alterations as they Shall think Best

Voted to accept the Report of the Committee Chose to consider on the Request of Robert Smith in regard of his being annexed to the School Quarter Commonly Called Smiths Roe which Report is as follows—viz—that in case M^r. Rufus Flagg removes into his new house & Dwells therein at the Time the S^d. Quarters are ready to expend their School money the currant year then M^r. Robert Smith is to remain to S^d. Quarter but if S^d. Flagg Should not remove as afore S^d. that then S^d. Smith is to belong to that Quarter wherein Capt. Smith Lives

Voted to Choose two assessors Living in the Center of the Town in addition to the Five Chose Last monday then Chose Capt. Samuel Flagg, & Doct^r. Elijah Dix

It was moved & Seconded to See if the Town would grant a Sum of Money to Purchase a Fire Engine, & the motion was put, & it passed in the Negative

Voted that Daniel Chadwick be annexed to Capt. Nathl. Brooks School Quarter So Called

Worcester Town Records, 1786. 73

Voted to allow Simeon Duncan his account for Diging a Grave for a Woman that Dyed at the Towns House & 1 pair of Cords

£ 0 .. 12 .. 0

Voted to allow William Jenison the Sum mentioned in his Request

19 .. 5 .. 2

£ 19 .. 17 .. 2

William Jenisons Request is as Follows——

To the Inhabitants of the Town of Worcester at their March Meeting 1786 William Jenison adm^r. on the Estate of his Father Israel Jenison Late of Worcester Gen^t. Dec^d. Humbly Shews

That his Said Father as a Committee man for the Town in June 1779 borrowed for their use of Sundry Persons the Sum of Seventeen hundred Pounds and gave his own private Note of hand therefor

That his Said Father rec^d. an order for S^d. Sum after it had been consolidated amounting to the Sum of £ 116 .. 16 .. 1½ which Sum included the interest to the first of January 1782 That Part of S^d. order has been paid S^d. William by M^r. Nathan Patch Collector vizt. the Sum of Sixty Eight Pounds Eleven Shillings & one penny half penny—that the Remainder of S^d. Sum being £ 4 .. 5 .. 0 is yet due & unpaid

That he has never been able to get the Said order discharged altho his S^d. Father in his Life Time made repeated applications therefor to the Treasurer and he also Sence his Father Death has has used his Endeavours by Further application that on y^e. 10 of march currant he gave up the old order & the present Selectmen gave him an order on M^r. Perry the Town Treasurer to receive the Said Sum of £ 48 .. 5/ but would not allow him any Interest on S^d. Sum but informed your Petetioner that it was without their Power to allow the S^d. Interest and advised that the matter be Laid before the Town for their Consideration—your Petetioner would therefore inform the Town that for want of S^d. money to discharge the S^d. Notes given by his S^d. Father he has been obliged to pay Interest on them to the amount of Nineteen Pounds five Shillings & two pence which will be too great a loss for him

Worcester Town Records, 1786.

to bear therefore prays the Town to grant Him that Sum of £19 .. 5 .. 2—And as Duty Bound Shall ever Pray

Willm. Jenison ad^r.

Voted to Choose a Committee to examine the accounts brought against the Town at this meeting then Chose Tim°. Paine Esqr., Doct^r. Elijah Dix, & Capt. Benjamen Heywood a Committee for Said Purpose

To the Selectmen of Worcester Gentlemen

We the Subscribers Freeholders & Inhabitants of the Town of Worcester Desire you would insert in your next warrant for calling a Town Meeting To See if the Town will Grant a Sum of money to provide a Fire Engine for the use of Said Town to be under Such Regulations as the Town Shall order according to Law and to act thereon as they Shall think Proper

Worcester Fe^b. 20th. 1786

Samuel Flagg, Tim°. Paine, Nathan Patch, Willm. Jenison, Joseph Allen, Elijah Dix, Daniel Goulding, Samuel Chandler, John Stanton, John Nazro

Voted that this Meeting be Further adjourned to Monday the third Day of April Next at one OClock in the afternoon then to meet at this Place & the Meeting was accordingly adjourned

A True Entry   attest   Daniel Goulding Town Clerk

At a Publick Town Meeting held at the Publick meeting house in Worcester on Monday the third day of April in the year of our Lord Seventeen hundred & Eighty Six for to Vote for. Govener Lieu^t. Govener, &c, then the Following Persons were Voted for Said offices & had the Number of Votes expressed against their Respective Names—Viz——

James Bowdoine Esqr.	45	
Thomas Cushing Esqr.	2	as Govener
John Hancock Esqr.	1	
Samuel Bridge	1	

Worcester Town Records, 1786.

Thomas Cushing Esqr.	25	
James Warren Esqr.	2	
Nathan^l. Gorham Esqr.	2	
Jonathan Warner Esqr.	1	as Lieu^t. Govener
Benjⁿ. Lincoln Esqr.	1	
Saml. Adams Esqr.	1	
Joseph Ball	1	
Aaron Bancroft	1	

Moses Gill Esqr	43	Benjamen Heywood	8
John Sprague Esqr.	42	Artimas Ward Esqr.	20
Saml. Baker Esqr.	44	Seth Washburn Esqr.	10
Rufus Putnam Esqr	21	Jonathan Warner Esqr.	3
Levi Lincoln Esqr.	18	Abel Wilder Esqr.	8

The Meeting was then Dissolved

        A True Entry   Attest   Daniel Goulding T C

At a Town meeting Continued by adjournment to Monday the Third Day of April A, D, 1786 & then Met Then the Following Votes were passed—viz—

Voted to abate M^r. Seth Hastings^s. State Tax in M^r. Barbers hands to Collect he having Paid the Same to Edmond Fowle   £

Voted to abate John Browns Pole Tax in M^r. Barbers hands to Collect he Producing a Certificate from the Town Clerk where he was Born proving that he was not Sixteen years of age when Said Tax was made   0..19..3

Voted to abate John Barbers Tax in M^r. Barbers hands to Collect he having paid his Taxes to Willm. Barber in Benson   0..

Voted that the Prayer of the Petetion of Othniel Taylor be granted So far as that his Poll Tax be abated & that Said Taylor have Liberty of Letting the Remainder of his Taxes lye for the Term of one year on Interest he giving Security to the Town with Sufficient Bondsmen   The Petetion is as follows

To the Inhabitants of Worcester assembled in Town meeting the first monday in April 1786 by adjournment from the 2^d. monday in march Last—

Othniel Taylor of Worcester humbly Shews — that for Some years past he has been in a poor State of Health & not been able to carry on his Farm that the Annual Payments he is obliged to make to his Step mother by order of his Father will with extraordinary Labor he has been obliged to hire to carry on his Farm has reduced him to Poverty, to Such a Degree that he is unable to pay his Taxes due to the Several Collectors vizt to M^r. Patch y^e. Sum of £19..4..5½ besides a paper money Tax of £5..19 — to Daniel Goulding 15/5½ To M^r. Joseph Barber y^e. Sum of £2..17..4 and to M^r. Jesse Taft y^e. Sum of — 11/5 That the S^d. Othniel among his other Difficultys he labors under is Deafness which Disanables him from Transacting any Business with his Fellow Citizens and cannot be in any wise Benefitted on that account in attending Publick worship & thinks that this misfortune Intitles him to an Exemption from his Poll Tax in all the Rates aforesaid, he therefore humbly prays that his Poll Tax in Said Rates may be abated and that the Town will So far indulge him as to the remainder of his Taxes as to take his Note of hand on Interest payable to the Town and give him orders on S^d. Collectors to discharge the Said Taxes and he will Endeavor to pay them as Soon as he possibly can otherwise your poor Petetioner must resign himself up to be comitted to Goal for Said Taxes—as in Duty bound Shall pray

Othniel Taylor

then Voted that this Meeting be further adjourned to may Next the Fifteenth Day at two OClock in the afternoon then to meet at this Place—& the meeting was adjourned accordingly

    A True Entry   Attest   Daniel Goulding Town Clerk

At a meeting of the Freeholders & others inhabitants of the Town of Worcester Qualified to Vote in Town affairs on wednesday the Tenth day of may 1786 then the Following Votes were passed—viz—

Chose Deacon Nathan Perry Moderator

It was moved & Seconded & the motion put to know the minds of the Town whether they were ready to come to a Choice of a person to Settle with them in the work of the ministery & it passed in the affirmative

It was then motioned & Seconded & the motion put to know the mind of the Town whether they would give M^r. Daniel Storer a call to Settle with them in the work of the ministery & it passed in the affirmative

Voted to Choose a Committee to Join a Committee of the Church to Draw Some proposals to offer M^r. Storer & Lay them before the Town at the adjournment then Chose Capt. Saml. Brooks, Joseph Wheeler Esqr. M^r. Robert Smith, Doct^r. Elijah Dix, M^r. John Chamberlain a Committee for Said Purpose

Then Voted that this meeting be adjourned to monday Next at Ten OClock in the forenoon then to meet at this Place—& the meeting was accordingly adjourned

  A True Entry Attest Daniel Goulding Town Clerk

At the above Town meeting held on the Tenth Day of May 1786 then the following Vote was passed—viz—

Voted to Choose a Committee to meet a Committee Chose by M^r. Bancrofts Society & agree with them in regard of the Ministerial Property belonging to this Town then Chose Capt. Samuel Brooks, Joseph Wheeler Esqr., Doct^r. Elijah Dix, & Deacon Thomas Wheeler, a Committee for S^d. purpose

   A True Entry attest Danl. Goulding T. C.

At a Town Meeting held on the Tenth Day of May A D 1786 & Continued by adjournment to Monday the fifteenth Day of the Same may & then Met then the Following Votes were passed viz

The Committee Chose to Joyn the Committee of the Church to draw Some proposals to offer M\`. Daniel Story made the Following Report—

The Committee appointed to take into consideration what may be proper to offer M\`. Daniel Story to Incourage him to Settle with us in the Gospel ministry beg leave to Report as follows viz —£ 300 Settlement to be paid in the following manner viz 100 in the first year of his ministry & 100 in the Second year & 100 in the third year of his ministry with us also to give him as an annual Sallery £ 120   all which is humbly Submitted

       p\`. order Jacob Chamberlain
Worcester may 12th. 1786 p\`. order Samuel Brooks

The above Report of the Committee having been read it was then Voted that M\`. Daniel Story have the Liberty of excepting of the proposals mentioned in Said Report or that the Town give him the Sum of one hundred & Fifty pounds annually exclusive of any Settlement

Voted that the above Said Committee Chose by the Town & Church wait on M\`. Story with the Votes of the Town

Voted then that this meeting be dissolved & it was dissolved accordingly

  A True Entry Attest Daniel Goulding Town Clerk

At a Publick Meeting of the Inhabitants of the Town of Worcester Qualified to Vote for Representatives Legally warned & assembled at the Publick meeting house in Said Town on Monday the Fifteenth day of may 1786

a motion was made & Seconded & the Question put whether the Town will Choose a Representative to represent this Town in the General Court the Current year & it passed in the affirmative   then the Town Chose Capt. Samuel Brooks for to represent Said Town in the Said Court for the Current year

At the Same Time & Place the Inhabitants of Said Town Qualified to Vote in Town affairs passed the following Votes viz—

Deacon Nathan Perry Chosen Moderator

Voted to Choose a Committee to provide the Town with a grammar School the Current year Then Chose M^r. Isaiah Thomas, Doct^r. Elijah Dix & M^r. John Nazro a Committee for Said Purpose

Voted that the Committee Chose March last to Provide the Town with Schooling be a Committee to consider on Some method that the Town may be Supplyed with a grammar School

Voted that the Selectmen agree with Some person or persons to take care of the meeting house & ring the Bell

Voted that the committee Chose to make Sale of the ministerial Land advertise the Same the way that they Shall think most proper & Sell the Same as Soon as there has been proper Notice given of Said Sale

Voted for a County Treasurer & the Following Persons were Voted for & had the Number of Votes expressed against their Respective Names   Timothy Paine 22, Nathan Perry 46, Samuel Flagg 33, John Chamberlain 1.

Voted that this Meeting be adjourned to monday the Twenty Ninth Day of this present may at Five OClock in the afternoon then to Meet at this Place & the meeting was accordingly adjourned

A True Entry   Attest   Daniel Goulding Town Clerk

At a Town Meeting held on the Thirteenth day of March 1786 and Continued by adjournments from Time to Time to this fifteenth day of may following & then met then the following Votes were passed viz—

Voted that the prayer of the Petition of Berzaliel Stearns & others be granted in regard of their being [formed into a] Destrict or Quarter for the purpose of Schooling   then Chose M^r.

Worcester Town Records, 1786.

Benjamen Flagg Ju^r. a School Committee man for Said Destrect or Quarter—the Petetion is as Follows viz

Worcester May 15th. 1786 To the freeholders and Other inhabitants of the Town of Worcester in Town Meeting assembled Gentlemen the Petition of us the Subscribers being inhabitants of Said Town Lately annexed to Said Town and also others formerly belonging to Said Town humbly Sheweth that whereas the first mentioned Persons are not as yet formed into a Destrect or Quarter for the Purpose of Schooling and the Last mentioned Persons not well accommodated, Pray that the Town would take this our Scituation under Consideration and form the Subscribers into a Destrect or Quarter for the Purpose above mentioned and as in Duty Bound Shall Ever Pray—Berzaliel Stearns, Benjn. Flagg Ju^r., Joshua Harrington Ju^r., Noah Harrington, Phineas Flagg, Benjamen Newton, Elijah Newton, Daniel Stearns, John Willard, Hilyer Tanner, Daniel Baird, Ruben Gray, John Stearns, Isaac Flagg

Voted to allow the Following accounts not examined by the Committee

to Flagg & Stanton for Articles dld M^r. Crosby £0..13..9
to Willm. Elder for Boarding John Spence 24
  Weeks from the 28th. of No^v. to this 15th.
  of May 1786 at 3/   3..12..0
to John Waters for Taking care of the Meeting House the year 85   3..0..0
                      £7..5..9

Voted to accept & allow the Report of the Committee Chose to examine Sundry accounts the Report is as Follows viz

The Committee appointed to Examine Sundrey accounts exhibited against the Town at march meeting 1786 report that they have exam^d. & allowed the following accounts viz—

N°. 1 to Levi Flagg for Sundrey^s. Supplyed
  Simon Glasco as by account   £1..1..6
  2 to Thomas Knight for keeping Tem-
    perance Cummings 10 Days   1..0..0

Worcester Town Records, 1786.

3 to Joseph Wheeler Esqr. his account for fees Relating to Sundrey Paupers	1 .. 10 .. 0
4 to Edward Knight for 5 Cord of Wood for Simon Glasco at 6/	1 .. 10 .. 0
5 to Thadeas Maccarty Sundry medicenes &c Supplyed Simon Glasco & Abiah Crosby	3 .. 1 .. 10
6 to Henery Taft going to Bolton to Serve a Sytation on account of Rosanna M^c.pine	0 .. 6 .. 8
7 to James Quigley for Boarding Agnes Brooks 44 Weeks at 3/4 and Elizabeth Brooks 52 Weeks at 2/8 p^r. week both Ending march 1st 1786	14 .. 5 .. 4
8 to the assessor for y^e. year 1785 for making a highway Tax Taking Valuatoin & making Town & County Tax	5 .. 14 .. 3
9 to Abel Stowel Expences conveying two poor Persons at Different Times to Shrewsbury	1 .. 12 .. 0
	£ 30 .. 1 .. 9

April 3^d. 1786   Tim^o. Paine P^r. Order

Then Voted that this meeting be adjourned to Wednesday the Twenty Ninth day of this Present may at Five OClock in the afternoon then to meet at this Place & the meeting was accordingly adjourned

    A True Entry   Attest   Daniel Goulding Town Clerk

At a Town meeting held on the Fifteenth day of may 1786 and continued by adjournment to the Twenty Ninth day of the Same may & then met then the Following Votes were passed viz—

Voted that the Grammar School to be kept in this Town the Current year be a moving School

Voted that the Sum of Sixty Pounds of the money granted march Last for the purpose of Supplying the Town with Schooling be appropriated for the purpose of Supporting & hireing a Grammar School master

Voted to excuse M^r. John Nazro & Doct^r. Elijah Dix from Serving as Committee men for hireing a Grammar School master

Voted that the Selectmen be desired to hire a Grammar School master to keep School in this Town the Current Year

Voted that this meeting be dissolved & the meeting was accordingly dissolved

  A True Entry Attest Daniel Goulding Town Clerk

At a Town meeting held on the thirteenth day of march and Continued by adjournment from Time to Time to this Twenty Ninth day of may A D 1786 & then met then the Following Votes were passed viz

Voted that John Woodward have Liberty of Letting the Ballance of his Taxes due to M^r. Nathan Patch lye for the present he giving his Security to the Town Treasurer on Interest—& that M^r. Nathan Patch be allowed the Same Sum

Voted to allow M^{rs}. Mary Boyds account Boarding Ritchard Morss from No^v. 28th. to may 28th. 1786 at 2/ p^r. week & 6/ for Curing him of the Salt Reume   £ 2 .. 18 .. 0

Voted to accept the Following Report of the Selectmen in regard of the money Due to the Town

A Return of the Subscribers of the Situation of the Bonds in favour of the Town of Worcester for the year 1785

In the hands of Phineas Ward Suretys Saml. Curtis & David Ritchardson £ 22 .. 15 .. 0 Interest P^d. to No^v. 1785
 in the hands of Stephen Dexter, Surety David Thomas
        33 .. 6 .. 8 In Paid to No^v. 1785
 in the hands of Ezekiel How Ju^r., Surety Ezekiel How
        20 .. 0 .. 0 In Due 36/ No^v. 1785
 in the hands of David Bigelow, Surety John Green
        35 .. 6 .. 8 1 years inter Due No^v. 85

in Palmer Gouldings hands Suretys Ignatius & Peter Goulding 46..13..4 2 years interest Due No^v. 1785
in the hands of Oliver Watson Suretys Oliver Watson & W^m. M^{c}farland   83..6..8 1 years interest Due march 1785
in the hand of Joseph Allen, Elijah Dix & Saml. Allen
51..1..1 Interest P^d. Oct 1785
in the hands of John Taylor, W^m. Young & W^m. M^{c}farland Suretys   42..3.4 Int. P^d. to No^v. 1785
In the hands of William Young Suretys Peter Johnson & John Taylor   48..10..0 Interest Not paid
In the hands of Simeon Duncan Suretys Joseph Blaire & Joseph Allen   40..0..0 In^t. P^d. Fe^{b}y 1786
In the hands of Joseph Allen Suretys Levi Lincoln & Ignatius Goulding   84..10..0 In^t. P^d. Fe^b. 1786
In the hands of Paul Gates Suretys Willm. Gates & W^m. Mahan   35..0..0 In^t. P^d. Fe^b. 1786
In the hands of Levi Lincoln Suretys Joseph Allen Ignatius Goulding   51..10..0 In^t. P^d. Fe^b. 1786
in the hands of Daniel Goulding Suretys Palmer & Ignatius Goulding   48..10..1 In^t. P^d. Fe^b. 1786
in the hands of John Stanton Suretys Saml. Flagg & Clark Chandler   36..10..0 1 years In^t. Due
in the hands of Willm. Treadwell Suretys Nathan Patch & John Stowers   152..10..0 In^t. P^d. Fe^b. 1786
in the hands of John Stanton & Danl. Goulding Surety Palmer Goulding   35..0..0 one years In^t. Due march 86

Pue Bonds

in the hands of Saml. Brown Dec^d. Suretys Elijah & Lem^l. Rice
39..5..0 1 y^{rs}. In^t. Due July 85
in the hands of Isaiah Thomas Suretys Joseph Allen & Nathan Patch   42..15..0 2 years In^t. Due July 85
in the hands of Nathan Patch Suretys Cornelius Stowel & Joshua Whitney   33..5..0 1 years In^t. Due July 85
in the hands of Elijah Dix Suretys Saml. Brown & Edward Bangs   39..5..0 In^t. P^d. July 85
Capt. Saml. Flaggs Lease Six pounds annually one years Interest Due march 1786

84   Worcester Town Records, 1786.

The Sum of Fifty-Six pounds fifteen Shillings & $6^d.\frac{1}{2}$ interest money Paid into the Town Treasurer Sence the Last Settlement

All which we humbly Submit

                        Nathan Perry   ⎞ Selectmen
                        John Chamberlain ⎬ of
                        Saml. Brooks   ⎠ Worcester

Voted then that this meeting be Dissolved and it was Dissolved accordingly

    A True Entry   Attest   Daniel Goulding Town Clerk

At a Town Meeting Legally assembled at the Publick meeting house in Worcester on Thursday the Tenth day of August A D, 1786 the following Votes were passed

Deacon Nathan Perry Chosen Moderator

then the Following Letter was red Derected to the Selectmen of Worcester

In Convention begun & held at Leicester by Delegates for a Number of the Towns in the County of Worcester on Monday the 26th. of June 1786   Voted that there be a Committee Chosen to write to the Towns in the above Said County which are not assembled with us to invite them to meet us in Convention by their Deligates to be holden by adjournment on Tuesday the 15th. Day of August Next at the house of George Bruce Inn holder in Leicester at Nine OClock, A. M, then and there to take under their Consideration Such Matters as Shall appear to them to be Grievances and for the Towns to instruct their Deligates concerning a Circulating Medium or Such means of Redress as they Shall think Proper—Voted that Doct^r. James Freeland of Sutton be one of the Committee and to write to the Town of Worcester Douglas & Northbridge

In Compliance with the above Vote I do hereby in behalf of the Conventions invite the Town of Worcester to meet us by their Deligate or Deligates at Time and Place and for the Purposes above mentioned

   Sutton July 29th. 1786   James Freeland ⎱ one of the
   To the Selectmen of Worcester   ⎰ Committee

A Motion was then made & Seconded to know the minds of the Town whether they would Send a Deligate or Deligates to meet in Convention agreeable to the Second Article in the Warrant for this meeting and the motion was put & it passed in the Negative

Voted then that this Meeting be Dissolved & it was Dissolved accordingly

  A True Entry Attest Daniel Goulding Town Clerk

At a meeting of the Freeholders & Other Inhabitants of the Town of Worcester qualified to Vote in Town affairs legally warned & assembled at the publick meeting house in Said Town on Monday the Twenty fifth day of September in the Year of our Lord Seventeen hundred & Eighty Six the Following Votes were Passed viz—

Deacon Nathan Perry Chosen Moderator

Voted that the address from the Selectmen of Boston to the Inhabitants of this Commonwealth be read

A motion was made & Seconded to See if the Town would Choose a Deligate or Deligates to Joyn the Convention adjourned to paxton agreeable to the Second article in the Warrant for this meeting & the question being put thereon it passed in the affirmative

The Vote for Sending was 47 against 39

A motion was then made to See if the Town would Choose two Deligates to Join in Said Convention & the question being put thereon & it passed in the affirmative—then the Town Chose M^r. David Bigelow & M^r. Daniel Baird for Said Deligates

Voted that the Delegates Chosen Lay there Doings before the Town at the adjournment of this meeting for there approbation

Voted that this meeting be adjourned to Monday the Second Day of October Next at four OClock in the afternoon then to meet at this Place & the meeting was accordingly adjourned

Worcester Town Records, 1786.

A Petition mentioned in the Second Article in the Warrant for the above meeting

To the Selectmen of the Town of Worcester Gentlemen The Petetion of us the Subscribers humbly Sheweth that whereas Not Long Sence there was a Town meeting held in this Town to See if the Town would Choose a Deligate to go to Leicester to Join in Convention agreeable to a Request of James Freeland one of the Committee of Said Committee of Said Convention and it was Voted Not to Send we conceive that the Reason must have been because the warning was Some What Short and the people were not well apprised of the importance of Sending and whereas the Said Convention is adjourned to the last Tuesday of September Next then to meet at Paxton we pray that you would call a Town meeting as Soon as may be to See if the Town will Choose a Deligate or Deligates to Join in Said Convention and for the Town to give instruction to their Deligate or Deligates if they Shall think proper Worcester August 25th. 1786 John Curtis, John Gleason, Ebenezer Willington, Benjamen Stowell, Jabez Tatman, Nathan White, William Mahan, Solomon Bixbee, Thomas Knight, Eli Chapen, Samuel Mower, Peter Slater, Thaddeus Chapen. Edward Knight, Nathl. Brooks, Willm. Knight, Ebenezar Willington Ju^r., Joshua Harrington Ju^r. Elijah Harrington

---

At a Meeting of the Freeholders & Other Inhabitants of the Town of Worcester Qualified to Vote in Town affairs begun & held at the meeting house in Said Town on monday the Twenty fifth day September A, D, 1786 & Continued by adjournment to monday the Second day of October Following and then Met

Voted that the Deligates Chose by this Town Last monday to Join the Convention at Paxton inform the Town of there doings

Then they Laid a Petetion before the Town from the Convention to the General Court

Voted that M^r. Daniel Baird be requested to inform the Town whether the Petetion read is agreeable to his mind, and he informed the Town that it was but that it was not agreeable to his mind to have it Sent to the General Court before it had been laid before the Town

Voted that the Petetion be read Paragraph by Paragraph and then the Town to Vote whether they will accept of the whole of it or not

The Petetion being read, a motion was made and Seconded to See if the Town would accept of the Petetion & the Question being put thereon, it passed in the Negative—it was then Voted that the deligates be dismissed from any further Service as Delegates

Voted that this meeting be dissolved, and the meeting was dissolved accordingly

  A True Entry Attest Daniel Goulding Town Clerk

The Petition of Joshua Whitney & Others

To the Gentlemen Selectmen of Worcester we the Subscribers petition that you will forthwith grant a Warrant for calling a Town meeting to See if the Town will Choose a Deligate or Deligates to meet in Convention at M[r]. Nathan Patch[s]. at Worcester on the Second Tuesday of November Next by adjournment from Paxton as in Duty bound Shall ever Pray—Worcester October 2[d]. 1786

Joshua Whitney, Joseph Barber, Elijah Harrington, Ruben Gray, Samuel Mower, Silas Harrington, Thadeas Chapen, Nathan White, Eli Chapen, Daniel Willington, Jon[a]. Glezen, Elisha Smith, Isaac Gleason, Jacob Hemenway, Robert Gray, John Moore 2[d]., Will[m]. Jeneson Sterne, Jonathan Osland, Thomas Nickols Ju[r]., James M[c]farland, John Moore, Daniel Heywood 2[d]. Ruben Hamilton Thaddeus Moore, Jabez Tatman, John Tatman, Jonathan Grout, Benjamen Stowell, Thomas Rice, Frances Harrington, Nathaniel Harrington, Joshua Bigelow, Joel Wesson, Will[m]. Taylor

The Petetion of Doct[r]. Dix & others

To the Gentlemen Selectmen of the Town of Worcester

Gentlemen your Petetioners earnestly request that you would

call a Town meeting as Soon as may be convenient for the following purposes To consider what measures are proper for the Town to adopt respecting the critical and alarming Situation of the Country that may tend to ease the minds of the people lessen their burdens & Secure to them the blessings of a free & equal Government

To See if the Town will instruct their Representative to enquire into the Expenditures of Publick monies the Salaries of the officers of Government the ways & means of Increasing the manufacteries of the Country—Promoting and rendering more Profitable the Business of husbandry and to use his best endeavours to diminish all Unnecessary publick expences—to remove every Grievance that the people may labour under at Present or that they may be exposed to in future And your Petetioners as in Duty bound Shall ever Pray

Worcester October 4th. 1786 Elijah Dix, Robert Smith, Wm. Bowles, Nathaniel Moore, Joseph Kingsbury, Isaiah Thomas, Timo. Bigelow, Daniel Waldo, Benjn. Flagg, John Pierce, Leml. Rice, John Goodwin, Jonathan Rice, Thomas Wheeler, Asa Moore, William Gates, Nathan Heard,

At a Meeting of the Freeholders and Other Inhabitants of the Town of Worcester Qualified to Vote in Town affairs legally warned and assembled at the Publick meeting house in Said Town on Monday the Sixteenth Day of October A. D. 1786

Mr. David Bigelow was Chosen Moderator

A motion was made & Seconded to See if the Town will Choose a Deligate or Deligates to meet in Convention at the house of Mr. Nathan Patchs. in Worcester on the Second Tuesday of November Next by adjournment from Paxton agreeable to a Petetion of Joshua Whitney & Others and the Question being put after Long Debates thereon & it passed in the affirmative 62 For & 53 against

the Town then Chose Mr. David Bigelow & Mr. Daniel Baird Deligates to meet in Said Convention

Voted that the Speech of the Honble Mr. Kings before the General Court be read

Worcester Town Records, 1786.

Voted to instruct our Representative agreeable to the Petetion of Doct^r. Elijah Dix & others—a Committee to form instructions for our Representative & lay them before the Town for acceptance were then Chosen viz Doct^r. Elijah Dix, M^r. David Bigelow, & M^r. Daniel Baird

Voted that the Deligates lay the doings of the Convention before the Town for their approbation or disapprobation at the Next Town meeting after the meeting of the Convention and that their be an Article in the Warrant for Said purpose

Voted to Choose a Committee to Examine the accounts brought against the Town & make report at the adjournment of this meeting then Chose Tim^o. Paine Esqr. Doct^r. Elijah Dix & Doct^r. Benjamen Green for Said Committee

Voted that M^r. Thomas be desired to Publish in his Magazine the Doings of this meeting & that the Town Clerk Supply him with an attested Coppy for that purpose

Voted that this meeting be adjourned to monday the Twenty third day of this Instant October at three OClock, P, M, then to meet at this Place & the meeting was accordingly adjourned

  A True Entry Attest Daniel Goulding Town Clerk

At a Town meeting held in Worcester on Monday the Sixteenth day of October A, D, 1786 & Continued by adjournment to monday the Twenty third of the Same October & then met then the following votes were passed viz

A motion was made & Seconded to See if the Town would accept of the instructions that Doct^r. Elijah Dix has formed & laid before the Town for their acceptance he being one of the Committee to form instructions for the Representative this motion being put it passed in the Negative—59 for the motion & 67 against

Then the Committee Chose to form instructions for the Representative for this Town laid the following instructions before the Town for their acceptance—

At a meeting of the Freeholders and Other inhabitants of the Town of Worcester held by adjournment October 23ᵈ. 1786 Voted that the following instructions be given to Capᵗ. Samuel Brooks Representative of this town the Present year—

Sir. Notwithstanding the good Opinion this Town entertain of your abilities and integrity yet in the present difficult and distressᵗ condition of this Commonwealth we think it proper to give you the following instructions viz—1ˢᵗ. that whereas the seting of the General Court in the Town of Boston is attended with great inconveniences we request you to use your endeavours that it be removed to Some inland Town

2ᵈ. that the Courts of Common pleas and general Sessions be aniolated and Some cheaper and more expeditious meathod be Substituted in their Room

3ᵈ. that the grant of the Supplementary fund to Congress for Twenty five years be emedeately repealed and the revenue arising by the impost and Excise be appropriated to the payment of the foreign Debt and if that Shall prove insufficient that anual grantes be made to make up Such Defficiency and that all other Supplys be with held from Congress till accompts between this Commonwealth and the Continent can be Setled

4ᵗʰ. That you indeavour to have the law repealed which obliges Each Town to keep a Grammer School at the Expence of the Town as we think it a burden to be oblidged to hire and pay a Grammer master when the Town at Large receives no advantage thereby these Sir are our Sentements with which we instruct you to use your Exercions in their Support

David Bigelow } Committee
Daniel Baird   }

the Town then Voted after Long debates to accept of the three first paragraphs in Said Petetion—the Number of Votes for accepting was 62 & 54 against accepting

Voted then that the Town Clerk Transmit a Coppy of the three first paragraps to Capᵗ. Samˡ. Brooks Representative for this Town for his instructions

Voted that Mʳ. Thomas be desired to Print the instructions to the representative for this Town in his Magazine

Worcester Town Records, 1786.

Voted to accept the following Report laid before the Town by the Committee Chose to examine accounts against the Town

Committee appointed to examine accounts against the Town report that they have examined the Following which they find due to the following Persons viz

N°.		
1	To Mary Boyd keeping Ritchard McDonalds Child from ye 28th May to the 16th. of Octr. being 37 Weeks at 2/ p^r. Week	£3..14..0
2	Daniel Johnson keeping Zachariah Johnson from 4th. April 1786 till Octr. 16th 27 & ½ Weeks at 4/	5..10..0
3	to Constable Trowbridge executing a Warrant agnst. Sarah McPune & Transporting her to Town of Bolton	1..3..0
4	to Edward Knight for two Cord wood Supplyed Simon Glasco	0..12..0
5	to Nathan Perry Sundreys Supplyed Ben^n. Crosby for his dafter	0..16..1
6	to Nathan Perry Boarding John Spence from 15 May 1786 to the Octr. 16 22 Weeks	3..19..2
6	John Goodwin for mending the Bell	0..4..0
7	Samuel Eaton Boarding & Keeping his mother from y^e. first of Sep^t. 1785 to the first of Sep^t. 1786 52 Weeks at 4/6 p^r.	11..14..0
8	Christiana Walker Boarding Jenny Dyar from 15 april 1786 to 15 Octr. 1786 being 26 weeks at 2/ p^r. Week	2..12..0
9	to D^r. John Green his account against Lydia Bowman by order of ye Selectmen	2..0..0
10	to John Knower his account of Carrying a Poor Person from Worcester to Ward	0..5..4
		£32..9..7

Tim°. Paine by order

Worcester Town Records, 1786.

Voted to allow the Following Persons their accounts to M^{rs}. Anna Chandler for Boarding Ministers & keeping horses   38 .. 7 .. 5
to Doct^r. Nahum Willard for Doctering Millicent Goulding being   2 .. 1 .. 4
to William Johnson the Ballance of his account for mending the Bell October 1785   0 .. 8 .. 8
                                                                      £73 .. 7 .. 0

Voted not to allow any Part of Doct^r. John Green accounts against M^{rs}. Hambelton George Tracy & Benjn. Crosby

A motion was made & Seconded to have this meeting Dissolved the motion was put & a Number Voted to have the meeting Dissolved & as the Contary Vote was Called for their was a Motion made to Dismiss the Deligates Chose by this Town to meet in County Convention—But after Long debates the Moderator Declared that it was a Vote to Dessolve the meeting and accordingly Declared the meeting Dissolved

    A True Entry   Attest   Daniel Goulding Town Clerk

[A Warrant was issued October 16th, 1786 with two articles as follows:

1 to Choose a Moderator

2^d For the Town to grant Such Sum or Sums of money as may be Sufficient to Defray the Charges for the Currant year]

Worcester October 23^d. 1786 The Town met & Voted not to act on the above Warrant

    A True Entry   attest   Daniel Goulding Town Clerk

At a Publick meeting of the Freeholders & Other Inhabitants of the Town of Worcester at the meeting house in Said Town on Monday the Twenty Seventh day of November A, D, 1786 then the following Votes were passed viz

Deacon Nathan Perry Chosen Moderator

Voted that this meeting be adjourned to monday the fourth day of December Next at Nine OClock in the forenoon then to meet at this Place & the meeting was accordingly adjourned[1]

  A True Entry attest Daniel Goulding Town Clerk

Met according to the above adjournment on Monday December the fourth and Voted that this meeting be further adjourned to Monday the Eleventh day of this Instant December at Nine OClock in the morning then to meet at this place—& the meeting was accordingly adjourned

  A True Entry Attest Daniel Goulding Town Clerk

At a meeting of the Freeholders & Other Inhabitants of the Town of Worcester Qualified to Vote in Town affairs at the publick meeting house in Said Town on Monday the fourth day of December A, D, 1786 then the following Votes were Passed viz

Deacon Nathan Perry Chosen Moderator

Voted that this Meeting be adjourned to monday the Eleventh day of this Instant December at Nine OClock in the forenoon then to meet at this Place & the meeting was accordingly adjourned

  A True Entry Attest Daniel Goulding Town Clerk

At a meeting of the Freeholders & Other Inhabitants of the Town of Worcester qualified to Vote in Town affairs begun & held at the Publick meeting house in Said Town on Monday the Twenty Seventh day of November A, D, 1786 & Continued by

---

[1] Article in the Warrant:—"For the Town to Come into Such measures as may be necessary Relative to the Ordination of Mr. Daniel Story"

94   *Worcester Town Records, 1786.*

adjournment from time to time to the Eleventh day of December following & then Met

Voted that M^r. John Nazro be Moderator Pro Tempore Deacon Nathan Perry being absent

Voted that this Meeting be further adjourned to friday the fifteenth day of this Instant December at Nine OClock in the forenoon then to meet at this Place—and the meeting was accordingly adjourned

 A True Entry Attest Daniel Goulding Town Clerk

At a meeting of the Freeholders & other Inhabitants of the Town of Worcester qualified to Vote in Town affairs begun & held at the Publick meeting house in Said Town on Monday the fourth day of December A, D, 1786 & Continued by adjournment to the Eleventh Day of the Same December and then Met

Voted that M^r. John Nazro be moderator Pro Tempore Deacon Nathan Perry being absent

Voted that this meeting be adjourned to friday the fifteenth day of this Instant December at Nine OClock in the Morning then to meet at this Place—and the meeting was accordingly adjourned

 A True Entry Attest Daniel Goulding Town Clerk

At a meeting of the Freeholders & Other inhabitants of the Town of Worcester Qualified to Vote in Town affairs begun & held at the Publick meeting house in Said Town on Monday the Twenty Seventh day of November A, D, 1786 & Continued by adjournment from Time to Time to the Fifteenth day of December following & then Met then the following Votes were passed viz—

Voted to Choose a Committee to consult with M^r. Story in regard of the Ordination—the vote was Scrupled & the house was devided & there was 97 for & 59 against the motion

then Chose Deacon Nathan Perry, Deacon Jacob Chamberlain, Deacon Thomas Wheeler, William Young Esqr. & Capt. Samuel Brook for Said Committee

Voted that this meeting be Dissolved & the meeting was Dissolved accordingly

  A True Entry Attest Daniel Goulding Town Clerk

At a meeting of the Freeholders & Other Inhabitants of the Town of Worcester Qualified to Vote in Town affairs begun & held at the Publick meeting house in Said Town on Monday the fourth day of December, A, D, 1786 and Continued by adjournments from time to Time to Friday the fifteenth Day of the Same December & then Met

Chose Capt. Micah Johnson a School Committee man in the room of Stephen Dexter who is moved out of this Town

A motion was made & Seconded to See if the Town will consent that the Society whereof the Rev^d. Aaron Bancroft is pastor be incorporated agreeable to the Following Proposals the motion being put after Long debates & it passed in the Negative there was 65 for the motion & 98 against it—the Proposals are as Followes viz

Proposals for accommodating all disputes respecting Ministerial matters Subsisting between the Town of Worcester & the Society whereof the Rev^d. Aaron Bancroft is Pastor & for uniting the Inhabitants of the Said Town in peace friendship mutual Satisfaction & kind offices towards one another and their respective Ministers

That Such Inhabitants of the Said Town as have or Shall become members of the Said Society by Signing or having Signed an Agreement for that purpose Shall as Soon as may be git incorporated into a Seperate parish with those Powers privileges & immunities common to other parishes Provided nevertheless that

Worcester Town Records, 1786.

nothing is to be construed So as to defeat or make void any of the articles or Clauses herein after expressed

Those persons only to be considered of the Said Society who Shall actually have Signed an Agreement for that purpose or Shall lodge their Names as is hereafter Expressed—That their Estates & families & Such persons as from Time to Time after the incorporation Shall Join the Said Society by Lodging their Names with the Town Clerk the first week in March annually for that purpose together with their families & Estates Shall be considered as belonging to & continuing of the Said Society or parish untill they Shall respectively express their desire of Joining the other Society by Lodging their Names with the Town Clerk expressive thereof in which case they are to be considered of the other Society the members of each Society having always free liberty to Join himself Estate & family to which Society he pleases by lodging his Name in manner as is above Expressed & Shall be held to pay only to the Society to which he professes to belong

That Such of the Said Inhabitants as now are or Shall become members of the Society afore Said together with their families & Estates Shall not be held or Subjected to pay have their property taken or appropriated or they be any ways assessed in any Sums of money for the Support of publick worship the ministry or the building repairing of a meeting house or houses excepting of that of their own Society or Parish from the thirteenth day of June A, D, 1785 being the Time when the Rev^d. M^r. Bancroft gave his answer to Settle over Said Society

That the Said Society Shall have Such apart of all the monies Estate or property or the interest thereof belonging to the Said Town that is or Shall be appropriated for the Support of the ministry or Publick worship annually applied by the Said Town to the use or benefit of the Said Society or parish as Shall be its proportion according to the interest that the inhabitants composing the Said Society from Time to Time Shall have in the Said monies Estate or property on the first Day of march annually according to the then last Town Rate

That all the property of the Church of the old Society is to remain their property & the meeting house to be Secured by the

Worcester Town Records, 1787.

Act of incorporation to the use of the old Society individuals retaining their private property in the pews which they own in Said Meeting house

Voted that this meeting be Dessolved & the meeting was Dessolved accordingly

  A True Entry Attest Daniel Goulding Town Clerk

At a meeting of the Freeholders & Other Inhabitants of the Town of Worcester qualified to Vote in Town affairs held at the Publick meeting house in Said Town on Monday the Eighth day of January A, D, 1787 Deacon Nathan Perry Moderator

Voted to accept the Following Report made by the Committee Chose to Proportion the School money

Worcester Nov : 20 1786   We the Subscribers being appointed a Committee by the Town of Worcester to ascertain each Quarters proportion of School money in S^d. Town report as follows

The Quarter in which $Doct^r$. Dix is Committee Man

		£ 45 .. 1 .. 2 .
Deacon Thomas Wheeler	D°.	6 .. 17 .. 8 . 3
Capt. $Nath^l$. Brooks	D°.	4 .. 7 .. 1 . 1
Deacon W^m. Bowles	D°.	6 .. 17 .. 0 . 1
M^r. Noah Harris	D°.	7 .. 4 .. 5 . 2
M^r. $Benj^a$. Flagg	D°.	3 .. 15 .. 7 . 2
M^r. $Eben^r$. Barber	D°.	4 .. 19 .. 5 . 3
Capt. Saml. Brooks	D°.	7 .. 14 .. 9 . 2
Capt. John Peirce	D°.	10 .. 9 .. 4 . 2
M^r. Thadeus Chamberlain	D°.	8 .. 2 .. 6 . 2
M^r. Stephen Dexter alias Capt. Micah Johnson	D°.	8 .. 11 .. 7 . 3
M^r. Gideon Smith	D°.	5 .. 19 .. 0 . 3
		£ 120 .. 0 .. 0 . 0

  all which is Humbly Submitted
    Elijah Dix p^r. Order

N. B. the Grammer School Proportion is half as much as what is Sett in this List

Worcester Town Records, 1787.

A motion was made & Seconded that all Disputes Respecting Ministerial matters in this Town between the two Societys be Setled agreeable to the Following proposals made by M^r. Nazro the motion being put passed in the Negative 58 For & 98 against the motion, the Proposals are as Follows

That Justice Equallity Peace Harmony & Friendship may take place in this Town—Voted that after the ordination of M^r. Daniel Story—This Town Consent that any of its Inhabitants who usually attend Public Worship under the Ministration of the Rev^d. Aaron Bancroft make application to the General Court, for an Act of Incorporation as Soon as may be, into a distinct Religious Society, Nor will this Town object to their being Secured by the Act of Incorporation to the annual use of the Said Society & members thereof for the Time being, Such a part of the Interest of the Ministerial property, belonging to Said Town as Shall be in proportion to the Right of the members composing Said Society, from Time to Time therein according to their then last Town Rate, Nor to the Securing to the Said Members their Families & Estates From paying being assessed or in any [way] made to contribute to ward the Support of Publick Worship, the ministry or building or repairing any other meeting house then for their own Worship from the Thirteenth day of June A, D, 1785

At which Time the Rev^d. M^r. Bancroft gave his answer provided that the Said Act Shall Secure to the residue of the Town the property of the meeting house in the Said Town excepting the right which individuals have or may have in & to the Pews therein——

And that the Said Act Shall Secure to all the Inhabitants of the Said Town respectively the priviledge of Worshiping with & of Joyning from Time to Time him or her Self family & Estate to which of the Said Societies he or She may Choose by Lodging his or her Name with the Town Clerk expressive of that purpose in any year in the month of march any agreement between the Rev^d. M^r. Bancroft & the persons under his Pastoral charge, to the contrary not withstanding, and Shall be held to pay only to the Society to which they profess to belong

Worcester Town Records, 1787.

The request mentioned in the third Article in the Warrant for this meeting is as Follows—viz—

To the Selectmen of the Town of Worcester   Gentlemen

We the Subscribers Freeholders & others within the Said Town request you to call a meeting of the Freeholders & other Inhabitants of the Said Town qualified to Vote in Town affairs to know the minds of the Town whether those persons who do or Shall belong to the Rev^d. M^r. Bancrofts Society Should finally be benefitted their Equal proportion of the Interest of the Ministerial property of the Town and be liable to ministerial assessments only for the Support of their own Minister & Publick Worship & to do and act thereon as the Town Shall think proper. And that an article may be inserted in the Warrant that may be issued for Said meeting in manner as above expressed—

Worcester December 23^d. 1786 John Nazro, Thomas Wheeler, Ruben Hambelton, James Trowbridge, W^m. Young, Daniel Waldo, Elijah Dix, Phineas Jones, John White, Samuel Jennison, William Buxton, Jonathan Gates, Daniel Waldo Ju^r. Simeon Duncan, Thomas Lynde

Voted that this meeting be adjourned to monday the fifteenth Day of this Instant January at one OClock P, M, then to meet at this Place & the meeting was adjourned accordingly

  A True Entry Attest Daniel Goulding Town Clerk

At a meeting of the Freeholders & other Inhabitants of the Town of Worcester Qualified to Vote in Town affairs begun & held at the Publick meeting house in Said Town on Monday the Eighth Day of January, A, D, 1787 & Continued by adjournment to this Fifteenth Day of the Same January and then Met a Motion was made & Seconded to See if the Town would have M^r. Storys answer read, the motion being Put passed in the Negative

A motion was made & Seconded to See if the Town will Settle all Disputes Respecting Ministerial matters in this Town agreeable to the Following proposals Laid before the Town by Judge

Lincoln the motion being put Passed in the Negative—the Proposals are as Follows—Viz—

Proposals to the Town by M^r. Bancrofts Society for the accommodation of ministerial disputes

1 That the members of M^r. Bancrofts Society be incorporated as Soon as may be with their Families and estates into a Seperate parish, and the act of incorporation to Secure the matters contained in the following articles

2dly That the inhabitants of the Town have Liberty from Time to Time & at all Times to Join him or her Self family and estate to which Society he or She pleases by Lodging his or her name with the Town Clark at any Time hereafter in the month of March for that purpose—any agreement or covenant to the contary notwithstanding

3^d. That the members of M^r. Bancrofts Society Shall not be assessed toward the Support of the publick worship of the old Society from the 7th day of June 1785

4th. That the ministerial property Shall remain to the uses for which it was originally granted, and to be appropriated only according to the Terms & force of the Said grants

5th. The meeting house to remain the property of the Town to be improved by the Society composed of the major part of the voters in Said Town and to be kept in repair by the Society which improves it

or 6^{thly} Instead of the two last articles, that the matters of dispute therein contained be refered to the Determination of three men of Discernment & integrity to be mutually Chosen as arbitrators and in case the men cannot be agreed on that it Shall be Left to either of the honorable Judges of the Supreme J Court to Choose the Said arbitrators & the Said arbitrators to determine what is right & equitable respecting the S^d. matter and to make report to the Town previous to the ordination of M^r. Storry—and the Town to vote an act of incorporation in conformity to the S^d. report

or 7^{thly} Instead of any of the foregoing articles that all matters in dispute be refered as afore S^d. to men Chosen as afore S^d who are to Determine & report as afore S^d. & the Town to pass a Vote as afore S^d. in conformity thereto

A motion was made & Seconded to See if the Town will Settle all disputes respecting Ministerial matters in this Town agreeable to the Following proposals laid before the Town by M^r. Daniel Baird the motion being put Passed in the Negative—The Proposals are as Follows—viz

The Town of Worcester consider that any Number of Persons Seperating from the rest of the Town, and Errecting themselves into a Religious Sociaty without the Leave of the Town or an Act of the General Court obtained for that purpose to be irregular unconstitutional and of A Dangerous tendancy Nevertheless they wish that Every one may Enjoy the fullest Liberty to worship agreeably to the Sentiments of their own minds which may consist with Peace and good order therefore the Town Consent that as many of its inhabitants as attend on the Reverend M^r. Bancrofts ministerial Labours and who are Disposed to apply to the General Court for an Act of incorporation Provided Nevertheless that the aforesaid inhabitants Do not Request any Priviliges But Such as are Common for other Pole Parrishes to have and they give up all Pretentions to any Right in the meeting house in Said Town Private Property in the Pews Excepted that on the aforesaid Conditions the Town will not interfere in the matter but confiding in the wisdom of the General Court will Leave the matter Entirely with them and Should the General Court incorporate the aforesaid inhabitants into a Sociaty or Parrish as aforesaid after the incorporation takes Place if the Town and the then Sociaty Cannot mutually agree about the apropriation of the interest arising from the ministerial fund in Said Town that then the Town Engage to Leave all Disputes Respecting the matter to be Setled by Disinterested Persons mutually Chosen for that purpose and the Town will abide the award

A motion was then made & Seconded to See if the Town will Settle all Disputes Respecting Ministerial matters in this Town agreeable to the Proposals laid before the Town by William Young

Worcester Town Records, 1787.

Esqr. the motion being Put Passed in the Negative—the Proposals are as Follows—viz—

Whereas A Number of the Inhabitants of the Town of Worcester have Seperated themselves from Said Town and have formed themselves into a Society for the purpose of Reliegeous worship and have placed them Selves under the Pastoral care of the Reverand Aaron Bancroft from Said Seperation have arisen Sundrey Disputes and Dificultys between Said Town & Society but more especially with respect to the destribution and improvement of the interest arising by a fund in possession of Said Town appropriated for the Sole purpose of Supporting of the Ministry therein

Said Town being desireous to remove all matters of Disputes and [difficulties] Subsisting between them and Said Society and ancious to Restore the peace and harmony of Said Town agree that upon Said Societys applying to the General Court to be incorporated into a destinct Releigeous Society as soon as conveniently may be they will not oppose Said Societys being incorporated and endowed with Such powers and Previledges as is Usual for Societys in Like circumstances to have and injoy—that upon Said Societys being incorporated Said Town will endeavour in a mutual way the Removeal of all disputes and Differences Subsisting between them & Said Society and the Said Town further agree that if they and Said Society cannot in a mutual way Settle Such Disputes and Differences as are or may be Subsisting between them Respecting the premises at the Time of incorporation they will Submit the Settlement thereof to three of five Judicious and disintristed persons to be mutually or indifferently Chosen by Said Town or Society for that purpose and neither of Said Referrees to be inhabitants of the Town of Worcester and that Said Town will abide Said Refferees determination of S^d. matter But it is to be under Stood that Said Town agree to Refer the above Said disputes and differances upon the conditions following viz—

That Said incorporated Society Relinquish all the Right title & Claim which they or either of them have in or unto the meeting house in Said Worcester their Private property in pews in Said hous Excepted—Secondly that it Shall be free any person that dos or may belong to Said Society at any Time to Remove themselves their Rateable Poles and Estates there from and Joyn themselves and afore Said to Said Town they proceeding in Such Removeal in an orderly and Legal way—and Likewise for any belonging to Said Town to Remove them Selves their Rateable poles and Estates and become members of Said Society they proceeding as above

A Motion was then made & Seconded to See if the Town will [settle] all Disputes Respecting Ministerial matters in this Town agreeable to the Proposals laid before the Town at this Time by Doct^r. Dix the motion being Put Passed in the Negative—the Proposals are as Follows viz

If the Town will Vote or agree not to oppose those Gentlemen who have placed themselves under the Pastoral care of the Rev^d. Aaron Bancroft in their giting incorporated as soon as may be and upon their obtaining S^d. Act of Incorporation Consent to Leave all disputes respecting the Interest arising upon Ministerial property to Disinterested men to be Mutually Chosen to determen in equity—and if the Gentlemen So Chosen Shall adjudge that any part of S^d. Interest belongs to the then Society The Town Grant to S^d. Society whatever proportion S^d. Gentlemen Shall award

A motion was made & Seconded that the all Disputes Respecting ministerial matters in this Town be Left wholly with the Judges of the Supreme Court to determine & if they Should refuse to give their Judgement then for them to appoint Such persons as they Shall See Fit to determin Said Disputes—the motion being put & passed in the Negative

A motion was made & Seconded to See if the Town will Choose a Committee to See if they cannot Settle the disputes respecting ministerial matters in this Town—the motion being put passed in the Negative

Voted then not to act any further on the matter Contained in the Third article in the warrant for this meeting

Worcester Town Records, 1787.

Voted that this meeting be adjourned to monday the thirtyeth Day of this Instant January at ten OClock in the morning then to meet at this Place & the meeting was accordingly adjourned

    A True Entry   Attest   Daniel Goulding Town Clerk

At a meeting of the Freeholders & Other Inhabitants of the Town of Worcester Qualified to Vote in Town affairs held at the publick meeting house in Said Town on Monday the fifteenth day of January A. D. 1787—the Following Votes were Passed viz—

    Chose Deacon Nathan Perry Moderator

    The Committee Lately Chosen to Set in County Convention were called on to make Report of their doings—and M^r. Baird Produced the address from the convention to the Inhabitants Published in a Late Worcester Magazine as their Doings

    A motion was made & Seconded to See if the Town will Dismiss the members Chose by this Town to meet in County Convention the motion being put passed in the affirmative

    Voted that the Selectmen be a Committee to make inquirey in regard of the Petetion mentioned in the fourth Article in the Warrant[1] for this meeting & make Report at the adjournment of the Other meeting held this Day

    To the Selectmen of the Town of Worcester We the Subscribers Desire that you would immediately call a Town meeting to See if the Town of Worcester will not dismiss their Deligates from any further attendance at the Convention as they have no further Business for them their December 10th. 1786

---

[1] ARTICLE 4 :—"to here the Request of Sundry Persons of the Town of Ward whether the Town of Worcester will grant them there Proportion of the Ministerial Money and their part of ammunition agreeable to their Request"

Worcester Town Records, 1787.

—Josiah Pierce, Joseph Kingsbury, Joel How, Ezekiel How Jonathan Lovell, James Fisk, Nathaniel Flagg, David Flagg Samuel Fisk, John Pierce, Benjamin Flagg, William Gates, David Chadwick, Joseph Ball.

To the Selectmen of the Town of Worcester Gentlemen We the Subscribers formerly Inhabitants of the Town of Worcester Humbly request that You would insert an Article in the Warrant for your Next Town meeting to know the mind of your Town whether they will grant to the Inhabitants of the Town of Ward who were Set off from the Said Town of Worcester and incorporated with the Town of Ward by an Act of the General Court their proportionable part of the ministerial Money, and also their proportionable part of the Town Stock of Ammunition which they helped to purchase & pay for with their money in So doing you will oblige your petetioners   Ward December 15th. 1786
Comfort Rice, Jonas Nichols, Jonah Cutting Thomas Baird administrator on the Estate of Darius Boyden, Timothy Bancroft, Joseph Dorr in the Right of Israel & Jacob Stephens, Thomas Drury, Jonathan Stone Ju^r. Jona Stone Thomas Baird, James Hart Ju^r.

Voted that this meeting be Dissolved, and the meeting was Dissolved accordingly

A True Entry   Attest   Daniel Goulding Town Clerk

At a Meeting of the Freeholders & Other Inhabitants of the Town of Worcester at the Publick meeting house in Said Town on Tuesday the Sixteenth Day of January A, D, 1787 then the Following Votes were Passed viz

Deacon Nathan Perry Chosen Moderator

Voted that this meeting be adjourned to one OClock this afternoon then to meet at this Place & the meeting was adjourned accordingly

A True Entry   Attest   Daniel Goulding Town Clerk

Worcester Town Records, 1787.

Met according to the above adjournment Jan[y]. 16th. 1787 at one OClock in the afternoon then the Following Votes were passed viz

[1] Voted that this Town engage to give the Sum of twelve Shillings to Eatch man as a Bounty that Shall engage agreeable to the orders Derected to the Militia officers for Raising a Number of men for the Support of Government—Voted that this Town engage to give the above mentioned men after the Rate of Forty Shillings p[r]. month for the Time they are out agreeable to the above mentioned orders & if the General Court Grant Larger Wages the Soldiers Shall have the Sum above the Forty Shillings allowed them

Voted to Choose a Committee to give Security to the Soldiers for their wages or the Town to Receive the Soldiers Pay from Government and that Said Committee Procure the money for their Bounty Then Chose Cap[t]. Samuel Brooks, Cap[t]. Phineas Jones, Cap[t]. Joel How, M[r]. Samuel Goddard, & Timothy Paine Esq[rs]. for Said Committee

Voted that M[r]. Samuel Goddard be excused & Chose Doct[r]. Dix in his Place

Voted that the Major Part of the above Committee be empowered to Act

Voted that this meeting be adjourned to Thursday the Eighteenth Day of this Instant Jan[y]. at one OClock in the afternoon then to meet at this Place & the meeting was accordingly adjourned

A True Entry   Attest   Daniel Goulding Town Clerk

Met according to the above adjournment January 18th. 1787 then the Following Votes were Passed—Viz—

Voted that the Soldiers that are engaged that cannot Provide

---

[1] ARTICLE 2:—"To See what measures the Town will take towards Raising their Quota of men for Supporting Government agreeable to a late Requisition for that purpose"

Powder have the Quantity that they are Derected to Provide out of the Town Stock & have the Value of it taken out of their Wages

Voted that this meeting be Dessolved & the meeting was dissolved accordingly

    A True Entry   Attest   Daniel Goulding Town Clerk

At a Meeting of the Freeholders & other Inhabitants of the Town of Worcester Quallified to Vote in Town affairs legally Warned & assembled at the public Meeting House in Said Town, on monday the 12th. day of March A D 1787 to act on the several articles contained in the foregoing Warrant

  M^r. John Chamberlain Chose Grand Juror

  Deacon Nathan Perry Chosen Moderator

  Theophilus Wheeler Town Clerk

  Voted To Choose 5 Selectmen—& Chose Deacon Nathan Perry, Capt. Saml. Brooks M^r. John Chamberlain, M^r. Daniel Baird, & Joseph Wheeler Esquire to be Selectmen

  Voted Deacon Nathan Perry for Town Treasurer

  Voted that the Selectmen be assessors, and Overseers of the poor the Currunt year

  Voted to Choose 2 men to Serve as Wardens & Chose Capt. David Moore and Robert Cook for S^d. Service

  M^r. Joseph Ball M^r. Samuel Mower Tythingmen

  M^r. Nathan Heard Sealer of tan^d. & Curried Leather

  M^r. Nathan Patch M^r. Samnel Bridge Clerks of the Market

  Capt. Joshua Whitney M^r. Samuel Mower Fence Viewers

  M^r. Clark Chandler M^r. Samuel Braizer Deer Rieves

  M^r. Thomas Knights Capt. John Pierce Field Drivers

  M^r. Ignatius Goulding M^r. Jed^h Healey Surveyors of Boards & Shingles

  M^r. Eben^r. Wiswall M^r. William Mahan M^r. Isaac Willard Junr.

M^r. Elijah Flagg M^r. Daniel Willington M^r. Isaac Putnam M^r. John Elder Junr. M^r. James Young M^r. William Trowbridge M^r. Solomon Gleason M^r. Samuel Fullerton Hog Rieves

Voted that all swine that are yoked & Ringed agreeable to Law go at large the Currunt year

Voted to Choose two Collectors of Taxes; then S^d Vote Reconsidered,

Motioned & Voted a Committee Consisting of three persons be chosen to treat with One or two persons to Collect public taxes this year

Voted that Timothy Paine Esqr. Joseph Allen Esqr. M^r. John Nazro be the Committee for S^d. purpose

Voted that the sum of One hundred & fifty pounds be assessed on the poles & Estates in this Town & Raised for the use of the Schools the Currunt year,: that out of said sum £50. be appropriated as it was the last year for the use of Grammar Schools in this Town

Doct^r Elijah Dix Capt. Samuel Brooks Leu^t Josiah Peirce Deac^n. Reubin Hamilton Mr Noah Harris Deac^n Thomas Wheeler M^r. James McFarland M^r. Jesse Taft M^r. Josiah Perry M^r. Thomas Stowell M^r. Benjamin Flagg Junr. a Committee to provide Schooling the Currunt year

Voted That Doct^r Elijah Dix Tim^o. Paine Esqr. Capt. Benj^a. Haywood Be a Committee to Settle accounts with the Town Treasurer

Voted that the Selectmen be a Committee to provide a Grammar master the Cur^t. year

Voted that the Sum of £200 be assessed and raised for the purpose of Repairing the Highways in this Town in the Same way & manner that it was the last Year, that if any persons have overworked their Last years highway taxes have Credit for so much as they have overworked, and those that are deficient have the privilidge of working the Same this year provided they do it before the first day of July next at the rate of 4/ p^r. day for a man, & for Oxen, Cart, & plows in proportion

Voted That Mr Noah Harris Mr Thomas Knights Doct^r Elijah Dix Samuel Curtis Esqr. Mr Saml. Moore Mr Robert Gray Capt. David Moore Deac^n. Thomas Wheeler Mr Isaac Willard Mr William McFarland Mr James Barber Mr Jesse Taft Deacon Ruebin Hamilton Mr Phineas Flagg Be Surveyors of Highways & Collectors of Highway taxes

at the adjournment, Voted to Dismiss Esqr. Curtis & Deacon R Hamilton, & Chose Mr Saml. Mower & Mr Charles Stearns in their room

Voted that the Selectmen be a Committee to Build the towns part of a fence round the land where Benj^a. Crosby lives, that the expence be paid out of the rent of the other part of the House

Voted to accept of the following Report of the Selectmen

The Selectmen have Laid out a Town road agreeable to the vote of the Town through the Ministerial Land So Called, and present the same to the Town at their annual Meeting in March 1787 for their acceptance, as follows, viz, beginning at the town road leading by Capt. Palmer Gouldings to Grafton at a Stake and heap of Stones placed 11 rods & an half west of the Bridge over Mill Brook from thence it runs North five & an half degrees East through said Ministerial land so called seventeen rods & an half then turns and runs West 26° North untill it meets with the Town road lately laid through said land up to the Southeast corner of a lot of said Ministerial land sold to Joseph Allen Esqr. The said road to lye on the westerly side of the first mentioned line, and the Southerly side of the other mentioned line, and said Road is laid out two rods and half wide

Nathan Perry	Selectmen
John Chamberlain	of
Jesse Taft	Worcester

Voted to adjourn this Meeting to the first monday in April next One of the Clock afternoon then to meet at this place, it was accordingly adjourned

A True Entery   Attest   Theoph^s. Wheeler Town Clerk

Worcester Town Records, 1787.

At the above mentioned adjournment from 12th March to the 2d. April 1787 The following Votes were passed, viz

Voted to Choose Mr Nathan Patch Collector of public taxes the Currunt year in the same manner as he proposed to the Committee Chosen to treat with some person or persons for that purpose, viz. to give good Security for the faithfull Discharge of his Trust & to be Intitled to three pence on the pound for Collecting—

Mr Nathan Patch Mr Jeddiah Healey Chosen Constables

Voted to pass over the 8th article in the foregoing Warrant [1]

Then Voted that this Meeting be Disolved and it was accordingly Disolved

A True Entry   Atts   Theophilus Wheeler Town Clerk

At a Town Meeting of the Freeholders & Other Inhabitants of the Town of worcester Quallified to Vote as the Law Directs for Govenor Liut Govenor & Senators. The following persons were Voted for as Govenor, Leut. Govenor & Senators & the Number of Votes Expressed against their respective Names viz

His Excellency James Bowdoin Esqr.   67 ⎫
His Excellency John Hancock Esqr.   111 ⎬ for Govenor

Honble Thomas Cushing Esq.   87 ⎫
Honble Benja. Lincoln Esqr.   62 ⎬ Luit. Govenour
Honble Nathl Goreham Esqr.   1 ⎭

Honble Moses Gill Esq.	51	Rufus Putnam Esq.	12
Honble Samuel Baker Esq.	52	Honble Artimas Ward Esq	10
Honble Seth Washburn Esq.	47	Timothy Paine Esq	19
Honble Abel Wilder Esq.	138	Honl. Levi Lincoln Esq.	2
Samuel Curtis Esq.	94	Genl. Jonathan Warner	1
Amos Singletary Esq.	92	Honble Israel Nichols Esq	1

---

[1] ARTICLE 8:—"To allow accounts to any to whome the Town is Indebted"

Worcester Town Records, 1787.

Jon^a. Grout Esq	94	Jno. Fessenden Esq	1
Hon^l. John Sprague Esq	54	Bezaleal Taft	1
Mr Stephen Maynard	94	Edward Crafts Esqr.	1

Senators

Voted that this Meeting be Disolved & it was accordingly Disolved

    A True Entry   Attest   Theophilus Wheeler Town Clerk

At a meeting of the Freeholders & Other Inhabitants of the Town of Worcester Qualified to Vote for Representatives; agreeable to Law, on the Second Day of April A D. 1787. The following persons were voted for for a County Treasurer, : the number of votes Expressed against their Respective Names—Viz—

The Honble Timothy Paine Esqr.	33
Deacon Nathan Perry	55
Capt Samuel Flagg	5
General putnam	1

Then Voted that this Meeting be Disolved, & it was Disolved accordingly

    A true Entery   Attest   Theophilus Wheeler Town Clerk

At a meeting of the Freeholders & Other Inhabitants of the Town of Worcester qualified to Vote in Town affairs on the 2^d day of April A. D. 1787.

Voted to Choose Deacon Jacob Chamberlain Moderator

Then Voted that this meeting be adjourned, it was accordingly adjourned till the 16th day of May next then to Meet at this place @ one of the Clock afternoon

    A true Entry   Att^s Theoph^s. Wheeler Town Clerk

Oath of Allegiance

I the Subscriber, Do truly and Sincerely acknowledge profess and Declare that the Commonwealth of Massachusetts is and of Right ought to be a free Soverign & Independent State, and I do Sweare that I will beare true faith & alleegiance to the Said Commonwealth and that I will defend the Same against Traiterous Consperacies and all Hostile attempts whatsoever, and that I do Renounce and abjure all allegiance Subjection and Obedience to the King Queen or Govenment of Great Brittain and every other forrign power whatever, and that no forrign Prince person, prelate, State or pottentate, hath, or ought to have, any Jurisdiction, Superiority, pre eminence, authority desposing or other power, in any matter, Civel Ecleasticle or Spiritual within this Commonwealth, except the Authority or power which is or may be Vested by their Constituents in the Congress of the United States, and I do further Testify and Declare, that no man or Body of Men hath or can have any Right to absolve or Discharge me from the obligation of this Oath, Declaration or affirmation, and that I do make this acknowledgement, profession Testimony, Declaration Denial Denunceation & abjuration heartily & truly according to the Common mean^g & acceptation of the foregoing words, without any Equivocation, Mental Evasion or secrete Reservation whatsoever—So help me God.

   Theophilus Wheeler   Nathan Perry
   Daniel Baird   Samuel Brooks
   Jedediah Healey   John Chamberlain
   Nathan Patch   Joseph Wheeler

Worcester ss March 23^d. 1787 personally appeared the above named Nathan Perry Samuel Brooks John Chamberlain & Joseph Wheeler Selectmen & assessors for the Town of Worcester for the Currunt year, & the s^d. Nathan Perry as Town Treasurer and took and Subscribed the above Oath Before me

        Theoph^s. Wheeler T, Clerk

Worcester ss. March 23^d. 1787. Personally appeared Theophilus Wheeler above named Town Clerk for the Town of Worcester the Currunt year & took & Subscribed the foregoing Oath Before   Joseph Wheeler J Pacis—

Worcester Town Records, 1787.

Worcester ss   March 28th 1787   Mr Daniel Baird Selectman & assessor personally appeared and took and Subscribed the foregoing Oath Before   Th^s. Wheeler Town Clerk

Mr Nathan Patch. Collector & Constable & m^r. Jed^h. Healey Constable for the Town of Worcester personally appeared & took & Subscribed the foregoing Oath of alleagince
                    Before Theoph^s. Wheeler Town Clerk
   A true Entery   Attest   Theophilus Wheeler T. Clerk

Worcester ss. 1787   Personally appeared, Nathan Perry Saml Brooks John Chamberlain, Daniel Baird & Joseph Wheeler Selectmen Overseers of the poor and assessors, Deacon Nathan Perry Town Treasurer Joshua Whitney Fence Viewer Saml. Brazer Deer Rieve, Capt. John Pierce Field Driver, Jed^h. Healey Surveyor of Boards & Shingles, William Mahan & John Elder Junr. Hog Rieves, Noah Harris, Thomas Knight, Doct^r. Elijah Dix Samuel Mower, Samuel Moore, Thomas Wheeler Isaac Willard William McFarland, James Barber Jesse Taft & Phineas Flagg Surveyors of Highways & Collectors of Highway Taxes, and were severally sworn to the faithfull Discharge of their Respective offices   Before Theophilus Wheeler Town Clerk
   A True Entry   Attest.   Theoph^s. Wheeler Town Clerk

Worcester ss.   March 19th 1787.   Capt. David Moore being Chosen a Surveyor of highways & Collector of highway taxes for the Town of Worcester for the Currunt year, personally appeared before me & took the Oath prescribed by law to Quallify him to act in S^d. Office   Jos. Allen Jus. Pacis

Worcester ss. March 23^d. 1787 Personally appeared Robert Gray and made solemn Oath, that in Executing the Office of Surveyor of highways for the Town of Worcester for the year 1787 —he would act faithfully & Impartially
                    Before me   Wm Young Just. Peace
      A true Entry   Attest   Theoph^s. Wheeler T. Clerk

Worcester Town Records, 1787.

At a Town Meeting by adjournment from the Second day of April A. D, 1787 to the 16th day of May 1787

Voted to accept of the Report of the Committee apointed to Settle with the Town Treasurer

Voted to accept of the Report of the Selectmen respecting the situation of the Town bonds—and that the Selectmen Call for the back Interest due on said Bonds That Should there appear to be any Deficiency in the security of any of the Town bonds, the Selectmen Call for new securities

Voted to Recommit the Report of David Bigelow and others, of the Sale of the Carriges lately belonging to the Cannon, in Order for them to Collect the proceeds of the Sale thereof

Voted that Mr   Haws have his Brother   pole tax abated which was Committed to Mr Nathan Patch to Collect in the year 1786

Then Voted this Meeting be Dissolved & it was accordingly Dissolved

The Reports afore Refered to are as follows

The account of Nathan Perry Town Treasurer, with the Town of Worcester May 16th 1787.—The said accountant Chargeth himself with the Balance of his account settled 28th Novr. 1785 Being
£1334 .. 11 .. 6

Also with the sum of £601 .. 5 .. 8 mentioned in said account due in new Emission Money, from Nathan Patch Setled with said Patch amounting to— lawfull money	320 .. 13 .. 8
Also with a sum mentioned in said account Drawn by the State Treasurer on Joseph Barber Collector for the year 1784	196 .. 14 .. 5
Also with a Tax Deld to Jesse Taft Collector 17 march 1786	221 .. 2 .. 9
Also with a tax Delivered to Mr Nathan Patch to Collect	150 .. –0 .. ——
Interest recieved of the Ministerial Money since the last settlement of the Selectmen	58 .. 18 .. 6½

£2282 .. 0 .. 10½

And Dischargeth himself by the payment of the following sums paid by order from the Selectmen, viz,

paid John Nazro £11..4..6½ paid Jon^a Stone & Cushing £9..19/	£21..3..6½	
p^d Samuel Brooks £6..11/11½ p^d Stephen Flagg 72/	10..3..11½	
p^d Thaddeus Maccarty 32/6 p^d Luther Gale 30/	3..2..6	
p^d Samuel Eaton £19..10/ p^d m^r. Kendell 60/	22..10..—	
p^d William Macfarland 9/6 p^d Eph^m Miller Ex^{er} £4..9/	4..18..6	
paid Phineas Gleason 6/ p^d Phineas Haywood 22/4	1..8..4	
p^d. W^m. Bowles £9..17/2 p^d David Bigelow 48/	12..5..2	
p^d Thaddeus Chapin 64/6 p^d John Walker 2/	3..6..6	
p^d William Trowbridge 32/ p^d John White £7..13/	9..5..—	
p^d John Waters Junr. 24/ p^d William Bowles 12/	1..16..—	
p^d Nathl Brooks £3–8/ paid David Bigelow £11..1/	14..9..—	
p^d William Brown 19/3 paid Simeon Duncan 47/	3..6..3	
p^d William Daws £13–4..2 paid Wm Jinson £48..5/	61−9−2	
p^d Samuel Brooks 36/ p^d Thad^s. Chapin 14/	2..10..—	
p^d Timothy Paine & Others £12 p^d Eben^r. wiswall 38/11	13..18..11	
p^d Joseph Miller 62/8 p^d Eben^r Lovel &c £11–7/	14−9−8	
p^d John Stowers 20/ p^d Robert Gray £9..6	10−6..—	
Paid Josiah Flagg 30/10 p^d Henry Patch 40/	£3..10..10	

paid Hep^s. Bowman 47/3.
    paid Samuel Brooks £8..15/10^d   11 – 3 – 1
paid Samuel Eaton £15..12/
    p^d Edward Knights 27/   16..19..—
p^d Nathan Perry 12/
    p^d Thomas Knight 74/1^d   4 – 6.. 1
p^d Jed^h. Healey £6..12/
    p^d Joshua Johnson £8..4/   14 – 16..—
p^d Elijah Dix £6..
    paid John Hamilton £7..16/   13..16..—
p^d Benjamin Whitney Ju^r. 66/10
    p^d Samuel Ward 30/   3..6..10
p^d Robert Crawford £13..15/10
    p^d Nathl Brooks 17/6   14..13 – 4
p^d Mary Bigelow £6..18/
    p^d Timothy Jones £15..2..11   22 – 0 – 11
p^d Nahum Willard 60/
    p^d Joseph Barber 6/   3..6 —
p^d James Quigley £15..12/
    p^d D^r. Willard £5..16/   21..8
p^d Samuel Brooks £8..10/
    p^d Solomon Bixby 18/4   9..8..4
p^d Joseph Wheeler Esq 47/8 D°. 9/   2..16..8
p^d Nathan Perry 26/7 p^d D° £4..1..6   5..8..1
p^d Thaddeus Chapin £11–5..6
    p^d Nathan Perry 30/7   12..16..1
p^d Edward Knight 63/
    Joseph Torrey 30/   4..13..
p^d William Elder 51/
    p^d Daniel Heywood &c £6..11..3   9..2..3
p^d School Committee £100
    p^d Flagg & Stanton 27/3   101 – 7 – 3
allowance for Counterfit money 67/11
    for Int^r. 13/7   4 – 1 – 6
p^d School Committee £150
    Allowance to M^r. Patch £131..12/5¾   581 – 12 – 5¾
p^d Mr Haven £13–10
    p^d m^r. Piper £10-10/   24 — —
p^d Mr Damin £6,,15/
    p^d m^r. Mills £7,,10/   14 – 5 —

Worcester Town Records, 1787.

p^d Mr Storey £ 12– d°. 40	14 ———
p^d Mr Haywood £ 18	18 ———
paid Joseph Wheeler £ 30/ Elijah Dix 46/4^d	3 .. 16 .. 4
William Taylor	1 – 19 – 0¾
Jesse Taft 6/6. Mary Boyd 68/6	3 – 15 ——
Simeon Duncan 12/	
Anna Chandler £ 38 .. 7 .. 5	38 .. 19 .. 5
William Elder 72/. Jed^h Healey 9/	4 – 1
	£ 1193 .. 16 .. 0½
Balance due	£ 1088 .. 4 .. 10

Errors Excepted   Nathan Perry Treasurer

Worcester May 16th. 1787. The Committee appointed by the Town to Examine the account of Mr Nathan Perry, have attended that Service by which it appears that he has charged himself with the sum of £ 2282 .. 0 .. 10½, that he has paid to the several persons in said account mentioned the sum of £ 1193 .. 16 .. 0½ that there is a balance in his hands after deducting the above sum £ 1088 .. 4 .. 10 which he is further to account with the Town for, as also for the Interest money that may arise upon the money due from Nathan Patch

{ Timothy Paine
{ Elijah Dix   } Committee
{ Benjⁿ. Haywood

A Return of the Situation of the Town Bonds for the year 1786

Stephen Dexter bond David Thomas Surety Interest paid to Novr. 1st 1785	£ 33 .. 6 .. 8
John Taylors bond, William Younge Esq W^m McFarland Sureties Interest Novr. 1st. 1785	42 .. 3 .. 4
Phineas Ward bond Saml. Curtis & David Richardson Sureties In^t. paid to Novr. 1st 1786	22 .. 15 —
David Bigelow Bond Jn°. Green Surety In^t. paid to Novr. 1st 1785	35 .. 16 .. 8
John Stanton & Daniel Goulding Bond Palmer Goulding Surety Interest paid to march 10th 1787	35 – 0 —

Joseph Allen Esq. Bond Doct^r Elijah Dix & Samuel Allen Sureties Interest paid to Octr. 1st 1785 — £51 .. 1 .. 1

Oliver Watson Junr. Bond Oliver Watson & William McFarland sureties Interest paid to march 28th 1785 — 83 – 6 – 8

Ezekiel How Bond, Ezekiel How Surety Interest paid to Novr. 1st 1785 — 20

Capt. Palmer Goulding Bond, Interest paid to nov^r. 1st 1783 Ignatius Goulding & Peter Goulding Sureties — 46 .. 13 – 4

Pew Bonds

Doct^r Elijah Dix and others now in the Hands of Jesse Taft; Sureties Josiah Lyon & Joseph Barber Interest paid to 21st July 1786 — 39 .. 5

Nathan Patch Bond Cornelius Stowell & Joshua Whitney Sureties Interest paid to July 21st 1784 — 33 .. 5

Isaiah Thomas Bond Jos: Allen Esq. & Nathan Patch Sureties given July 21st 1783 no Interest pd. — 42 .. 15

Samuel Brown d^o Bond Doct^r. Elijah Dix & Lemuel Rice Sureties Interest paid July 21st 1785 — 37 .. 5

Proceeds of the Ministerial Land——

Joseph Allen Esq. Bond Levi Lincoln & Ignatious Goulding Sureties Int. paid to Feby 15th 1786 — 84 .. 10

Daniel Gouldings Bond Palmer Goulding & Ignatious Goulding Sureties Interest paid to Feby. 15th 1786 — 48 .. 10

Levi Lincolns Bond Joseph Allen Esq & Ignatious Goulding Sureties Int. paid to Feby 21st 1786 — 51 .. 10

John Stantons Bond Samuel Flagg & Clark Chandler Sureties no Interest paid Feby 21st 1785 — 36 .. 10

William Treadwell Bond, Nathan Patch & John Stowers Sureties Int paid Feby 21st 1786 — 152 .. 10

Worcester Town Records, 1787.

Simeon Duncan Bond, Joseph Blair & Joseph Allen Sureties Int^r paid Feby 21st 1786 } 40 —

Paul Gates Bond William Gates & W^m. Mahan Sureties Int^r paid Feby 21st 1787 } 35 —

William Young Bond Peter Johnson & John Taylor Sureties no Interest paid given Feby 15. 1785 } 48 .. 10

Samuel Flagg Lease not paid since the 9th day of March A, D. 1785 which is £6 .. p^r. year

The Subscribers Rec^d. of Interest money £9 .. 16 - 4

All which we Humbly Submit { Nathan Perry / Jno. Chamberlain / Daniel Baird } Selectmen

Worcester March 1787

The foregoing are true Entries
    Att Theophilus Wheeler T. Clerk

At a meeting of the Freeholders & other Inhabitants of the Town of Worcester Quallified to Vote for Representatives, at the public meeting House in Worcester on the 16th day of May A. D. 1787—Voted to send but one Representative this year, then Voted that Capt. Saml. Brooks, Represent this Town in the General Court the Current year

At the same time and place the Freeholders & other Inhabitants of this Town of Worcester Quallified to Vote in Town affairs —passed the following Votes viz, Voted that Deacon Nathan Perry be moderator

A motion was made & Seconded to see if the Town would act upon the Petition & order of Court mentioned in the 2^d. article of the above warrant.[1] the Town voted to act upon said Petition & order

---

[1] SECOND ARTICLE:—"To hear the petition of Levi Lincoln and others, requesting the General Court to Incorporate them into a parrish in the Town of Worcester, and the Order of the General Court thereon"

Worcester Town Records, 1787.

Then Voted to Deferr the Consideration of matters respecting S^d. petition & order for the present—Voted that this Meeting be adjourned to monday the 28th day of May Ins^t. @ 3, o Clock afternoon   it was accordingly adjourned

  A true Entry Att^s Theophilus Wheeler Town Clerk

At a Meeting of the Freeholders and other Inhabitants of the Town of Worcester at the public meeting House on the 28th day of May A. D. 1787 by adjournment from the 16th day of May 1787

Voted that the Town object to the petetion of Levi Lincoln & others mentioned in the Second article in the Warrant

Voted that a Committee be Chosen to appear before the great & General Court to shew cause in behalf of the Town why the prayer of the petition of Levi Lincoln and others Inhabitants of S^d Town praying to be Incorporated into a Seperate parrish should not be granted

Voted that the above s^d Committee Consist of three

Then Voted that Capt. Samuel Brooks, M^r. Daniel Baird & M^r. John Chamberlain be the Committee for S^d purpose

Then Voted that this Meeting be Disolved, it was Disolved accordingly

  A true Entry Att^s Theo^s Wheeler Town Clerk

To the Gentlemen Selectmen of Worcester,   The petitioners pray that you would forthwith Grant a Warrant for Calling a Town Meeting for the following purposes.—first to Choose a Moderator 2^d. as there has been Sundry conveyances by individuals of the Land Called millstone Hill, which we Humbly conceive belongs to the Town, to See if the Town will take the Matter into Consideration, to do and act on the premises as the Town shall see fit—as in duty Bound shall ever pray

                                                          John Curtis
                                                          Eben*r*. Willington
                                                          Thaddeus Bigelow
Worcester May 19th 1787   David Bigelow
                                                          Daniel Willington
                                                          Samuel Jenison
                                                          William Taylor
                                                          Joseph Barber
                                                          Thomas Stowell
                                                          Cornelius Stowell

At a Legal Town Meeting of the Freeholders and other Inhabitants of the Town of Worcester Quallified to Vote in Town affairs on the 28th. day of May A D. 1787 at the public Meeting House in said Town

Capt. Samuel Brooks Chosen Moderator

Voted to Choose a Committee to Enquire into the Records, & Examine with Respect to the Towns Right & title to Millstone Hill so Cald. to take advice and Obtain what light they can respect.g the premises, and to make Report to the Town at some future meeting

Then Voted that this Committee Consist of three

Voted that Mr. David Bigilow Capt. Saml. Brooks & Timothy Paine Esqr be the Committee

Voted that This Meeting be Disolved and it was accordingly Disolved

        A true Entry   Atts.   Theophs. Wheeler Town Clerk

Worcester ss. Septr. 13th 1787 Mr. Isaac Putnam personally appeared and was Sworn to the faithfull Discharge of the office of Hog Rieve the present year

                      Before Theophs. Wheeler Town Clerk

122 *Worcester Town Records, 1787.*

At a meeting of the Inhabitants of the Town of Worcester Quallified to vote in Town affairs on monday the 15th day of October A D 1787

Deacon Nathan Perry Chosen Moderator

Motion made and Seconded to See if the Town will accept of M^r. Daniel Storys Answer, he Relinquishing all Right to the ministerial property in said Town

Voted to accept M^r. Storys answer, he Relinquishing as above motioned

Voted to Choose a Committee Consisting of five to Consider of a propper time for Ordination and Report to this Meeting Deacon Jacob Chamberlain Capt John Curtis, Deacon Nathan Perry, Joseph Wheeler Esq & Mr John Chamberlain Chose for S^d Committee

Motioned That Deacon Perry be Directed to Lodge M^r. Storys Explanatory, or Second answer to the town—Which Motion passed in the negative

The above mentioned Committee Report that the Last wednesday in Novr. next is a propper time for the Ordination of M^r. Story

Voted that S^d Day be appointed for Ordination

Voted to Choose a Committee of Seven men to make provision for the Ordination—Capt Joshua Whitney, Mr John Chamberlain Capt Nathl Brooks Mr Daniel Baird, Mr Jonathan Rice Deacon Thomas Wheeler

Voted to add the Selectmen Mr Nathl Harrington Mr Tyler Curtis & Mr Isaac Willard to this Committee

Then voted that this meeting be adjourned One fortnight, then to meet at this place 3 o,Clock afternoon, it was accordingly adjourned

A true Entry   Attest   Theophilus Wheeler Town Clerk

M̄ Daniel Storys answer

To the Church of Christ in Worcester, and the Inhabitants of said Town

Honored & Beloved

The Great affection and respect you have been pleased to mannifest towards me has not failed to excite the warmest emotions of gratitude in return, and when I consider your Unanimity in the Invitation given me to Settle with you in the Gospell ministry I feel myself laid under Still more lasting obligations, and esteem it a Circumstance of the most engageing nature

Reflecting upon the arduousness, Solemnity and Importance of the Work to which you have Called me, I am Ready to Exclaim; who is sufficient for these things; But being Convinced that I hear the voice of God in your Call, and humbly Relying, as I trust, upon Support and assistance from the Great head of the Church who has promised that he will be with his ministers to the end of the world—I Chearfully, tho' trembling, accept your Invitation—Intreating your prayers, that the work allotted me may be So performed that I may not, after haveing preached to others be myself a Castaway—and whilst I request an Interest in your addresses at the throne of Grace I shall never cease to bow my knee before God even the father, for your Spiritual prosperity —May the divine Spiritt enable me to come to you from [   ] —in the fullness of the blessing of the Gospell of peace and assist me to Dispence Divine truth in such a manner that I shall both save myself and them who hear me, and whilst we attempt to strengthen each others hands & to encourage each others hearts in the path of duty, may we be like a City sit on a hill, which cannot be hid and whose benign Influence shall be extensive— may we live together in Unity & the firmest attachment till we shall be gathered to our Father   Then may our Speritts be admitted to the presence and enjoyment of the Lord, where ordinances will be unnecessary, as we shall with open face behold the Glory of God.   there the Church will appear in the perfection of Beauty and will weare an Immortal unfadeing Crown—Wishing you Grace mercy & peace from him who holdeth the Stars in his right hand & walkith in the midst of his golden candlesticks—I am honored & beloved with sentiments of affection & Respect your Servant in the Gospell of Christ Jesus

Worcester November 11th 1786   Daniel Story

N B Whereas in the above answer I have not Signified my choice of the two proposals which the town have generously made me, I hereby Declare my acceptance of the one hundred & twenty pounds annual Salary with the Settlement   Daniel Story

   A true Entry   Att^s Theoph^s. Wheeler Town Clerk

At a Meeting of the Freeholders & other Inhabitants of the Town of Worcester Quallified to vote in Town affairs, (by adjournment from the 15th day of this Ins^t Oct^r) on the 29th day of Octr. 1787

Voted, to Reconsider the vote of the last Town Meeting appointing the time for the Ordaination of Mr Daniel Story

Voted. that this Meeting be adjourned to the 12th day of Novr. next at One of the Clock in the afternoon then to meet at this place—and the Meeting was accordingly adjourned

   A true Entry   Att^s Theoph^s. Wheeler T Clerk

At the above mentioned adjournment from the 29th day of Octr. to the 12th day of November A. D. 1787

It was motioned and Seconded to adjourn this meeting for four weeks, which passed in the negative

Then voted that this meeting be adjourned to the 26th Day of Novr. Ins^t at one of the Clock in the afternoon then to meet at this place, and the meeting was accordingly adjourned

   A true Entry   Attest   Theoph^s Wheeler T Clerk

Worcester Town Records, 1787.   125

At a Meeting of the freeholders and other Inhabitants of the Town of Worcester Quallified to vote in Town affairs on the 19th day of November A. D. 1787

Deacon Nathan Perry Chosen Moderator

Voted to Choose a Committee consisting of three, to Converce with Millicent Goulding Respecting her future Subsistance Deacon Wheeler, Esquire Paine & Deacon Chamberlain Chosen for said Committee, who are to make report at the adjournment of this meeting

Voted to choose a Committee to Examine the accounts that are now Exhibited & that may be Exhibited to them, against the Town—Timothy Paine Esq. Joseph Allen Esq. & Mr John Chamberlain Chosen for S^d Committee

Voted that the Selectmen procure a Gravestone or Gravestones for the Rev^d. Mr Thads Maccarty & Mrs Maccarty his wife Deceased

Voted that this meeting be adjourned to the 3^d Day of December next at two of the Clock afternoon and it was adjourned accordingly

   A true Entery   attest   Theophilus Wheeler Town Clerk

Millicent Gouldings Petition

To the Selectmen of Worcester   Gentlemen   I Desire you would insert an article in the Warrant for Calling the next Town Meeting to See if the Town will agree with some person for a certain sum to support me during my Natural Life—and thereby save me a great deal of trouble in repeated applications for Support

I am now Destitute of house or home or Decent Cloathing & Daily Suffering for the Necessaries of Life

   Worcester July 18th 1787   Millicent Goulding
   A true Entry   attest   Theophilus Wheeler Town Clerk

126   *Worcester Town Records, 1787.*

At a Town meeting by adjournment from the 12th of Novr. 1787 to the 26th of the same month, a motion was made & seconded to Disolve the meeting which passed in the Negative

then Voted to adjourn this meeting to the 10th of Decr. next to meet at this place 1, of the Clock afternoon, and it was accordingly adjourned

 A true Entry Atts Theophilus Wheeler Town Clerk

At a Town Meeting of the Inhabitants of the Town of Worcester on the third day of Decr. 1787 by adjournment from the 19th day of November last, The following votes were passed

Voted to pass over the Second article in the Warrant[1] for this Meeting

Voted that the following Report of the Committee appointed to Examine accounts against the Town, be allowed (Excepting the assessors account of £11-15/)—

The Committee appointed to Examine accounts Exhibited against the Town have receved and Examined the following Ones, viz—

N°			
1	Deacon Nathan Perry for sundries supplyd for the Support of the poor	£7..17..1	
2d.	John Walker for Supporting Mary Walker from the 26th march 1786 to the 10th April 1787 54 weeks at the Request of the Selectmen. £5..8/ and mendg the tonge of the Bell 5/	5.13—	
3	Samuel Eaton for the Support Mrs Sarah Eaton from the first of September 1786 to Sept. 1787 52 weeks @ 4/6	11–14—	
4	Jacob Hemmenway for Plank for bridges	1–10	
5	Jesse Taft for Sundreys Supplyd the Poor of the Town &c	10–3–1	

---

[1] The petition of Millicent Goulding.

6	Edward Knight Supplying Simon Glasco 12 Cords of Wood	3 – 12 —
7	Samuel Mower Plank for bridges	19 – 9
8	Mary Boyd Keeping Richard McDonald to 13th Novr 1787	5 .. 12 —
9	Phineas Flagg, Potatos & Wood Del^d to Crosby	8 . 6
10	The assessors for makeing taxes take^g Valuation &c	11 15 . 0
11	James Quigley, Supporting agness Brooks & her child to the first of May 1787	13 .. 17 – 4
12	to Daniel Johnson Boarding and Cloathing Zacheus Johnson to 5th Feby 1787	4 – 16 —
13	To James Blake Boarding & Nursing Thomas Whaland a Stranger who died at his house	12 – 1 – 4
14	Joseph Wheeler Esq Sundreys Supplyed S^d Whaland	17 – 2
15	Joseph Wheeler hearing and Determining a Cause between the Town and Fitchburge respecting Eph^m. Smith &c	12 —
19	Martha Wiley boarding and Cloathing Lydia, Child of Joanna Parker to the 16th of Novr. 1787 19 weeks @ 2/	1 – 18 —
20	John Chamberlain for Sundrey Cloathing for Joanna Dyar to the 15th Novr. 1787 £ 1–17/ to D^o. Supplys to Simon Glasco 2/11	1 – 19 – 11
21st	Daniel Baird Sundrys Supplyed the poor of the Town & for an horse to transport Eph^m Smith to Fitchburge	14 – 4
22	Capt Samuel Brooks Sundrys Supply^d Simon Glasco £ 2 .. 10 .. 7 D^o. Boarding Sally Walker to 29 Septr. 25 weeks £ 2 . 10/	5 – 0 – 7
23^d.	To Nathan Patch his account as on file	2 . 5 —
		£ 103 – 6 . 1

All which is Submitted to the Town for their acceptance & allowance Worcester Decr. 3^d. 1787

Tim^o. Paine
John Chamberlain } Committe
Jos : Allen

Voted to accept the following Report of a Committee Chosen to hire money for the Soldiers Bounty, January 1787—Viz

The Committee appointed by the Town of Worcester in January 1787 to hire money for paying a Bounty of twelve Shillings to Each Soldier who should inlist for the Support of Government agreeable to the then Requisition of the Commander in chief &c Report that they have Borrowed the following sums from the following persons, viz,

of Levi Lincoln	£1..16..0	of Stephen Salisbury	£ 2 - 8—
of Charles Adams	6 —	of David Moor	18.8
of Samuel Allen	12 —	of Daniel Clap	1 - 4—
of Samuel Braizer	12 —	of Samuel Goddard	12—
of Samuel Bridge	6 —	of Nathan Patch	12—
of John Stowers	6 —	of Ephraim Moore	6—
of John Chamberlain	6 —	of Samuel Flagg	1 - 16—
of Samuel Chandler	12 —	of Daniel Waldo	10 - 16—
of Isaiah Thomas	2 . 8 —	of John Nazro	2 - 8—
of Joseph Wheeler	- 6 —	of Doct John Green	1 - 4—
of Elijah Dix	1 16 —	of Nathl Paine	- 12—
of Joseph Allen	- 13 4	of Nath^n Heard	12—
of Timothy Bigelow	- 12 —		
of Samuel Brooks	1 16 —	£ 35 - 15—	

and the same has been paid for the purpose for which it was borrow^d except 36/. which is in the hands of Capt Phinias Jones

Phinias Jones per Order

Voted to let the accounts respecting Thomas Whaland lay on file untill they can be sent to the Govenor & Council for allowance

Voted to return the thanks of the Town to Col. Samuel Flagg for his services as assessor

Voted to return the thanks of the Town to Doct^r Elijah Dix for his Services as assessor

Voted to allow M^r. John Chamberlain the one half of his account for Services as, assessor, & paper found £3..9/—& to return him the thanks of the Town

Voted to return the thanks of the Town to M^r. Daniel Baird for his services as Assessor

Voted to return the thanks of the Town to Deacon Nathan Perry for his services as assessor.

they having generously given the same

Voted that the Selectmen (as soon as may be) call in what is due to the Town from Mr Nathan Patch & Mr Joseph Barber to be appropriated for the payment of Town Debts

Voted that the Selectmen Call in the Interest due on the bonds belonging to the Town

Voted to accept the following Report of a Committee—

The Committee appointed to examine accounts against the Town besides those contained in their Report Delivered in, had exhibited to them the following accounts, viz.

From Joseph Wheeler Esqr. for keeping Mr Storys Horse from the 21th of Novr. 1786 to the 21th of Feby 1787: 13 weeks @ 4/ p^r week	£2..12 – 0
From John Chamberlain attending the General Court as a Committee man	3.. 6 —
From Daniel Baird as a Committe man at the General Court	3.. 6 —
	9.. 4 —

As the above accounts are of a parochial Nature the Committee are of oppinion that they ought not to be considered as a Town, but a parrish Charge

Timothy Paine } Committee
Joseph Allen

Worcester Decr. 3^d. 1787

Worcester Town Records, 1788.

[Second article in a Warrant dated November 25th, 1787 :—
"To Choose a Delegate or Delegates to meet at the State House in Boston on the Second wednesday in January next to take into consideration the Constitution or frame of Government for the United States of America agreeable to a Resolve of Congress and the Recommendation of the Genl. Court."]

At A Meeting of the Freeholders and other Inhabitants of the Town of Worcester Quallified to vote for a Representative on the 3^d. day of Decr. A D 1787—Voted that the Selectmen preside as moderators

Voted to send two Delegats to the State Convention Samuel Curtis Esqr. & Mr David Bigelow Chosen for S^d Delegates

  A true Entery Attest Theophilus Wheeler T. Clerk

At a Town Meeting by adjournment from the 26th of Novr. 1787 to the 10th Day of Decr. 1787. Motioned & Seconded to Disolve the Meeting which passed in the negative—Then Voted that this Meeting be adjourned to the 7th Day of January next at one of the Clock afternoon then to Meet @ this place and the Meeting was accordingly adjourned

  A true Entry Att^s Theophilus Wheeler Town Clerk

At a Meeting of the Freeholders & other Inhabitants of Worcester Quallified to Vote in Town affairs, by adjournment from the tenth Day of December 1787 to the 7th Day of Jany. 1788 .. – Voted that this Meeting be adjourned to the 8th Day of Feby. Next and it was accordingly adjourned

  A true Entry Att^s. Theophilus Wheeler Town Clerk

At the above mentioned adjournment on the 18th of Feby 1788. Voted that this Meeting be adjourned to the 10th Day of March next @ 1 of the Clock afternoon—the meeting was accordingly adjourned

A true Entry   Att^s   Theoph^s Wheeler T Clerk

At the annual Meeting of the Freeholders & other Inhabitants of the Town of Worcester Quallified to vote in Town affairs on the 3^d day of March 1788

Samuel Curtis Esqr. Chosen Moderator, he being absent Joseph Wheeler Chosen protempore

Theophilus Wheeler chosen Town Clerk

Voted to Choose 5 Selectmen

Nathan Perry Samuel Brooks Jno. Chamberlain, Jos: Wheeler Daniel Baird Selectmen

Nathan Perry Town Treasurer

Motioned that the Town Choose assessors to perform the services without any pay   passed in the negative

Voted that the Selectmen be assessors the Current year

Voted that the Selectmen be overseers of the poor

Voted not to Choose Wardens; Reconsidered & voted to Chose 2 Wardens

Voted to adjourn this Meeting half an hour—

Robart Cook Rufus Flagg Wardens

Voted to Choose 2 Tytheingmen   Isaac Prat Eli Gale Tythingmen

Nathan Heard Sealer of tanned & Curried Leather

Voted to Choose 2 Clerks of the market

Samuel Bridge John Paine Clerks of the market

Voted to Choose 2 fence viewers   Joshua Whitney Thad^s. Bigelow Fence Viewers

Voted to Choose 2 Dear Rieves   Joseph Ball Benj^a. Whitney Jun Dear Reaves

Voted to Choose 2 field Drivers   Joseph Barber Capt Jno. Pearce field Drivers

Voted to Choose 2 Surveyors of Boards & Shingles   Ignatius Goulding David Bigelow Surveyors of Boards & Shingles

Voted to Choose the same number of hogg Reeves theire was last year

Abel Heywood Simon Gates Thos. Rice Eben^r. Willington Junr. Wil^m Jineson Thomas Gates Wil^m Elder Saml Kingston Joel Bixby Silas Henry Nathl Coolidge Jesse Taft Hogg Reives Sworn

Voted that the Swine go at large the Currunt year being yoked & Ringed according to Law

Voted that the lowest bidder be Collector of taxes the year Ensuing he giving bonds with good sureties

Voted to Deferr the Choice of a County Treasurer for the present

Voted that the Schools be Supply^d. in way & manner as they were the last year

Voted that the sum of Two hundred pounds be granted Levied & assessed for the support of the Schools the Currunt year

Doct^r Elijah Dix Capt Saml Brooks Samuel Moore Saml Mower Benj^a. Haywood Esq Joel Wesson James Moore Josiah Lyon Tim^o. Taft Joseph Barber Ruebin Gray Eben^r. Mower School Committee

Voted to Choose a Committee of three men, to Settle with the Town Treasurer

Tim^o Paine Esq Benj^a. Haywood Esq Doct^r Elijah Dix the Committee

Voted that Nathan Patch be Collector of taxes the Current year he giving good Security, & Demanding no pay from the Town for his trouble

Voted to Choose 2 Constables   Nathan Patch Eli Gale Constables

£200 Granted to be Worked on the Highways in way & manner as was the last year

Saml. Goddard Nathl Paine Esq Saml Braizer Joshua Whitney Jon^a. Gates 2^d Jno. Mower Nathl Harrington Benj^a. Haywood Esq Thad^s Chamberlain Robart Smith Elisha Smith Junr. Hellyer Tanner Saml. Moore Simon Gates Highway Surveyors & Collectors of highway taxes

Voted to Choose a Committee to take care of the Towns Property on Millstone Hill, who are Empowered to prosecute Every trespasser on the same and to Dispose of the property to the best advantage of the Town

David Bigelow Saml Brooks John Chamberlain Said Committee

Voted to accept the following Report of a Committee—

The Committee Chosen in May last to Enquire into the Records & Examine with respect to the Towns right & title to Millstone Hill so Called to take advice & obtain what light they could with respect to the premises & to make report @ some future meeting Beg leave to report, that at a Meeting of the Propriators of the Town of Worcester in the year 1733 it was voted that 100 acres of the poorest land on Millstone hill be left Common for the use of the Town for building stones,[1] That in the year 1750 a Committee of said propriators appointed to sell their Common & Undevided lands, gave a Deed to Danl Haywood of all their Common & undevided Lands on Millstone Hill not yet Disposed of amount^g to 97 acres more or less, That in 1751 Daniel Haywood Deeded the same to John Chadwick and Asa Flagg, & they in 1761 Deeded it to Bezaleel Gleason, That in 1763 Bezaleel Gleason brought an Action of covenant broken against the said John Chadwick & Asa Flagg for Covenanting in their Deed that they were seized of said land avering in his Declaration that the Inhabitants of the Town of Worcester were seized of the same to which Declaration @ the Superior Court in Worcester in Septr the same year they pleaded that they had Kept their Covenants and the Jury found Specially viz, That if by the vote aforesaid such a right passed to the Town of Worcester in the hundred acres of Land

---

[1] See page 235, Vol. 3, Collections of The Worcester Society of Antiquity (Records of the Proprietors), or page 191 of the original.

aforesaid as that the propriators of the Common lands of Worcester could not afterwards grant the same lands to any other person or persons, then the Jury find for the plf £43 , , 8/ damages & costs, otherwise the Jury find for the Defendent costs upon which special verdict the Court gave Judgement that the said Bezaleel should recover against the said John Chadwick & Asa Flagg the sum of £43 . .8/ Damages & costs, afterwards on the first day of march 1770 Daniel Haywood for the consideration of £7 - 1 - 4 from said propriators and £9 . 1 - 4 from the heirs of the Committee aforesaid released, to the heirs of the said Committee, all actions on account of any of the Covinants mentioned in their Deed to him, and after that on the 26th day of the same march 1770 at a Meeting of the said proprietors, it was voted that whereas it appears to the proprietors that m^r. Daniel Haywood purchased nearly 100 acres of land on Mill stone Hill of the proprietors Committee, the same being recovered from his assigns in due Course of Law, therefore Voted that John Chandler pay the said Daniel Haywood £7 . . 1 - 3. of their money in his hands provided he gave sufficient release to the proprietors for any claim relative to the sale aforesaid [1] and on the 28th of the same month the said Daniel Haywood acknowledged the receipt of the said sum and released the proprietors accordingly, on which facts your Committee have asked advice of Council in law & received confirmation in their Oppinion that the fee of said land is in the Town of Worcester

          David Bigelow
          Samuel Brooks

 Voted, to adjourn this Meeting to the 17th day of this Instant march A. D 1788 @ 2 of the Clock afternoon

  A true Entry Att^s Theophilus Wheeler Town Clerk

 At a meeting of the Freeholders & Other Inhabitants of the Town of Worcester on the 10th day of march A D 1788 by adjournment from the 18th day of Feby Last past

---

[1] See page 311, Vol. 3, Collections of The Worcester Society of Antiquity (Records of the Proprietors).

Voted to Choose Joseph Wheeler Esq Moderator of this meeting protempore the moderator being absent

Voted that the Church be requested to Communicate to the Town what has passed between them & M^r. Story

Voted to Reconsider the vote of the Town accepting of Mr Danl Storys last answer—Motioned & Seconded to see if the Town will accept of Mr Storys answer in Conjunction with his Explanatory or Second answer which passed in the negative

Motioned to adjourne this meeting 1 fortnight which passed in the negative

Voted that this meeting be Disolved, it was Disolved accordingly

   A true Entry att^s Theophilus Wheeler T Clerk

At a Town Meeting of the Inhabitants of the Town of Worcester Quallified to vote in Town affairs on Monday the 17th day of March 1788 by adjournment from the 3^d Day of S^d March

Voted to Discontinue the action brought by the Committee Chosen @ the last Town Meeting to take care of the Towns property on mill stone Hill against David Chadwick

Voted that the Town Treasurer be Directed to pay the cost of the presentment against the Town for not keep^g a Grammar School upon the bills being made up

Voted to Dismiss the Committee appointed the last meeting to take care of the Towns property on Millstone Hill

Voted to Choose a Committee Consisting of three to Examine into David Bigelow Jun^{rs} petetion to this Meeting[1]

Voted That Capt Whitney appear before s^d Committee to answer their Questions, being duly notified to attend

---

[1] 12th ARTICLE:—"To hear the Petition of David Bigelow Junr relative to his being obliged to pay to Capt Whitney one half of a bounty given by the Town June 1778."

136   *Worcester Town Records, 1788.*

Cap* Nath¹ Brooks Benjᵃ Haywood Esq. & Mʳ Daniel Baird Chosen for said Committee

Voted that those who have not worked out their last year highway taxes have the liberty of working them this year provided they do it before June next, and those who have overworked theirs be allow so much out of their this years highway taxes

Voted that the Selectmen be a Committee to bring actions [against] all who are indebted to the Town who have not paid up the Interest—& be Impowered to prosecute the same to final Judgement & Execution for the Recovery of the Interest, and also the principal of those they think not Secure unless they procure sufficient Securities

Voted to allow the following accounts—viz—

To James Fisk	£1 .. 8 .. 11
To John Elder	6 .. 9 .. 10
To Rufus Chandler	5 . 14 —
To Levi Flagg	1 - 5 —

Voted that this Meeting be Disolved & it was accordingly Disolved

    A True Entry   attˢ Theophilus Wheeler T Clerk

Worcester ss. April 3ᵈ. 1788   I hereby Certify to the Town Clerk of Worcester that I have Joined no persons in marrage since my last return in April 1787   Jos : Allen Jus Pacis

---

At a Meeting of the Freeholders & Other Inhabitants of the Town of Worcester Quallified to Vote for Representatives (Legally Warned) on Monday the 17ᵗʰ Day of April A D 1788—

The following persons were voted for, for Govenor, Leuᵗ. Govenor & Senators and the number of Votes Expressed against their respective names

Viz His Excellency John Hancock Esq.	92	
Hon¹. Elbridg. Garey Esq	37	for Govenor
Exellency James Bodoin Esq	1	

Worcester Town Records, 1788.

Hon.ble Benjamin Lincoln Esq	66	
Hon! James Warren Esq.	45	
Hon.ble Sam.ll Adams Esq.	10	Leu.t Govenour
Hon! Elbridge Gerry Esq.	5	

Hon! Abel Wilder Esq.	67	Hon.ble Artemas Ward Esq.	3
Hon! Timothy Paine Esq.	67	Hon! Seth Washburn Esq.	5
Hon! Moses Gill Esq.	70	Jon.a. Grout Esq.	48
Hon! Sam.l Baker Esq	67	Hon! Amos Singletary	51
Hon! Jn°. Sprague Esq	68	Hon! Jn°. Taylor	47
John Fessenden Esq.	48	Hon! Peter Penniman	50
	James Bodoin Jun.r. Esq		

Senators

A True Entry   Att.s.   Theophs Wheeler Town Clerk

At a meeting of the Freeholders and other Inhabitants of the Town of Worcester Quallified to vote for Representatives (duly warned & assembled) on monday the seventh day of April A D. 1788

The following persons were voted for, for a County Treasurer, viz

Timothy Paine Esq.r.	83
Nathan Perry	32
Samuel Allen	1

Oath   I do truly and Sincerely acknowlidge profess testify & Declare that the Commonwealth of Massachusetts is and of right ought to be a free Sovereign & Independent State. and I do Swere that I will bear true faith & Alliegance to the said Commonwealth, & that I will defend the Same against traiterous Conspirators and all hostile attempts whatsoever, and that I do renounce and abjure, all alliegance, subjection & obedience to the King Queen or Government of Great Brittain & every other foreign power whatsoever and that no forrign prince, person prelate, State or potentate hath or ought to have any Jurisdiction, Superiority, preminence, authority Dispencing or other power in any matter Civel,

Worcester Town Records, 1788.

Ecleisasticle or Spiritual within this Commonwealth—except the authority and power which is or may be vested by their Constituents in the Congress of the united States of America, and I do further Testafy & Declare that no man or body of men hath any right to absolve or discharge me from the obligation of this Oath —and that I do make this acknowledgement proffession Testamony &c heartily & truly according to the Common meening & acceptance of the foregoing words without any Equivocation mintal Evasion or Secrete reservation whatever   So help me God

Worcester ss   March 1788
Personally appeared the five last subscribers to the foregoing Oath, & took & Subscribed the same before   Theoph^s. Wheeler
Town Clerk

{ Theoph^s Wheeler
Joseph Wheeler
Jno. Chamberlain
Daniel Baird
Nathan Patch
Samuel Brooks }

A True Entry   attest   Theoph^s. Wheeler

At a Meeting of the Inhabitants of the Town of Worcester Quallified to Vote for Representatives agreeably to the Constitution of Massachusetts on the 15th of May A D. 1788 Legally warned and assembled.

Honble Timothy Paine Esq Chosen by a Majority of Votes to represent the Town of Worcester in the General Court the year Insueing   The meeting then was Disolved

A true Entry   attest   Theoph^s. Wheeler Town Clerk

At a meeting of the Inhabitants of the Town of Worcester Quallified to vote in Town affairs on the 15th day of May A. D. 1788[1]

---

[1] ARTICLE 3 of the Warrant for this Meeting is as follows:—"To hear the Petition of Deacon Thomas Wheelers & others requesting that the assessors may be directed to take a View of all the Estates in Town in order that they may be better able to Judge of every mans Interest"

Joseph Allen Esq Chosen Moderator

Voted to allow Jacob Hemenways account for bridge plank	£2 .. 8 – 0
to allow Phineas Flagg for wood supply^d Crosby	19 —
Voted to allow James Fisk's account	1 – 8 – 11
Voted to accept the report of the Selectmen respect^g the Situation of the Town bonds, The Selectmen Chargeable with the Sum of	£57 .. 4 .. 3.

Voted not to abate John Stearns Jun^{rs} taxes in Wm Taylors hands to collect—that it Subside for the present.

Voted that Capt. Nathl Brooks, Benj^a Haywood Esq. & John Chamberlain be a Committee to Examine into the taxes of Jno. Welch & others in Nathan Patches hands to Collect, also to Examine James Quigleys acc^t.

Voted not to Build a Ministerial toomb

Voted that this Meeting be Disolved it is Disolved accordingley

     Att^s Theophilus Wheeler Town Clerk

At a Meeting of the Freeholders & other Inhabitants of the Town of Worcester Quallified to vote in Town affairs, on the 20th day of October 1788

Deacon Nathan Perry Moderator

Voted that the accounts brought against the Town be refered to the Committee now outstanding for Examination & allowance &c., Viz, Capt. Nathl Brooks John Chamberlain & Benj^a. Haywood Esq.—& make report at some future meeting

Voted to pass over the third article in the Warrant[1] to some future Meeting

Voted that the Town purchase a new pall

---

[1] ARTICLE 3 :—"To hear the report of the Outstanding Committees"

Voted that the Sum of Six pounds be granted for the purpose of purch[as]ing a pall & that the Selectmen purchase the same as Soon as possible

Voted that this Meeting be adjourned one fortnight from this day one of the Clock afternoon, it was adjourned accordingly

  A true Entry attest Theoph^s Wheeler T Clerk

At a Meeting held by the above adjournment on Novr. 3^d 1788 Voted to accept the following report of the Committee Chosen to Examine accounts.

Voted to abate William Brown Jun^{rs}. pole tax for 1786

Voted to Omit the abatement of taxes pray^d for by M^r. Patch till some future Meeting

The Committee appointed to Examine such accounts as are brought against the Town have attended that service and beg leave to report that there be allowed and paid to the following persons, the sums set against the respective names agreeably to their accounts, viz,—

N° 1	to Jesse Taft £1 .. 2 .. 6	
(2^d)	To Daniel Baird £5 .. 15/ 2½	£6 .. 17 − 8½
3	To John Chamberlain	3 .. 14 − 11
4	To Edward Knights	2 .. 14 ———
5	To Deacon Jacob Chamberlain	3 − 18 ———
6	To Nathan Patch	1 − 10 ———
7	To Deacon Nathan Perry	— 17 − 8
8	To Martha Wiley	5 − 4 ———
9	To Mary Boyd	5 − 4 ———
10	To Eli Gale 18/6 (11) To Abigail Grout £5 - 8/	6 − 6 − 6
12	To John Elder	5 − 12 − 11
13	To Saml Eaton	11 − 14 ———
14	To David Bigelow & Capt Saml Brooks	1 − 8 ———
15	To Capt. Saml Brooks	2 − 5 − 8

16	To Thad^s Bigelow		9 —	7
17	To Deacon Nathan Perry & others assessors		7 — 7 —	6
18	To James Quigley		8 .. 13 —	4
		£ 73	16,	9½

All which is humbly submitted

p^r Nathl Brooks
Benj^a Haywood } Committee
John Chamberlain

Voted that M^r. Saml Eaton be allowed 3/8 per week for keep^g his Mother the Current year if she lives

Voted that £ 80 be granted levied & assessed on the poles & Estates of the Inhabitants of this Town, in order to defray the Town Charges the Current year, to be paid into the Treasurey by the first of march next

Voted that this Meeting be Disolved, it is accordingly Disolved

   A true Entry   attest   Theoph^s. Wheeler Town Clerk

At a Meeting of the Freeholders and other Inhabitants of the Town of Worcester on the 18th day of December A D. 1788 agreeably to the above Warrant

The following persons were voted for to represent the Destrect of Worcester County in the Congress of the United States of America the number of Votes set against their respective names, Viz,

Hon^l. Timothy Paine Esq.	46
Hon^l Jonathan Grout Esq.	25
Hon^l Abel Wilder Esq.	3
Hon^l Artemas Ward Esq.	1

Also at the same time & place the following persons were voted for as Candidates for an Elector of President & vice president of the United States of America Viz.,

Hon^be Abel Wilder Esq	61
Hon^l John Sprague Esq	28
Hon^l Artemas Ward Esq	21
Hon^l Saml Curtis Esq	16
Hon^l Timothy Paine Esq	5
Hon^l Moses Gill Esq	1
Joseph Allen Esq	3
Hon^l Saml Baker Esq	2
Hon! Jon^a Grout Esq	1
Joseph Wheeler Esq	1

Voted this Meeting be Dissolved & it was accordingly Disolved

A true Entry att^s Theoph^s. Wheeler T Clerk

At a Meeting of the Freeholders & Other Inhabitants of the Town of Worcester Quallified to Vote for Representatives Legally warned and assembled on the 29th day of Jany. A. D. 1789, The following persons were voted for to represent the District of Worcester in the Congress of the United States of America, the number of votes set against their respective names viz

Honble Tim^o. Paine Esq	61
Hon! Jon^a. Grout Esq	40
Hon! Artemas Ward Esq	15
	116

Voted that this meeting be Dissolved, and it was Dissolved accordingly

A true Entry att^s Theoph^s Wheeler T. Clerk

At a Legall Town Meeting of the Inhabitants of the Town of Worcester Quallified to Vote in Town affairs on the 29th day of Jany. A. D. 1789

Deacon Nathan Perry Chosen Moderator

Motioned and Seconded to see if the Town will refer the matters contained in the afore mentioned petition, to a Committee, which passed in the negative[1]

Motioned and Seconded to see if the Town will Grant the prayer of s^d petition, which passed in the negative

Motioned & Seconded to see if the Town will reconsider the Vote up on the first motion for Choosing a Committee passed in the Negative

Voted to put over the third article in the Warrant[2] to march meeting

Voted that this meeting be Disolved it was disolved accordingly

  A true Entry   att^s Theoph^s. Wheeler Town Clerk

At a Meeting of the Freeholders & other Inhabitants of the Town of Worcester Quallified to Vote in Town affairs Legally warned & assembled on the 2^d day of March 1789 The following Votes were passed, viz,

 Samuel Curtis Esqr. Chosen moderator

 Theophilus Wheeler Town Clerk

---

[1] SECOND ARTICLE:—"To hear the petition of Josiah Peirce & Others which petition is as follows, To the Selectmen of Worcester in the County of Worcester Greeting We the Subscribers freeholders of the Town of Worcester, Desireous of adjusting all the Difficulties and disputes among the Inhabitants of said Town respecting Ministerial matters do hereby request that you would forthwith call a Town meeting for the Express purpose hereafter mentioned, viz, To see if the Town will agree that all public property that is has been or may be appropriated to ministerial purposes and all assessments therefor since the association of M^r. Bancrofts Society may be so adjusted that each Society may have their Just and Equal share thereof and to do and act thereon as may be Judged proper"

[2] THIRD ARTICLE:—"To see if the Town will abate sundry persons taxes in Mr William Taylor's hands to Collect"

Voted to Choose 5 Selectmen

Deacon Nathan Perry Capt. Saml Brooks M^r. John Chamberlain Joseph Wheeler Esq Mr Daniel Baird Selectmen and overseers of the poor

Voted to Choose three assessors

Samuel Curtis Esqr. Capt. Saml Flagg Mr Danl Baird assessors
March 2^d 1789 Sworn

Deacon Nathan Perry Town Treasurer March 2^d 1789 Sworn

This meeting adjourned 1 houre

Voted to Choose two Wardens

John Moore & Moses Miller Wardens, Sworn March 2^d 1789

Elijah Harrington | Sworn | William Taylor Tythingmen

Nathan Heard Sealer of tan^d & Curried Leather

Abraham Lincoln ⎫ March 2^d 1789 Sworn
               ⎬ Tythingmen
Eph^m Mower ⎭ March 12th 1789 Sworn

Joseph Kingsbury Micah Johnson Junr. Fence Viewers
March 2^d. 1789 Sworn

Nathan Patch Dear Rieve

Joseph Barber Josiah Peirce Eli Chapin Field Drivers

Ignatious Goulding David Bigelow Surveyors of Boards & Shingles

Eben^r Wiswall Jur ⎫	Sworn
John Barnard	
Isaac Willard Junr	March 2^d 1789 Sworn
Eben^r Willington Junr	
Tyler Curtis	March 2^d 1789 Sworn
Nathan Patch ⎬	Hogg Reives
John Elder Junr	march 2^d 1789 Sworn
Increase Blair	Sworn before Esqr Young March
William Trowbridge	11th 1789
Eben^r Whitney	march 2^d 1789 Sworn
Elisha Smith Junr	
Simeon Duncan	March 2^d 1789 Sworn
Daniel Stearns ⎭	Sworn

Voted that the Swine go at large the Current year being yoaked & Ringed

Voted to Choose 1 Collector, the article put over to the adjournment

Simeon Duncan } Constables
Eli Gale } march 2^d. 1789 Sworn

Cornelius Stowell
Nathl Flagg   March 4th 1789 Sworn
Samuel Mower   march 2^d 1789 Sworn
Micah Johnson Junr. march 2^d 1789 Sworn
John Mower   d^o Sworn
Nathan Patch
Jonathan Rice   march 2^d 1789 Sworn
William McFarland Junr. d^o
Rufus Flagg
Jesse Taft   march 2^d 1789 Sworn
Ruebin Gray   d^o
Samuel Moore   Sworn June 2^d 1789
Saml Hemenway   march 14th 1789 Sworn
John Stanton   march 3^d 1789 Sworn
Benjamin Flagg Junr. march 2^d 1789 Sworn
Phineas Jones   Sworn May 21st 1789

Highway Surveyors & Collectors of highway taxes

£ 200 , , Granted to be worked on the Roads this year at the same rate it was last year

Those persons who over worked their taxes last year to be allowed the overplus out of this years taxes, & those who have not worked out their last years rates have liberty to do it this year provided they do it by the last of June next

Voted that £ 200 be granted Levied & assessed on the poles & Estates of the Inhabitants of this Town for the Support of the Schools which are to be kept & the monies proportioned in the same way & manner as they were last year

Samuel Brazer Samuel Brooks Samuel Moore Saml. Mower Jonathan Rice Nathan Patch Thad^s. Chamberlain Thad^s. Chapin Thomas Stowell Benj^a Whitney Junr. Helyer Tanner Joel How School Committee

Voted to return to Mr William Taylor the list of taxes, to collect, which he presented for abatement

Worcester Town Records, 1789.

Voted to pass over the 11th article[1]

Voted that the Select men dispose of the poor named in a list this day presented to the Town to the best advantage & Saveing to the Town they can & make return to the adjournment of this meeting

Voted that the 14th article in the Warrant[2] be put over to the adjournment of this meeting

Voted to accept the following Report of the Committee

The Report of the Select men of Worcester in laying out a road from the House of Daniel Baird to the road leading by Helyer Tannars which is as follows viz,, begining @ the County road leading to Sutton by said Bairds & running as the wall now stands to the northeast end of the wall thence in a Strait line to a Small Walnut tree marked thence to a large white Oak a line tree between Nathl Moore & said Baird thence to a small black Oak, thence to a black Oake marked on said Tannars road, said road being on the Northerly side of s^d line & is laid out two rods wide said road is laid out upon Condition that the proprietors give the lands, and said road going through Daniel Baird & Nathl Moores land

Worcester Feby. 19,, 1789   Nathan Perry ⎫ Selectmen
                               John Chamberlain ⎬ of
                               Joseph Wheeler ⎭ Worcester

and as a Compensation for the land taken up by the aforesaid road belonging to Nathl Moore & Benj^a Haywood Voted that the said Nathl Moore & Benj^a Haywood, their heirs and assigns shall forever have the uninterrupted priviledge of keeping open a free Course for the Water to run in the manner that it now does down

---

[1] ARTICLE 11 :—"To see if the Town will Grant a sum of money to defray Contingent Charges"

[2] ARTICLE 14 :—"To see if the Town will accept of an alteration in the Cross road Southeast of John Stearns agreeable to the request & plan exhibited by Phineas Flagg and others provided the alteration be made without any expence to the Town—Also to see if the Town will discontinue the old Cross road leading from said Stearns to the County road leading by Nathl Moores & Suffer the same to lye Common."

the road from the House of John Stearns between his land & land of Jonathan Rice to the County road lead^g to Uxbridge

Voted that this Meeting be adjourned to the first monday in april next. 4 o Clock afternoon. It was accordingly adjourned

  A true Entry att^s Theophilus Wheeler Town Clerk

At A Meeting of the Freeholders and other Inhabitants of the Town of Worcester Quallified to vote for Representatives legally warned & assembled on the 2^d day of March A D 1789

The following persons were Voted for to represent them in the Congress of the United States of america, the number of votes set against their respective names viz,

    Hon^l. Timothy Paine Esq 62
    Hon^l. Jon^a. Grout Esq. 60
    Hon^l. Artimas Ward Esq. 15

Voted that this meeting be Disolved it was Disolved accordingly

    A true Entry Att^s Theoph^s Wheeler T Clerk

Worcester ss At a meeting of the Freeholders & other Inhabitants of the Town of Worcester Quallified to vote for a Representative duly warned & assembled on the 6th day of april 1789 The following persons were voted for for Govenor the number of Votes set against their respective names,, viz,

    His Excellency John Hancock Esq 78 }
    His Excellency James Bodoin Esq 37 }

For Liu^t. Govenor

    The Honb^{le} Benj^a. Lincoln Esq 45
    The Honb^{le}. Saml. Adams Esq 64

For Senators

Worcester Town Records, 1789.

Honb^{le}. Moses Gill Esq	80	Hon^l. Israel Nichols Esq	27
Honb^{le}. Abel Wilder Esq	78	Hon^l. Peter Penniman Esq	25
Honb^{le}. Saml. Baker Esq	62	Martin Kinsley Esq	22
Hon^{bl}. Artemas Ward Esq	48	M^r. David Bigelow	22
Hon^l. Amos Singletary Esq	47	Hon^l. John Fessenden Esq	14
Hon^l. Timothy Paine Esq	44	Benj^a. Haywood Esq	1
Hon^l. Seth Washburn Esq	37	Jonathan Warner Esqr.	1
Hon^l. Saml Curtis Esq	29	Doct^r Joseph Wood	1

At the same time and place Voted for the following persons for a County Treasurer viz,

Tim° Paine Chosen moderator

  Nathan Perry 46
  Saml Allen 45
  Samuel Flagg 1

Voted that this Meeting be Disolved, it was Disolved accordingly

       att^s Theoph^s Wheeler Town Clerk

At a Meeting by adjournment from the 2^d day of march A D 1789 on 6th April A D 1789

Timothy Paine Esq chosen moderator protempore

Voted that John Barnard be Collector the year Insuing giving Sufficient bonds for the faithfull discharge of his trust and that he be allowed 4^d on the pound for his trouble—and that he be Constable Sworn

Voted that David Bigelow & others assessors for 1784 be a Committee to Examine a list of taxes pray^d to be abated by M^r. Joseph Barber & by Jesse Taft

Voted to allow M^r. Simeon Duncans acc^t. £1,,8,,4

Voted that Abraham Lincoln be a Hogg Reive

Voted to accept the following Report, & to Discontinue the Road lead^g by Jn°. Stearns.

Voted to allow William Knights ac^t. for beef & pork Del^d to Simon Glasco £1,,5.10

Voted to abate 3/10 a pole tax to Capt Nathl Brooks
                                                    3.10

Voted That instead of the plan refered to which was to be exhibited by Phinias Flagg the proposed alteration be as follows viz, begining on the south side of the County road leading to Grafton one rod & half from the northeast corner of John Stearns land, thence on a Circular line till it comes to the fence on the cross two rods South of said Corner also begining on the east side of said Cross road three rods from the southwest corner of Elijah Harringtons land, thence on a Curve line till it comes to the County road leading to Uxbridge two rods East of the aforesaid corner

Voted that this Meeting be disolved

Theoph^s Wheeler Town Clerk

Worcester ss March 26th 1789 We the Subscribers being appointed by the Selectmen of our respective Towns to renew the bounds between Worcester & Boylston have attended that Service, the bounds are as follows, viz, begining at a heap of stones betwen Nathl Haywoods and Jonathan Lovells then runing over the East corner of said Lovells House to a heap of Stones in said Lovells Orchard thence to a heap of stones Northerly of Eames Brook thence to a Walnut tree marked thence to a heap of Stones, thence to a pine tree marked, thence to a Large white Oak tree marked, thence to a Swamp white Oak with stones about it being Holden corner

Joseph Wheeler	for	Ezra Beaman	
Saml Brooks	Worcester	Jonas Temple	for
		Tim^o. Whitney	Boylston

March 26th 1789 We the Subscribers being appointed by the Selectmen of our respective Towns to perambulate and renew the bounds betwen our respective Towns have attended that service and report that the bounds are as follows, viz, beginning @ a black Oak tree marked near the North end of Long pond, thence Northerly to a maple tree marked in Nathl Haywoods land, thence to a heap of Stones betwen said Nathl Haywoods & Jonathan Lovells it being the Corner of Shrewesbury & Boylston

Joseph Wheeler } In behalf of } Ross Wyman } In behalf of
Samuel Brooks } Worcester } Isaac Harrington } Shrewsbury

In Obedience to a Notification from the Selectmen of Worcester to renew and preambulate the line betwixt Holden & Worcester We the Subscribers have attended that service by meeting at the Northwest corner of Worcester on Leicester line & preambulated & renewed make^g a Strait line rewewing Easterly to a corner on Boylston this 26th march 1789

Josiah Stratton } Selectmen   John Chamberlain Selectman
John Davis   } of Holden   of Worcester
Richard Flagg } by ap-
Nathan Harrington } point^t Saml Moore by appointment

To the Gentlemen Selectmen of Worcester Greeting—We the Subscribers Certify that we have appointed Capt David Henshaw and Capt John Southgate a Committee to meet you or such of you as you shall appoint at the time and place by you notified to preambulate the line & renew the bounds between the Towns of Worcester & Leicester   Leicester March 19th 1789

Edwd Rawson }
Saml Green } Selectmen of Leicester
David Henshaw }

March 26th 1789   These may certify that we the subscribers meet @ the line notified by the Selectmen of Worcester & preambulated the line and renewed the bounds between the Towns of Worcester & Leicester to Holden Line

David Henshaw
John Southgate

Worcester 2ᵈ April 1789

We the Subscribers being appointed by the Selectmen of Worcester & the Selectmen of Ward to run the line and Establish the bounds betwen the Said Towns have attended the business of our appointment & have began @ the Northeast corner of Ward & have Established the line from the said Corner to the southwest corner of Worcester & the Southeast corner of Leicester on Ward line being on Lamsur[?] Hills, by Erecting Sundry heaps of Stones & a range of marked trees on said line

Daniel Baird } on the part of Worcester
Jnᵒ. Pierce

Charles Stearns
Jonᵃ. Stone Junʳ.
Thoˢ. Drewry
Jos. Stone
} on the part of Ward

Entered from the Originals ℔ Theophˢ. Wheeler Town Clerk

Worcester March 26ᵗʰ 1789—We the Subscribers according to appointment met and perambulated the line and renewed the bounds between Worcester & Sutton

Nathan Perry
Samuel Goddard
Thadˢ. Chapin
Barthʷ Woodbury
Jedʰ. Barton
Ezra Lovel

Worcester ss At a Meeting of the Freeholders & other Inhabitants of the Town of Worcester Quallified to vote for Representatives on the 14ᵗʰ day of May 1789

Honˡ. Timᵒ. Paine Esq Chosen to Represent this Town in the Great and General Court of this Commonwealth the year Insueing

At the Same time and place the following Votes were passed viz

Capᵗ Samˡ Flagg Chosen moderator

Worcester Town Records, 1789.

Voted to Choose a Committee consisting of three, viz, Danl. Clap Robert Smith & Benjamin Heywood Esqr., to pitch upon a Suitable place for a Gun House   Voted that Timothy Bigelow & Nathl. Brooks be Joined to the above Committee

Voted that the proprietors of the two buildings standing west of the burying ground on the Common remove them

Voted that the Officers of the Artillery have liberty of Erecting a Gun house where the Old stable now stands @ the west end of the burying ground leaving 12 feet between the Gate leading into s^d burying ground, & sd Gun house

Voted that the proprietors of the School house be allowed one month to remove the same school house

Voted to abate the following taxes, viz.

Stephen Hassums 19/3   Daniel Whitneys 19/3 £1 .. 18 .. 6
Crosbys 19/3   Ellis Gray Blake £1 .. 9/4   2 .. 8 . 7
Uriah Ward 21/5.   Elisha Dunham 12/10   1 - 14 - 3
   In m^r. Joseph Barbers hands to Collect

Joseph Bigelow 3/7¾   Jabez Bigelow 3/7¾   7 .. 3½
Duncan Campbell £1 .. 6 - 1¼
               James Campbell 3/7¾   1 .. 9 .. 9
Edward Jordan 3/7¾   Daniel Raymond 3/7¾   7 .. 3½
Uriah Ward 3/7¾   Solomon Johnson 10/9¾   14 .. 5½
Paul Gates 5/5¾   William Moore 3/7¾   9 .. 1½
   In M^r. Jesse Tafts hands to Collect

The case of Jacob Smith & wife refered to the Selectmen

[Article in a Warrant dated May 8th, 1789 :—"To hear the petition of Mesr^s Saml Chandler & Daniel Clap—which petition is as followeth viz   We the Subscribers in behalf of the proprietors of the Cotton & Linen manufactory in said Town request that the Select men would call a Town Meeting to see if the Town will Grant liberty to said proprietors to Errect a building on Common land in said Town between the House & Shop of Mr John Waters for the purpose of Carrying on said manufactory and to remove the same in Case said proprietors should hereafter think proper so to do."]

[May 14th, 1789.] Upon the petition of Samuel Chandler & Daniel Clap

Voted That the petitioners have [liberty] to Errect a Building as prayed for in the petition for the use of the Cotton and Lining Manufactory and that said Building be Errected on the Common land betwen the House & Shop belong^g to Mr John Waters in such a manner as to leave at least four rods betwen the same and the fence leading from Waters to Capt. Gouldings on the East of the Common, provided the proprietors of said Building will consent on their part to remove the same when the Town shall require it

Voted that the foregoing meetings be Disolved and they were Disolved accordingly

The foregoing are true Enteries, Att^s

Theoph^s. Wheeler Town Clerk

At a meeting of the Inhabitants of the Town of worcester Quallified to vote in Town affairs on the 19th Octr A D, 1789

Deacon Nathan Perry chosen Moderator

Voted not to act on the Second article [1]

Voted to choose a Committee consisting of three to examine accounts M^r. Jno. Chamberlain, Tim^o. Paine Esqr. & Capt Saml. Brooks chosen upon s^d Committee

Voted to pass over the 4th article [2] to the adjournment of this meeting

---

[1] ARTICLE 2:—"To see if the Town will annex Silas Harrington to Capt. Tanners School Quarter District agreeable to his request"

[2] ARTICLE 4:—"To make such Grants of money as the Town Shall think proper"

Worcester Town Records, 1789.

Voted to pass over the 5th article [1] to the adjournment of this meeting

Voted that this meeting be adjourned for three weeks 2, oClock after noon that the Select men post up a notification thereof

the meeting was accordingly adjourned

    A true Entery   Att^s.   Theoph^s. Wheeler Town Clerk

At a Meeting of the Inhabitants of the Town of Worcester by adjournment from the 19th of Octr. A D 1789 to the 9th day of Novr A D 1789

Voted to accept of the following report of the Committee for allowing accounts

Voted not to allow m^r Benj^a Butmans account for boarding & Cloath^g Clarissa Cunninghams ac^t

Voted that £140 be granted Levied & assessed on the poles & Estates of this Town to defray the Town expences the Current year

Voted That whoever has any proposals to make with respect to the poor apply to the Select men on the first monday in the month @ their meeting, that the Select men act therein according to their best discretion & prudence

Voted that this Meeting be Disolved it was Disolved accordingly

    A true Entry   Att^s Theophilus Wheeler Town Clerk

The Committee appointed by the Town at Town Meeting held at Worcester on the 19th of October A. D. 1789 to examine accounts exhibited against the Town report that they have examined the following accounts due to the following persons for the Towns allowance and payment, viz,

---

[1] ARTICLE 5 :—"For the Town to take such measures as they shall think proper for the Support of the poor."

Nº. 1	To Samuel Brooks to Sundrys supply^d Simon Glasco	£2 .. 6 .. 6
	Sundries Supplyd Thomas Gleason	6 —
2	Moses Miller boarding & Cloathing Anna White 9 weeks & half ending 10th march 1789 @ 3/9	1 .. 15 - 7
3^d	To William Taylor keeping & Cloathing Anna White 34 weeks ending 2^d Novr. 1789	6 .. 7 - 6
	Extraordinarys found her in sickness	£0 - 8 - 0
4	William Trowbridge account for plank & timber	1 .. 9 - 0
5	Mary Boyd boarding & Cloathing Richard McDonald to 6th March 1789 21½ weeks @ 2/	2 - 3 —
6	To Palmer & Daniel Goulding sundrys dd Crosby	1 3 6½
	To d^o. del^d. Thomas Gleason	16 —
7	To Ashbell Johnson for boarding & Cloathing Zacheus Johnson 2 years ending 4th feb^y. 1789 @ 3/	15 - 12 —
8	To Edward Knights for 21 Loads wood del^d. to Simon Glasco	3 .. 3
9	To Nathan Perry for sundries supplyd Mis^{rs}. Benj^a. Crosby & Thomas Gleason addition 5/4	2 .. 13 6½
10	To Daniel Waldo & Son for 2 years & 8 months Interest of £10 . 16 Loaned to the Town	1 .. 7 —
11	Abigail Grout for boarding & Cloathing Sally Walker 1 year ending 13th October 1789 @ 2/	5 - 4 —
12	To Cornileus Stowell to Supplying Thomas Gleason with milk 147½ Quarts @ 2^d	1 - 4 - 7
13	To John Elder to boarding John Spence 1 year ending 20th Octr 1789 & finding sundries of Cloathing	10 .. 13 .. 6
14	Benj^a. Haywood Esqr. for pork supplyed Thomas Gleason	9 - 4½

15	To John Chamberlain part of his account, viz,	4 – 7 – 5
	The remainder of his account being for Supporting Nathan Houghton to the 15th Octr 1789 the Committee are of oppinion ought to be paid out of the Estate of said Nathan Houghton	£7 – 16
16	To Martha Wiley & Thomas Nichols for boarding & Cloathing Lydia, an Indian Child 1 year ending Octr 15th 1789	5 – 4 —
17	To Samuel Eaton for boarding his mother Sarah Eaton 1 year ending Septr 1789 &c	9 . 15 . 8
18	To Nathl. Moore for 15½^{lb} pork del^d Thos. Gleason by Selectmens orders @ 6^d 7/9 addition on account 1/6 also 5/7½	9 – 3 5 – 7½
19	Saml. Brooks Daniel Baird & Jno. Chamberlain assessors for the year 1788 making a Town & County tax 6 days at 4/	1 – 4 —
20	To Joseph Wheeler Esqr. sundries supply^d the poor of the Town 18/11 and his service relateing to paupers 36/ as by ac^t. on file	2 . 14 - 11
21	To Eli Gale Constable carrying Clarissa Gale to Princeton & Abraham Newton to Shrewsbury by order of Justice Wheeler	1 .. 4 —
22	To Simeon Duncan Constable carrying Abigail Phelps & Child to Boylston by order of Justice Haywood & Abigail Taylor to Boylston & John Chatfield to Shrewesbury by order of Danforth Kyes Justice Peace	1 .. 10 —
23	To Daniel Baird sundrys supplyed M^r. Crosby	1 – 0 —
24	To Helyer Tanner sundries supplyed Jacob Smith	8 . 3
25	To Nathan Patch Sundries as constable	3 .. 0 —

26 The assessors for the year 1789   10 .. 13 . 4
All which is humbly Submitted

                          John Chamberlain } Committee
                          Samuel Brooks

Worcester Novr. 3^d 1789

Octr 9th 1789 At a Town Meeting of the Inhabitants of the Town of Worcester Quallified to vote in Town affairs on the 9th day of November A. D. 1789[1]

Voted that the sum of Forty pounds be Granted for the Incouragement of the removal of the Leicester Acadamy into the Town of Worcester to be paid annually so long as said Acadamy shall remain in said Worcester

Voted that this meeting be Disolved, it is accordingly Disolved

        A true Entry   att^s Theophilus Wheeler Town Clerk

At a Meeting of the Inhabitants of the Town of Worcester on monday the 21st day of December A. D. 1789

Deacon Nathan Perry Chosen moderator

Voted that the Selectmen be and hereby are appointed to settle the demand of Benjamin Butman against the Town for keep^g & Cloathing Clarissa Cunningham in the best way & manner they can, and if they cannot settle the same upon reasonable terms, The Town hereby appoint the said Selectmen or any two of them agents for the Town to appear & defend the law suit commenced against the Town by said Butman to be heard and tried before John Child Esq a Justice of the peace on monday the 28th day of Decr. Ins^t. to final Judgement

Voted not to act on the third article at Present[2]

---

[1] On the petition of Timothy Paine and others.

[2] ARTICLE 3d :—"To receive the report of the Committee who were appointed to Examine the taxes in M^r. Nathan Patches hands @ a former meeting"

Worcester Town Records, 1790.

Voted that the third article be refered to march meeting & an article be Inserted in the Warrant for that meeting for that purpose

Voted that this meeting be Disolved, it was disolved accordingly

 A true Entry Attest Theophilus Wheeler Town Clerk

Worcester ss At a Meeting of the Inhabitants of the Town of Worcester Quallified to vote in Town affairs Legally warned & assembled on this 1st day of March Anno Domini 1790

 Capt Samuel Flagg Moderator

 Theophilus Wheeler Chosen Town Clerk Sworn 2^d March 1790 before J Wheeler J Pacis

 Voted to Choose 5 Selectmen

 Capt. Samuel Flagg. Samuel Curtis Esq. Capt Samuel Brooks. Mr John Chamberlain Joseph Wheeler Esq. Selectmen

 Capt Samuel Flagg Town Treasurer, who was excused

 Benjamin Haywood Esqr. Chosen Town Treasurer & *Sworn* 2^d march 1790

 Voted to Choose 3 assessors

Samuel Curtis Esq. ⎫ May 3^d 1790 Sworn
Capt Samuel Flagg ⎬ Assessors
M^r. Jno. Chamberlain ⎭ Sworn march 1st 1790

 Voted to adjourn 1 hour

 Voted to Choose two wardens for the insueing year

 Mr William Trowbridge Mr Henry Patch Wardens Sworn Ap^l 1st 1790

 Voted to Choose Tytheing men

 Capt John Stanton Capt. Joshua Whitney Tytheingmen Sworn may 21st 1790

 Mr Nathan Heard, Sealer of Tanned & Curryed Leather

Benjamin Flagg Junr. ⎫ aug^t 3^d 1790 Sworn
         ⎬ Fence Viewers
Noah Harris   ⎭

Samuel Goddard Dear rieve

Voted to choose two field drivers

Cap¹. Joshua Whitney Benjamin Whitney Jun' Field drivers

David Bigelow Ignatius Goulding Surveyors of Boards & Shingles

Daniel Goulding July 30 ⎫ 1790 Sworn
Benjamin Stowell
Robert Cook
Levi Pierce   Ap¹ 5th 1790 Sworn
Daniel Willington   Ap¹. 20th 1790 Sworn
William Taylor   Ap¹. 5th 1790 Sworn
William Elder   ⎬ Hogg Rieves
Samuel Kingston   ap¹ 29th 1790 Sworn
Samuel Griggs
Eben'. Whitney march 3ᵈ ⎪ 1790 Sworn
Benj³. Whitney Ju'. Sworn ⎭
Elijah Newton Ap¹ 12th 1790 Sworn

Voted that the Swine go at large the currunt year being yoked and rung according to law

Voted to Choose one Collector

Voted That £ 200 be granted for the Support of Schools the Currunt year

Samuel Brazier Samuel Brooks David Bigelow John Barnard Nathan Perry Nathaniel Harrington William M°Farland Jun'. Nathan White Nath¹ Brooks Benjamin Whitney Jun'. Daniel Baird Joel How School Committee

Voted that said Committee prepare a plan for the apportionment of the School money so as shall best answer the law, & be most for the benefit of the town and make report at the adjournment of this meeting

Voted That Cap¹. David Moore be allowed to take his proportion of the School money from the usual apportionment and apply it in Schooling some other way the year insuing

Voted To annex M' Isaac Gleason to Cap¹. Curtis School Quarter

Voted That Timothy Paine Esq. Doct Elijah Dix Benjamin

Worcester Town Records, 1790.

Haywood Esq Committee to Settle with the Town Treasurer & to transfer the necessary papers to the new Treasurer

Voted that £200 .. be granted to be worked on the highways @ 4/ per day—That those who did not work out their highway taxes the last year have liberty of working them out this year if they do it before the last of June next. & those that have over worked be allowed the same this year

Noah Harris
Nathaniel Flagg
Capt. Joshua Whitney   March 5th 1790 Sworn before Joseph
Increase Blair   May 29th 1790 Sworn   [Wheeler
John Mower
Thaddeus Bigelow   Sworn
Jonathan Rice
Thad^s. Chamberlain   Sworn March 8 1790
James Barber   Ap^l. 12th 1790   Sworn
Eben^r. Barber   Ap^l 15 1790   Sworn
Danl Stearns
Benj^a Childs   Ap^l 5th 1790   Sworn
Eben^r. Lovel
Daniel Haywood   Ap^l. 7th 1790   Sworn
Stephen Haywood   Sworn
Phineas Jones
John Totman
    Highway Surveyors & Collectors of Highway [Taxes]

Voted That the Selectmen Settle the account with M^r. Nathl Boynton in the best way they can, and make application to Gloucester for payment of the expence & cost in the case of Worcester against Maj Moore

Voted that Samuel Goddard Timothy Taft and Moses Perry be a Committee to view the Bridge near M^r. Wards mill and make the necessary prepareation of meterials for repareing it & lay their account before the Town

Voted that this meeting be adjourned to the first monday in April next nine oClock forenoon—it was adjourned accordingly

  A true Entrey   attest   Theoph^s. Wheeler Town Clerk

Worcester Town Records, 1790.

Att the above mentioned adjournment

Voted that this meeting be further adjourned to One of the Clock afternoon of this day

Att the above mentioned Meeting by adjournment. on the fifth day of April 1790

Voted to allow the widow Judah Rice her account for timber £0..6..0

Voted to Choose Daniel Baird, Timothy Paine Esq & Benjamin Haywood Esqr. Committee to adjust accounts

Voted that this meeting be adjourned 1 hour

Voted to pass over the 11th article in the warrant[1] for this meeting

Voted To abate Timothy Taylors tax of 6/3. and that he have an order for the repayment of it

Voted to abate the following taxes prayed for by m^r. N Patch viz

Oliver Mossmans	£0 - 16 - 0
[ ] 17/4 Benj^a. Edward £1..9..1¾	2 . 6 . 5¾
Jacob Smith Junr. 17/4 —— Smith 17/4	1 - 14 . 8
John Welch £5 - 6 - 1¾ John Quigley 25/7	6 - 11 - 8¾
George Thayer £2 - 4 - 1 Daniel Grout 19/	3 - 3 - 1
Jacob Smith 9/ Luther Ward 19/9	1 - 8 - 9
Richard Dickinson 5/4½ Isaac Stearns 19/3	1 - 4 - 7½
Chandler 19/9 —— Houghton 19/9	1 - 19 - 6
John Kendrick 19/9 Saml. Stow 19/9	1 - 19 - 6
William Tracy 19/9 Charles Warren 19/9	1 - 19 - 6

Voted that this Meeting be adjourned to the 12th day of this Inst april 2, oClock afternoon   it was accordingly adjourned

A true Entry   att^s Theophilus Wheeler Town Clerk

---

[1] ARTICLE 11 :—"To see if the Town will grant a sum of money to Defray Contingent charges"

Worcester Town Records, 1790.

At a Meeting of the Freeholders & other Inhabitants of the Town of Worcester Quallified to Vote for Representatives Legally warned & assembled on the 5th day of April A D. 1790. The following persons were voted for, for Govenor the number of votes set against their respective names. Viz,

His Excelency John Hancock Esq 51 } Govenor
His Excelency James Bowdoin Esq 20 }

The Honble Samuel Adams Esq 56 } for Leut. Govenor
The Honble Benj^a. Lincoln Esq 1 }

Abel Wilder Esq.	50	Seth Washburn Esq		19
Samuel Baker Esq	51	John Fessenden Esq		15
Moses Gill Esq	55	Peter Penniman		10
Artemas Ward Esq	35	Jeremiah Larned		9
Timothy Paine Esq	35	David Bigelow		8
Amos Singletary Esq	16	Saml Curtis		3
	Israel Nichols Esq	1		

Senators

Worcester ss At a meeting of the Inhabitants of the Town of Worcester Quallified to vote for Representatives legally warned and assembled on the 5th day of Ap^l. A D 1790. The following persons were voted for, for a County Treasurer, & the number of votes set against their respective names, viz,

Capt Saml Flagg moderator

Saml. Allen 50 }
Saml. Flagg 15 } County Treasurer
Nathan Perry 12 }

Voted that this meeting be dissolved and it was dissolved accordingly

A true Entrey att^s Theophilus Wheeler Town Clerk

At a meeting of the Freeholders & other Inhabitants of the Town of Worcester Quallified to Vote in Town affairs by adjournment from the first day of march A D 1790 to the 5th day of April follow^g & from thence to the 12th day of April 1790.

Voted that the Selectmen Settle the Accounts of Heath for Gleason in the Easyest way they can

Voted to allow M^r. Danl. Gouldings Account   £9,, 11-2

Voted to allow Capt. Brooks what he paid Benj^a. Butman   3,, 15-8

Voted that the Selectmen Select out one Quarter part of the list of Jurors to Serve as Jury men at the Supreme Judicial Court

Voted to Choose 4 fire wards the insuing year

> Doct^r Elijah Dix
> Capt. Saml Flagg
> Mr Stephen Salisbury
> M^r. John Stanton
} fire Wards

Voted that Mr John Barnard be Collector of taxes for the town of Worcester the present year he giving Sufficient bonds, for the faithfull discharge of Said trust who is to be allowed 6^d. on the pound for Collecting &c

Voted to Choose M^r. John Barnard & M^r. Simeon Duncan Sworn Ap^l. 15th 1790   Constables

Voted that the Condition in part of the Collectors bonds be that if it is necessary any abatements should be made he represent the Same to the Town at their meeting next after one year from the date of s^d taxes

Motioned and Seconded to see if the Town will choose a Committee to Examine into Doct^r Dix & others taxes & report to the Town passed in the negative

Voted to Excuse Maj^r. Jones as highway Surveyor &c
M^r. Abel Haywood Chosen in his room—May 22^d 1790 Sworn

Voted to Excuse M^r. Noah Harris highway Surveyor &c
M^r. Moses Perry Chosen in his room—June 1st. 1790

Voted to Excuse M^r. John Barnard Constable
M^r. Eli Gale chosen in his room—May 4th 1790 Sworn

Voted that the Consideration of the report of the School Committee be refered to the may meeting

Voted that Mr Benj^a. Stowell keep Thomas Gleason & be allowed 3/2 p^r. week for it

Voted that this meeting be Disolved, it was disolved accordingly

    A true Entry   Att^s Theoph^s Wheeler Town Clerk

Worcester ss At a Meeting of the freeholders and other Inhabitants of the Town of Worcester Quallified to Vote for Representatives on the 10th Day of may A. D. 1790

Capt Samuel Flagg Chosen to Represent this Town in the General Court of the Commonwealth of Massachusetts the year Insuing

At the Same Time and Place the following Votes were Passed viz,

    Capt Samuel Flagg Chosen Moderator

    2 Joseph Wheeler Esqr. Chosen Clerk Pro Tempore

    3^d Voted to Give the Land Near Cippio Hemmenways which is Proposed for a County Road. S^d Road to be Laid out west of a Pitch pine Tree which is to be one of the Easterly Boundaries of s^d Road

    4th Voted to accept of the Report of the Committee appointed to Settle with the Late Town Treasurer

    5th Voted to accept of the Report of the Selectmen Respecting the Town Bonds

    6th Voted to accept of the Report of the Committee Respecting the Grammer School

The Question being Put whether the Town will Divide the money for the English School agreeable to the Number of Children under age in Each District

Voted that the School Committee be a Committee to ascertain the number of minors in each School District and apportion the money agreeable to the aforesaid Question

Voted that M^r. Samuel Braizer Capt. Samuel Flagg & Joseph Wheeler Esq be a Committee to Conferr with the Center Quarter to See if they will accept of the vote of the Town now passed respecting Grammer School money

Worcester Town Records, 1790.

The report of the Committee respecting Grammer School

The within Committee have attended the service agreeable to the within vote and beg leave to report as follows, Viz, That twenty pounds out of the two hundred granted for the use of Schools be paid to the Center Quarter or Individuals of the same on Condition of their Keeping a Grammer School agreeable to Law for the said Town of Worcester the Current year & the remainder for the use of English Schools to be apportioned as the Town Shall direct—all which is humbly Submitted

Samuel Brazier p^r. Order

Worcester March 24th 1790

The Town of Worcester to Nathan Perry Treasurer D^r.

N°.			
1, &, 2	To cash paid Stephen Salisbury £4,,16. 10		
	D^o p^d M^r. Shittlesworth £18	£22 - 16 ,, 10	
3 & 4	d^o. p^d Esther Mower 32/		
	do p^d Abel Stowell £2. 14	4 - 6 -	
5 & 6	d^o. p^d William Bowls 24/.		
	do p^d Danl. Goulding 19/6	2 - 3 . 6	
7 & 8	d^o. p^d Daniel Goulding £4,,8/		
	D^o. p^d Danl. Johnson £5-10/	9 - 18	
9 & 10	d^o. p^d Jacob Chamberlain 32/		
	d^o. p^d Jesse Taft. 52/	4 - 4	
11 & 12	d^o paid Nathan Patch £74..3..5¾		
	d^o. Saml Brooks 16/	74..19 - 3¾	
13 & 14	d^o. p^d. Saml Brooks 56/		
	d^o p^d. James Blake 30/	4.. 6 -	
15 & 16	d^o p^d James Quigley £7,,5..4		
	d^o. p^d Nathⁿ Patch 30/	8,,15 - 4	
17 & 18	d^o. p^d. Nathⁿ Perry 12/		
	d^o p^d Mary Boyd £5-12/	6.. 4 -	
19 & 20	d^o p^d John Curtis 40/		
	John Stanton £11-14/	13..14 -	
21 & 22	d^o. p^d Daniel Goulding £7,,10-3		
	Jesse Taft 12/	8.. 2 3	
23 & 24	d^o p^d Samuel Brigham £9-6-5		
	John Green 40/	11 - 6 - 5	
26	d^o. p^d Christⁿ Walker	2 - 12 -	

Worcester Town Records, 1790.

27 & 28	dº. pᵈ Wilᵐ Jenison £19..5–2	
	John Chamberlain 49/1	21 - 14 - 3
29 – 30	dº. pd. Wilᵐ Jenison 8/8	
	Clark Chandler £7	7 - 8 - 8
31 – 32	dº. pd. Thoˢ. Wheeler 72/	
	Samuel Goddard 56/	6 - 8 -
33 – 34	dº. pᵈ Martha Wiley 38/	
	John Waters Junʳ 24/	3 - 2 -
35 – 36	do pᵈ Nathan Patch £33–15	
	Nathan Perry £4 - 15 - 3	38..10 - 3
37 – 38	pᵈ. Nathⁿ Perry 22/	
	Danl Storey £7–1–5	8.. 3 - 5
39 – 40	pᵈ. Samuel Brigham £15	
	John Pierce 40/	17.. 0 -
41 – 42	pᵈ. Edward Knights 42/	
	Nahum Willard 41/4	4.. 3 .. 4
43 – 44	pᵈ. Mary Boyd £4..3..18/	
	Sarah Jones 28/8	6.. 6.. 8
45 – 46	pᵈ. Daniel Baird £5 . 2–2	
	Samˡ Eaton £11–14	16..16.. 2
47 – 48	pᵈ. John Waters £5–2–6	
	John Chamberlain 74/11	8..17 - 5
49 – 50	pᵈ Nathˡ Paine 12/	
	Thomas Stowell 32/	2 - 4 -
51 – 52	pᵈ David Moore 18/8	
	Jonathan Rice 52/	3 ..10 - 8
53 – 54	pᵈ. John Elder £6–9–10	
	Mary Boyd £5 ..4/	11 – 13 – 10
55 – 56	pᵈ John Chamberlain £5–14–11	
	Jnº Green Junʳ. £15–18–6	21 – 14 – 5
57 – 58	pᵈ John Walker £5 . 13/	
	Samuel Eaton £11–14	17 – 7 –
59 – 60	pᵈ David Bigelow 14/	
	Daniel Baird £5–18–6½	6 – 12 – 6½
61 – 62	pᵈ Martha Wiley £5–4/	
	Jesse Taft £7 .. 15 11	12 – 19 . 11
63 – 64	pᵈ. Jacob Hemenway 30/	
	Levi Flagg 25/	2 – 15 –
65 – 66	pᵈ Phineas Flagg 8/6	
	Thadˢ Bigelow 9/7	£ 0 – 18 – 1

67 – 68	p^d Elijah Dix £35-8/	
	Jesse Taft 22/6	36 - 10 - 6
69 – 70	p^d Joseph Barber £18-2-11	
	John Elder £5-12 . 11	23 - 15 - 10
71 – 72	p^d Thads maccarty 61/10	
	Samuel Bridge 6/	3 .. 7 .. 10
73 – 74	p^d Edward Knights £6-6/	
	Saml Brazer 12/	6 - 18 -
75 – 76	p^d John Chamberlain £3-19-6	
	Jesse Taft £4-9-0¾	8 - 8 - 6¾
77 – 78	Samuel Brigham £8-16/9	
	William Taylor 19/10	9 - 16 - 7
79 – 80	p^d Phineas Flagg 19/	
	Danl Story £11-18/10	12 - 17 - 10
81 – 82	p^d Danl Story £10-7-2	
	James Blake 10-11-4	20 - 18 - 6
83 – 84	p^d Flagg & Stanton 13/9	
	Jonathan Rice 28/10	2 - 3 - 7
85	pd John Waters 48/	2 - 8 -
87 – 88	p^d School Committee £120	
	d^o £100	220 - 0 -
89 to 93	See next page	
94 – 95	p^d School Committee £150	
	Saml Brooks 81/8.	154 - 1 - 8
96 – 97	p^d Jacob Gray 12/	
	Charles Adams 6/	18 -
98 – 99	p^d Robert Smith 14/10	
	Clark Chandler 66/3^d ¼	4 - 1 - 1¼
100 - 101	p^d Nathan Perry 17/8.	
	Joseph Barber 19/3	1 - 16 . 11
102 - 103	p^d John Waters 28/1	
	Joseph Allen 13/4	2 - 1 - 5
104 - 105	p^d Saml Allen 13/	
	James McFarland 19/3	1 - 11 - 3
106 - 107	p^d Joseph Willard £10-10/	
	Mary Brown 28/7¾	11 - 18 - 7¾
108 - 109	p^d Abigail Grout £4-18-2	
	Benj^a Stone £4-8-3	9 - 6 - 5
110 - 111	p^{d.} Samuel Flagg 36/	
	John Nazro £6 .. 14-5	8 .. 10 .. 5

112 - 113	paid Simeon Duncan 58/4	
	Jacob Hemenway 48/	5 - 6 - 4
114 - 115	p^d. Joseph Barber £8..19-1	
	T & W mCarty £7	15 - 19 - 1
116 - 117	p^d Joseph Wheeler 17/	
	D^o. £2..12-0	3..9..2
118 - 119	p^d. D^o. 6/. D^o. 12/.	18—
120 - 121	p^d. Saml Goddard 12/.	
	Danl Goulding £7-18..6	8..8..6
122 - 123	p^d. Isaiah Thomas 48/	
	Levi Lincoln £9-10	11..8—
124 - 125	p^d Elijah Dix £8.	
	Danl Johnson 96/	12 - 16 —
126 - 127	p^d. Nathan Patch £31-14-6	
	Jesse Taft 47/2	34 - 1 - 8
128 - 129	p^d. Jesse Taft 67/11	
	David Thomas 14/5	4 - 2 - 4
130	p^d Thad^s. & W^m. McCarty	16 - 6 10½
131 - 132	p^d. Danl Waldo £7-3-4	
	Elijah Dix £7-5-8	14 - 9 - 0
	p^d on Nathan Perrys Order	18..3 —

To Sundry notes of hand &c Del^d to my Successor—vizt

89	To a note signed by Samuel Fullerton	
	Decr. 13th 1785 on In^t	12 - 16..6
90	To 1 d^o. Signed Thomas Tracy dated	
	Decr. 12th 1785 on In^t.	4 - 10 - 7
91	To 1 d^o. Signed by Uriah Ward dated	
	Decr. 12th 1785 d^o	12 - 14 - 10
92	To 1 d^o. signed by Wil^m Croxford dated	
	Decr. 12th 1785 on In^t.	4 - 11 - 6¾
93	To 1 d^o. Signed by John Woodard dated	
	may 29th 1786 on In^t.	6..8..7
133	To Cash paid Thad^s & W^m. Maccarty	
	pr order 17/	17
134	p^d. David Bigelow & Nathan Perry per	
	Order	1 - 0 - 6
135	To a note signed by W^m. Taylor dated	
	Feby 3^d 1783 on Interest part paid	
	remains due of the principal	22 - 10 - 0¾

136	1 note signed by Daniel Goulding dated Novr 7th 1785 on Int	24 - 7 - 9
137	1 note signed by Cyrus French dated Decr 16. 1784 not on In^t.	6 - 0
138	1 d^o in the hands of Levi Lincoln Esq Signed by Wm Jenison Dated Septr 9th 1783	36 - 18
139	1 D^o. Signed by Nathan Patch dated Novr 7th 1785 on Int^r part paid remains due the principal	128 - 0 - 3¼
	To Interest due on William Jenisons note prior to nov^r. 7th 1785 the time that I received it of M^r. Patch	5 - 6 - 8
	To Sundry sums due from Collectors, viz,	
140	From Danl. Goulding Collector for the year 1783	£7..15.. 0½
141	To Balance due from Joseph Barber Collector for the year 1784	39..10..11¼
142	To 1 State treasurers Order on Joseph Barber	196..14.. 5
143	to 4 State treasurers Orders of Jacob Severy	96.. 1 - 10
	To the balance remaining in Nathan Patchs hands on a new Emission tax assessed in the year 1781 £410.18..1. reduced to Spiece @ 1 & ⅞ for 1	219.. 2 - 11¾
	To balance due from Nathan Patch on Other taxes committed to him to Collect	5 - 18 . 7¾
		£1909..18.. 7¾

Supra C^r.

By Balance due to the Town
@ the last settlement May
16 1787   £1088. 4-10

By a tax for the year 1787
Committed to Nathan Patch
to Collect   153. 9- 7

By do. for 1788 Com^td to do.	289.10- 5
By rent rec^d. of Flagg & Stanton	24. 0 —
By John Cutlers note	3.15- 6
By Interest rec^d of John Chamberlain on Town bonds &c	156.11- 3
By David Thomas Wages	6. 5- 2
By an order drawn on John Barnard	1. 5.5½
By do. on do	1 - 4- 0
	1724 - 6 - 3
Bal due to the Treasurer	£ 185 - 12 - 4¾

May 10th 1790   Errors Excepted
                        Nathan Perry

We the Subscribers appointed a Committee to settle with the late Town Treasurer have attended that service and find, on examining his accounts that he charges the Town with the sum of Ninteen hundred & nine pounds 18/7¾ — Seven hundred and thirty pounds five shillings & eight pence farthing of which consists of Debts still due to the Town the particular papers & accounts respecting this last mentioned sum we have transferred to Benjamin Haywood the present treasurer for which he will account, That the said late Treasurer Credits the Town with the sum of Seventeen hundred & twenty four pounds 6/3. Which being deducted from the aforesaid debt leaves a balance due to him of £185. 12, 4¾ but as there are sundry Orders given by the said late Treasurer on the Collectors, which have been not yet taken up & which must be charged to him the final balance will probably be reduced by that meens much below the above sum   all which is Submitted

                              Elijah Dix   } Committee
May 10th 1790   Benj^a. Heywood }

   Voted that this meeting be disolved, it was accordingly disolved

     A true Entry   att^s

Worcester ss   Att a Meeting of the Inhabitants of the Town of Worcester Quallified to vote for Representatives, Legally warned & assembled on the first monday in October A. D. 1790 The following persons were voted for to Represent the district of Worcester in the Congress of the United States of America, with the number of votes set against Each persons Name viz

Hon^l. Jon^a. Grout Esq.	26
Hon^l. Artemas Ward Esq	24
Hon^l. John Sprague Esq	14
Hon^l Levi Lincoln Esq	2
Dwight Foster Esq	2
Hon^l Tim^o. Paine Esq	1

Voted that this meeting be Disolved   it was disolved accordingly

    A true Entry   att^s Theophilus Wheeler Town Clerk

Worcester ss   At the Meeting of the Inhabitants of Worcester Quallified to vote in Town affairs, on the fourth day of October A D. 1790

Capt Samuel Flagg moderator

Voted to Grant the sum of £1,,16,,2 to Joseph Wheeler Esqr. for taxes he over paid in 1781   £1 .. 16 - 2

Voted to choose a Committee to examine accounts & report at the adjournment—Timothy Paine Esq Benjamin Heywood & Saml Curtis Esq^{rs} Chosen

Moved and Seconded to see if the Town will give directions respecting Doct^r Dix being overtaxed the year past

Voted that this meeting be adjourned to the 11th day of Octr 1790 to meet at 2 oClock afternoon, it was adjourned accordingly.

    A true Entry   attest   Theophilus Wheeler Town Clerk

At a Meeting of the Inhabitants of Worcester Quallified to vote in Town affairs by adjournment from the 4th day Oct\\r 1790 to the 11th day of the same month

Voted to accept of the Report of the Committee to examine accounts

Voted that the sum of £140..15..10½ be granted levied and assessed on the poles and estates of the Inhabitants of the Town of Worcester for the support of the poor & other expences. that the same be paid into the Town Treasury by the first of January next one half & the other half by the first day of march next.

Voted that the Town Treasurer be desired to Loan the old Continental money in his hand, in behalf of the Town.

Voted That the Representative apply to the State Treasurer with the Orders in the hands of the Town Treasurer, for Settlement & in case he has not power to Settle the same, then he to apply to the General Court respecting the payment of them

Voted that Jacob Smith Jun\\r. have his taxes abated that are not paid in M\\r. Patches hands

Voted That the sum of thirty pounds, in Lieu of the Twenty pounds part of the two hundred pounds already granted for Schools, be appropriated towards Supporting a Grammar School according to law in the Center of the Town, in that case the proprietors of the Center School engage to keep said Grammar School for one year and indemnify said Town from any fine in case of neglect.— always provided that this vote is not to take Effect untill M\\r. Hosey the present Grammar School master Shall have fulfilled his engagement or given up the School by agreement.

Voted that Benjamin Stowell Nath\\l Flagg, & Jonathan Rice be a Committee to procure the meterials for widening the Bridge by Co\\l. Bigelows Shop, that was

Voted to Reconsider the last above vote

Voted that Doct\\r. Dix, Nathan Patch, & Joseph Wheeler Esq be a Committee to provide meterials for widening the above s\\d Bridge the expence to be deducted from the Highway taxes the year insuing

Voted that Mr. Salisbury be requested to procure a Cloth pall in the best way & manner he can, according to Mr Thayers Estimate

Voted to Grant the further sum of £12 to defray Contingent charges

Voted to abate the following taxes in Mr. Barbers hands to Collect viz

―― Childs 19/3 ―― Richardsons 19/3	£1 „ 18 .. 6
Asa Noyce 21/5 Reubin Rice 21/5	2 .. 2 .. 10
George Philmore 15/9. William Croxford 14/5	1 - 10 ―
Ruebin Parks 11/10	11 10
	£6 3 - 2

Voted that the following report be accepted

The Committee appointed to examine Sundry accounts exhibited against the Town of Worcester at a Town meeting held on the 4th day of Octr 1790 have attended that service and report the following sums due to the following persons, viz.

N°		£ s d
1	To Samuel Brooks Sundries supplied Simon a negro man and for a coverlid found Thomas Gleason	£2 .. 4 - 8½
2	To Charles and Saml Chandler Sundries Supplied Thomas Gleason by order of the Selectmen	8 . 8
3	Nathl Paine, account for Timber for Wards Bridge del{d} Mr Saml Goddard & Nath{n} Perry	1 ,, 2 ―
4	Samuel Goddard for timber for wards Bridge	17 - 6
5	Nathan Perrys account for sundries supplied Gleason	2 - 11 ―
6	Timothy Greens account, for Service @ Haverhill about Kimballs Family	1 - 4 ―
7	Benjn. Heywood for a Book to keep Treasurers ac{ts} in	7 - 6
8	Micah Johnson Junr. for Plank for Bridges 854 feet @ 8/ pr hundred	3 - 8 ―

9	Phineas Ward for Sawing plank for Bridges	19 - 3
10	William Taylor Boarding and Cloathing & nursing Nancy White, board & Cloath^g. 48 Weeks at 3/. the remainder for nursing	9 - 12 —
11	To John Elder Boarding and Cloath^g John Spence to the 4th of Octr 1790 49 weeks	7 - 18 . 5
12	To William Elder for 72 feet timber for mowers Bridge	— 6 —
13	To Benjamin Stowell Sundries found Thos. Gleason & family & boarding 26 weeks end^g 13th Septr 1790	16 - 9 - 7
14	To John Stowers 5 feet wood for Thos Gleason	3 - 9
15	To Cornileus Stowell milk and vinegar for T Gleason	6 - 6
16	To Joseph Wheeler Junr. for St[r]aw Bunk for T Gleason	7 - 6
17	To Capt Saml Flagg sundries supplied Thos Gleason	1 .. 8 . 6
18	To Simeon Duncan the following sums for the following services	

Jany. 1790 Viz, Carrying Eliza Spalding & Daughter & Effects to Boylston & keep^g them one week £0-19-0

march for Burying a Daughter of Thos. Gleason   8

d^o moveing Elisha Newhall & wife & 4 Children & Effects to Leicester & find^g them &c   15

Ap^l. moving a poor woman to Grafton & her Effects & find^g them 11/   11

July moveing a poor woman to Leicester   6

removeing a poor person to Shrewsbury   8 - 2

moveing Mrs Kimball and Children

		to Haverhil time and expence exclusive of horses & waggon 2 5 —	
		moveing Eliz^a. Willson to Ward & finding her 8 10	6 .. 1 —
N°.	19	To Nathan Patch Sundries found for Mrs Kimball including 2 horses to Haverhil	£ 2 - 2 - 1
	20	To Joseph Wheeler Esq Sundries Supplied the wife & family of Nathl Kimball includ^g a waggon to remove them to Haverhil	1 - 17 - 7
	21	To Joseph Wheeler for Sundries Supplied Thos Gleason	15 - 7
	22	To James Quigley Keeping agness Brooks from the 1st may 1788 to 1st Octr 1790 125 weeks @ 2/4	20 - 16 - 8
	23	To Abigail Grout for boarding & Cloath^g Sally Walker one year End^g 13 Octr. 2/	5 4 —
	24	Martha Wiley for boarding & Cloath^g Lydia, an Indian Child one year end^g 15th Octr. 1790 @ 2/	5 4
	25	To John Chamberlain for board^g & Cloath^g Nathan Houghton 52 weeks @ 3/. p^r. week	7 - 16 —
		extraordinary trouble part of the time he being now blind	1 ———
		To John Chamberlain for boarding and Cloathing Jenny Dyre 52 weeks @ 1/2½	3 - 2 - 5
	26	To William McFarland for a bed blanket del^d M^r. Chamberlain for Thomas Gleason	12 - 9
	27	To Elizabeth Rice for dressing Thomas Gleasons sore lagg 3^d [ ]	1 - 0
	27	To the Selectmen to Enable them to discharge the accounts that may be exhibited against the Town for the Support of the Widow Eaton her Doct^g & funeral charges they to adjust s^d accounts & to be answerable for said Sum	18 - 0 —

28	To Samuel & Stephen Salisbury their account for Town Stock of amunition to be allowed Interest till paid	10 - 12 - 3

£ 133 .. 19 2½

N B. The accounts exhibited against the Town by M^r. Joseph Barber Collector for the year 1784 for abatement & for cost paid on M^r. Dinglys Execution, we report to the Consideration of the Town—The accounts exhibited against the Town for the expences encured by Anthony Heards Sickness it is proposed that the Selectmen make out all the accounts relateing thereto and send them to the Genl Court for their allowance he being one of the States poor

All which is Humbly Submitted p^r.

Octr 11th 1790
Timothy Paine
Saml Curtis
Benj^a. Heywood

Voted to allow the Assessors account being £6 , , 16 , , 8

Voted that this Meeting be dissolved it was accordingly disolved

A true Entry att^s Theophilus Wheeler Town Clerk

Worcester ss At a Meeting of the Freeholders and other Inhabitants of the Town of Worcester Quallified to Vote for Representatives Legally Warned and assembled on the 26th day of Novr. Anno Domini 1790 The following persons were voted for, to represent the district of Worcester in the Congress of the United States of America, Viz,

Honble Artemas Ward Esq   53
Honble Jonathan Grout Esq   26

A True Entery attest. Theophilus Wheeler Town Clerk

At a Meeting of the freeholders & other Inhabitants of the Town of Worcester Quallified to vote in Town affairs Legally warned & assembled on the 26th day of November A. D. 1790

Col. Samuel Flagg chosen moderator

Voted That Phineas Jones Solomon Bixby & John Barnard, be a Committee to view the Bridge near Mr. William Trowbridges to see what repairs are necessary

Voted That Benjamin Heywood Esq Col Saml. Flagg & Timothy Paine Esq be a Committee to Confer with Mr. Nathl Patch or others with respect to the Town orders not reduceing their nominal Sum

Voted That the Selectmen Settle the affair respecting William Jenisons Note with Mr Nathan Patch & make report at the adjournment of this meeting

Voted that William Sever Esq. be, and hereby is appointed agent for the Town to prosecute to final Judgement & Execution two actions already commenced in behalf of said Town viz, One against Luther Rice as Trustee to John Gould upon a bond. One other against Nathan Patch on a note of hand, at the next Court of Common pleas to be held at Worcester in said County on the first Tuesday of December next unless said actions are Settled

Voted to allow Edward Knights account for wood found Simon Glasco £3–1–6

Voted that this meeting be adjourned to the first day of Decr. next @ 2 oClock afternoon, it was accordingly adjourned

        A true Entry   att{s}   Theophilus Wheeler T Clerk

At a Meeting of the Freeholders and other Inhabitants of the Town of Worcester Quallified to vote in Town affairs by adjournment from Novr 26th 1790 to the 1st Decr. 1790

Voted to abate the following persons taxes, in Mr. Nathan Patches hands to Collect, viz,

    Thomas Gates £1,,2,,10 Uriah Ward £0-18..7 £2 ,, 1 ,, 5
    Rubin Rice 18/7. Billings 3/2. Mills 25/2.   1 ,, 10 ,, 6
    Brown 2/2 Abraham Lincoln 24/8½ Norris 1/   1 ,, 5 ,, 8½
    John Carters   £0 ,, 11 - 5

178   *Worcester Town Records, 1791.*

Voted that the Selectmen Obtain of Mr. N Patch Security for Jenisons Debt

Voted that this Meeting be disolved   it was disolved accordingly

   A true Entry Att{s} Theoph{s} Wheeler T Clerk

Worcester Ss.   At a Town meeting of the Freeholders & other Inhabitants of the Town of Worcester Legally Warned & assembled on the Seventh day of March A. D. 1791

Samuel Curtis Esqr. Chosen Moderator

Theophilus Wheeler Chosen Town Clerk

Voted to Choose five Selectmen

Samuel Flagg Samuel Curtis Samuel Brooks Jno. Chamberlain Joseph Wheeler Selectmen & Overseers of the Poor

Benjamin Heywood Esqr. Town Treasurer

Samuel Flagg Samuel Curtis Jno. Chamberlain Assessors

Noah Harris Daniel Willington Wardens

Daniel Baird John Walker Tytheingmen

Nathan Heard Sealer of Leather

Joshua Whitney Joseph Ball Fence Viewers

Samuel Mower Josiah Knights Field Drivers

Walter Tufts Thomas Rice Silas Flagg Samuel Fisk Ebenr. Hastings Peter Slater William Chamberlain John How William Young Ju{r}. Benja. Newton Hogg Reives

John Stanton Dear Reive

David Bigelow Ignatius Goulding Surveyors of boards & shingles

Simeon Duncan Eli Gale Nathan Patch Constables

Jonathan Grout James Fisk Joshua Whitney John Mower Samuel Gates Benjamin Stowell Thaddeus Chamberlain Jonathan Gleason Benjamin Childs Noah Harrington David Bigelow Ebenr. Lovel Samuel Brazer Joshua Harrington Ebenr. Wiswall Junr. Highway Surveyors & Collectors of highway taxes

Voted that the Swine go at Large the year Insuing being yoaked and Ringed according to Law, Excepting those belonging to the Center School Quarter

Voted that the sum of £300 be granted Levied and assessed on the poles & Estates of the Inhabitants of S^d Town, to be worked out on the highways to be applyed in the Same way & manner, as the last year, the Same wages to be allowed as was the last year

Voted that this meeting be adjourned 1 Hour

Voted Then that Theophilus Wheeler be Clerk of the market

Nathan Patch Collector of taxes, to be allowed 6^d p^r pound for Collecting

Voted That £200 be granted Levied and assessed on the poles and Estates of the Inhabitants of said Town for the Support of the Schools the Current year, to be Kept & the money proportioned in the same way and manner as the last year—£30 for the Center Quarter to Keep the Grammar School, to take place when the other £30. is Expended

Timothy Paine Esq. Daniel Baird David Bigelow Committee to Settle with the Town Treasurer

Samuel Brazer Samuel Brooks David Bigelow Phineas Jones Jon^a. Rice Nathl Harrington James M^cfarland Peter Slater Nathl Brooks Eben^r. Barber Phineas Flagg Jonathan Gates School Committee

Voted that this meeting be adjourned to the 18th day of march Ins^t @ one Clock afternoon

A true Entry att^s.   Theophilus Wheeler T Clerk

(Oath) Worcester ss March 7th 1791 Personally appeared Benj^a Heywood Esq. Samuel Curtis Esq John Chamberlain, Noah Harris Daniel Willington, Daniel Baird, John Walker, Joshua Whitney, Joseph Ball, Samuel Mower, Josiah Knights, Silas Flagg, Wm Chamberlain Jonathan Grout, James Fisk, Joshua Whitney, John Mower, Benjamin Stowell, Thaddeus Chamberlain, Jona-

Worcester Town Records, 1791.

than Gleason, Benjamin Childs, Noah Harrington, David Bigelow, Sam¹ Brazer, Joshua Harrington & Ebenr. Wiswall Junr. and made Solemn Oath to the faithfull discharge of the several offices to which they are chosen   Before Theophilus Wheeler T. Clerk

Worcester ss. March 7th 1791 personally appeared Theophilus Wheeler and made Solemn Oath faithfully to discharge the office of Town Clerk, Before Joseph Wheeler J Pac.

At a meeting of the Inhabitants of the Town of Worcester Quallified to vote for Representatives, on the Seventh day of March Anno Domini 1791—being annual Town meeting

Samuel Curtis Esqr. was Chosen Moderator

The following persons were voted for. for County Treasurer, the number of Votes set against their respective names viz,

Mr. Samuel Allen	94
Col. Samuel Flagg	56
Benja. Heywood Esq	13
Col. Danl Clap	1	&

and for Register Deeds for said County the following persons had the number of Votes set against their respective names viz,

| Col. Samuel Flagg | 120 |
| Col. Danl Clap | 66 |

Voted that this meeting be Disolved, it was accordingly Disolved.

A true Entry   attest   Theophilus Wheeler Town Clerk

At a Meeting of the Inhabitants of the Town of Worcester on the 18th day of March A. D 1791 by adjournment from the 7th day of the same month

Voted that those persons who have over worked their taxes the last year be allowed out of their taxes the present year and those who are Deficient have liberty to work them out this year provided they do it in the month of June

Motioned and Seconded to se if the Town will grant a sum to defray Contingent Charges—passed in the negative

Voted to pass over the Eleventh article [1] untill April meeting

Voted not to grant M^r. Amos Wheeler & others Petition [2]

Voted not to grant M^r. Eli Chapin & others Petition [2]

Voted that Capt Joshua Whitney Benj^a. Heywood Esq. & Deacon Thomas Wheeler be a Committee to take care of Millstone Hill, that no Trespass is Committed thereon [3]

Voted to Excuse M^r. Danl Baird from being Tythingman

Voted That Mr Moses Perry be Tythingman

Voted to accept of the Town Treasurers verbal report with respect to the Towns old money

Voted That the motion for reconsidering the vote of the Town respecting the Swine going at Large, be put over to April meeting

Voted not to allow Ashbel Johnsons account

Voted That the accounts lay, untill some future meeting

Voted not to abate any taxes to m^r. Danl Henshaw

Voted That M^r. John Barnard Collect the remaining taxes in his hands as soon as possible

Then Voted that this meeting be adjourned to the first monday in April next at One of the Clock. It was accordingly adjourned

    A true Entry att^s Theoph^s Wheeler Town Clerk

---

[1] ARTICLE 11:—"To See what measure the Town will take for the Support of the poor the Insuing year"

[2] ARTICLE 13:—"To hear the petition of Eli Chapin & others to be set off to John Barnards School Quarter and also the petition of Amos Wheeler and others that they may have the Disposal of their own School monies"

[3] ARTICLE 14:—"To see if the Town will choose a Committee to make Inquirey what Trespas has been Committed, upon Millstone Hill in Cutting & Carrying off wood, Timber &c and to make report to the Town of the same"

Worcester Town Records, 1791.

At a meeting of the freeholders & other Inhabitants of the Town of Worcester Quallified to Vote in Town affairs Legally Warned and assembled, on the 18th day of march A. D. 1791

Sam¹. Flagg Esq. Chosen Moderator

Voted That Benjamen Heywood Esq Timothy Paine & Wm Sever Esq^{rs}. or the major part of them be and hereby are appointed, agents for the Town to appear in behalf of the Inhabitants of said Town, before Nathaniel Paine Esq. one of the Justices of the Peace for the County of Worcester on monday the 21st day of march Current, @ two of the Clock afternoon at his Dwelling House & then & there answer in behalf of the Inhabitants of s^d Town to Nathan Patch of said Town, In a plea of the Case, and defend the s^d action to final Judgement, and the said agents or the major part of them are hereby impowered to referr the said action & all demands Subsisting betwen the Inhabitants of said Town and the said Nathan Patch if they should think proper and generally to do act and transact every thing necessary for Defending said action—and to acknowledge the service of the said writt on the said Town if they shall finde it necessary to be done before said Justice or any other Court

Voted That Mr Joseph Ball be set to Capt Curtis School Quarter

Voted That this meeting be disolved, it was accordingly disolved

A True Entry   att^s.   Theophs Wheeler Town Clerk

Worcester ss   At a meeting of the Inhabitants of the Town of Worcester Quallified to vote for Senators & Representatives duly warned and assembled on the first monday in April 1791 The Votes were as follows viz the number set against Each respective name

For Govenor { His Excellency John Hancock Esq   68
            { The Honble Francis Dana Esq   1

Leu^t Govenor The Honble Samuel Adams Esq   43

Worcester Town Records, 1791. 183

The Honble Moses Gill Esq	43	Jon^a. Warner Esq	12
Abel Wilder Esq	38	Hon^l. Jno. Fessenden Esq	8
Saml Baker Esq	30	Martin Kinsley Esq.	7
Tim^o Paine Esq	24	Seth Washburn Esq	7
Timothy Newell Esq	24	Saml Curtis Esq	4
Hon^l. Jon^a. Grout Esq	22	Amos Singletary Esq	2
Dwight Foster Esq	1		

Senators

At a Town meeting of the Inhabitants of Worcester by adjournment from the 18th day of march last to ap^l. 4th 1791

Voted to Reconsider the Vote of the Town, Suffering the Swine to go at large excepting the Center School Quarter

Voted that the Swine go at large the Current year, being yoaked & ringed according to Law

Voted that the Selectmen assist in the Support of Saml Danna & family so far as they shall think proper

Voted that application be made to the Judge of Probate for a Guardian for Othnial Taylor

Voted that the Selectmen write to M^r. James Quigley that the Town will not pay him any thing more for the Support of Agness Brooks and that if he will not keep her for what she Earns to return her to Worcester

Voted that the Selectmen are requested to derict Ashbel Johnson to return Ephraim Johnson to Worcester unless he will relinquish his present demand for his keeping and keep him in future without charge to this Town therefor

Voted That the Selectmen apply to Doct Chenery to know on what terms he will take Gleason under his care

Voted to make sale of Wigwam Hill so called &, the ministerial lands

Voted that Benjamin Heywood Esq Saml Flagg Esq. & Capt. Samuel Brooks Be a Committee to make sale of said lands

and that this Committee Enquire into the Records & see in what manner the lands came to the Town and report at may meeting

Voted to accept the following report of the Situation of the Town Bonds

Report of the Selectmen Shewing the Situation of the Town Bonds A. D. 1791

John Stantons Bond dated Feby 1785 for   £ 36 - 10 - —
Samuel Flagg & Clark Chandler Sureties, Interest paid.

Simeon Duncans Bond dated 15th Feby 1785   40 - 0 - —
Joseph Blair, Joseph Allen Sureties two years Interest due

William Gates Bond dated Novr. 1st 1789   15 - 11 - 2
Thomas Wheeler, Nathaniel Harrington Sureties. Interest paid

Henry Patchs Bond dated 15. February 1789   152 - 10 - —
Nathan Patch Eli Chapin Sureties
One years Interest due

Stanton and Goldings Bond dated 10th march 1784   35 - 0 - —
Palmer Goulding Surety four years Interest due

Daniel Gouldings Bond dated 15th February 1785   48 - 10 - —
Palmer Goulding & Ignatius Goulding Sureties 3 years Interest due

Ezekiel Hows bond dated 1 November 1776   20 - 0 - —
Ezekiel Howe Surety—Interest paid

Oliver Watson Jun^rs Bond dated 28th march 1785   83 - 6 - 8
Oliver Watson, William McFarland Sureties
One years Int due

Zebulon Cuttings bond dated 3^d Sept 1790   50 - 0 - —
Peter Johnson Jacob Holmes Sureties Interest paid

Samuel Browns bond dated 21st July 1783   39 - 5 - —
Elijah Dix Lemuel Rice Sureties one years Interest due

Levi Lincolns Bond dated 15th Feby 1785   51 - 10 - —
Joseph Allen Ignatius Goulding Sureties Interest paid

Worcester Town Records, 1791.

John Chamberlains Bond dated 20th May 1790   101 ,, 0 - 0
   Ignatius Goulding Daniel Goulding Sureties
   Interest paid
Joseph Allens Bond dated 13th August 1784   34 - 11 - 1
   Elijah Dix, Saml Allen Sureties
   Interest paid
Nathan Patches Bond dated 21st July 1783   33 - 5 - —
   Cornelius Stowell Joshua Whitney Sureties
   One years Int due
Nathan Patches Bond dated 21st July 1787   42 - 15 - —
   Timothy Bigelow John Walker Sureties
   One years Int due
Jesse Tafts Bond dated 21st July 1786   39 - 5 - —
   Josiah Lyon Joseph Barber Sureties
   One years Interest due
Paul Gates Bond dated 15th Feby 1785   35 - 0 - —
   William Gates William Mahan Sureties
   2 years Int due
Phineas Wards bond dated 1st Novr 1773   22 - 15 - —
   Samuel Curtis David Richardson Sureties
   Interest paid
David Bigelows Bond dated 1st Novr. 1782   35 - 16 - 8
   John Green Surety.   Interest paid
John Goulds Bond dated 1st Novr 1788   33 - 6 - 8
   Josiah Jenison, Josiah Jenison Sureties
   One years Interest due
William Youngs Bond dated 1st November 1787 42 - 3 - 4
   Robert Henry William Young Junr Sureties

Flagg and Stantons Lease of Store ground two }
   years rent due
Interest money paid late Treasurer Perry as
   per receipt   156 - 11 - 3½
D°.   D°. paid present treasurer Heywood
   as per recep^t   76 - 3 - 2
Interest money now due Exclusive of William }
   Youngs bond now in Suit and unsettled }   63 - 11 - —

Worcester Town Records, 1791.

Balance now due the Selectmen as per ac^t 2 - 11 - 3½

all which is Humbly Submitted

    Saml Flagg
    Samuel Curtis   Selectmen
    John Chamberlain   of
    Joseph Wheeler   Worcester
    Saml Brooks

Worcester April 4th 1791

Voted that this meeting be disolved

A true Entry   att^s Theophilus Wheeler Town Clerk

At a Meeting of the Freeholders & other Inhabitants of the Town of Worcester Quallified to Vote for Representatives on the ninth day of may A. D. 1791

Capt. Samuel Flagg chosen to represent this town in the Great & General Court the Current year

At the Same time & place, Capt Saml Flagg chosen moderator

Voted to dismiss the 2^d Article in the Warrant [1]

Voted to accept of the report of the Committee respecting Wigwam Hill

Voted to Choose a Committee to Petition the General Court to Confirm the sales already made of ministerial & School lands & to Grant leave for the sale of the remaining Ministerial and School lands the proceeds to be appropriated according to the original design

Capt Samuel Flagg Timothy Paine Benjamin Heywood Esq^{rs} Chosen for said Committee

The Committee appointed to Examine the title the Town has to the lands at Wigwam Hill have attended the service and report—

---

[1] ARTICLE 2:—"To see if the Town will Choose a Committee to make enquiry what Trespass has been Committed upon the land belonging to said Town on Millstone Hill in Cutting and Carrying off wood Timber &c and make Report to the Town respecting the same."

That at a Proprietors meeting on the 17th day of Feby. 1752 it appears that the plan of forty nine acres and forty rods of land with an allowance of 106 rods for highways at Wigwam Hill was Exhibited by a Committee for that purpose, and the same accepted and Ordered that the said land remains to the use of the Town forever as part of a third devission for the Support of the School[1] also that on the 24th of January 1755 the said propriators purchased of John Chandler Esq. & William Johnson as appears by their deed of that date runing to John Chandler Junr. Esq. Town Treasurer & his Successor in that Office & recorded in the Registers Office Book 35 page 332/ ninteen acres of land on Wigwam Hill being the Northwardly part of 32 acres which they had bought of said proprietors, which ninteen acres under the Reservation of a road of two rods wide to the remaining part of said 32 acres, also one half of all oar or mines of all sorts was granted to the Town, to make up all deficiencies of ministerial or School lands belonging to the Town—So that it appears to the Committee that the title the Town has under the reservations aforesaid to Sixty-eight acres and one Quarter as Specified in said plan & Deed or Record is incontestable all which is Submitted

       Benjamin Heywood } Committee
       Samuel Flagg

Worcester May 9th 1791

Voted to accept the following Settlement with the Town Treasurer

  Dr. The Town of Worcester in act Current with B. Heywood Treasurer

1790 May 3d By John Chamberlains note on Interest from Octr. 15th 1789 being due from Nathl Houghton £6 .. 12 - 11
    10th By Sundry obligations for money due to the Town

---

[1] See Volume III., Collections of The Worcester Society of Antiquity (Proprietors' Records), page 280; or pages 235-236 of the original volume.

rec[d] of Deacon Nathan Perry former Treasurer viz

Samuel Fullertons note dated Dec[r] 13th 1785 on Int £12 - 16 - 6

Thomas Tracys d[o]. Dec[r]. 12th 1785 on d[o] 4 ,, 10 ,, 7½

Uriah Wards d[o]. same date on d[o] 12 - 14 - 10¼

William Croxfords d[o]. same date on d[o] 4 - 11 - 6¾

John Woodwards d[o]. same date on d[o]. 6 - 8 - 7

an Order signed by Thad[s]. & W[m]. M[c]Carty — 17 -

William Taylors note dated Feb[y] 13th 1783 on Int[r]. part paid, remainder due of the principal 22 - 10 - 0¾

Daniel Gouldings dated Nov[r] 7th 1786. on Int 24 - 7 - 9

Cyrus Frenches Note Dec[r]. 16. 1784. not on Int[r] — 6 -—

William Jenisons Note dated Sept[r] 9th 1783. given to Nathan Patch and in the hands of L Lincoln Esq to be put in suit 36 - 18 - 0

Interest due on said note prior to Nov[r]. 7th 1785 £5 - 6 - 8

Nathan Patches Note dated Nov[r]. 7th 1785. on Interest part paid remains due of the principal 128 - 0 - 3¾

An Order given by State Treasurer on Joseph Barber 196 - 14 - 5

4 orders given by d[o] on Jacob Severy 96 - 1 - 10

Due from former Collectors, viz—

Daniel Goulding on taxes assessed in the year 1783 7 - 15 - 0½

Joseph Barber on d[o]. in 1784 39 - 10 - 11¼

Nathan Patch on a New Emission Tax. in the year 1781 being £410.18.1 which reduced to Specie @ 1⅞ for 1	219 - 2 - 11¾	
Nathan Patch on other taxes 5 - 18 - 7¾		830 - 5 - 8¾
By the assessors return of a Tax committed to Joseph Barber Col^r for 1784		5 - 0 - 5
By the assessors do. of fractional parts contained in the State tax of Sept 28 1789 Committed to John Barnard		10 - 1 - 1
By the assessors return of a tax committed to Jno. Barnard Col^r for 1789		356 - 4 - 10½
Sept. 4 By Cash Rec^d of Jno. Chamberlain p^r. my receipt		3 - 0 - —
Oct. 11 By the Assessors return of a tax Com^{td} to Jno. Barnard Col^r for 1790		392 - 14 - 11
By a mistake in the assessors Return of a Tax made in the year 1782 & Committed to Nathⁿ Patch to Collect		110 - 8 - 11

1790
Oct 4th By Interest rec^d of Nathan Patch on a Judgement of Confession   17 - 7¾

1791
Jany 21 By Interest recd of Daniel Goulding on his note of hand   3 - 17 - 7¼

By Interest recived on the debt due from William Jenison   10 - 3 - 4

Feby 11th By cash receved for old Continental money Sold   3 - 10 - 8

March 4th By a payment recieved of Deacon Nathan Perry being the amount of Sundry Orders Drawn by him on Nathan Patch Col^r. & Others charged in the foregoing account, viz, N°. 18.–23–29 31–32. 33–34–35. 36–37. 50–66. 99–100–101– & 95   140 - 2 - 10¼

By Cash &c Rec^d. of the Selectmen being for Interest by them rec^d on obligations for money due to the Town exclusive of £3 - 0 credited in this account Sept 4th 1791   73 - 3 - 2

Worcester Town Records, 1791.

March 26. By Cash receved of William Henshaw Esq being a fine by him imposed on W^m. J Stearns for prophane Swearing   5

£ 1946 - 9 - 1½

1790
- N°. 1. To Cash p^d School Committee p^r order of Selectmen   150 - 0 - —
- 2. To do. p^d Joel Wesson p^r d^o   14 - 3
- 3. To d^o p^d John Elder p^r d^o   10 - 13 - 6
- 4. To d^o p^d John Stanton p^r d^o   9 - 15 - 8
- 5. To do. p^d Nathan Patch p^r d^o   3 - 0 - —
- 6. To do p^d Capt Saml Brooks pr. d^o   5 - 0 - 7
- 7. To d^o p^d Cornelius Stowell p^r d^o   1 - 4 - 7
- 8. To d^o p^d Jno Chamberlain p^r d^o   4 - 7 - 5
- 9. To d^o p^d Micah Johnson p^r d^o   19 - 2
- N°. 10 To Cash paid Daniel Baird p^r d^o   4 - 2 - 0
- 11. To d^o p^d Edward Knights p^r d^o   3 - 3 - —
- 12. To d^o p_d Martha Wiley p^r. d^o   5 - 4 - —
- 13. To d^o p^d Nathan Perry p^r d^o   2 - 13 - 6½
- 14. To d^o p_d Mary Boyd p^r. d^o   2 - 3 - —
- 15. To d^o p^d Eli Gale p^r d^o   1 - 4 - —
- 16. To d^o p^d Ashbell Johnson p^r d^o   15 - 12 - —
- 17. To do. p^d Saml & S. Salisbury in part of an Order in favour of E Dix & by him indorsed to John Green   9 - 9 - —
- 18. To d^o. p^d. on Execution in favour of Saml Moore on an order given by Dⁿ Perry upon Nathⁿ Patch   2 .. 10 - 9

19	To d⁰ pᵈ Samˡ Eaton per order of Selectmen	2 - 0 - —	
20	To do. pd Nathan Patch pr do	6 .. 13 - 11½	
21	To do. pd. Nathˡ Brooks pr do	3 - 10	
22	To do. pd. Jn⁰. Chamberlain pr do	1 - 4 - —	
23	To do. pd. Martha Wiley pr. order of Dⁿ. Perry on N. Patch	1 - 6 - —	

July 22ᵈ

24	To do. pd Abigail Grout pr. order of Selectmen	5 - 4 - —

Augᵗ 13

25	To Interest pd Thadˢ & Wilᵐ maccarty	5 - 11 - —

16

26	To do. paid Nathⁿ Patch pʳ Order of Selectmen	23 - 3 - 10

Sept 11

27	To do. pd the Inhabitants of Heath pr do	10 - 19 - 2
28	To do pd Jos Allen Esqʳ. & others pr. do	12 - —

13

29	To do. pd Dⁿ. Nathan Perry pʳ his order in favour of Jos Barber	11 14 - 10
30	To do pd Thadˢ & Wᵐ Maccarty in part of a bond against the Town	17 - —

23

31	To do. pd Dennis Smith per Orders of Dⁿ Perry on Nathⁿ Patch	12 - —

Oct 4

32	To do. pd Jn⁰. Paine for do on do	4 - 0 - —
33	To do pd James McFarland for do on do	3 . 12 - —

34	To d⁰ p^d Elijah Dix p^r d⁰ on d⁰	39 - 8 . 10¼
35	To d⁰ p^d. Martha Wiley p^r d⁰ on d⁰	1 - 6 - —
36	To d⁰. p^d. Sally Denny p^r d⁰. on d⁰.	12 - —
37	To d⁰ p^d William Barber p^r. d⁰ on d⁰	3 - 12 - 10½
38	To d⁰ p^d Jos. Wheeler Esq per order of Selectmen	1 - 2 - —
39	To d⁰. p^d Daniel Storey in part of his note ags^t the Town	30 - 0

11
40	To d⁰. p^d Saml Brooks per order of Selectmen	2 - 6 - 6

Nov. 12
41	To d⁰. p^d Jn⁰ Parks p^r d⁰	8 . 2 - —

22
42	To d⁰ p^d Benj^a. Hasey p^r. d⁰	8 - 10 - —
43	To d⁰. p^d John Elder p^r d⁰	7 . 18 - 5

26
44	To d⁰. p^d Anna Bigelow p^r d⁰	2 - 3 - —

Dec. 6
45	To d⁰. p^d Nathan Patch p^r d⁰	68 . 9 - 1
46	To d⁰ p^d Joseph Wheeler p^r d⁰	1 - 16 - 2
47	To d⁰ p^d. Nathan Patch p^r d⁰	2 - 2 - 1
48	To d⁰. p^d Jn⁰. Chamberlain p^r. d⁰	11 - 18 - 5
49	To d⁰ p^d Simeon Duncan p^r. d⁰	6 . 1 - —

N° 50 To Cash paid Benj[a] Stowell per order of Deacon Perry on N Patch £2 - 0 - 0

Dec. 28th.

51 To d[o] paid James Quigley per order of Selectmen 15 - 5 - 7
52 To d[o] p[d] Benj[a] Stowell p[r]. d[o] 16 - 9 - 7

Jan[y]. 13 1791

53 To d[o]. p[d] Sam[l] Brazer p[r]. d[o]. 18 - 15 - 6
54 To d[o]. p[d] Eph[m] Mower p[r]. d[o] — - 6 - —
55 To d[o] p[d] Benj[a]. Heywood p[r]. d[o] 7 - 6

19

56 To d[o]. p[d]. Sam[l] Flagg p[r] d[o] 4 - 5 - 2
57 To d[o] p[d] d[o] p[r] d[o] 3 - 12 - 0
58 To d[o] p[d] d[o] p[r] d[o] 4 - 5 - 4
59 To d[o] p[d] Phineas Ward p[r] d[o] 19 - 3
60 To d[o] p[d] Nath[l] Paine p[r] d[o] 1 - 2 - —
61 To d[o] p[d] Tim[o] Green p[r] d[o] 1 - 4 - —
62 To d[o] p[d] Nathan Patch p[r] d[o] 6 - 3 - 8
63 To d[o] p[d] Edward Knights p[r] d[o] 3 - 1 - 6
64 To d[o] p[d] Capt Sam[l] Brooks p[r] d[o] 1 - 8 - —
65 To d[o] p[d] d[o] p[r] d[o] 6 - 0 - 4
66 To d[o] p[d] d[o] p[r] order of De[n]. Perry on Nathan Patch } 1 - 15 - 1½

21

67 To d[o] p[d] James Quigley per order of Selectmen 12 - 18 - 10
68 To d[o]. p[d]. P. & D. Goulding p[r]. d[o] 1 - 19 - 6½
69 To d[o]. p[d]. Dan[l] Goulding p[r]. d[o] 8 - 13 - 4
70 To d[o] p[d] d[o] p[r] d[o] 9 - 11 - 2

24
71	To do p^d Joseph Barber on a note given to Reubin Spalding	18 - 12 - 6½

31
72	To do p^d Hilyer Tanner p^r. order of Selectmen	8 - 3
73	To do p^d Samuel Eaton p^r do	2 - 0 - —
74	To do p^d Benj^a Heywood p^r do	9 - 4½
75	To do p^d Judith Rice pr do	6 - —
76	To do p^d James Fisk pr do	1 - 8 - 11
77	To do p^d Moses Miller pr. do	1 - 15 - 7
78	To do p^d Eli Gale p^r. do	18 - 6
79	To do p^d Daniel Waldo p^r do	4 - 6
80	To do p^d do & Son p^r do	1 - 7 - —
81	To do p^d do p^r do	3 - 12 - 8
82	To do p^d William Trowbridge p^r. do.	1 - 9 - —
83	To do p^d John Barnard p^r. do	10 - 4 - 4
84	To do p^d Saml Curtis pr. do	3 - 6 - —
85	To do p^d Joseph Wheeler p^r do	2 - 14 - 11
86	To do p^d William Knights p^r do	1 - 5 - 10
87	To do p^d Alexander Murray p^r order of assessors	6 - 2
88	To do paid Jacob Smith Junr p^r do	6 - 3
89	To do pd. Saml Brazer pr. do	4 - 2½
90	To do p^d Nathl Paine pr do	9 - —
91	To do p^d Joseph Allen p^r do	2 - 3
92	To do p^d Isaac Chenery p^r do	2 - 2
93	To do p^d Jno. Barnard p^r do	6
94	To do p^d Nathl Moore per order of Selectmen	14 - 10½
95	To do. p^d John Waters per order of D^n. Perry on Nath^n Patch	2 0 - 2¾

Feby 21

96	To d^o p^d Saml Eaton per order Selectmen	5 10 - —
97	To d^o p^d David Bigelow p^r d^o	10 - 0 -

25

98	To d^o p^d Jno Chamberlain p^r d^o	2 - ——
N°. 99	To d^o p^d Abigail Grout p^r order of D Perry on N Patch	£1 - 14 - 3
100	To d^o p^d Nathan Patch p^r. Order of D^n. Perry	54 - 8 - —
101	To d^o p^d Danl Goulding p^r. d^o	12 - 0 - 11½

1791
March 4

102	To d^o p^d Nath^n Perry p^r. order of Selectmen in part of the balance of his Treasurers ac^t.	140 - 2 - 10¼
103	To d^o p^d d^o p^r. d^o	2 - 11 - —

5

104	To d^o p^d Elizabeth Rice p^r d^o	1 ———

7

105	To d^o p^d Joseph Blair pr. d^o	2 - 2 -
106	To d^o. p^d Joseph Barber p^r d^o	6 - 3 - 2
107	To d^o. p^d. William Trowbridge p^r. d^o	2 ———
108	To d^o p^d Capt David Mower p^r d^o	1 - 4 - —
109	To d^o p^d Micah Johnson Ju^r. p^r d^o	3 - 8 - —
110	To d^o p^d Cornelius Stowell p^r. d^o.	6 - 6

18

111	To d^o p^d John Stanton p^r. d^o	6 - 10

112	To do pd John Chamberlain pr. do	1 - 8 - 9		
113	To do pd Martha Wiley pr. do	5 - 4 - —		
114	To do. pd. in part of Danl Storys note against the Town per John Heards receipt	7 - 0 - —		
26				
115	To do. Saml. Mower per order of Selectmen	19 - 9		
28				
116	To do pd Doct John Green pr order do	1 - 4 - —		
117	To do. pd. William Taylor pr. do	6 - 15 - 6		
118	To do. pd. do	9 - 12 - —		
119	To do. pd Joseph Allen Esq pr do.	7 - 2 - 10		
120	To do paid Jno Chamberlain pr do	18 - 3 - 8		
121	To do. pd the School Committee pr. do	157 - 0 - —		
Apl. 1st				
122	To do pd John Barnard do	1 - 4 - —		
124	To do. pd Jona Lovel per order of Selectmen	6 - 3		
123	To do. pd Jno Barnard by order of assessors	15 - 6		
125	To do. pd Jno. Stowers pr. Order of Selectmen	1 - 3 - 9		
126	To do. pd. Charles & Saml Chandler pr do	8 - 8		
127	To do. pd. Stephen Salisbury pr. do	2 - 8 - —		
128	To do. pd Rufus Chandler pr do	5 - 14 - —	1157 - 7 - 10¼	

    Balance to be further accounted for   £789 - 1 - 3¼

    Errors Excepted   Benja. Heywood Town Treasurer

The Committee appointed to Examine the Town Treasurers account report that they have attended that Service whereby it appears he has charged himself with the Sum of £1946.9.½ That he has paid out by orders from the Selectmen to Sundry persons the Sum of £1157-7-10¼ which leaves a Balance due to the Town of Seven hundred eighty nine pounds 1/ 3¼ which the said Treasurer is further to account for — your Committee would further Report that Sundry orders contained in the within ac^t. drawn by the said Selectmen on the Treasurer were drawn without a previous grant made by the Town for the allowance and payment of s^d Sum   Worcester April 4th 1791

all which is humbly Submitted

       Tim^o Paine }
       David Bigelow } Committee
       Danl Baird }

A true Entry att Theo Wheeler Town Clerk

At a Town meeting of the Inhabitants of the Town of Worcester on the 15th day of August 1791 legally warned and assembled

Samuel Flagg chosen moderator

Voted That Benjamin Heywood Timothy Paine & William Sever Esq^{rs} or the major part of them be and hereby are appointed Agents for the Town of Worcester to appear in behalf of Said Town before Nathaniel Paine Esqr. one of the Justices of the peace for the County of Worcester on Monday the twenty ninth day of August 1791 at two of the Clock afternoon at his Dwelling House in said Town and then and there answer in behalf of the Inhabitants of said Town to Nathan Patch of said Worcester & Joseph Patch of Stratton in the County of Windham & State of Vermont in two Seperate Actions, commenced by them respectively against said Inhabitants and defend the same to final Judgement, or otherwise compromise and settle the Same according to their best discression & Judgement and the said agents or the major part of them are hereby empowered to refer the said actions and all demands Subsisting betwen the Inhabitants of said Town

Worcester Town Records, 1791.

and the said Nathan Patch & Joseph Patch if they should think proper and generally to do act & transact every thing for defending said actions before said Justice or any other court

Voted that the Selectmen settle the action brought by Anna Chandler against the Town before trial

Voted that Benj^a. Heywood Esq be School Committee man in the room of Jon^a. Rice deceased

Voted that this meeting be dissolved, it is accordingly dissolved

    A true Entry   Att^s Theophilus Wheeler Town Clerk

At a Town Meeting on Monday the 17th of October A. D. 1791

Col. Samuel Flagg chosen moderator

Voted That Benj^a. Heywood Esq Col Saml Flagg & M^r. Jno. Chamberlain be a Committee to receive & examine accounts

Voted to repair the County road leading by Eli Chapins to Comfort Rices land [1]

Voted To pass over the 4th article to the adjournment [2]

Voted To pass over the 6th article for the adjournment [3]

Voted to choose a Committee to see if there is any convenient place to Errect Stables on the Common & report @ the adjournment—Selectmen chosen for said Committee [4]

Voted to Choose a Committee to apply to the Genl Court for

---

[1] ARTICLE 5:—"To See what measures the Town will take relative to the contents of a Letter from the grand Inquest of said County directed to the Selectmen of said Worcester respecting necessary repairs of the County road leading by Eli Chapins"

[2] ARTICLE 4:—"To grant such sum or sums of money as the Town shall think proper to defray necessary expences"

[3] ARTICLE 6:—"To see whether the Town will take any measures to recover what is due to them for transporting the poor of other Towns"

[4] ARTICLE 7:—"To see if the Town will grant leave to Capt Joshua Whitney and others to Erect Stables on any part of the Common for their Horses on public days"

leave to sell the remainder of the ministerial & School lands in said Worcester, and also to confirm the titles of what has been sold—& that said Committee be impowered to sell the School land on Wigwam Hill so called & to make and execute good & Sufficient deed or deeds thereof agreeable to a resolve of the Great & Genl Court passed last Session Tim^o. Paine Benj^a. Heywood & Saml Flagg chosen for said Committee

Voted That this meeting be adjourned to the first monday in Novr next it is accordingly adjourned

    A true Entry att^a Theo. Wheeler Town Clerk

At a Meeting of the Freeholders & other Inhabitants of the Town of Worcester on the 7th day of Novr. A. D. 1791 by adjournment from Octr. 17th 1791

Voted to grant the sum of £144„14„7 & that the same be Levied and assessed on the poles & Estates of the Inhabitants of this Town

Voted to abate to Danl Goulding Ruebin Rices taxes

	£ „ 5-4
Richard Dickinsons /8^{d}½	
Wil^m Stearns £1 „ 12 „ 8½	1 - 13„5
Stephen Flaggs Class rate	8 - 4
	2„ 7„ 1

The Committee appointed to Examine Sundry accounts exhibited against the Town of Worcester at a Town meeting held on monday the seventeenth day of October 1791 have attended that service and report the following Sums due to the following persons, viz,—

N° 1.	To Charles Adams for sundries supplied wid^o. Tracy & Children from 16th June 1791 to 15th august following	£2 „ 1„ 4
2	To Isaiah Thomas for two Books for the use of the Town	2 - 2 —

3	To Benj^a. Heywood Esq for a Journey to Ipswich to settle an action brought against ye Town by John Heard & pay ye Debt	1 ,, 4 —
4	To Abel Stowell for meet supplied Thos Gleason in Nov. 1789	5 . 7½
5	To Abigail Grout for Boarding & Cloathing Sally Walker from 18th Octr 1790 to 19 Jany 1791 13 weeks @ 2/ being the time the Selectmen put the girl out	1 ,, 6 —
6	To Francis Salvage and wife the sum of five pounds four Shillings as a Reward for their takeing one of Thomas Gleasons Children to bring up from 4 years old	5 ,, 4 —
7	To William Taylor for Boarding & Cloathing anna White from 4th Octr 1790 to 17th Octr 1791 Being 54 weeks @ 3/	8 - 2 —
8	To Charles & Samuel Chandler for Sundries of Cloathing d^d Benj^a. Stowell for Thos Gleazen £3-0--1^d & D^o d^d. John Elder for Jno Spence £1-1-8^d	4 - 1 - 9
9	to John Elder for Boarding & Cloathing Jno Spence from 4th Octr 1790 to 17th Octr 1791 Being 54 weeks @ 3/ Including 22/2 for Cloathing	9 - 4 - 2
10	To John Chamberlain for Boarding & Cloathing Nathan Houghton & Jenny Dyer from 15th Octr 1790 to 15th Octr 1791 Being 52 weeks @ 6/ for the two & 3/ for one Load of wood D^d Samuel Denny family	15 - 15 - —
11	To Simion Duncan for time & Expence Carrying William Powers to Boylston & Bringing William Tracy &c	1 - 0 - 0
12	to the Town of Marlboro 35/10 which they paid their Constable for Carrying Mary Moore from S^d Marlboro to Lynn on a Warrant from the town of Worcester	1 - 15 - 10
13	To Theophilus Wheeler for 3½ y^{ds} Baize d^d Benj^a Stowell for Gleazens wife @ 2/	7

14	to Joseph Wheeler Esq for sundries d^d Simon Glasco being necessaries in his Sickness		12 - 4
15	to Isaac Gleazen for 128 lb Beef Supplied Simon Glasco by order of Joseph Wheeler Esqr @ 2^d		1 - 0 - 2
16	to Samuel Flagg for Sundries d^d Simon Glasco & other Poor of the Town		2 - 3 - 9
17	to Benjamin Tucker for Sundries Supplied Thomas Gleazens family from Decr 19th 1789 to ap^l 12th 1791		3 - 10
N° 18	To Ebenezer Lovell for 315 feet of Plank Supplied the Town for Repairing Bridges	£	1 - 11 - 6
19	to Daniel Goulding for Sundries Supplied Thomas Gleasons & Wid^o Tracys family Towns Poor to nov^r 7th 1791		3 - 15 - 3
20	to Doct^r Jno Green for medicine & attendance on Lydia Gleazen one of the Towns Poor deceased		1 - 3 - 6
21	to Eunice Follinsbee for nursing & for Linnen @ the Burial of Lydia Gleazen a Poor Child deceased		1 - 4 —
22	Jed^h. Healy for makeing Coffin for Lydia Gleason		4 —
23	to Col. Eben^r Lovell for Timber & Plank for Bridges		17 —
24	to Benjamin Stowell for Supporting Gleasons Family &c		24 - 15 - 2
N B	The Sum of Twenty six pounds eight shillings has been paid out of the Treasurey for alterations in the County roads in said Town by order of the Court of Sessions		26 - 8 - —

$£$116 . 7 ,, 2½

all which is Submitted by

Benj^a Heywood
Saml Flagg
Jno Chamberlain

Voted to allow the foregoing report

Voted to allow the following accounts in addition to the above

To Capt Samuel Brooks	5 - 5 - 1½
To John Stanton and Daniel Goulding	5 - 10 - 3
To the Assessors	8
	£135 - 2 ,, 7
To Mr Salisbury	9 - 12 —
	144 4 7

Voted that the above sum of £144. 14 - 7 be granted Levied and assessed on the poles & Estates of the Inhabitants of this Town

Voted That the Selectmen be a Committee to use such measures as they shall think proper to recover what is due for transporting the poor of other towns

Voted to pass over the Seventh Article in the Warrant[1]

Voted that this meeting be disolved, it is accordingly disolved

A true Entry att.^s   Theo.^s Wheeler Town Clerk

At a meeting of the Freeholders and other Inhabitants of the Town of Worcester Quallified to vote in Town affairs on the Seventh day of Novr A. D. 1791

Voted Saml Flagg moderator

Voted that Daniel Baird be a Committee man in the room of Phineas Flagg deceased

Voted That the Collection of taxes be put up to the lowest bidder,[2] which was Struck off to Mr Nathan Patch at 6^d on the Pound he being the lowest bidder — A motion was made and Seconded to see if the Town will accept of Nathan Patch as Collector of taxes which passed in the negative

---

[1] See note, page 198.

[2] ARTICLE 3:—"To see if the Town will choose a Collector of taxes in the room of the one they choose at their annual meeting in march last who has not given bonds agreeable to the former Custom of the Town"

Voted That John Barnard be Collector of taxes the ensuing year and that he be allowed 6^d. on the pound for collecting he giveing bond to the acceptance of the Selectmen for the faithfull discharge of S^d trust

Voted this meeting be disolved it was disolved accordingly

A true Entry from the moderators minutes

                Att^s.   Theophilus Wheeler Town Clerk

At a meeting of the Freeholders & Other Inhabitants of the Town of Worcester Qualified to vote in Town affairs legally warned and assembled at the publick meeting house of the first Parish in Worcester on Monday the fifth day of march A, D, 1792 the following votes were passed & the following persons were chosen into office viz

Benjamen Heywood Esqr. Chosen Moderator

M^r. Theophelus Wheeler Town Clerk & was Excused

Daniel Goulding Town Clerk Sworn by Benjamen Heywood Esqr.

Voted to Choose five Selectmen

Samuel Flagg Samuel Curtis Samuel Brooks John Chamberlain Benjamen Heywood Selectmen

Benjamen Heywood Esqr Town Treasurer

Samuel Flagg Samuel Curtis John Chamberlain Assessors

Ebenezar Lovell Joshua Harrington Wardens

Joseph Ball Thomas Nickels Tything Men

Nathan Heard Sealer of Tanned & Tanned & Curryed Leather

Nathan White Stephen Haywood Fence Viewers

Charles Adams Henery Patch Field Drivers

Ignatius Goulding Elias Mann David Bigelow Surveyors of Boards & Shingles

Simeon Duncan Nathaniel Flagg Cullers of Hoops & Staves

Samuel Brazer Benjamen Andrews Jesse Crage Measurers of Wood & Bark

Increase Blake Sealer of Weights and Measures

Abel Stowell to Execute the Deer Act

Elijah Dix Samuel Flagg Stephen Salsbury John Stanton Fire wards

Jesse Crage Paul Gates Silas Flagg Joseph Chadwick Samuel Bigelow John Elder Ju^r. William Chamberlain Clark Goulding Jason Blake Hog Reeves

Voted that the Swine go at large the Current year being Yoked & ringed according to law

Voted that the last vote be reconsidered so far as respects the Swine on the Main Street in the Town from M^r. Samuel Chandlers farm House to Timothy Paines Esqr. inclusively

Samuel Brazer Daniel Waldo Ju^r. Clerks of the Market

Joseph Allen John Chamberlain Samuel Flagg Committee to Settle with the Town Treasurer

Simeon Duncan Abel Stowell Constables

Voted to Choose one Collector of Taxes the Current year

Nathan Perry Samuel Jenison Thadeas Chapen Ebenezer Mower Thomas Rice William M^{c}farland Ju^r. Samuel Andrews Simeon Fish Hy^l Tanner Samuel Moore Ebenezer Lovell Elijah Dix Daniel Goulding Solomon Bixbee William Moore Ebenezar Hastings Surveyors of Highways & Collectors of Highway Taxes

Voted that the Sum of three Hundred pounds be levied and assessed on the Poles & Estates in this Town for the purpose of keeping the Public Roads in repair the Current year

Voted that those persons that were Taxed in the Highway Taxes the Last year & have not been Notified of S^d. Tax have liberty of working S^d Taxes out provided they do it before the first of June Next

The meeting was adjourned at half after one oClock in the afternoon for one hour and met according to adjournment and proceeded to business

Voted that the Sum of two hundred Pounds be granted levied and assessed on the Poles & Estates in this Town for the Support of Publick Schools the Current Year

Voted that the money granted for the Support of Schools be proportioned and laid out in the Same way and manner it was the last year except no individual Shall not have any right to draw his owne money

Voted that Thirty pounds of the money granted for the Support of Schools be allowed to M^r. John Chamberlains School Quarter for the Support of a Grammer School Provided Said Quarter keep Said School agreeable to Law

Levi Lincoln Esqr. Nathaniel Flagg Joseph Kingsbury Phineas Jones Elijah Harrington William Gates John Tatman Nathaniel Brooks Simeon Fish Joel How John Chamberlain Daniel Baird School Committee

Voted that the Town meetings in this Town for the futer be warned by the Constables Posting a True and an Attested Coppy of the warrant for the Meeting two Sabbaths previous to the meeting at the Publick meeting Houses of Each Society in this Town

Voted that this Meeting be adjourned to the first Monday in April Next at three OClock in the afternoon then to meet at this place   The Meeting was accordingly adjourned

  A True Entry Attest Daniel Goulding Town Clerk

At a meeting of the Inhabitants of the Town of Worcester Qualified as the Constitution prescribes on monday the Second day of April A. D. 1792 for the purpose of Voting for a Govenor Lieu^t. Govenor & Senators & Counsellors Then the following persons were Voted for, for Govenor Lieu^t. Govenor & Senators & Counsellors and had the Number of Votes Expressed against their respective Names viz

Worcester Town Records, 1792.

For Govenor	His Excellency John Hancock Esq	24
	The Honble Francis Dana Esq	5
	Samuel Phillips Esqr	18
	Elbridge Gerry Esqr	1

For Lieu^t Govenor The Honble Samuel Adams Esq   48

Senators & Counsellors

Honble Moses Gill Esqr.	57	Dwight Foster Esqr.	1
Samuel Baker Esqr.	58	Timothy Paine Esqr.	1
Abel Wilder Esqr.	60	Caleb Amidown Esqr.	1
Jonathan Warner Esqr.	60	John Fessendon Esqr.	1
Timothy Newhall Esqr.	43	Benjamen Reed Esqr.	1
Samuel Flagg Esqr.	14	Jonathan Grout Esqr.	1
	Martin Kinsley Esqr.	1	

It was then Voted that the above meeting be Dissolved & the meeting was Dissolved accordingly

    A True Entry   Attest   Daniel Goulding Town Clerk

At a meeting of the Inhabitants of the Town of Worcester Qualified to Vote for Representatives on Monday the Second Day of April A. D. 1792

    Benjamen Heywood Esqr. Chosen Moderator

    Then M^r. Samuel Allen had 94 Votes for County Treasurer

    Voted that this meeting be dissolved & the meeting was Dissolved accordingly

    A True Entry   Attest   Daniel Goulding Town Clerk

At a meeting of the Freeholders & other Inhabitants of the Town of Worcester Qualified to Vote in Town affairs legally warned & assembled at the Publick meeting House of the First Parrish in Worcester on Monday the Second Day of april A, D, 1792

    Capt. Samuel Flagg chosen Moderator

2dly   Voted that the two School Quarters or Destricts formerly called Tatnick School Destricts be reduced to one School Destrict agreeable to the Petetion of Joseph Blair and others mentioned in the Second Article in the Warrant

On the third article Voted that Timothy Paine Esqr. Benjamen Heywood Esqr. & Colo Samuel Flagg a Committee appointed on the 17th. of October last be and they hereby are further impowered to make and execute to Saml. Gates or his order a Deed of S^d. Twenty two acres & an half of Land at Wigwam hill which was laid out for compleating the ministerial & School Land as mentioned in S^d. Article the Town having obtained leave to sell the Same by a resolve of the General Court [1]

4^thly   Voted that the fourth Article in the Warrant for this meeting be Desmissed [2]

Voted that this meeting be Dissolved & the meeting was Dissolved accordingly

   A True Entry   Attest   Daniel Goulding Town Clerk

At a Meeting of the Freeholders & other Inhabitants of the

---

[1] ARTICLE 3:—"Whereas the Committee appointed by the vote of the Town on the 17th Day of October last to make Sale of the School land on Wigwam Hill did in Consequence of the Said Vote make Sale of about Twenty two acres and an half of Land adjoining thereto laid out for compleating the ministerial and School land Supposing by Said Vote they were empowered So to do but upon examining the Town Book they found the vote so expressed as makes doubt their authority to give a Deed to Samuel Gates to whom they Sold the Same for four pounds one Shilling per acre— To See if the Town will empower Said Committee or any others to execute a Deed of the premises to Said Samuel Gates or his order the Said Town being now empowered to Sell the Same by a resolve of the General Court passed in February 1792"

[2] ARTICLE 4:—"To See if the Town will exempt Mr Samuel Chandler and Such others as it may be necessary to Summons as Witnesses in the action now pending at ye Supreme Judicial Court between the Inhabitants of the Said Town and Nathan Patch from any part of the expence or Damage attending the Same"

Town of Worcester on Monday the Second Day of april A, D, 1792 by adjournment from march the 5th. 1792

Voted that M^r. John Barnard be Collector of Publick taxes the Current year he giving Sufficient bonds for the faithfull performance of his trust to the Satisfaction of the Selectmen & that he be allowed the Sum of fifteen Pounds for Said Service

Voted that M^r. William M^cfarland Ju^r. be excused from Serving as Heighway Surveyor & Collector of Heighway Taxes the Current year

Then Chose M^r. Thadeas Chamberlain Heighway Surveyor and Collector of Heighway Taxes in the room of M^r. William M^cfarland Ju^r. excused

Voted that the Sum of four Shillings p^r. day be allowed for Work at the Heighways the Current year & Oxen Carts & Plows in the Usual Proportion

Voted that M^r. John Chamberlain & Capt. Joel How be excused from Serving School Committee men in the Quarters they were Chosen for at march meeting

Voted that the Sum of Thirty pounds that was Voted to be allowed to M^r. John Chamberlains School Quarter be now allowed to the Tatnick School Destrict this day reduced from two School Destricts to one Provided they Keep a Grammer School agreeable to Law the Term of one Year

Chose Capt. Joel How School Committee man for the Tatnick School Destrict

Voted that the Town Treasurer & Town Clerk be a Committee to procure a Case for the Safe keeping the Town records

Voted that the Resolves of the General Court in respect to the Sale of the Ministerial and School Lands be Recorded in the Town Book

Voted that M^r. John Barnard make out a List of the Taxes he has a Desire to have abated and Lay before the Town at the Next Town meeting

Voted that this Meeting be Dissolved & the meeting was Dissolved accordingly

    A True Entry   Attest   Daniel Goulding Town Clerk

At a Meeting of the Freeholders & other Inhabitants of the Town of Worcester legally warned & assembled on monday the Seventh Day of may A. D. 1792 Qualified to Vote for Representatives

Capt. Samuel Flagg was Chosen to Represent this Town in the General Court the Current year   the meeting was then Dissolved

At another meeting of the Freeholders & Other Inhabitants of the Town of Worcester Qualified to Vote in Town affairs Legally warned and assembled at the publick meeting House of the first Parish in S^d. Town on Monday the Seventh day of May 1792

Capt. Samuel Flagg was Chosen Moderator

Voted to accept of the Report of the Selectmen of a Road Laid out by the Selectmen to millstone Hill by Deacon Thomas Wheelers & Charles Adams^s. it being no expence to the Town Either in Purchasing the Land for the Road or in fenceing the Same

Voted to accept the Report of the Selectmen of an alteration made by the Selectmen of a Road leading from Capt. Joshua Whitneys through y^e. Land of Ephraim & Thomas Mowers to y^e. Post Road near halfway River—& that the old road So far as respects the alteration be Discontinued

Passed over the alteration made by the Selectmen of a Road beginning near the Quigley House and running through part of John Walkers land to Danl. Chadwicks

Voted that the Selectmen direct the Heighway Surveyors to mend & repair the County Road through Thadeas Chapen & Eli Chapens farms and the Town Road leading by John Elders to Samuel Curtis Esq^{rs}. meaning that Part of the Road that Lays in the Limits of the Town of Worcester

Upon the fifth article Voted that Timothy Paine Benjamen Heywood Esq^{rs}. & Capt. Samuel Flagg be a Committee to make further Examination into the Demands the Town has against Nathan Patch for Sundrey Sums of money by him received on orders for which he had been previously paid and to confer with S^d. Patch on the Subject & that S^d. Committee be impowered to

Settle the affair with him and upon his refusal to commence an action in behalf of the Town for the recovery of S^d. Sums at any Court proper to try the Same & that S^d. Committee or the major part of them pursue S^d. action to final Judgment & Execution

Voted that [this] meeting be Dissolved and the meeting was Dissolved accordingly

 A True Entry Attest Daniel Goulding Town Clerk

Laid out in the Town of Worcester a Town or private way as Follows vizt

Begining (on the Road leading from the first Parish meeting House to Nathan Patch's Farm and by M^r. William Taylors) at a large apple tree at the entrance of a lane leading from Said road to Deacon Thomas Wheelers House thence by Said lane to a large apple Tree marked Standing about four Rods westward of Said Wheelers Barn thence by Several Turnings by Stakes and Stones through Said Wheelers and M^r. Charles Adam's land to an apple Tree marked Standing about ten Rods Short of Said Adam's House thence by the East End of Said Adam's House to a Small Black Oak Tree marked Standing at y^e. Corner of his Field, Thence Turning westwardly and runing to a Large Gray Oak Tree Standing on the East Side of millstone Hill and near the Said Adam's West line and Said Road or way to be one Rod and an half wide, and to lie on the Easterly Side of Said Courses, also made the following alteration in the Town Road leading through the land of Eph^m and Thomas Mower vizt. Begining on the County Road leading by Capt. Joshua Whitneys to Ward Meeting House, at a Stake & Stones Standing in the South line of Eben^r. Wiswall Jun^{rs}. Land on Said County Road and Opposite to the Northeast Corner of Said Mowers land thence on S^d. Wiswalls line to a White Oak tree, thence on Said line to another white Oak tree, thence through Said Mowers land as the fence now Stands by a white Oak and a Walnut Tree to the Corner of Capt. John Peirces Land thence as the Road is now Trod to the County Road at half way River and Said Road to be two Rods wide and to lie on the South Side of Said Courses

Dated at Worcester aforesaid this 5th. Day of April A. D. 1792

Samuel Flagg   Selectmen
Sam¹. Curtis   of
John Chamberlain   Worcester

A True Entry   Attest   Daniel Goulding Town Clerk

Petition for Town Meeting 1792 We the Subscribers Freeholders in the Town of Worcester in behalf of ourselves & many Other Inhabitants of the Said Town hereby Signify our request to the Selectmen of Worcester aforesaid that they would, as Soon as conveniently may be call a Meeting of the Inhabitants of the Said Town to take into consideration the expediency of Establishing one or more hospitals in Said Town for inoculating for the Small Pox & to act thereon as the Town may Seem Meet

Worcester Sep^{tr}. 3^d. 1792

Samuel Brazer, Abel Stowell, Nathan Heard, Thos. Shepard, Nathan Blackman, John Stowers, Nathan Patch, Abraham Lincoln, Benj$^a_{,,}$ Butman, Isaiah Thomas, Theoph^s. Wheeler, Edw Bangs, Jesse Craig, Joel How,

At a Meeting of the Freeholders & Other Inhabitants of the Town of Worcester Qualified to Vote in Town affairs held on Monday the Seventeenth Day of September A, D, 1792

Samuel Flagg Esqr. was Chosen Moderator

A motion was made & Seconded to see if the Town would consent to have one or more hospitals for inoculating for the Small Pox Established in the Town of Worcester agreeable to the Second article in the Warrant, and after Some debate on the matter the motion was put and passed in the Negative

Voted then that the meeting be Dissolved & it was Dissolved accordingly

       A True Entry   Attest   Daniel Goulding Town Clerk

Worcester Town Records, 1792.

We the Subscribers Freeholders of the Town of Worcester request the Selectmen of the Said Town to issue their Warrant as Speedely as may be to assemble the Freeholders of Said Town of Worcester for the purpose of taking into consideration the expediency of Licencing one or more houses for innoculation for the Small Pox or to act thereon as the Town may think proper

Worcester September 19th 1792

To the Selectmen of Worcester

Isaiah Thomas, EDW. Bangs, Joel How, Amos Wheeler, Jonathan Gates, James Fisk, John Barnard, Joseph Barber, William Chamberlain, Lot Hutchinson, Thomas Stowel Nathaniel Flagg

At a Legal meeting of the Inhabitants of the Town of Worcester held on Monday the 1.st Day of October A, D, 1792

Chose Samuel Flagg Esqr. Moderator

Voted that Such Hospitals as the Selectmen Shall direct be opened for the purpose of Inoculating for the Small Pox & that the Same be under the Derection of the Selectmen

Voted that this Town do approve of Doct^{rs} John Green, Elijah Dix, John Green Junr. and Oliver Fisk as Physicians to attend Said Hospitals, and also

Voted that the aforesaid Physicians be not at liberty to Inoculate any Persons with the Small Pox after the 31st. day of this Present month

Voted that this meeting be Dissolved and it was Dissolved accordingly   Attest   Samuel Flagg Moderator

    A True Entry   Attest   Daniel Goulding Town Clerk

Worcester Ss. April 19th. 1792 M^r. Nathan Heard came before me this Day & took the oath prescribed by Law to qualify him to execute the duty of his office as Sealer of Leather in the Town of Worcester   Jos. Allen Jus. Paces

    A True Entry   Attest   Daniel Goulding Town Clerk

Worcester Town Records, 1792.

Pursuant to a Resolve of the General Court passed the 30th Day of June 1792 The Inhabitants of the Town of Worcester Qualified according to the Constitution to Vote for Representatives to the General Court upon due warning given met together on Friday the Second day of November 1792 for the purpose of giving in their votes for federal Representatives to Congress as the Said Resolve of the General Court directs

Votes for the following Persons were given in counted and Sorted, and declaration thereof made in open Town meeting, as the Said Resolve provides (viz)

For the County of Hampshire	William Lyman Esqr.	28
	Samuel Lyman Esqr.	19
	Samuel Henshaw Esqr.	1
	Simeon Strong Esqr.	1
For the County of Worcester	Jonathan Grout Esqr.	26
	Timothy Paine Esqr.	3
	Dwight Foster Esqr.	3
	Artimas Ward Esqr.	16
	Nathaniel Paine Esqr.	2
For the County of Berkshire	Theodore Sedgwick Esqr.	34
	Thompson T Skinner Esqr.	16
	John Bacon Esqr.	1
For the 2^d. Destrict at Large vizt. Hampshire Worcester & Berkshire	Samuel Lyman Esqr.	31
	Theodore Sedgwick Esqr.	18
	Thomson T. Skinner Esqr.	1
	Samuel Henshaw Esqr.	1
For the 1st. 2^d. & 3^d. Distrects	David Cobb Esqr.	20
	John Bacon Esqr.	29
	Charles Jarvis Esqr.	2

A True Entry   Attest   Daniel Goulding Town Clerk

Pursuant to a Resolve of the General Court passed the 30th day of June 1792—the Inhabitants of the Town of Worcester Qualified according to the Constitution to Vote for Representatives to the General Court upon due warning given mett together on Friday the Second day of November 1792 for the purpose of giving in their votes for Electors of Presedent & Vice Presedent of the United States within & for the Second Distrect consisting of the Counties of Hampshire Worcester & Berkshire as the Said Resolve of the General Court Directs the Following Persons were Voted for & had the Number of Votes Set against their Respective Names vizt.

Honble Moses Gill Esqr.	18	William Lyman Esqr.	2
Samuel Baker Esqr.	17	William Shepard Esqr.	1
Martin Kinsley Esqr.	20	Andrew Peters Esqr.	1
Samuel Flagg Esqr.	20	Elijah Dwight Esqr.	1
Samuel Fowler Esqr.	20	Thomas Dwight Esqr.	1
David Smead Esqr.	21	Simeon Strong Esqr.	1
Thomson T Skinner Esqr.	38	John Bacon Esqr.	1
Samuel Lyman Esqr.	18	Jonathan Warner Esqr.	1
Samuel Henshaw Esqr.	13	Joseph Allen Esqr.	1

 A True Entry Attest Daniel Goulding Town Clerk

At a meeting of the Freeholders & Other Inhabitants of the Town of Worcester Qualified to Vote in Town affairs legally assembled at the Publick meeting house of the First Parish in Said Town on Friday the Second Day of November A, D, 1792 then the Following Votes were Passed vizt.

Samuel Flagg Esqr. was Chosen Moderator

Voted to Choose a Committee to Receive & Examine account brought against the Town at this meeting Then Chose Benjamen Heywood Esqr. Daniel Goulding & Deacon John Chamberlain a Committee for S^d. Purpose

Voted that this meeting be adjourned to Monday the Nineteenth Day of this Instant November at one OClock in the afternoon then to meet at this Place, the meeting was accordingly adjourned

 A True Entry Attest Daniel Goulding Town Clerk

Commonwealth of Massachusetts

In the House of Representatives June 13th. 1791

On the petition of the inhabitants of the Town of Worcester in the County of Worcester, shewing that there is in Said Town a lot of unimproved land containing about fifty acres laid out for school land and praying that they may be empowered to make Sale of Said land for reasons Set forth in Said petition :—Resolved that the prayer of Said petition be granted & that the Said inhabitants be and they are hereby empowered to make sale of Said land and to execute good and sufficient deed or deeds to pass the same—and the money arising by the sale or sales of Said Land shall be put out on interest and the annual interest arising on the amount of such sale or sales shall be applied for the support of schools in said Town of Worcester

Sent down for concurrence   David Cobb Speaker

In Senate June 14 1791   Read & concurred

                           Samuel Phillips president

Approved   John Hancock

True Coppy   Attest   John Avery Junr. Sec^y

    A True Entry   Attest   Daniel Goulding Town Clerk

Commonwealth of Massachusetts

In the House of Representatives Feby 2^d 1792

On the petition of the Inhabitants of the Town of Worcester in the County of Worcester shewing that there is in Said Town twenty two acres & an half of land laid out for the purpose of compleating the ministerial and school lot divisions in said town situate in the extreme part of said town & unimproved and for reasons set forth in said petition praying that they may be impowered to make sale thereof—also shewing that the said inhabitants have heretofore made sale of other ministerial & School lands in said town without first having the leave of Government therefor & praying that such sales may be confirmed

Resolved that the prayer of Said petition [be] granted and that the Said inhabitants be & they hereby are impowered to make Sale of Said Twenty two acres and an half of land, and to make & execute a good & Sufficient deed or deeds to pass the Same — And it is further

Resolved that the sales and titles to the other ministerial and School lands which the said inhabitants have heretofore sold be and they hereby are established and confirmed to the original purchasers in as full and ample a manner as if licence had been first obtained from the General Court therefor provided that the money which has arrisen & Shall arise from the sale or sales of Said land shall be put out at interest on good security & that the annual interest arising on the amount of Such sale or sales Shall be applied for the Support of the ministry & Schools in Said Town agreeably to the original design for which the said lands were reserved any law or resolve to the contrary notwithstanding

 Sent up for concurrence   D Cobb Speaker
 In Senate Feby 27th. 1792 Read and concurred
           Samuel Phillips Presid
 Approved John Hancock
 A True copy   Attest   John Avery Junr. Sec^y
   A True Entry   Attest   Daniel Goulding Town Clerk

At a Town Meeting held on Monday November the Nineteenth A, D, 1792 by adjournment from the Second day of the Same month, Benjamen Heywood Esqr. was Chosen Moderator in the room of Samuel Flagg Esqr. he being absent, then the Following Votes were passed vizt.

Voted to accept of the Report of the Committee Chose to Examine accounts exhibited against the Town & that the Same be allowed & paid to the persons therein mentioned the Report is as follows

The Committee appointed by the Town of Worcester at a Town Meeting held on Friday the 2^d. day of November A, D, 1792 to

Worcester Town Records, 1792.

Examine accounts exhibited against the Town, Report that they have examined the following accounts due to the following Persons for the Towns allowance & payment (viz)

N°		
1	To Capt. Saml. Brooks for Supplies for Simon Glasco	£ 5 ,, 17 ,, 6½
2	To William Taylor for Boarding and Cloathing anna White from Octr. 7th. 1791 th No^v. 2^d 1792 inclusive being 56 weeks at 3/6	9 ,, 16 ,, 0
3	To John Elder for boarding & Cloathing John Spence from Octr. 17th. 1791 to No^v. 5th. 1792 being 55 weeks	9 ,, 2 ,, 1
4	to John Barnard for Boarding Thos. Gleason 5 weeks at 4/	1 ,, 0 ,, 0
5	To Charles & Saml. Chandler for Sundry articles of Cloathing for John Spence	0 ,, 18 ,, 10
6	To Dea^n. John Chamberlain for Boarding and Cloathing Nathan Houghton & Jenny Dyer one year ending Octr. 15th. 1792 and for sundries Supplyed Saml. Denny	18 ,, 0 ,, 6
7	To Benj^a. Stowel for Boarding Thos. Gleason his wife and Child 5 Weeks Ending No^v. 19th. 1791	2 ,, 10 ,, 0
8	To Daniel Goulding for Supplies del^d. M^{rs}. Tracy & Children to No^v. 16th. 1792	19 ,, 16 ,, 10
9	To Simeon Duncan for Transporting Anthony Taylor to Boylston & W^m. Park to Shrewsbury and Burying a Child of the widow Tracy & 1 p^r of Cords	1 ,, 6 ,, 6
10	To Simon Gates for 64 feet of Chestnut Timber	0 ,, 5 ,, 4
11	To Col^o. Eben^r. Lovell for 115 feet of Bridge Plank	0 ,, 7 ,, 0
12	To David Griggs for 160 feet of D^o.	0 ,, 8 ,, 0
13	To Asa Ward for 300 feet of D^o.	0 ,, 18 ,, 0

14	To the Assessors for making Taxes and taking a Valuation the present Year	12 ,, 4 ,, 9
15	To Thomas Rice for Covering Stones for the Bridge near the Goal & Labour	1 ,, 6 ,, 3
16	to Benj^a. Stowell for D^o.	3 ,, 0 ,, 3
17	To the Widow Eunice Rice for D^o.	2 ,, 12 ,, 8
18	To Benj^a. Heywood for Carting Covering Stones for S^d. Bridge and Sundry disbursements of Cash for the benefit of the Town	7 ,, 3 ,, 6
N° 19	To the Selectmen to enable them to fulfill their contract with James Quigley for the Support of Agnus Brooks for the Term of one Year ending the 1st. of May next the S^d Selectmen to be accountable for the appropriation of the Same	5 ,, 4 ,, 0
20	To Moses Miller for Boarding and nursing Lydia Gleason a Daughter of Thos. Gleason	2 ,, 5 ,, 0
21	To John Nazro for Interest due to him on a demand of £10,,11,,3¼ for Supplies at the funeral of Rev^d. Tha^d. Maccarty	3 ,, 8 ,, 9
22	To Major Willm. Treadwell for making a Case for the Town Records and finding meterials for the Same	3 ,, 7 ,, 2
23	To Nath^n. Patch for boarding Lydia Gleason 29 Weeks ending 21st of August last	3 ,, 7 ,, 0
24	To Capt. Joel How for a Journey to Brantree for Robert Hoit in the Case between Worcester & Shrewsbury	0 ,, 12 ,, 0
25	To Danl. Waldo & Son	2 ,, 8 ,, 4
		£117 ,, 6 ,, 3½

all which is Submitted

November 19th. 1792

Benj^a. Heywood
John Chamberlain } Committee
Daniel Goulding

Voted to allow to Benjamen Heywood Esqr. The Sum of Nine Pounds for his extraordinary Services as Town Treasurer the two last Years

Voted to accept the Report of the Committee Chose Some Time Sence to make Sale of the Ministerial & School Lands at Wigwam Hill So Called the Report is as follows

The Committee appointed to make Sale of the Ministerial & School Lands at Wigwam Hill So called have attended the Service assigned them and report. That having caused the Said Lands to be Surveyed and divided into five Several lots (a plan of which is annexed) the Committee then proceeded to advertise and make Sale of the Same at Publick Vendue as Follows vizt.

Lot N°. 1 Containing fifteen acres and three Quarters Sold to Capt. Samuel Brooks for the Sum of Twenty four pounds Eight Shillings and three pence	£24 ,, 8 ,, 3
Lot N°. 2 Containing Twelve acres and an half Sold to M^r. John Barnard for Forty Nine pounds Seven Shillings and Six pence	49 ,, 7 ,, 6
Lots N°. 3 & 4 together Containing Twenty Nine acres to M^r. Willm. Mahan Ju^r. and by him Released to M^r. Ignatius Goulding Capt. Daniel Goulding and Capt. Daniel Heywood Jointly for the Sum of Ninety Seven pounds ten Shillings	97 ,, 10 ,, 0
and Lot N°. 5 being that part Called ministerial Land Containing Twenty two acres and an half Sold to Ebenezer Hastings for the Sum of Ninety one pounds two Shillings & Sixpence	91 ,, 2 ,, 6
The Committee further account for Eighteen Shillings & four pence earnest money Rec^d. of Jon^a. Lovell to Whom Lot N°. 1 was Struck of to but he refusing to take a Deed and give Security for ye purchase money the Same became forfiet	0 ,, 18 ,, 4
Which makes the whole amount Rec^d. by ye Committee	£263 ,, 6 ,, 7

and y^e. Committee request allowance for the following Sums vizt.

Capt. Samuel Brooks Bond on Interest	£23 ,, 10 ,, 0	
M^r. John Barnards Bond on D^o	48 ,, 9 ,, 6	
Ignatius Gouldings & Others d^o. on D^o.	95 ,, 14 ,, 0	
Eben^r. Hastings Bond on D^o	90 ,, 4 ,, 6	
Expence of Surveying & Selling Said Land	2 ,, 15 ,, 8	
The Committees Time and trouble in ye Business in-Cluding writing Deeds and Bonds	2 ,, 4 ,, 11	262 ,, 18 ,, 7
Balance		£ 0 ,, 8 ,, 0

There Remains a Balance of Eight Shillings which the Committee have left in the hands of the Town Treasurer for the use of the Town   all which is Submitted

Samuel Flagg } Committee
Benj^a. Heywood }

Worcester 31 Octr. 1792

Voted that the above mentioned Bonds for which the Land was sold Lay in the Hands of the Selectmen for the use of the Town of Worcester

Worcester 10th January 1792
Surveyed by J^no. Pierce
Protracted by a Scale of 30
Rods to an inch

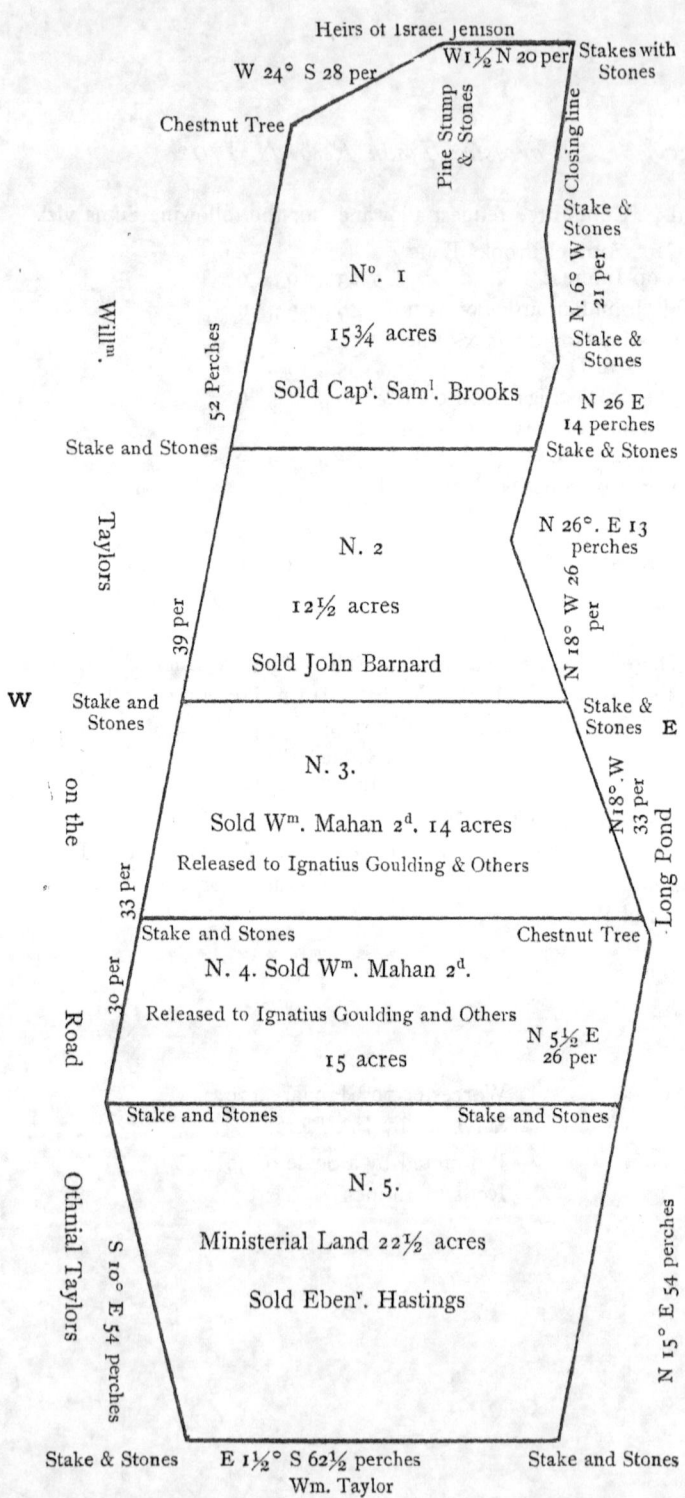

Worcester Town Records, 1792.

Voted to accept the Report of a Committee Chose Some Time past to Examine into the Demands the Town has against Nathan Patch for which he has been previously paid and to Recover the Same which Report is as follows

1786 D^r,, M^r. Nathan Patch in an account Current with ye Inhabitants of the Town of Worcester   C^{rs},

March 11th, To Cash pd by an order for abatement of James Gates Taxes	£2 ,, 2 ,,	1
To ditto an abatement of Nathan Johnsons ditto	1 ,, 15 ,,	7
To ditto an abatement of Cato Walkers ditto	4 ,, 19 ,,	7
To ditto paid Commissions on State Tax of £1849 ,, 3 ,, 0	15 ,, 8 ,,	0
To ditto paid Commissions on State Tax new Emmission £1664 . 10/3	7 ,, 8 -	3
1788 Febry 25th.		
To an order for James Gates Tax abated	2 - 2 -	1
To ditto for Nathan Johnsons Tax abated	1 ,, 15 ,,	7
To ditto for Cato Walkers Tax abated	4 ,, 19 ,,	7
To paid Commissions on Town Tax dated 19 Septr. 1781	9 ,, 12 ,,	0
To paid Commissions on State Tax dated 22 Decr. 1781	14 ,, 9 ,,	3
To paid ditto on Town & County Taxes, 21 Janry 1782	10 ,, 8 ,,	11
To paid ditto on Continental Tax 1 June 1782	9 ,, 9 -	8
To paid ditto on ditto Second Moiety 24 January 1783	9 ,, 12 -	0
To paid ditto on Town Tax Same date	1 ,, 14 ,,	10
1789 Febry 24th.		
To paid Commissions on Tax made 28 February 1781 and another Tax dated 28 June 1781	33 ,, 15 ,,	0

1790 Novem^r. 15th.
   To paid Commissions for Collecting Sundry Taxes   68 ,, 9 ,, 1

               £198 ,, 1 ,, 6

1781 June ye 28th.
   By his Commissions on £1664 ,, 10 ,, 3 new Emmission money Reduced to hard Money at 2^d. on the pound   7 ,, 6 ,, 8

   By his Commissions on State Tax for £1849 ,, 3/ @ 2^d 15 ,, 8 ,, 2

Septr. 19th By his Commissions on Town Tax for £1140 ,, 7 ,, 4 @ 2^d 9 ,, 10 ,, 1

Decem^r. 22^d
   By his Commissions on a State Tax of £1735 ,, 10 ,, 9 @ 2^d 14 ,, 9 ,, 3

1782 January 21st
   By his Commissions on a Town and County Tax of £1263 ,, 19 7 at 2^d. on the pound in three Tax Bills   10 ,, 10 ,, 8

June 1st. By his Commissions on the first moiety of Continental Tax for £1138 ,, 6 ,, 8 at 2^d. on the pound   9 ,, 9 ,, 8

1783 Jan^{ry} 24th
   By his Com^s. on ye 2^d Moiety of ye Cont^l. Tax being £1148 ,, 6 ,, 8 @ 2^d 9 ,, 12 ,, 0

Janry 24th. By his Commissions on a Town Tax of £209 0 0 @   1 ,, 14 ,, 10

1786 Septr 11th
   By his Com^s. on a State Tax of £1800 8/ @ 2^{d}½   18 ,, 15 ,, 0

Septr. 11th By his Com^s. on a County Tax of £52-9-7 @ 2^{d}½   ,, 11 - 0

1787 Janry 8th
   By his Com^s. on a Town Tax £150 ,, 0-0 @ 2^{d}½   1 ,, 11 ,, 3

June 2^d By his Com^s. on a County Tax of £69 ,, 13 ,, 6 @ 3^d ,, 17 ,, 6

Worcester Town Records, 1792.

1788 Janry 14th.
  By his Com[s]. on a Town Tax of
   £150.0-0 @ 3[d]   1 ,, 17 - 6
1783 Nov[r]. 3[d].
  By abatement of James Gates Tax   2 ,, 2 - 1
1784 May By abatement of Nathan Johnsons
   Tax   1 - 15 - 7
1785 Dec[r]. By an abatement of Cato Walkers
   Taxes   4 ,, 19 ,, 7
              _____
              £110 ,, 10 ,, 10
1790 Nov[r]. 15 Balance due to the Town   87 ,, 10 ,, 8
              _____
              £198 ,, 1 ,, 6
Worcester 7 May 1792   Errors Excepted
        p[r] Samuel Flagg   ⎫
         Samuel Curtis   ⎪ Selectmen
         Jn[o]. Chamberlain ⎬ of
         Benj[a]. Heywood ⎭ Worcester

The Committee appointed to Settle the within demand against Nathan Patch, Report the Following Settlement viz[t].

1792 Aug[st]. 9th M[r]. Nathan Patch to the Town of Worcester D[r].
To the Balance from the other side within £87 ,, 10 ,, 8
To y[e] Interest on £68 ,, 9 ,, 1 part of s[d]
 Balance from 15 Nov[r]. 1790 to this Time   7 ,, 3 ,, 4
To the Interest on £19-1-7 the Remainder ⎫
 of the said Balance from the 24th February ⎬   4 ,, 0 ,, 0
 1789 to this Time   ⎭
To the Balance of Interest due on an Exe- ⎫
 cution the Town had against you on Set- ⎪
 tlement of the said Ex͡con agreeable to ⎬   1 - 6 - 0
 your obligation dated 4 October 1790   ⎭
              _____
              £100 - 0 - 0

Worcester 9 August 1792   Received of Nathan Patch above named a note of hand for the above sum of one hundred pounds payable in one year to Benjamin Haywood Esq[r]. Towns Treasurer for the use of the Inhabitants of said Town, with Interest, which when paid will be in full of this account

Tim⁰. Paine ⎫
Sam¹. Flagg ⎬ Committee

A Copy of yᵉ a/c Revised

Same day Received of yᵉ abovesᵈ Committee the abovesaid note against Said Patch, for the Said Sum of one hundred pounds payable as aforesaid, and for the use of the Inhabitants of said Town of Worcester   Benjᵃ. Heywood Town Treasurer

The Committee request an allowance for Time and Trouble, in adjusting the foregoing account, the Sum of Twenty four Shillings

Voted to allow the above Said Committee Chose Some Time Sence to Examine into the Demands the Town has against Nathan Patch the above mentioned Sum of Twenty four Shillings for their Time and Trouble in adjusting Sᵈ. accounts

Voted that Mʳ. John Barnard have untill march Next to See if he cannot Collect a part or all the Taxes he has brought in a List of this day to have abated

Voted that the Thirty pounds mentioned in the fifth article in the Warrant for this meeting[1] be made use of for the Support of English Schools in this Town and proportioned in the Same way the Other money Granted for the Support of English Schools & with it

Voted that Capᵗ. Joshua Whitney & Others have leave to Erect Horse Sheds on the Common & that the Selectmen be a Committee to view the Ground and direct where they may be build So as to not inconveen the meeting House

Voted to Build a Small Brick Building for the purpose of Holding the Towns Stock of Amunition & that their be a Committee Chose for Said purpose & that they provide a Sutable Spot of

---

[1] ARTICLE 5:—"To See in what way and manner yᵉ. Town will dispose of the Sum of £30 granted to the Centre School District in March A, D, 1791 on Condition the Said District Should keep a Publick Grammar School for the Benefit of the Town Dureing the Term of one year, the Same not having been applied for that purpose"

Ground to Build S^d. Building on & that they Lay their Accounts before the Town for an allowance then Chose Benjamen Heywood Esqr. Samuel Flagg Esqr. & M^r. John Nazro for S^d. Committee

Voted Joyn with M^r. Samuel Chandler in Setling a new division line between his House Lot and Land belonging to the Town on the North Side of the Common and

Voted then that the Selectmen be a Committee to transact the business and impowered to give and take Deeds of the Same in behalf of the Town of Worcester

Voted to accept the Following Settlement made with the Treasurer for the Town

The Account of Benjamen Heywood Treasurer of the Town of Worcester, who credits the Inhabitants of Said Town by Sundry Sums as follows (viz)

	£	s	d
By the Balance of his last account settled April 4th. 1791	789	1	3¼

1791

August 15th By Cash rec^d. of John Chamberlain as Interest on Obligations for money due to the Town   5 ,, 19 ,, 10

Novr. 21st. By Interest rec^d of Nathan Patch included in his confession of the debt due from Willm. Jenison   4 ,, 10 ,,

28th By Cash rec^d. of John Chamberlain as Interest on Obligations for money due to the Town   4 ,, 10 ,,

Decr. 2^d By the assessors Return of a Tax committed to John Barnard to Collect for 1791   387 ,, 1 ,, 7

13th By Cash rec^d. of John Chamberlain as Interest on Obligations for money due to the Town   8 ,, 5 ,,

1792

April 26th. By Cash Rec^d of Saml. Flagg one of the Selectmen in

part of a Note given by the State Treasurer for what was due to the Town for the Support of Thomas Whayland	7	18	3
May 15th By one years Interest rec^d. on 292 „ 16 „ 3 due from the Treasury of the Commonwealth	17	11	4
18th By Cash rec^d. of John Chamberlain as Interest on Obligations for money due to the Town	15	1	4
August 9th By Nathan Patches Note on Interest for the Balance due to the Town on Settlement made by Timothy Paine and Others a Committee for that purpose	100		
Sep^t. 26th. By Cash rec^d. of John Childs Esqr.being the amount of fines imposed on Sundry persons for profane cursing and Swearing	1	2	6
22^d. By Interest on Nathan Patch^s. dated Novr. 7th 1785	61	18	8¾
No^v. 2^d By Cash rec^d. of Deacon John Chamberlain as Interest on Obligations for money due to the Town in the hands of the Selectmen	18		

£1420 „ 19 „ 10

And the Said Accountant Chargeth the Said Inhabitants with Sundry payments by him made as p^r. Receipts (viz)

1791
April 7th N 1. To Cash paid John Heard in full of a Note given by Deacon Nathan Perry Town Treasurer to M^r. Daniel Story and cost of Suit thereon	£49	11	2
2 To Ditto paid James Quigley in full of an Order given him by the Selectmen	5	11	1
June 13th 3 To Interest money paid Thad & W^m. Maccarty	5	10	0½

Worcester Town Records, 1792.

August 6th	4	To Cash paid Saml. Moore p^r. Order of the Selectmen	2 ,,	5 ,,	0
Novr. 21st	5	To Ditto p^d. Benj^a. Heywood p^r. Ditto	4 ,,	1 ,,	0
Dec^m. 8th.	6	To Cash p^d. John Elder p^r. Order of the Selectmen	9 ,,	4 ,,	2
	7	To Ditto p^d. John Chamberlain p^r. Ditto	15 ,,	15 ,,	0
13th	8	To Ditto p^d. Benj^a. Stowel p^r. Ditto	24 ,,	15 ,,	2
1792 Feb^y	9	To Ditto p^d. Samuel Brazer p^r. Ditto	30 ,,	0 ,,	0
march 3^d	10	to Ditto p^d. Willm. Taylor p^r. Ditto	8 ,,	2 ,,	0
20th	11	to Ditto p^d. Nathan Patch p^r. Ditto	18 ,,	8 ,,	1
may 18th	12	to Ditto p^d. Daniel Goulding p^r. Ditto	2 ,,	7 ,,	1
	13	to Ditto p^d. Ditto and John Stanton p^r. Ditto	5 ,,	10 ,,	3
	14	to Ditto p^d. Elijah Dix on Note given p^r. Ditto	19 ,,	13 ,,	4
	15	to Ditto p^d. Ditto on Interest p^r order of D^o.	10 ,,	14 ,,	4
30th	16	to Ditto p^d. the School Committe p^r. D^o	168 ,,	16 ,,	0
	17	to Ditto p^d. Nathl. Heywood in full of an order given to Doct^r. Elijah Dix	17 ,,	15 ,,	0
	18	to Ditto p^d. Isaac Gleason p^r. Order of y^e. Selectmen	1 ,,	0 ,,	2
	19	to Ditto p^d. Eunice Follinsbee p^r. Ditto	1 ,,	4 ,,	0
	20	to Ditto p^d. Capt. Saml. Brooks p^r. Ditto	2 ,,	3 ,,	10
	21	to Ditto p^d. Moses Miller p^r. D^o	0 ,,	5 ,,	11
	22	to Ditto p^d. Willm. Elder p^r. D^o	0 ,,	6 ,,	0
	23	to Ditto p^d. Samuel Flagg p^r. D^o	3 ,,	0 ,,	0
	24	to Ditto p^d. John Barnard p^r. D^o	15 ,,	10 ,,	5
	25	to Ditto p^d. James Quigley p^r. D^o	10 ,,	4 ,,	0
	26	to Ditto p^d. Frances Savage p^r. D^o	5 ,,	4 ,,	0
	27	to Ditto p^d. Simeon Duncan p^r. D^o	1 ,,	0 ,,	0
	28	to Ditto p^d. W^m. McFarland p^r. D^o	0 ,,	12 ,,	9
	29	to Ditto p^d. Jonathan Lovell p^r. D^o	1 ,,	0 ,,	0
	30	to Ditto p^d. Abigail Grout p^r. D^o	5 ,,	4 ,,	0
	31	to Ditto p^d. Nathan Perry p^r. D^o	7 ,,	17 ,,	1

32	to Ditto p^d. Isaac Chadwick p^r. D^o	0,, 8,, 0
33	to Ditto p^d. John Barnard p^r. D^o	15,, 3,, 4
34	to Ditto p^d. Martha Wiley p^r. D^o	1,, 10,, 0
35	to Ditto p^d. John Chamberlain p^r. D^o	2,, 12,, 0
36	to Ditto p^d. Benjamin Tucker p^r. D^o	0,, 3,, 10
37	to Ditto p^d. David Moore p^r. D^o	1,, 4,, 0
38	to Ditto p^d. Samuel Flagg p^r. D^o	4,, 10,, 8
39	to Ditto p^d. Joseph Kingsbury p^r. D^o	1,, 0,, 0
40	to Ditto p^d. Charles Adams p^r. D^o	2,, 1,, 4
41	to Ditto p^d. Joseph Wheeler Ju^r. p^r. D^o	0,, 7,, 6
42	to Ditto p^d. Samuel Goddard p^r. D^o	0,, 17,, 6
43	to Ditto p^d. Samuel Curtis Esqr. p^r. D^o	2,, 8,, 0
44	to Ditto p^d. D^o. ——— p^r. D^o	2,, 0,, 0
45	to Ditto p^d. Samuel Flagg Esqr. p^r. D^o	2,, 3,, 9
46	to Ditto p^d. Nathan Patch p^r. order of the assessors	0,, 3,, 9
47	to D^o. p^d. Samuel Flagg Esqr. p^r. order of the Selectmen	6,, 2,, 6
48	to D^o. p^d. Abigail Grout p^r. order of the Selectmen	1,, 6,, 0
49	to D^o. p^d. Joseph Wheeler Esqr p^r. Ditto	0,, 12,, 4
50	to D^o. p^d. Capt. Samuel Brooks p^r. Ditto	5,, 5,, 1½
51	to Ditto p^d. Charles & Saml. Chandler p^r. D^o.	4,, 1,, 9
52	to Ditto p^d. Benj^a. Stone p^r. Ditto	9,, 1,, 9
53	to Ditto p^d. — Ditto — p^r. D^o.	1,, 6,, 10
54	to Ditto p^d. Saml. & Stephen Salsbury p^r. D^o	23,, 6,, 8
55	to Ditto p^d. Stephen Salsbury p^r. D^o	10,, 0,, 0
56	to Ditto p^d. Deacon Nathan Perry p^r. D^o	6,, 0,, 0
57	to Ditto p^d. Ditto — p^r. D^o	50,, 6,, 9
58	to Ditto p^d. Ditto — p^r. D^o	45,, 9,, 6½
Octr. 11 59	to Ditto p^d. Thad^s. & William Maccarty being one years Interest on a Bond due from the Town to them dated march 2^d. 1789 which is also endorsed on S^d Bond	5,, 10,, 0½

Nov. 2 60 to Cash pd. the Town of Marlborough pr. Order of the Selectmen	1 „ 15 „ 10	
Octr. 31 to an Execution vs. Nathan Patch extended on 69 acres of Land for the benefit of the Town	189 „ 19 „ 0	
	846 „ 11 „ 8	
Ballance Due to the Town carried to new account	£ 574 „ 8 „ 2	
Errors Excepted	Benja. Heywood	

Worcester November 17th. 1792   We the Subscribers being the major part of a Committee appointed by the Town of Worcester to adjust & Settle the account with Benjamen Heywood Esqr. The Treasurer of Said Town, beg leave to report that he has charged himself with the Sum of fourteen hundred & Twenty pounds Nineteen Shillings & ten pence, that he has paid out by Orders from the Selectmen & by discharging Notes of hand given in behalf of the Town &c. the Sum of Eight hundred & forty six pounds Eleven Shillings & Eight pence, which leaves a ballance due to the Town of five hundred & Seventy four pounds Eight Shillings & two pence, which the Said Treasurer is further to account for, all which is humbly Submitted

Joseph Allen
John Chamberlain

Voted that the Several Sums of Money allowed at this meeting be Granted Levied and assessed on the Poles & Estates in this Town and the Collector directed to Collect and pay the Same to the Town Treasurer on or before the first day of march Next

Voted to accept the following report of the Selectmen of the Situation of the Towns Bonds — viz —

Report of ye. Selectmen Shewing the Situation of the Towns Bonds 2d. Nov. 1792

Simeon Duncans Bond dated 15 February 1785 for £40 - 0 - 0
    Messs. Joseph Allen & Joseph Blair Sureties   Interest paid

Worcester Town Records, 1792.

Daniel Gouldings Bond dated 15 February 1785 for   48 - 10 - 0
   Mess^s. Palmer & Ignatius Goulding Sureties, four years Interest due

Samuel Browns Bond dated 21 July 1783 for   39 - 0 - 0
   Mess Elijah Dix & Lemuel Rice Sureties three years Interest due

Jesse Tafts Bond dated 21 July 1786 for   39 - 5 - 0
   Mess^s. Josiah Lyon & Joseph Barber Sureties, one years Interest due

Reuben Lambs Bond dated 1 September 1791 for   42 - 3 - 4
   Mess^s. John Heart & Levi Eddy Sureties Interest paid

Alpheas Eatons Bond dated February 15th 1792 for   36 - 10 - 0
   William Eaton & Samuel Flagg Sureties Interest paid

Ezekiel Howes Bond dated 1 November 1776 for   20 - 0 - 0
   Ezekiel How Surety two years Interest due

Levi Lincolns Bond dated 15th February 1785 for   51 - 10 - 0
   Mess^s. Joseph Allen & Ignatius Goulding Sureties two years Interest due

John Chamberlains bond dated 20th may 1790 for   101 - 0 - 0
   Mess^s. Ignatius Goulding & Daniel Goulding Sureties two years Interest due

Joseph Allens Bond dated 30 August 1784 for   34 - 11 - 1
   Mess^s. Elijah Dix & Samuel Allen Sureties Interest paid

Phineas Wards Bond dated 1 November 1773 for   22 - 15 - 0
   Mess^s. Samuel Curtis & David Ritchardson Sureties one years Interest due

David Bigelows Bond dated 1 November 1782 for   35 - 16 - 8
   M^r. John Green Surety two years Interest due

William Gates^s. Bond dated 1 November 1789 for   15 - 11 - 2
   Mess^s. Thomas Wheeler & Nathaniel Harrington Sureties one years Interest due

Paul Gates Bond dated 15th February 1785 for   £35 - 0 - 0
   Mess^s. William Gates & William Mahan Sureties Interest paid

Zebulon Cuttings Bond dated 3^d. September 1790 for 50 - 0 - 0
   Peter Johnson & Jacob Holmes Sureties one years Interest due

John Stanton & Daniel Gouldings Bond dated 10 march 1784
for   35 - 0 - 0
Mess⁵. Palmer Goulding

Oliver Watson Junʳˢ. Bond dated 28 march 1785 for   83 - 6 - 8
Mess⁵. Oliver Watson & Wᵐ. Mᶜfarland Sureties Interest paid

Nathan Patchˢ. Bond dated 21 July 1787 for   42 - 15 - 0
Mess⁵. Timo Bigelow & John Walker Sureties two years Interest due

Nathan Patchˢ. Bond dated 21 July 1783 for   33 - 5 - 0
Mess⁵. Cornelius Stowell & Joshua Whitney Sureties two years Interest due

Henery Patchˢ. Bond dated 15 February for   152 - 10 - 0
Mess⁵. Nathan Patch & Eli Chapen Sureties one years Interest due

John Goulds Bond dated 24ᵗʰ January 1791 for   33 - 6 - 8
Mess⁵. John & Holloway Taylor Sureties Interest paid

Flagg & Stantons Lease of Store Ground Rent paid up

amount of Interest Received Sence last
Report made 4 april 1791   £81 - 7 - 8
Balance then due to yᵉ Selectmen £2-11-3
Cash pᵈ. yᵉ Treasurer pʳ. Sundry
Receipts   78-16-5
                                  ─────   81 - 7 - 8

Interest money now due on yᵉ aforesaid Bonds £74 - 18 - 7
Worcester 19ᵗʰ. Noᵛʳ. 1792   all which is Submitted

               Samuel Flagg   ⎫ Selectmen
               John Chamberlain ⎬   of
               Benjᵃ. Heywood   ⎭ Worcester

Voted that the Selectmen be directed to call for the Interest money that is due on the above mentioned Bonds and if there is any one or more that in their oppinion does not lay secure that they Imeadiately Call for the principle unless there is Sufficient Security given

Voted that this meeting be dissolved and the meeting was Dissolved accordingly

        A True Entry   attest   Daniel Goulding Town Clerk

Worcester Town Records, 1793. 233

Cap.[t] William Gates being appointed by the Selectmen of Worcester November 17.th 1792 Searcher & Packer of Beef & Pork designed for Sale within the Town of Worcester & to Continue for Such for the Term of one year Personally appeared before me and took the Oath to Qualify him for Said office

 1793 January   Daniel Goulding Town Clerk

Pursuant to a Warrant from the Supreme Executive of the Commonwealth of Massachusetts bearing date the 10.th of December A D 1792 The Inhabitants of the Town of Worcester Qualified according to the Constitution to Vote for Representatives to the General Court upon due warning given met together on Monday the fourteenth day of January 1793 for the purpose of giving in their Votes for two Federal Representatives to Congress as the Said Warrant directs—Votes for the following persons were given in counted and Sorted and declaration thereof made in open Town meeting as the Said Warrant provides viz.[t]

For the County of Hampshire	Samuel Lyman	39
	William Lyman	8
Second District	Dwight Foster	41
	Samuel Lyman	8
	Jonathan Grout	1

then the above meeting was Dessolved

 A True Entry   Attest   Daniel Goulding Town Clerk

At a Publick meeting of the Inhabitants of the Town of Worcester Qualified to Vote in Town affairs Legally warned and assembled at the meeting House of the first Parish in Said Town on Monday the 14.th day of January A D 1793

Samuel Flagg Esq.[r] was Chosen Moderator then the following Votes were passed

 Voted that Cap.[t] David Moore be an agent to take care of the

Land mentioned in the Second article in the warrant for this meeting[1]

Voted that Nathaniel Paine Esqr. be an agent to assist Simon Glasgow in obtaining a Pension from the United States on account of the disability which befell him while a Soldier in the Continental Army

Voted that in case the General Court Shall make a Law making this Town the Seat of Government the Lot of Land North of the Town Common that Remains unSold be Granted for the Use of Government for the purpose of Erecting a State House on

Voted to grant a Sum of money to procure a good Fire Engine for the use of the Town

Voted to Choose a Committee to procure a good Fire Engine then Chose Samuel Flagg Esqr., Doct^r. Elijah Dix, & Nathaniel Paine Esqr. a Committee for Said Purpose

Voted to accept the Report of the Selectmen of the Situation of the Town Bonds which Report is aded & Recorded with the doings of the Town meeting held November 19th. 1792

Voted that this Meeting be dissolved and the meeting was Dissolved accordingly

    A True Entry   Attest   Daniel Goulding Town Clerk

At a meeting of the Freeholders and Other Inhabitants of the Town of Worcester Qualified to Vote in Town affairs legally warned and assembled at the Publick meeting house of the first Parish in Worcester on monday the fourth day of march A, D, 1793 then the following persons were Chosen into the Offices Expressed against there Names & the Following Votes passed viz

    Daniel Goulding Town Clerk

---

[1] ARTICLE 2:—"To See if the Town will appoint an agent to take care of the Land lately Set off to its Inhabitants by an Execution against Nathan Patch"

Samuel Flagg Esq[r]. Samuel Curtis Esq[r]. Cap[t]. Samuel Brooks Deacon John Chamberlain Benjamen Heywood Esq[r]. Selectmen

Voted that the Selectmen be overseers of the Poor the Current year

Benjamen Heywood Esq[r]. Town Treasurer

Samuel Flagg Esq[r]. Samuel Curtis Esq[r]. Deacon John Chamberlain Assessors

John Moore 2[d]. & Simeon Duncan Tythingmen

Nathan Heard Sealer of Tanned & Curryed Leather

Joshua Whitney & Benjamen Flagg Ju[r]. Fence Viewers

Samuel Gates & Eli Chapen field Drivers

Ignatius Goulding Elias Mann David Bigelow Surveyors of Boards & Shingles

Simeon Duncan & Nathaniel Flagg Cullers of Hoops & Staves

Robert Smith to Execute the Deer act

Doct[r]. Elijah Dix, Samuel Flagg Esq[r]. M[r]. John Nazro M[r]. John Stanton Fire Wards

M[r]. John Nazro & M[r]. Thomas Payson Clerks of the market

Thomas Sheperd Nathaniel Stowell Abijah Pierce Levy Flagg William Taylor Henery Patch Ezekiel Smith Timothy Johnson Daniel Stearns Hog Reeves

Voted that the Swine be under the Same restrictions the Current year they was the Last year

Noah Harris Tyler Curtis Nathan White Eben[r]. Moore Isaac Willard Thomas Nickels Ju[r]. Thomas Stowell Laben Smith Jason Blake Daniel Heywood 2[d]. Samuel Moore Daniel Goulding William Trobridge Moses Miller Phineas Jones Thomas Wheeler Jonathan Gates 2[d]. Jesse Craige Surveyors of Highways & Collectors of Highway Taxes

Voted that the Sum of three hundred Pounds be levied and assessed on the Poles & Estates in this Town for the purpose of keeping the Publick Roads in repair the Current year

Voted that the Price of Labour Oxen Carts. &c be the Same the Current year at the Heighways that it was the Last year

Worcester Town Records, 1793.

Voted that those Persons that have over worked there Heighway Taxes the Last year be allowed towards there Heighway Taxes this year — and Voted that if there is any Persons that have not worked out there Heighway Taxes the last year that they have liberty of working them out the Current year

Doct^r. Elijah Dix John Nazro Thomas Payson Committee to Settle accounts with the Town Treasurer

Voted that the Committee to Settle accounts with the Town Treasurer make Report of there Doings to the Town

John Nazro James Fisk Edward Knight Simon Gates Thomas Rice Nathaniel Harrington Henery Patch Nathaniel Brooks Simeon Fish John Chamberlain Joshua Harrington Committee to provide the Town with Schooling

Voted that the Sum of two Hundred Pounds be Raised levied & assessed on the Poles & Estates in this Town for the purpose of Supporting Publick Schools the Current year

Voted that the Publick Schools be kept in this Town the current year in the Same way & manner they were the Last year

Voted that Benjamen Heywood Esqr. Deacon John Chamberlain and Nathaniel Paine Esqr. be a Committee in behalf of the Town to prosecute to final Judgment and Execution any Person or persons who have Committed or may hereafter Committ any Trespass on the property of the Town at Mill Stone Hill[1]

Worcester ss. March 4th. 1793 Personally appeared Daniel Goulding and made Solemn Oath to the faithfull discharge of the Duty of Town Clerk for the year ensuing

    Before me   Benjn. Heywood Ju^s. Pacis.

Voted to Choose a Committee to view the Road mentioned in the Ninth article in the Warrant for this meeting Lately Laid out or alteration made between Gouldings & Bairds & if they Suppose

---

[1] ARTICLE 12:—"To See if the Town will at the request of David Chadwick relinquish to him all Claim to Millstone Hill except the prevelege of gitting building Stones or adopt measures to prosecute for any trespasses that have or may be committed on the Same"

that there can be an alteration made for the better that they Petition in behalf of the Town to the Court of General Sessions for a New Committee to be appointed for Said purpose then Chose Capt. Samuel Brooks, Capt. Joshua Whitney, and M^r. Samuel Brazer a Committee for Said Purpose [1]

Voted to Choose a Committee to adopt a method for the appropriation of the Interest money arising from the Towns Bonds now in the hands of the Selectmen agreeable to the 10th article in the Warrant for this meeting then Chose Joseph Allen Esqr., Benjamen Heywood Esqr., & Deacon John Chamberlain a Committee for Said purpose

Voted that the Selectmen be a Committee to Select out of the list they have laid before the Town of Persons Qualified for Jurors one fourth Part to Serve as Jurors at the Supreme Court they then Presented the following Lists and it was then Voted that they Should be put into the Boxes agreeable to Law—

For the Supreme Court

Benjamen Andrews	Stephen Salsbury	Phineas Jones
David Bigelow	Robert Smith	Abraham Lincoln
Samuel Brazer	Benj^a. Stowell	Elias Mann
Samuel Chandler	Hyler Tanner	John Nazro
Samuel Curtis	Leonard Worcester	John Pierce
Noah Harris	Saml. Brooks	John Stanton
Joseph Kingsbury	John Barnard	Charles Stearns
Eben^r. Lovell	Daniel Baird	Isaiah Thomas
James M^{c}farland	John Chamberlain	Thomas Wheeler
John Mower	Daniel Goulding	William Gates
Thomas Payson	Daniel Heywood	

For Court of Common Please

Increase Blair	Simon Gates	Saml. Moore
Joseph Barber	Ignatius Goulding	John Moore

---

[1] ARTICLE 9:—"To See if the Town will take any measures to prevent the Exceptance of the alteration lately laid out in the County roade between Capt. Gouldings and Daniel Bairds"

Worcester Town Records, 1793.

Samuel Bigelow	William Goulding	John Moore 2^d
Thadeas Bigelow	Ruben Gray	Moses Miller
Joseph Ball	Samuel Gates	Eben^r. Mower
Benjamen Bemiss	Samuel Goddard	Thomas Nickels Ju^r.
Benjamen Butman	Jonathan Grout	Byfield Pierce
Nathan Blackman	Jonathan Gates 2^d.	Moses Perry
William Barker	Jonathan Gleason	Josiah Perry
Solomon Bixbee	Jeremiah Hawkins	Henery Patch
David Chadwick	Phineas Heywood	Abel Stowell
Joseph Chadwick	Daniel Heywood 2^d.	Peter Stowell
Gardiner L. Chandler	Abel Heywood	Thomas Stowell
Nathl. Coolidge	Nathan Heard	Thomas Sheperd
Jesse Craige	Jedediah Heley	John Stowers
Tyler Curtis	Asa Hambleton	Elias Stowell
Thadeas Chamberlain	Nathl. Harrington	Daniel Stearns
William Chamberlain	Eben^r. Hastings	Peter Slayter
Daniel Chadwick	Elijah Harrington	John Tatman
Eli Chapen	Joshua Harrington	Willm. Trobridge
Thadeas Chapen	James Haywood	Tim^o. Taft
Saml. Curtis Ju^r.	Stephen Haywood	Joseph Torry
Simeon Duncan	William Johnson	Nathan White
Alph^s. Eaton	Samuel Johnson	John White
Benja Flagg Ju^r.	Samuel Jenison	Daniel Waldo Ju^r.
James Fisk	Wil^m. Jenison	Joseph Wheeler
Josiah Flagg	Edward Knight	Asa Ward
Elijah Flagg	William Knight	Eben^r. Wiswall Ju^r.
Simeon Fish	Samuel Kingston	Amos Wheeler
Nathl. Flagg	Samuel Mahan	Benjamen Whitney Ju^r
David Flagg	Thomas Mower	John Walker
Ezekiel Fowler	Willm. M^{c}farland	

Voted that this meeting be adjourned to monday the first Day of April Next at three OClock in the afternoon then to meet at this Place and the meeting was accordingly adjourned

  A True Entry attest Daniel Goulding Town Clerk

Worcester Town Records, 1793.

At a meeting of the Freeholders and Other Inhabitants of the Town of Worcester Qualified as the Constitution or frame of Government of the Commonwealth prescribes on Monday the first day of april A, D, 1793 for the purpose of Voting agreeable to the Several Articles Contained in the above Warrant then the Votes for the following persons were given in counted & Sorted in open Town meeting viz

For Governour
- His Excellency John Hancock Esq[r]. 31
- Hon[ble] Elbridge Gerry Esq[r]. 31
- Thomas Russell Esq[r]. 1
- Samuel Phillips Esq[r]. 2

For Lieu[t]. Governour
- Hon[ble] Samuel Adams Esq[r]. 42
- Elbridge Gerry Esq[r]. 1
- Samuel Phillips Esq[r]. 5
- Thomas Russell Esq[r]. 6

Hon[ble] Moses Gill Esq[r].	61	Hon[ble] Amos Singletary	1
Hon[ble] Jonathan Warner Esq[r].	46	Josiah Stearns Esq[r].	21
Hon[ble] Samuel Baker	62	Samuel Flagg Esq[r].	15
Hon[ble] Tim[o]. Newhall	40	Martin Kinsley Esq[r].	8
Hon[ble] John Sprague	33	Elijah Brigham Esq[r].	5
Hon[ble] Seth Washburn	5	David Bigelow Esq[r].	1
Hon[ble] Jonathan Grout	7		Senators

Votes for Representatives to Congress

Dwight Foster Esq[r]. 61 } For Representative for
John Sprague Esq[r]. 1 } the Destrict

Samuel Lyman Esq[r]. 58 For the County of Hampshire

Then Chose Samuel Curtis Esq[r]. Moderator

Then M[r]. Samuel Allen had 91 Votes for County Treasurer

Then Voted that this meeting be Dissolved and the meeting was Dissolved accordingly

  A True Entry Attest Daniel Goulding Town Clerk

Worcester ss March 28th. 1793
  Personally appeared Jason Blake and took the Oaths Neces-

sary to qualify him for a Collector of Heighway Taxes and Surveyor of Highways for the year ensuing

    Before me Benjamen Heywood Jus. Pacis
 A True Entry attest Daniel Goulding Town Clerk

At a Town Meeting held in Worcester on Monday the first day of April A, D, 1793 by adjournment from March 4^(th). 1793 the Following Votes were passed viz

Voted that M^(r). John Barnard be Collector of Publick Taxes the Current year he giving Bonds to the Satisfaction of the Selectmen for the faithfull performance of his trust, and that he be allowed the Sum of Fifteen pounds for Collecting the Town & County Taxes & if there is a State Tax he to be allowed Sixpence on the pound for Collecting that

Then Chose M^(r). John Barnard and M^(r). Abel Stowell Constables

Then Chose M^(r). Samuel Rice Hogreeve

Voted that the Report of the Committee respecting the Interest money be put by untill may meeting

Voted that this meeting be Dissolved & the meeting was Dissolved accordingly

 A True Entry Attest Daniel Goulding Town Clerk

Worcester ss. Personally appeared Benjamen Heywood Esq^(r)., John Moore 2^(d). Elias Mann, John Nazro, Thomas Payson, Thomas Sheperd, Henery Patch, Ezekiel Smith, Samuel Rice, Noah Harris, Tyler Curtis, Isaac Willard, Laben Smith, Jesse Craige, John Barnard, and Abel Stowell and took the Oaths Necessary to Qualify them for the Several offices to which they were chosen at a meeting in march last and this Day

Worcester April 1^(st). 1793
    Before me Daniel Goulding Town Clerk

Personally appeared Samuel Curtis Esqr., Samuel Flagg Esqr., and Deacon John Chamberlain, and took the Oath to Qualify them for the office of assessors they being Chosen at the annual meeting in march last
Worcester May 13th. 1793
      Before me Daniel Goulding Town Clerk

Personally appeared Phineas Jones, Nathan White, Jonathan Gates, 2^d. Ebenezer Mower, Moses Miller, William Trobridge, Samuel Moore, Daniel Heywood 2^d, Thomas Nickels Ju^r., Thomas Stowel & Thomas Wheeler & took the Oaths Necessary to Qualify them for the Offices of Heighway Collectors & Heighway Surveyors for which offices they were Chosen at a meeting in March last
      Before me Daniel Goulding Town Clerk
Worcester May 13th. 1793

         Worcester may 30th. 1793
This may Certify that Daniel Stearns being Chosen a Hogreve for the Town of Worcester for the Current year made Oath that he would faithfully perform the Duties of Said office
    Before me   EDW Bangs Jus Pacis
   A True Entry Daniel Goulding Town Clerk

At a Meeting of the Freeholders and Other Inhabitants of the Town of Worcester Qualifyed to vote for Representatives at the Publick meeting House of the first Parish in Worcester on Monday the thirteenth day of may A. D. 1793

Samuel Flagg Esqr. was Chosen to Represent this Town in the Great & General Court the Current year
  A True Entry attest Daniel Goulding Town Clerk

At a meeting of the Freeholders and other Inhabitants Quallified to Vote in Town affairs on Monday the thirteenth day of may A, D, 1793 at the Publick meeting House of the first Parish in Worcester

Samuel Flagg Esq'. was Chosen Moderator

It was moved and Seconded that the Interest money arising from the Towns Bonds be equally divided between the two Clergymen in this Town the motion was then put and passed in the affirmative

The house was divided & there was 37 against the motion & 39 for it

Voted that this meeting be adjourned to the first monday in June Next at four OClock in the afternoon then to meet at this place & the meeting was accordingly adjourned

A True Entry   attest   Daniel Goulding Town Clerk

At a Town meeting on Monday June the third day A, D, 1793 by adjournment of a meeting held in Worcester on may 13th. A, D, 1793

Chose Benjamen Heywood Esq'. Moderator Pro Tem

Then Voted that the Vote passed at the Town meeting held on the thirteenth day of may last Respecting the Interest arising from the Towns Bonds be Reconsidered

Voted that this meeting be Dissolved and the meeting was Dissolved accordingly

A True Entry   attest   Daniel Goulding Town Clerk

At a meeting of the Freeholders & Other Inhabitants of the Town of Worcester Qualified to Vote in Town affairs legally warned & assembled at the meeting House of the first Parish in Said Town on monday the twelvth day of august A, D, 1793 the Following Voters were passed viz

Chose Samuel Flagg Esq'. moderator

Voted to Choose one person for an agent to make application to the Court of General Sessions of the Peace in behalf of the

Town of Worcester for the further Support of Susanna Smith wife of Capt. Elisha Smith, and for the repayment of the monies already expended by the Selectmen for that purpose, then Chose Benjamen Heywood Esqr. an agent for Said purpose

Voted to Choose one person for an agent to prosecute and defent to final Judgement & Execution any Suits that may be brought for or against the Town of Worcester, then Chose Benjamen Heywood Esqr. an agent for Said purpose

Voted that this meeting be disolved, & it was disolved accordingly

A True Entry Attest   Daniel Goulding Town Clerk

At a Town meeting legally assembled at the Publick meeting House of the first Parish in Worcester on monday the Twenty first day of October A D 1793 for the Purpose of acting on the Several articles contained in the Warrant for Said meeting then the Following Votes were passed vizt.

Chose Samuel Flagg Esqr. Moderator

Voted to Choose a Committee to Examine the accounts brought against the Town at this meeting and make Report to the Town then Chose Samuel Flagg Esqr. Benjamen Heywood Esqr. and Capt. Nathaniel Brooks a Committee for Said purpose

Voted that M^r. Samuel Brazer be desired to Collect the Tools mentioned in the Sixth article in the Warrant[1] and bring them to this Place at the adjournment of this meeting and that they then be Sold at Publick Vendue

Voted that Benjamen Heywood Esqr. be an agent in behalf of the Town to make and Execute a Quit Claim deed of the Land Lately Set of by Ex^n. against Nathan Patch in Favour of Said Town being a Part of the Real Estate of Said Nathan Patch

Voted to Choose a Committee to take into Consideration the

---

[1] "Entrenching Tools now in the possession of M^r. Stephen Salsbury and others."

Rent of the Ground where Samuel Flagg Esqr. Store Stands & make Report at the adjournment then Chose M^r. Robert Smith Capt. Joel How & Benjn. Heywood a Committee for S^d. purpose

Voted to Choose a Committee to view and measure the new proposed Road mentioned in the Eighth article in the Warrant[1] and make report to the Town then Chose Deacon David Bigelow, Capt. Nathaniel Brooks, Capt. John Perce, M^r. Robert Smith, and Capt. Joel How, a Committee for S^d. Purpose

Voted to Choose a Committee to ascertain the Cost of a House convenient to hold the Fire Engine and Herse and ascertain a proper Place for S^d. House then Chose Benjamen Heywood Esqr. M^r. William Trobridge and Samuel Flagg Esqr. a Committee for Said Purpose

Voted to accept the report of the Committee Chose Some Time past to petition to the Court of General Sessions of the Peace which report is as Follows vizt.

The Committee Chosen to Petition to the Honourable Court of Sessions to alter the Road laid out by their Committee from Capt. Daniel Goulding^s to M^r. Daniel Bairds beg leave to report that they have attended that Service and the honourable Court ordered the report of their Committee recommited, the petitioners paying the expence

Which expence is as follows Capt. Samuel Brooks One pound Nine Shillings and four pence   Samuel Brazer one Pound Ten Shillings, as by Receipts   Samuel Brooks
Worcester Octr. 21st. 1793   Samuel Brazer

Voted that this meeting be adjourned to Monday the fourth day of November Next at One OClock in the afternoon then to meet at this Place & the meeting was accordingly adjourned

    A True Entry   attest   Daniel Goulding Town Clerk

---

[1] ARTICLE 8 :—"To See if the Town will take any measures to prevent ye. Laying out of a new County Road through the Land of Joseph Kingsbury and Others agreeably to the Petition of Ezra Beaman Esqr. and Others"

Worcester Town Records, 1793.

At a Town meeting held at the Publick meeting House of the first Parish in Worcester on Monday the fourth day of November A, D, by adjournment from the Twenty first Day of October Last the following Votes were passed vizt.

Voted to accept the Report of the Committee Chose to Examine the Demands brought against the Town and make Report which report is as follows

The Committee appointed by the Town of Worcester at their meeting held on monday the 21st. day of October 1793 to examine accounts exhibited against the Town, ask leave to Report that they have examined the following acc^{ts} due to y^e. following persons for ye Towns allowance & payment vizt.

N°.		£ s d
1	to Capt. Samuel Brooks for Sundreys Supplied Simon Glasgow	£ 4 ,, 3 .. 11
2	to Deacon John Chamberlain for Supporting & Cloathing Nathan Houghton and Jenny Dyer 52 weeks at 6/ ending the 15 day of October 1793	15 ,, 12 ,, 0
3	To Ditto for cash paid Abel Johnson in full for bringing Zac Johnson one of y^e. Towns poor from Dumerston in the State of Vermont	0 ,, 12 ,, 0
4	To Ditto for Sundries Samuel Dennys Family	4 ,, 3 ,, 3
5	To Nathan White for 104 feet of Timber for Bridge by Mowers	0 ,, 17 ,, 4
6	To John Elder for Boarding John Spence from 5 Novr. 1792 to 22^d Octr. 1793 and making him two Shirts	8 ,, 4 ,, 0
7	To Isaac Chadwick for making a pair Stocks for ye Town & finding Lock and hinges	0 ,, 12 ,, 0
8	To John Perce for Surveying the Road to Danl. Bairds	0 ,, 6 ,, 8
9	To Nathl. Moore for Pork Supplyed Simon G[l]asgow	0 ,, 7 ,, 3
10	To William Trobridge for 275 feet of Bridge Plank	1 ,, 4 ,, 0

11	To John Stanton for Sundries d^d. Daniel Goulding & John Elder for Clothing Jno. Spence and William Tracys Children Towns poor	1,,13,, 8
12	To Joel Bixbee for 538 feet of 3 Inch Yellow Pine Plank for the Bridge	2,, 8,, 5
13	To Willm. Taylor for Boarding and Cloathing anna White from 2^d. No^v. 1792 to 2^d. No^{vr}. 1793 being 52 weeks at 3/6 p^r. Week	9,, 2,, 0
14	To Jesse Taft for Boarding Thomas Gleasons Child from 6 Dec^m. 1792 to 20th. April 1793 being 19 weeks at 2/	1,,18,, 0
15	To Samuel Flagg for Sundry Supplies to Simon Glasgow in 1792 & 1793 38/10 and Grain for Samuel Denny in may last 9/	2,, 8,,10
16	To the assessors for making Taxes and preparing Valuation y^e. present year & Recording the Same	8,,11,, 9
17	To Doct^r. Jno. Green Ju^r. for medicine and attendance on William Tracys Famely £4,,18,, 8	
	Ditto for Ditto for Simon Glasgow 6,, 7,,10	
	Ditto for Ditto for Thos Gleazen & Famely 3,,10,, 6	
	£14,,17,, 0	
	Deduct what the Town paid for Doctering Thomas Whayland more than was allowed by y^e. General Court 5,, 0,, 4	
		9,,16,, 8
18	To the Estate of Tim^o. Paine Esqr. Dec^d. a Ballance as appears by Settlement on file to be recorded	0,,11,, 8
19	To C & S Chandler for Trimings for ye Clerks desk	0,,10,, 4
20	To Thomas Shepperd for painting Said Desk	0,,18,, 0

Worcester Town Records, 1793.

21	To Gard^r. L. Chandler for eight String pieces for Trobridges Bridge	1,, 0,, 0
22	To Danl. Goulding for Supporting Willm. Tracys famely from No^v. 1792 to 4 No^v. 1793	18,, 5,, 9½
22	To Ditto paid for Labour and Stones and Boarding men at the new Bridge	9,, 8,, 10½
23	To Deacon Thomas Wheeler for work and Stones at the Said new Bridge	4,, 4,, 0
24	To Eben^r. Williams for work at Said Bridge	1,, 4,, 9
25	To Levi Flagg for Labour at Said Bridge	1,, 7,, 0
26	To Silas Gleazen for Covering Stones and Other Stones for Said Bridge	5,, 0,, 0
27	To Thomas W. Millet for Labour done at Said Bridge	0,, 19,, 6
28	To William Sever for Carrying on & Defending the Suit of Nathan Patch vs the Town together with disbursements in Said action	6,, 11,, 8
29	To Micah Johnson Ju^r. for 383 Feet of Bridge Plank delivered in ye years 1790 1792 & 1793	1,, 10,, 8
30	To Benj^a Heywood as agent for the Town for Time & expences in defending ye action brought against y^e. Town by Nathan Patch	6,, 13,, 0

£130,, 6,, 0

Worcester 4th. November 1793

all which is Submitted by   Samuel Flagg
                                       Benj^a. Heywood } Committee
                                       Nathl. Brooks

Voted to allow to Doct^r. Elijah Dix the Ballance of his account for Labour and Stuf for the Bridge near M^r. Salsburys being

£16,, 2,, 6½

Voted that the Town Treasurer pay the demands brought against the Town at this meeting and allowed out of the money in his hands the property of the Town

Voted that the Town Treasurer pay for the fire Engine when delivered and the Damage allowed to Sundrey Persons by the General Sessions of the Peace for the alteration in the Road leading from the South meeting House to M^r. Daniel Bairds, out of the money in his hands

Voted to accept the Report of the Committee Chose to view & measure the new proposed road by M^r. Kingsburys which is as follows vizt.

Pursuant to a Vote of the Town of the Twenty first of October last, We your Committee agreeable to the 8th. article in the Warrant have attended Said business, and beg leave to report as follows Viz Upon an accurate measurement of both Roads we find the new proposed road to be Seventy Nine rods the Shortest, and it is the oppinion of your Committee the new proposed Road will be attended with great expence and is unnecessary

Worcester No^{vr}. 4th 1793

David Bigelow
Nathl. Brooks
Jno. Peirce } Committee
Robert Smith
Joel How

Voted to Choose an agent to oppose the laying out of the New proposed Road by M^r. Kingsburys & Lieu^t. Pierces & that if he thinks proper to employ an attorney at the expence of the Town then chose Samuel Flagg Esqr. an agent for Said purpose

Worcester ss November 4th. 1793

I hereby Certify, that at a Court of General Sessions of the peace held at Worcester, at August term 1793 the Sums herein after mentioned were ordered to be paid by the Town of Worcester to the following persons respectively, being in full of the Damages they Severally sustained by the alteration of the Heighway from Worcester Meeting house to Sutton Town line

viz	to Benjamen Heywood Esqr	£ 2 .. 8 .. 0
	to Elijah Harrington	16 .. 0 .. 0
	to Jacob Holmes	25 .. 0 .. 0
	to Silas Harrington	9 — —
	to Benjamin Lathe	15 — —
		67 .. 8 —

Attest   Jos Allen Cler

Voted to accept the Report of the Committee Chose to Settle accounts with the Town Treasurer which report is as follows vizt.

The account of Benjamin Heywood Treasurer of the Town of Worcester, who Credits the Inhabitants of Said Town by Sundrey Sums as follows (viz)

1792 No^v. 19th By the Ballance due to the Town brought from his last account settled this day £574,, 8,, 2

By Cash Rec^d. of the Committee for Sale of lands at Wigwam Hill 8,,—

Dec^m. 6 By the assessors Return of a Town Tax committed to John Barnard to Collect 332,, 12,, 1

31 By Cash rec^d. of Dea^n. John Chamberlain p^r my Rec^t. of this date being Interest money arising on obligations for money due to the Town in the hands of the Selectmen 58,, 13,, 8

1793 Jan^u. 8 By Cash rec^d. of John Childs Esqr. being a Fine by him imposed for profane cursing & Swearing 4,,—

April 29 By Ditto Rec^d. of the Selectmen p^r. Rec^d. on account of the Support of Thos Whayland & Temp^l. Comins 14,, 19,, 10

June 18 By Ditto of Ditto p^r. Deacon John Chamberlain and gave a Rec^t. being on Town Bonds in there hands 3,, 16,, 2½

29 By Ditto of Ditto p^r. Rec^t. on acc^t. of the Support of Thos Whayland and Temp^{le} Comins 8. 11,, 4

By one years Interest on two thirds of 292,, 16,, 3 Rec^d. of the Treas^r of the Commonwealth 11,, 14,, 3

By four months Interest on one third of of 292,, 16,, 3 Rec^d. of Ditto 1,, 19,, 0½

Sep^t. 11th. By Sundry Obligations on Interest received of Nathan Patch being the Redemption of his land Set of by Ex^n. in favour of the Town Octr. 1792 200,, 5,, 8

1207,, 12,, 3

Worcester Town Records, 1793.

1792 And the Said accountant chargeth the Said Inhabitants with Sundry payments by him made as p^r. Receipts for which he requests allowance————vizt.

Octr. 26 N. 1. to Cash p^d. John
  Nazro p^r. order of Selectmen £3 ,, 8 - 0
 2 to Cash p^d. Benj^a. Stowell p^r.
  Ditto   3 ,, 0 ,, 3
 3 to Ditto p^r. Ditto — p^r. Ditto   2 ,, 10 ,, 0
31 4 to Ditto Deacon John Chamberlain p^r. D^o 18 ,, 0 ,, 6
 5 to Ditto Capt. Daniel Goulding
  p^r. D^o 19 ,, 16 ,, 10
1793 Jany. 2^d. 6 to Ditto John Elder
  p^r. Ditto   9 ,, 2 ,, 1
7 7 to Ditto p^d. Doct^r. Elijah
  Dix p^r. Order of assessors   0 ,, 9 ,, 0
 8 to Ditto p^d. Ditto p^r. Order of
  Selectmen   1 ,, 8 ,, 7½
 9 to Ditto p^d. Ditto p^r. — Ditto 12 ,, 1 ,, 8½
10 to Ditto p^d. Ditto p^r. — Ditto   3 ,, 10 ,, 2
11 to Ditto p^d. Capt. Samuel
  Brooks p^r. Ditto   5 ,, 17 ,, 6½
12 to Ditto p^d. Hon Tim^o. Paine
  Esqr. p^r. Ditto   0 ,, 8 ,, 0
13 to Ditto p^d. Jesse Craige p^r.
  order of assessors   0 ,, 2 ,, 3
14 to D$^{o\cdot}$ p^d. John Barnard p^r.
  Order of Selectmen   1 ,, 0 ,, 0
15 to D^o. p^d. John Chamberlain
  p^r. Di^{t}to   3 ,, 12 ,, 0
16 to D^o. p^d. Col Eben^r. Lovell
  p^r. Ditto   2 ,, 8 ,, 6
17 to D^o. p^d. Samuel Flagg Esqr.
  p^r. Ditto   5 ,, 8 ,, 9
18 to D^o. p^d. Isaiah Thomas p^r.
  Ditto   2 ,, 2 ,, 0
19 to D^o. p^d. Ditto p^r. order of
  assessors   3 ,, 12 ,, 7
23 20 to D^o. p^d. D^n. Nath^n. Perry
  p^r. order of Selectmen   10 ,, 8 ,, 4

21 to D⁰. p̃ᵈ. Rebeckah Bill pʳ.
    Ditto   0 „ 15 „ 0
1793 Janᵘ. 23
22 to Ditto paid School Committee
    pʳ. order of Sellectmen   200 „ 0 „ 0
23 to Ditto paid Selectmen for
    Support of the Grammer School 30 „ 0 „ 0
24 to Ditto p̃ᵈ. James Quigly pʳ.
    order of Selectmen   5 „ 4 „ 0
April 8ᵗʰ 25 to D⁰. p̃ᵈ. Thaᵈ. &
    Wᵐ. Maccarty pʳ. Bond given
    by Nathan Perry former Treas-
    urer   97 „ 15 „ 8
June 4 26 to Ditto p̃ᵈ. Lowis Smith
    pʳ. order of Selectmen   1 „ 4 „ 0
27 to Ditto p̃ᵈ. Benjamen Hey-
    wood pʳ. Ditto   16 „ 11 „ 6
July 3ᵈ. 28 to Ditto p̃ᵈ. Lowis
    Smith pʳ. D₀.   1 „ 10 „ 0
29ᵗʰ. 29 to Ditto p̃ᵈ. Eli Gale
    pʳ. D₀.   13 „ 19 „ 9
August 15ᵗʰ. 30 to Ditto p̃ᵈ. Danˡ.
    Baird pʳ. order of assessors   0 „ 3 „ 9
Sepᵗ. 9 31 to Ditto p̃ᵈ. Lowis Smith
    pʳ. order of Selectmen   1 „ 10 „ 0
Octʳ. 32 to Ditto p̃ᵈ. Daniel
    Goulding pʳ. D⁰.   1 „ 15 „ 3
33 to Ditto p̃ᵈ. Moses Miller pʳ. D⁰ 2 „ 5 „ 0
34 to Ditto p̃ᵈ. Abel Stowel pʳ. D⁰   0 „ 5 „ 7½
35 to Ditto p̃ᵈ. Simon Gates pʳ. D⁰   0 „ 5 „ 4
36 to Ditto p̃ᵈ. Samuel Curtis Esqʳ.
    pʳ. Ditto   3 „ 12 „ 0
37 to Ditto p̃ᵈ. John Elder pʳ.
    Ditto   0 „ 8 „ 0
38 to Ditto p̃ᵈ. Jedʰ. Heley pʳ.
    Ditto   0 „ 4 „ 0
39 to Ditto p̃ᵈ. Thos Rice pʳ. Ditto 1 „ 6 „ 3
40 to Ditto p̃ᵈ. Thoˢ. Wheeler pʳ.
    Ditto   0 „ 7 „ 0

41	to Ditto p^d. Danl. Waldo & Son pr. Ditto	2 ,, 8 ,, 4	
42	to Ditto p^d. David Griggs pr. Ditto	0 ,, 8 ,, 0	
43	to Ditto p^d. Willm. Treadwill pr. Ditto	3 ,, 7 ,, 2	
44	to Ditto p^d. Capt. Joel How pr. Ditto	0 ,, 12 ,, 0	
45	to Ditto p^d. Simeon Duncan pr. Ditto	1 ,, 6 ,, 6	
46	to D^o. p^d. Col Phineas Jones pr. order of assessors	0 ,, 5 .. 11	
47	to Ditto p^d. John Tatman pr. Ditto	0 ,, 3 ,, 9	
Octr. 31 48	to Ditto p^d. Lowis Smith pr. Order Selectmen	1 ,, 10 ,, 0	497 ,, 10 ,, 11

Ballance due to the Town further to be accounted for   £710 ,, 1 ,, 4
  Errors Excepted Benj^a. Heywood

Worcester No^v. 4 1793

We the Subscribers being a Major part of the Committee appointed by the Town of Worcester to examine and adjust the accounts with Benj^a. Heywood Esqr. Treasurer of S^d. Town — Beg leave to report that he has charged himself with the Sum of Twelve Hundred & Seven pounds twelve Shillings & three pence & has paid out by Orders from the Selectmen &c & by discharging a Bond given by the former Treasurer the Sum of four Hundred & Ninety Seven pounds ten Shillings & Eleven pence which leaves a ballance of Seven Hundred & Ten pounds one Shilling & four pence due to the Town which the S^d. Treasurer is further to ac^t. for   all which is Submitted by us

        Elijah Dix
        Thos Payson

Voted that the List M^r. John Barnard Collector Lays before the Town at this time for abatement be abated and if it is ever hereafter in his power to Collect all or any part of them that [he] does it and be accountable to the Town for What ever he Collects which list is as follows viz

M^r. John Barnard applies for an abatement of Sundrey persons Taxes for 1789 vizt.

Silas Bardwell out of Town before the Tax was delivered	£ 0,, 6,,	0
Joseph Browning gone before Tax was made	0,, 4,,	0
Thad^s. Brown was Committed to Goal & let out on letter of licence	0,, 19,,	0
Benj^a. Converse one of the poor of Leicester	0,, 7,,	11
James Campbell poor Foriner	0,, 6,,	3
Winthrop Chandler poor & Deceased Insolvent	0,, 18,,	9
Luke Duffe Lame and Swipsey	0,, 6,,	3
Jeffrey Hemenway poor	0,, 6,,	3
Barnabas Jrom a Transcient person and ran away	0,, 6,,	3
Joseph King very Lame & poor	0,, 6,,	3
Jack Mansey or Melvin poor Negro	0,, 2,,	3
John Milline a Stranger and very poor	0,, 2,,	3
William Ramsey a Stranger a Soldier to ye Ohio	0,, 6,,	3
Solomon Smith Dec^d. and left a poor Widow	0,, 6,,	3
John Sikes a poor Dutchman a thief & ran away	0,, 6,,	3
Thomas Tracy a poor man & a Family to Support	0,, 2,,	3
Willard Wheelock gone to New York befor Tax was made	0,, 6,,	3
Cato Worthington a Negro thief and ran away	0,, 6,,	3
Joseph Wheelock poor he & his wife Sick	0,, 6,,	3
Benj^a. Fuller gone befor Tax made	0,, 6,,	3
For 1790 John Brown gone to new York befor Tax made	0,, 6,,	0
Thad^s. Brown gone to New York befor Tax made no Estate	0,, 15,,	0
John Brooks Went to Vermont before Tax was made	0,, 6,,	0
Joshua Davis lived with man and ran away	0,, 6,,	0
Elisha Dunham poor and ran away	0,, 6,,	0
Ezra Estabrook a minor Taxed in Holden	0,, 6,,	0
Samuel Green at Providence before Tax made	0,, 6,,	0
Barth Hutchinson a minor did not belong to Town	0,, 6,,	0

Worcester Town Records, 1793.

Lansing Morse p{d}. at Leicester and produced Receipt	0,, 6,, 0
Frances Newton was out of Town before 1 of may	0,, 6,, 0
Ithamer Smith very poor and Family to Support	0,, 6,, 0
Thomas Tracy poor and a Family	0,, 6,, 0
Joseph Woodward left Town and went to New York	0,, 6,, 0
William W Woodward Same	0,, 6,, 0
Willard Wheelock Same	0,, 6,, 0
Joseph Wheelock very poor & a Family	0,, 6,, 0
Newton Adams out of the State	0,, 6,, 0
1791 Abel Blakeley ran away	0,, 5,, 11
Samuel Denny Ju{r}. for 1790 and for 1791 poor	0,, 11,, 11
Elisha Dunham poor and ran away	0,, 5,, 11
Thomas S Eayas a Madman gone to Boston	0,, 12,, 3
Nathl. Harwood a Minor paid at Leicester	0,, 5,, 11
John Hair very poor and a Family	0,, 5,, 11
Thomas Knight Sick and did not improve the farm	0,, 4,, 0
Frances Newton gone the year before the Tax was made	0,, 5,, 11
John Nickols gone ye year before	0,, 7,, 5
James Osburn paid at Danvers produced Receipt	0,, 5,, 11
Henery Pratt lived with man and ran away	0,, 5,, 11
Thomas Tracy poor as before	0,, 5,, 11
Prince Trueman poor Negro & Dec{d}.	0,, 5,, 11
Joseph Wheelock poor and a Family	0,, 6,, 8
John Woodward poor and a Family	0,, 5,, 11
	18,, 10,, 2

Voted that this meeting be adjourned to monday the Twenty fifth day of this present month of November at One OClock in the afternoon then to meet at this place the meeting was then accordingly adjourned

   A True Entry   attest   Daniel Goulding Town Clerk

Met according to the above adjournment November 25th. 1793
Chose Samuel Curtis Esqr. Moderator Pro Tem

Voted that their be Built at the Expence of the Town a House Convenient to hold the Town fire Engine & Herse and that Said House be Set at the South East end of the Gun House then Chose Doct^r. Elijah Dix M^r. John Barnard & M^r. Samuel Brazer a Committee to See that Said House is built

Voted to allow John Elder his account exhibited at this time for Cloathing John Spence being } £ 2,,5,,4

Voted to Choose One other agent to act with Samuel Flagg Esqr. in opposing the laying out of the New proposed Road by M^r. Kingsburys & Lieu^t. Peirces then Chose Benjamen Heywood Esqr. an agent for Said purpose

Voted to acept the report of the Situation of the Towns Bonds which report is as Follows vizt.

Report of ye Selectmen Shewing the Situation of y^e. Town Bonds—

Reuben Lambs Bond Dated September 1st 171 for   £42 ,, 3 ,, 4
    John Heart & Levi Eddy Sureties   Interest paid up

Paul Gates Bond dated 15 February 1785 for   35 ,, 0 ,, 0
    William Gates & William Mahan Sureties   one years Interest due

Joseph Allens Bond dated 30 August 1784 for   34 - 11 - 1
    Elijah Dix & Samuel Allen Sureties   one years Interest due

Eben^r. Hastings Bond dated 5 January 1792 for   90 - 4 - 6
    William & Samuel Gates Sureties   Interest paid up

Phineas Wards Bond dated 1 November 1773 for   22 - 15 —
    Samuel Curtis & David Ritchardson Sureties   Interest paid up

Samuel Browns Bond dated 21 July 1783 for   39 - 5 —
    Elijah Dix & Lemuel Rice Sureties   four years Interest due

Jesse Tafts Bond dated 21 July 1786 for   39 - 5 —
    Josiah Lyon & Joseph Barber Sureties   one years Interest due

Oliver Watson Ju^r. Bond dated 28 march 1785 for   83 - 6 - 8
    Oliver Watson & William M^cfarland Sureties   Interest paid

William Gates Bond dated 1 November 1789 for   15 - 11 - 2

Thomas Wheeler & Nath[l]. Harrington Sureties one years Interest due

Elias Manns Bond dated 1 November 1792 for 20 ———
Daniel Heywood & Jed Heley Sureties one years Interest due

Zebulon Cuttings Bond dated 3[d]. September 1790 for 50 ———
Peter Johnson & Jacob Holmes Sureties two years Interest due

Simeon Duncans Bond dated 15 February 1785 for 40 ———
Joseph Allen & Joseph Blair Sureties one years Interest due

Ignatius Gouldings Bond dated 5 January 1792 for 95 - 14 —
Daniel Goulding & Daniel Heywood Sureties one years Interest due

John Chamberlains bond dated 20 may 1790 for 101 ———
Ignatius Goulding & Dan[l] Goulding Sureties one years Interest due

David Bigelows Bond dated 1 November 1782 for 35 - 16 - 8
John Green Surety one years Interest due

Alpheas Eatons Bond dated 15 Fe[b]. 1792 for 36 - 10
W[m]. Eaton & Sam[l]. Flagg Sureties one years Interest due

John Barnards Bond dated 5 Jan[u]. 1792 for 48 - 9 - 6
Benj[a]. Stowell & Ephraim Mower Sureties one Years Interest due

Daniel Gouldings Bond dated 15th Fe[b]. 1785 for 48 - 10 - 0
Palmer Goulding & Ignatius Goulding Sureties one years Interest due

John Stanton & Daniel Gouldings Bond dated 10 march 1784 for 35 ———
Palmer Goulding Surety one Years Interest due

Samuel Brooks Bond dated 30 April 1792 for 23 - 10 —
Benj[a]. Stowel & David Bigelow Sureties Interest paid up

Levi Lincolns Bond dated 15 Feb[y]. 1785 for 51 - 10 —
Joseph Allen & Ignatius Goulding Sureties two years Interest due

John Goulds Bond dated 24 January 1791 for 33 - 6 - 8
John Taylor & Holl[y] Taylor Sureties one yearsInterest due

Leonard Worcester[s] Bond dated 13 August 1793 for 33 ———
Nathan Patch & Theop[s]. Wheeler Sureties no Interest due

Ignatius Gouldings Bond dated 27 No^v. 1786 for   42 - 10 —
  John Chamberlain & Daniel Goulding Sureties   two years Interest due
John Stanton & Daniel Gouldings Bond dated 27 No^v. 1786 for
                                                                19 - 10 —
  Palmer Goulding Surety   Seven Years Interest due
Joseph Patchs Bond dated 11 Septr. 1793 for   143 ————
  Benj^e. & Aaron Flagg Sureties   no Interest due
Henery Patch^s. Bond dated 11 September 1793 for   52 - 10 —
  Nathan Patch & Eli Chapen Sureties   no Interest due
Abel Stowels Bond dated 7 may 1792 for   26 - 14 - 7
  Cornelius & Thos Stowell Sureties   one years Interest due
William Gouldings Bond dated 7 may 1792 for   14 - 10 —
  Igna^s. Goulding & W^m. Johnson Sureties   one years Interest due
Igna^s· Gouldings Bond dated 27 No^v. 1792 for   20 - 9 —
  Willm. Goulding & Willm. Johnson Sureties   one Years Interest due

Samuel Flaggs Lease of Store Ground Rent paid up

  Amount of Interest money Received & p^d. into y^e. Treasury Sence the last Report   62 - 9 - 10½
  In the hands of y^e. Selectmen to be paid into the Treasury imediately   31 - 5 —

Worcester 4 No^v. 1793

  Saml. Flagg, Saml. Brooks John Chamberlain
                              Selectmen of Worcester

Voted that the Bonds the property of the Town be all renewed and dated the first of December & that the Selectmen be impowered to transact the Business

Voted that Samuel Flagg Esqr. pays for the rent of the Ground where his Store Stands the Sum of three pounds twelve Shillings p^r. Year and no more during the pleasure of the Town agreeable to a Verbel report of a Committee Chose to consider of the Said Ground rent

Voted that this meeting be dissolved and the meeting was dissolved accordingly

         A True Entry   attest   Daniel Goulding Town Clerk

Worcester Town Records, 1794.

At a Town meeting Legally warned and assembled at the Publick meeting House of the first parish in Worcester on monday the Twenty fifth day of November A, D, 1793

then Samuel Curtis was Chosen Moderator

A motion being made and Seconded to See if the Town would direct the money granted in march last for the Support of Schools the Current year together with the last Granted State & County Taxes to be paid out of the debts and money now in the hands of the Town Treasurer agreeable to the Second article in the warrant for this meeting the motion being put passed in the affirmative

Voted then that the above Vote be reconsidered

Voted then that the County Tax last granted be paid out of the debts & money now in the Treasurers hands

Voted that this meeting be disolved & it was disolved accordingly

 A True Entry attest Daniel Goulding Town Clerk

At a meeting of the Freeholders and other Inhabitants of the Town of Worcester Qualified to Vote in Town affairs legally warned and assembled at the publick meeting house of the first Parish in Said Town on monday the third day of march A, D, 1794 the the following Votes were passed & the following persons were Chosen into the Offices expressed against there respective Names (viz)

Chose Deacon John Chamberlain Moderator

Daniel Goulding Town Clerk

Voted to Choose five Selectmen

Samuel Flagg Esqr. Samuel Curtis Esqr. Deacon John Chamberlain Benjamen Heywood Esqr. Nathaniel Paine Esqr. Selectmen

Voted that the Selectmen be overseers of the Poor the Current year

Worcester Town Records, 1794. 259

Voted to Choose three assessors for the Current year
Samuel Flagg Esqr. Samuel Curtis Esqr. Deacon John Chamberlain assessors

Benjamen Heywood Esqr. Town Treasurer

Eli Gale & Charles Stearns Tythingmen

Nathan Heard Searcher & Sealer of leather

Joshua Whitney & Elijah Flagg Fence Viewers

Joseph Kingsbury & Joel How field Drivers

Simeon Duncan & Nathaniel Flagg Cullers of Hoops & Staves

David Bigelow Elias Mann & Ignatius Goulding Surveyors of Lumber meaning Boards & Shingles &c

David Bigelow & Jesse Craige Deer Reeves

Joseph Allen Samuel Flagg John Stanton Abraham Lincoln Fire Wards

Daniel Heywood & Ephraim Mower Clerk of the market

Abraham Lincoln Ephraim Brooks Jonathan Lovell Ju^r. Ebenezer Williams Joseph Bigelow Timothy Taft Amos Whitney William Moore Daniel Baird Ju^r. Joel Bixby Hog Reeves

Voted that the Swine be under the Same restrictions the Current year in this Town they were the two last years

Voted that this meeting be adjourned to two OClock this afternoon then to meet at this Place and the meeting was accordingly adjourned

    A True Entry   attest   Daniel Goulding Town Clerk

At a Town meeting held on Monday the third day of March A D 1794 at two OClock in the afternoon by adjournment of a meeting held in the forepart of the Same day then the following Votes were passed & the following persons Chosen into the offices expressed against there respective Names (viz)

Noah Harris John Barnard Samuel Curtis Joel How Nathaniel Stowell Thadeas Chamberlain James Barber Benjamen Thaxter

Daniel Baird Abijah Peirce Silas Harrington Ephraim Mower William Chamberlain Nathaniel Harrington Luke Rice Jedediah Heley Surveyors of Highways & Collectors of Highway Taxes

Voted that the Sum of three hundred Pounds be assessed on the poles & Estates in this Town and raised for the purpose of keeping the Publick Roads in repair the Current year

Voted that the Same wages be allowed for labour of men Oxen Carts Plows &c as was the last year

Voted that those that have over worked there last years Taxes be allowed what they have over worked towards the present years Tax —— — and

those that have not worked there Highway Taxes out have liberty of Working out the Same provided they do it by the first of June Next

Voted that the Sum of two hundred pounds be assessed on the poles & Estates in this Town & raised for the purpose of Supplying the Town with Schooling the Current year and that the Same be expended in the Same way and manner it was the last year

Voted that the School committee take the Number to divide the money by on the first day of November Next

Nathan Heard John Barnard Ebenezer Willington Ju^r. Asa Ward Benjamen Heywood Samuel Gates Eli Chapen David Chadwick Benjamen Thaxter James M^{c}farland Joshua Harrington School Committee

Nathaniel Paine Esqr. M^r. Saml. Chandler Samuel Flagg Esqr. Committee to Settle with the Town Treasurer

Voted to Choose an agent to prosecute and defend to final Judgment and Exc^n any Suit or Suits at law that may be brought for or against the Town of Worcester then Chose Benjamen Heywood Esqr. an agent for Said purposes

Voted that one Shilling be paid by the Treasurer of the Town of Worcester as a bounty for Each & every Crows head delivered to him by any inhabitant of the Said Town within one year he certifying the Same was killed within Said Town

Voted that M^r. William Mahan be Collector of publick Taxes in the Town of Worcester the current year he giving Sufficient Bonds for the faithfull performance of his Said Trust to the Satisfaction of the Sellectmen and that he be allowed Seven pence three farthings on the pound on the Sum he Collects

Then Chose M^r. Simeon Duncan & M^r. William Mahan Constables

Voted that this meeting be dissolved and the meeting was dissolved accordingly

    A True Entry   Daniel Goulding Town Clerk

Worcester ss march 12th. 1794

Daniel Goulding of Worcester in the County of Worcester Gentleman, was Sworn before me, to execute the dutys of the office of Town Clerk in Worcester for the present year and untill another person is elected in his place and at the Same time took and Subscribed the oath of allegeance and abjuration

            Nathl Paine Jus Paces

  A True Entry   attest   Daniel Goulding Town Clerk

            Worcester ss March 1794

Personally appeared Samuel Flagg, Samuel Curtis, John Chamberlain, Benjamen Heywood, Charles Stearns, Elijah Flagg, Joseph Kingsbury, Elias Mann, Jesse Craige, Ephraim Mower, James Barber, Danl. Baird, William Mahan, Abraham Lincoln, Jonathan Lovell Ju^r. Tim^o. Taft, Daniel Baird Ju^r., Joel Bixby, Benjamen Thaxter, Abijah Peirce, Nathaniel Harrington, Jedediah Heley Amos Whitney Luke Rice, Joel How, & William Chamberlain, and made Solemn oath to the faithfull discharge of the Several offices to which they are Chosen

        Before me   Daniel Goulding Town Clerk

We the Subscribers met and Preambulated run and renewed the bounds between the Towns of Worcester and Sutton agreeable to a law of this Commonwealth

Worcester march 31st 1794
  John Tatman } Appointed
  Timothy Taft }
  Abijah Tainter } Selectmen
  Asa Goodell } of Sutton

Received April 1st. 1794 and Entered from the Original
  Attest   Danl. Goulding Town Clerk

To Mess^s. John Chamberlain and John Barnard both of Worcester Greeting

We the Subscribers by Virtue of a Law of y^e. Commonwealth in Such case made & provided do hereby nominate and appoint you on the part of the Town of Worcester to meet those that Shall be appointed on the part of ye Towns of Shrewsbury and boilstone on the 31st. day of march Instant at ten OClock in the forenoon at Samuel Jenisons & at Eleven OClock at Deacon David Bigelows to preambulate run and renew the dividing lines between Said Towns and make return of your proceedings into the Clerks office of each of Said Towns as Soon as may be

Given under our hands this 10th day of march A, D, 1794

  Samuel Flagg } Selectmen
  Samuel Curtis } of
  John Chamberlain } Worcester
  Nathl. Paine }

Worcester March 31st. 1794 and Shrewsbury meets by their Committee at y^e. North Side of long Pond at a gray Oak tree and preambulated y^e. line to Boylston Corner

John Chamberlain } Committee   John Bragg } of Shrews-
John Barnard } of Worcester   Nathl. Heywood } bury

We the Subscribers meet for the purpose of preambulate ye line beetweext Worcester and Boylston met at y^e. Corner by Nathl. Heywood at heap Stones then running over Lovels house to heap Stone then to a heap Stone northerly of W^m. Emses brook thence to a walnut tree thence to a heap of Stones thence to pine tree thence to corner on holden

John Chamberlain } of Worcester   Jonas Temple }
John Barnard   James Holland } of
                                  Aaron Sawyer } Boylston

To Mess$^\text{rs}$. Phinehas Jones and John Peirce both of Worcester in the County of Worcester — Greeting —

We the Subscribers, by Virtue of a Law of y^e Commonwealth in Such case made & provided, do hereby Nominate and appoint you to preambulate run and renew the dividing lines between the Towns of Worcester and Leicester and make return of your doings or proceedings into the Clerks office of each of Said Towns as Soon as may be

Given under our hands this 10th day of March A, D, 1794

Leicester are Notifyed to meet you at Colo Phinehas Newhalls the 31st day of march Instant for the above purpose at ten of the Clock in y^e. Forenoon

Saml. Flagg   }
Saml. Curtis   } Selectmen of
John Chamberlain   } Worcester
Nathl. Paine   }

March 31st. 1794

This may Certify that we the Subscribers Inhabitants of Worcester & Leicester meet at a heap of Stones at the North west Corner of Worcester and preambulated run and renewed the bounds to the South west corner of Worcester being a heap of Stones at each of the afore mentioned corners between the afore Said Towns

David Henshaw   }
Nathan Waite   } Committee from
John Sargeant   } Worcester &
Phineas Jones   } Leicester
John Peirce   }

True Entry from the original
    attest   Daniel Goulding Town Clerk

At a meeting of the Inhabitants of the Town of Worcester qualified to Vote for Governor Leiu^t. Governor Counsellors &

Worcester Town Records, 1794.

Senators held at the Publick meeting House of the first Parish in Said Town on Monday the Seventh day of April A, D, 1794 then Votes for the following Persons were given in, Counted & Sorted viz—

For Govenor		For Lieu^t. Govenor	
Honble Samuel Adams	55	Honble Moses Gill	28
Honble William Cushing	38	Samuel Adams	36
		Samuel Phillips	1

Senators & Counsellors			
Honble Moses Gill	59	David Bigelow Esqr.	22
Saml. Baker	65	Martin Kinsley Esqr.	4
Jon^a. Warner	47	Salem Town Esqr.	5
Josiah Stearns	59	Samuel Curtis Esqr.	1
John Sprague	23	Edward Bangs Esqr.	1
Samuel Flagg Esqr.	20	Benj^a. Heywood Esqr.	1
Elijah Brigham Esqr.	6	Pliny Merrick Esqr.	1

Town meeting held april 7th. A, D, 1794 To Vote for County Treasurer

Samuel Curtis Esqr. Chosen Moderator

Then Votes for the County Treasurer were brought in and there was for M^r. Samuel Allen Eighty Six Votes

the above meetings were then dissolved

    A True Entry   attest   Daniel Goulding Town Clerk

To Mess^s. Thadeus Chapen and William Trobridge both of Worcester in ye County of Worcester — Greeting

We the Subscribers by Virtue of a Law of the Commonwealth in Such case made and provided do hereby Nominate and appoint you (on the part of the Town of Worcester to meet those that Shall be appointed on the part of Ward on the 31st day of March Instant at ten OClock in the Forenoon at y^e. Corner of Leicester and Ward) to preambulate run and renew the dividing lines between y^e. S^d. Towns of Worcester and ward, and make return of your proceedings into the Clerks office of Each of Said Towns as Soon as may be

Given under our hands this 10th day of march A. D. 1794

        Samuel Flagg
        Samuel Curtis   Selectmen
        John Chamberlain of
        Nathl. Paine   Worcester

Worcester march 31st. 1794 We the Subscribers have met according to our appointment & preambulated the Lines between Worcester and Ward & Renewed the Corners

        Thadeus Chapen
        William Trobridge
        Jonathan Stone Ju^r.
        James Heart

    A True Entry   attest   Daniel Goulding T Clerk

At a Legal Town meeting held on Monday the fifth day of may A D. 1794 at the Publick meeting house of first parish in Worcester for the purpose of Choosing one or more Representatives to Represent Said Town at the General Court appointed to be convened and held at Boston on the last Wednesday of this present may

Voted to Send but one Representative the Current year

Then Samuel Flagg Esqr. was Chosen to Represent the Town of Worcester the Current year in Said General Court

the meeting was then dissolved

    A True Entry   attest   Daniel Goulding Town Clerk

March 27th. 1794 Agreeable to the Derections of the Selectmen of Worcester and the Subscribers have met at the South west Corner of Holden and North west Corner of Worcester near by David & Jesse Moore^s. and have preambulated run and Renewed

Worcester Town Records, 1794.

the Bounds between Said Towns to the North East Corner of Worcester and South East Corner of Holden and we also agree that it is a Straight line from one Corner to the other

Samuel Hubbard } Selectmen of Holden
Eben^r. Estabrook }

Joel How } Committee of Worcester
Eben^r. Mower }

1796 Feb. 11th. Received & Recorded

Daniel Goulding Town Clerk

The Town of Worcester in a/c with y^e. Estate of Tim^o. Paine Esqr. late Chairman of a Committee for the Sale of Publick Lands

1785
Feb. 15th. To Cash paid expences at y^e. first Sale vizt. paid Stowers 16/8 writing deeds 48/ I Thomas 48/ William Young for Surveying   £5 ,, 18 ,, 8

To Interest on the Same to 28^d October 1793   3 ,, 1 ,, 8
To Cash in hand to pay the Committee   3 ,, 18 ,, 0

1786
No^v. 26th. To Cash paid expences at the Second Sale vizt. John Peirce Surveying 12/ Eph^m. Mower for his Bill at S^d Sale 9/6 I Thomas advertizing 24/   2 ,, 5 ,, 6

To Interest on the Same to 23^d October 1793   0 ,, 19 ,, 0

1792
May 7th. To Cash in hand to pay the Committee   2 ,, 0 ,, 0
to Cash paid expences at ye 3^d Sale vizt. advertizing 3/ Committee 8/ Eph^m. Mower 4/ writing 6 Bonds 6/   1 ,, 1 ,, 0

1793
Octr. 23^d   To Cash paid David Moore a Dep^y Sheriff a Judgment that Eben^r. Bradish recovered against the Town of Worcester p^d. 20th. April 1774 as p^r. S^d. Morses Rec^t. to be produced   6 ,, 18 ,, 4
To Interest on the Same to 23^d. Octr. 1793   8 ,, 1 ,, 9

£34 ,, 3 ,, 11

1785
Fe^b. 15th. By Cash received of y^e. Several purchasers of Land as Earnest money for 9 Lots sold 30/ Each as appears on ye Town Book Recorded page 308 ... 13,,10,,0

By Interest on the Same to 23^d. of Octr. 1793 ... 7,,0,,3

1786
No^v. 26 By Cash received as Earnest money of three purchasers vizt. 15/ 20/ 20/ ... 2,,15,,0

By Interest on y^e. Same to 23^d October 1793 ... 1,,2,,10

1792
may 7th By Cash received as Earnest money of three purchasers vizt. 10/ 20/5 20 ... 2,,10,,5

By Interest on y^e. Same to 23^d. October 1793 ... 0,,4,,5

1792
No^v. 7 By Cash received as Interest money on Lot N°. 3 Sold to Benjamen Convers ... 6,,2,,7

By Interest on the Same to 23^d October 1793 ... 0,,6,,9

1793 ... 33,,12,,3
Octr 23 By Ballance due to the Estate ... 11,,8

£34,,3,,11

Worcester 23^d Octr. 1793   Errors Excepted

P^r. Saml. Paine attorney to Sarah Paine Executrix of the Will of Tim^o. Paine Esqr.

A True Entry   attest   Daniel Goulding Town Clerk

At a meeting of the Freeholders & other Inhabitants of the Town of Worcester Qualified to Vote Town affairs at the meeting House of the First Parish in Said Town on Monday the Eighth day of September A D 1794 the following Votes were passed Viz^t.

First Samuel Flagg Esqr. Chosen Moderator

2dly Voted that there be paid one dollar out of the Town Treasury as a bounty to Each Soldier that has or Shall Engage in this Town to Serve in the Continental army to Compleat ye Said Towns Quota and if they are called upon to march that there be an addition to their wages to make them up to Eight Dollars p^r. month during the time they are in Service including the allowance for Clothing and that the Selectmen be directed to draw orders on the Town Treasury for the Same[1]

3dly Voted that the Selectmen be impowered to cause to be taken an accurate plan of the Town of Worcester agreeable to a Resolve of the Legislative passed June last in the best way they Can at the expence of the Town

Voted that this meeting be dissolved the meeting was then dissolved accordingly

  A True Entry attest Daniel Goulding Town Clerk

At a meeting of the Inhabitants of the Town of Worcester Qualified to Vote in Town affairs legally warned and assembled at the meeting House of the first Parish in Said Town on Monday the 20th. day of October A D 1794 The following Votes were passed viz

 Samuel Flagg Esqr. Chosen Moderator

 Voted to Choose a Committee to Examine accounts brought against the Town at this meeting and make Report at the adjournment

 Then Chose Saml. Flagg Esqr. Benjamen Heywood Esqr. and Deacon John Chamberlain a Committee for Said Purpose

 Voted that this meeting be adjourned to monday the third day of November Next at one OClock in the afternoon then to meet at this place

   A True Entry attest Danl. Goulding T Clerk

---

[1] ARTICLE 2:—"To See if the Town will give any Bounty, or make any additional Grant to the wages of their Quota of Soldiers who have or Shall engage to Serve in the Continental Army agreeable to a late law of Congress"

At a meeting of the Inhabitants of the Town of Worcester Qualified to Vote in Town affairs on monday November the third day A D 1794 by an adjournment from October the Twentyeth A D 1794 the following Votes were passed vizt.

Voted to allow the following Report made by the Committee Chose to Examine the accounts brought against the Town — vizt.

The Committee appointed by the Town of Worcester at their meeting held on monday the 20th of October last to Examine accounts exhibited against the S^d. Town ask leave to Report that they have examined the following accounts due to the Following persons for the Towns allowance and payment vizt.

N°. 1	To William Knight for carting y^e. Towns Standards from Boston to Worcester	£0,, 6,, 0
2	To Moses Miller for Boarding &c Zac^{us} Johnson from 2^d December 1793 to 11 march 1794 at 3/ p^r. Week	2,, 8,, 5
3	To Thomas Nickols for Boarding & Cloathing Zac^h. Johnson from 11 march 1794 to 22^d. October 1794 being 32 weeks at 3/6 p^r. Week	5,, 12,, 0
4	to Samuel Brazer for 2 Shirts for Zachriah Johnson 11/1 and 7 yards Ravens duck at 2/6 d^d. Deacon Chamberlain to Cover the Hearse 17/6	1,, 8,, 7
5	To Samuel Brazer for his account of Building and Compleating the Engine & Hearse House agreeable to y^e. Report of ye Committee	31,, 13,, 5½
6	To William Taylor for Boarding and Cloathing anna White from 2^d. No^v. 1793 to y^e. 10 march 1794	2,, 11,, 3
7	To Martha Wiley for Boarding & Clothing Anna White from 10 march 1794 to the 3^d. No^v. 1794 being 34 Weeks at 3/	5,, 2,, 0
8	To Curtis & Lincoln for Iron work for the Burying yard Gate & for the Hearse	0,, 15,, 1
9	To Josiah Flagg for 50^{lb} Beef Del^d. Simon Glasgow	0,, 12,, 0

10	To Oliver Fisk for Vissiting & Medicen for Anna White one of the Towns Poor	2,, 4,, 7
11	To John Elder for Boarding John Spence from Oct\(^r\). 22\(^d\). 1793 to November 3\(^d\). 1794 being 53 & ½ Weeks at 5/ the Week and mending his Shoes 5/6	13,, 13,, 0
12	To Samuel Flagg for Grain and meat Supplyed Simon Glasgow & Samuel Dennys Families from 15 march last to 11 September 1794	3,, 8,, 0
13	To the assessors of the Town of Worcester for the year 1794 for making Heighway Taxes State County & Town Taxes &c	8,, 15,, 4
14	To Daniel Goulding for his account of Supplies and Support of William Tracys Widow and three Children from 4\(^{th}\). November 1794 to 1 No\(^v\). 1794	19,, 10,, 6
15	To Deacon John Chamberlain for Boarding and Cloathing Nathan Houghton & Jenny Dyer from 15\(^{th}\) Oct\(^r\) 1793 to 15\(^{th}\). Oct\(^r\). 1794 being 52 Weeks at 7/ and Sundries of Wood and Provisions Supplied Sam\(^l\). Dennys Famely 69/4 and part Cloathing Zach\(^s\). Johnson 9/	22,, 2,, 4
16	To Increase Blake in full for Nine Camp Kettles he made for the Towns Stock	1,, 16,, 0
17	To Elisha Smith for 6 Days work making the Hearse Gate & Gate posts for the Burying yard at 3/6	1,, 1,, 0
18	To Deacon John Chamberlain for 6 days work on the Herse & Gate & Gate posts for y\(^e\) Burying yard finding Timber Boards paint & Iron for y\(^e\). Same	2,, 12,, 6
19	To James Fisk for Supplying Simon Glasgow with wood two years Ending this day being astimated at 16 Cords at 7/	5,, 12,, 0

20	To John Barnard for Cash paid Silas Gleason for Blowing a large Rock near M`r`. Willingtons and Boarding y`e` man 12 Days & finding Powder	4 ,, 4 ,, 0
21	To Cap`t`. Samuel Brooks for Sundries Supplied Simon Glasgow & Zach Johnson Towns poor to this Time	3 ,, 11 ,, 11½
22	To Charles and Samuel Chandler for Sundries of Cloathing dld for Zach Johnson Peter Willard and Charles Henery and making them	2 ,, 12 ,, 9½
23	To Nathaniel Paine Esq`r` for Costs in the Suit of the Inhabitants of Worcester vs Elisha Smith Ju`r`.	1 ,, 8 ,, 0
24	To Benjamen Heywood Esq`r`. for Cash paid Witnesses &c in the Same action & Fees to M`r`. Merrick for advice and pleading against Beamans New Road	1 ,, 12 ,, 6
25	To Nath`l`. Paine Esq`r`. for a Harness Suitable for the Hearse	4 ,, 10 ,, 0

Worcester 3`d`. No`v`. 1794 £149 ,, 3 ,, 3½

all which is Humbly Submitted

Sam`l`. Flagg
Benj`a`. Heywood } Committee
John Chamberlain

Voted that the Sum of One hundred Ninety three pounds Seven Shillings & three pence half penny be granted levied & assessed on the Estates & Poles in this Town for the purpose of paying the demands brought against the Town and for Paying Sundrey Persons for their damages occasioned by highways being laid through their lands the Same being allowed them by the Court of General Sessions of the peace for the County of Worcester — viz Joseph Kingsbury £16 ,, 10 Josiah Pierce £13 ,, 10 Doct`r` Elijah Dix £5 Nathan Patch £8 M`r`. Stephen Salsbury £1 ,, 4

Voted to discontinue a Road formerly laid out between the lands now owned by M`r`. Elijah Harrington & Daniel Stearns

Voted that the Selectmen View the Road mentioned in the fifth article in the Warrant leading from the House lately owned

Worcester Town Records, 1794.

by John Stearns to the South East Corner of Silas Harringtons land & make report to the Town whether it is expedient that it Should be kept open as a Road or discontinued

Voted to accept the Report of the Committee Chose to Settle with the Town Treasurer which Report is as follows — vizt.—

The account of Benjamin Heywood Treasurer of the Town of Worcester who credits the Inhabitants of Said Town for the following Sums (viz)

1793
Novr. 4 By Ballance due to the Town brought
 from last account this day Settled and
 allowed in Town meeting   £710,, 1,, 4
By Cash rec^d. of the Selectmen arising on
 the Sale of Intrenching Tools   3,, 11,, 5
Dec^m. 2^d. By Ditto rec^d. of Joseph Walker
 for House rent   2,, 8,, 0
9th. By Ditto rec^d. of John Chamberlain
 adm^r. on the Estate of Benj^a. Crosby dec^d. 1,, 19,, 10½
By Ditto rec^d. of the Selectmen to money
 expended on acc^t. of Thos. Eyers 17,, 11,, 9
By Interest rec^d. on Dea^n John Chamberlains Note   1,, 12,, 10
By Sundries rec^d. of the Selectmen by the
 hand of Deacon John Chamberlain as Interest on Obligations in their hands for
 money due to the Town viz
Willm. Youngs Note on Interest
 from may 19th. 1792 £2,, 15,, 6
Nathan Patches D^o. on Interest
 from Augt. 13th. 1793 3,, 5,, 8
Henery Patches D^o. on Interest
 from Sep^t. 11th. 1793 14,, 7,, 7
Ignatius Gouldings D^o. on Interest from Jan^u. 16th. 1793 1,, 4,, 6
Cash and a Rec^t. given for y^e.whole 26,, 4,, 7½ 47,, 17,, 10½
16 By Ditto rec^d. of Ditto as Interest on
 Said Obligations and gave a Receipt 22,, 6,, 9½
1794 Jan^u. 6 By the assessors return of a Tax
 Committed to John Barnard to Collect 250,, 13,, 2

Fe^by. 10 By Interest rec^d. of Deacon John Chamberlain arising on Obligations for money due to the Town in the hands of the Selectmen   14,, 2,, 0
March 31 By Interest on Jon^a. Moores Note   1,, 5,, 2
April 4 By Interest on William Taylors Note   22,, 10,, 11¾
May 19 By Interest rec^d. of Saml. Curtis Esqr. for money loaned   0,, 14,, 3
 20 By Interest rec^d. of Eph^m. Mower for D^o   2,, 15,, 6
Sep^t. 8 By Interest on Town Bonds rec^d. of the Selectmen by the hand of Nathaniel Paine Esqr.   15,, 18,, —
                                             ──────────────
                                              £1115,, 8,, 11¼

And the accountant requests to be allowed for the following payments by him made on Orders of the Selectmen &c

1793 Dec^m. 9th
N 1 Paid Capt. Saml. Brooks   £7,, 12,, 10
   2 Nathan Patch   3,, 7,, 0
   3 Minestry
   4 Deacon Jno. Chamberlain   20,, 7,, 3
   5 Capt. John Stanton   1,, 13,, 8
   6 Nathl. Moore   7,, 3
   7 Benj^a. Heywood   2,, 8,, —
   8 Ditto   6,, 13,,
   9 Jesse Taft   1,, 18,, —
14th 10 Deacon Thomas Wheeler   4,, 4,,
   11 Silas Harrington   9,, ──────
   12 Levi Flagg   1,, 7,,
   13 Capt. Danl. Goulding   9,, 8,, 10½
16th 14 Ditto   18,, 5,, 9½
   15 William Seaver Esqr.   6,, 11,, 8
Dec^m. 16th
   16 Doct^r. John Green Ju^r.   9,, 7,, 8
1794 Feb. 7
   17 Nath^n. Patch p^r. Execution 57,, 13,, 1
   18 Ditto p^r. Order of Selectmen   1,, 4,,

19	Ditto	3 ,,		
20	Levi Lincoln Esqr.	2 ,,	2 ,,	8
21	Saml. Denny Ju^r.	1 ,,	10 ,,	
22	Eli Gale	3 ,,	11	
23	Jacob Holmes	25		
24	Elijah Harrington	16		
25	Capt. John Pierce	— ,,	6 ,,	8
26	William Taylor	9 ,,	16 ,,	—
27	Ditto	9 ,,	2 ,,	—
28	John Bigelow for 4 Crows heads		4 ,,	—
29	Capt. Samuel Brooks	4 ,,	3 ,,	11
May 16 30	Saml. Graves for 4 Crows heads	—	4 ,,	—
31	Saml. Curtis Esqr.	2	12 ,,	—
32	Benj^a. Lathe	15		
27 33	Phineas Gleason for 2 Crows heads	—	2 ,,	—
34	Israel Whitney 1 Ditto	—	1 ,,	—
35	Luther Moore 3 D^o	—	3 ,,	—
36	Robert Gray 14 D^o	—	14 ,,	—
37	Joshua Harrington 2 D^o	—	2 ,,	—
38	William Moore for 2 D^o	—	2 ,,	—
39	Col Phineas Jones for 5 D^o	—	5 ,,	—
40	Jon^a. Gates for 5 D^o	—	5 ,,	—
41	Phineas Heywood	—	12 ,,	—
42	James Quigley	5	4 ,,	—
43	Simeon Duncan	1	16 ,,	—
Sep^t. 44	Paid School Committee	1 70		
45	Simeon Duncan	2	2 ,,	—
46	John Paine	—	6 ,,	—
47	John Crowley for 1 Crows head	—	1 ,,	—
Octr 48	Simeon Smith 3 D^o		3 ,,	—
No^v. 1 49	Daniel Waldo Esqr.	1	8 ,,	—
50	Gardner L Chandler	1		
51	Lowis Smith	1 ,,	3 ,,	—

52	Doct^r. John Green Ju^r.	1 ,, 3 ,, 6
53	Ruben Gray	— 2 ,, 10
54	Samuel Brazer	1 ,, 10 ,, —
55	William Jones	9 ,, —
56	Lowis Smith	1 ,, 10 ,, —
57	Thomas W Millet	19 ,, 6
58	Joel Bixbee	2 ,, 8 ,, 5
59	Charles & S Chandler	10 ,, 4
60	Ditto	18 ,, 10
61	Asa Ward	18 ,, —
62	Silas Gleason	5 —
63	John Chamberlain	2 ,, 12 ,, —
64	William Trobridge	1 ,, 4 ,, —
65	Col Daniel Clap	1 ,, 4 ,, —
1794 No^v. 1 66	Benj^a. Andrews	6 ,, —
67	M^{rs}. Eunice Rice	2 ,, 12 ,, 8
68	M^r. John Barnard	18 ,, 10 ,, 2
69	Samuel Flagg Esqr.	2 ,, 8 ,, 10
70	John Elder	8 ,, 4 ,, —
71	Doct^r. Elijah Dix	16 ,, 2 ,, 6½
72	Daniel Willington	2 ,, 10
73	John Barnard	15 ,, —
74	Thomas Shepard	18 ,, —
75	William Eaton	8 ,, —
76	Saml. Flagg Esqr.	3 ,, 7 ,, 9
77	Capt. Saml. Brooks	1 ,, 9 ,, 4
78	Isaac Chadwick	12 ,, —
79	Col Eben^r. Lovel	7 ,, —
80	Elias Stowel	2 ,, 10
81	Eben^r. Williams	1 ,, 4 ,, 9
82	John Elder	2 ,, 5 ,, 4

To my Time and trouble in
Transacting Treasurey Business } 18 ———
for three years past

£552 ,, 2 ,, 9½

No^v. 3^d. 1794 Balance due to the Town   £563 ,, 6 ,, 1¾
to be further accounted for

Errors Excepted   Benj^a. Heywood Town Treasurer

Worcester No^v. 3^d. 1794   We the Subscribers having been appointed a Committee to Examine & Settle the accounts of Benjamin Heywood Esqr. Treasurer for the Inhabitants of Worcester & attended to Said business beg leave to report that the Said Benjamin Heywood has charged himself with Eleven hundred & fifteen pounds Eight Shillings & Eleven pence one farthing out of which he has paid by orders drawn on him and has accounted for the Sum of Five hundred & Fifty two pounds two Shillings & Nine pence half penny, that there is now remaining in the hands of the S^d. Heywood Five hundred Sixty three pounds Six Shillings & one penny three Farthings to be accounted for by him —
all which is Submitted by   Nathan^l. Paine
                              Saml. Chandler
                              Saml. Flagg

N B We have in the Settlement of the Treasurers account allowed him Eighteen pounds for three years Service in his office of Treasurer which is Submitted for the Consideration of the Inhabitants of the Town of Worcester   N Paine
                              Saml Chandler
                              Saml Flagg

Voted to accept the Report of the Surviving members of a Committee Chose March 1786 to Survey Lot out & take an accurate Plan of the Ministerial & School Land lying East off and near the late Capt. Palmer Gouldings and to make Sale of y^e. Same at Publick Vendue which report is as Follows vizt.

The Committee appointed by y^e. Town of Worcester in the month of March A. D. 1786 to Survey, Lot out and take an accurate Plan of the Ministerial & School land lying East off and near the Late Capt. Palmer Gouldings and to make Sale of ye Same at Publick Vendue — Now ask leave to Report their doings as Follows vizt.—

That they have caused a Survey thereof to be made by Capt. John Peirce (a Plan of which is herewith exhibited and after duely notifying the time and Place of Sale proceeded to Sell the Same at Publick Vendue at the House of M^r. Ephraim Mowers

Innholder in Said Worcester at two Several times and then and there Sold the Following lots to the following persons they being the highest Bidders vizt.—

Lot N°. 1 Containing one acre three Quarters and Sum Rods Sold to Daniel Goulding for the Sum of Twenty pounds   £20 - ———

Lot N°. 2 Containing one hundred & Twenty one Rods Sold to Silas Harrington for the Sum of Nineteen pounds Ten Shillings and by him released to Jn°. Jacob Wagoner who Sold ye Same to Jacob Miller ye present posseser   19 - 10

Lot N°. 3 Containing one hundred and ten Rods Sold to Benjamin Converse for the Sum of Twenty pounds Nine Shillings which his Guardean has Sence Sold to Ignatius Goulding   20 - 9

Lot N°. 4 Containing Eighty two Rods Sold to Nathan Patch who forfeited his Earnest money and the Same has Sence been Sold to William Goulding for the Sum of Fifteen pounds Ten Shillings   15 - 10

Lot N°. 5 Containing Five acres three Quarters and fourteen Rods Sold to Jonathan Gates who forfeited his Earnest money and the Same has Sence been Sold to Abel Stowel for the Sum of Twenty Seven pounds fifteen Shillings   27 - 15

Lot N°. 6 Containing two acres and fifty Eight Rods Sold to Ignatius Goulding for the Sum of Forty two pounds ten Shillings   42 - 10

            Amount of y^e. Sales   £145 - 14

And your Committee have taken Bonds of the Several purchasers to the Selectmen of Said Town and their Successors in Said office for the following Sums payable in one year with Interest as Follows vizt.—

    of Daniel Goulding Jn°. Stanton & Palmer Goulding For   £19 ,, 10 ,, 0

    of Jacob Miller Jedediah Heley & Peter Stowell for   18 ,, 15 —

of Ignatius Goulding Danl Goulding & John Chamberlain for	20 ,, 9 —
of William Goulding Ignatius Goulding & Willm. Johnson for	14 ,, 10 —
of Abel Stowell Cornelius Stowell & Thomas Stowell for	26 ,, 14 ,, 7
of Ignatius Goulding Danl. Goulding & John Chamberlain for	42 ,, 10 —
Net proceeds of ye Sale	£142 ,, 8 ,, 7

Which afore mentioned Bonds are now in ye hands of the Selectmen of Said Town

This Report with the plan of Said lots your Committee think ought to be Recorded in the Town Book

The Committee further Report that the account of the Earnest money expence of Survey and Sale of Said Lots has already been Settled by the Executors of the Late Tim^o. Paine Esqr. Dec^d. late Chairman of Said Committee and Recorded in y^e. Town Book dated the 23^d. October 1793

All which is Humbly Submitted

Elijah Dix } Surviving members
Samuel Brooks } of Said Committee

See the Plan the Next Page

Voted that this meeting be Dessolved the meeting was dissolved accordingly

A True Entry   attest   Daniel Goulding Town Clerk

At a meeting of the Inhabitants of the Town of Worcester on Monday the 3^d. day of November A. D. 1794 after being legally warned for the purpose of giving in their Votes for Some person Suitable to Represent the Inhabitants of the fourth western District in the Commonwealth of Massachusetts in the Congress of the United States of America agreeably to a Law of Said Commonwealth passed the Last Session of y^e. General Court of S^d. Commonwealth, the Inhabitants being assembled gave in their

Vote for the following Persons & the Number of Votes Expressed against their Names vizt.

    For the Hon Levi Lincoln Esqr. 38
    For the Hon Dwight Foster Esqr. 30

 The meeting was then Dessolved

  A True Entry attest Daniel Goulding Town Clerk

 At a meeting of the Freeholders & Other Inhabitants of the Town of Worcester Qualified to Vote in Town affairs Legally warned and assembled at the meeting house of the first parish in Said Town on Monday the Second day of March A, D, 1795 the following Persons were Chose into office and the following Votes passed (vizt.)

 Nathaniel Paine Esqr. Chosen Moderator

 Daniel Goulding Town Clerk

 Samuel Flagg Esqr. Samuel Curtis Esqr. Deacon John Chamberlain Nathaniel Paine Esqr. Benjamen Heywood Esqr. Selectmen

 Voted that the Selectmen be the Overseers of the Poor the Current year

 Samuel Flagg Esqr. Samuel Curtis Esqr. Nathaniel Paine Esqr. assessors

 M^r. Samuel Allen Town Treasurer

 Jason Blake & Silas Gleason Tythingmen

 Nathan Heard Searcher & Sealer of Leather

 Joshua Whitney Nathan White & Jonathan Lovell Fence Viewers

 James M^{c}farland Silas Bigelow field Drivers

 Simeon Duncan Ignatius Goulding Cullers of Hoops

 Samuel Porter Elias Mann Surveyors of Lumber

 Joel How Jonathan Gates 2^d. Deer Reeves

 Capt. Daniel Heywood Daniel Goulding Clerks of the Market

Samuel Flagg Esqr. Capt. John Stanton Joseph Allen Esqr. M^r. Ephraim Mower Fire Wards

Daniel Goulding Nathaniel Paine John Chamberlain Committee to Settle with the Town Treasurer

David Stowell Samuel Case Josiah Knight Ju^r. Tyler Curtis Samuel Denny Ju^r. Stephen Hawes William Mahan Laben Smith John Elder Ju^r. Rufus Flagg Hog Reeves

Voted that the Swine be under the Same restrictions the Current year in this Town they were the last three years

Timothy Taft John Barnard Samuel Curtis Esqr. Ebenezer Mower Thomas Rice John Chamberlain Joseph Barber Amos Whitney Daniel Baird Jonathan Gleason 2^d. Ephraim Mower Samuel Kingston Samuel Curtis Ju^r. Jonathan Gates 2^d. William Trobridge Simeon Duncan Surveyors of Highways & Collectors of Highway Taxes

Voted that the Sum of three hundred Pounds be assessed on the Polls and Estates in this Town & raised for the Purpose of keeping the Publick Bridges & Roads in repair

Voted that those that have not worked their Highway Tax Last Season have Liberty of Working out the Same provided they do it before the first of June Next—& that those if any the[re] be that have over Worked their Last Year Taxes be allowed towards their Highway Tax this year

Voted that the Same Sum be allowed p^r. Day for a man, Yoke of Oxen, Carts & Plows that was the Last year

Voted that the Same encouragement be given for distroying mischievous Birds called crows within this Town that was given Last year

Voted to Choose a Committee of Eleven persons to Destrect the Town into School Squadrons & See what money will be Necessary to raise to furnish the Town with Schooling & in what way and manner will be most beneficial to expent the money

then Chose Levi Lincoln, John Chamberlain, Asa Ward, Samuel Curtis, Capt. Samuel Brooks, David Bigelow, Willm. Gates, Benjamen Thaxter, Stephen Haywood, Benjamen Heywood,

Nathaniel Brooks, a Committee for Said purpose S^d. Committee to make Report at the adjournment of this meeting

Voted that the article for Choosing a Collector be passed over untill the adjournment of this meeting

Voted to Choose a Committee to See if they can find any Sutable place on the Common for Capt. Whitney & Others to Erect Horse Sheds on and Say in what manner the Sheds Shall be Built and make report at the adjournment of this meeting then Chose Ephraim Mower, Samuel Brazer, Daniel Goulding, Daniel Baird & John Nazro a Committee for S^d. Purpose

Chose M^r. Alpheus Eaton Constable

Voted that this meeting be adjourned to the first monday of April Next at two OClock in the afternoon then to meet at this Place and the meeting was adjourned accordingly

  A True Entry   attest   Daniel Goulding Town Clerk

At a meeting of the Freeholders & Other Inhabitants of the Town of Worcester on Monday the Second day of March 1795 Continued by adjournment to this Sixth day of april 1795 & then met then the following Votes were passed viz

Voted to Excuse M^r. Samuel Allen from Serving Town Treasurer the Current year

Voted to Excuse Saml. Curtis Esqr. from Serving Selectman assessor and Highway Surveyor & Collector of Highway Taxes the Current year

Then Chose M^r. Samuel Chandler Town Treasurer

Daniel Goulding Selectman

Deacon John Chamberlain assessor

Capt. Joshua Whitney Surveyor of Highways & Collector of Highway Taxes

M^r. Thomas Rice Constable

Voted that M^r. Thomas Rice be Collector of Taxes the Current year he giving Bonds with Suretys to the Satisfaction of the Selectmen for the faithful performance of his Trust and that he be allowed for Said Service Seven pence three farthings on the pound for the Sums he Shall Collect

Voted to Excuse M^r. Thomas Rice from Serving Highway Surveyor and Collector of Highway Taxes the Current year

Then Chose M^r. Benj^a. Stowell Highway Surveyor & Collector of Highway Taxes

Voted that the Schools be kept in this Town the Current year in the Same way & manner they were the last year

Voted that the Sum of two hundred & fifty pounds be raised and assessed on the Polls & Estates in this Town for the purpose of Supplying the Town with Schooling the Current year

Then Chose John Stanton, John Barnard, Daniel Heywood 2^d, David Andrews, Joshua Whitney, John Tatman, Nathaniel Harrington, Nathaniel Brooks Benjamen Thaxter, Moses Miller & Stephen Haywood Committee to Supply the Town with Schooling the Current year

Chose Nathaniel Paine Esqr. an agent to prosecute and defend to final Judgment and Execution any Suit or Suits at Law that may be brought for or against Said Town

Voted to accept the Following Report of the Selectmen in regard of the Situation of the Town Bonds

Report of y^e. Selectmen of the Town of Worcester Shewing the Situation of the S^d. Town Bonds

Thomas Wheelers Bond dated 1 Dec^m 1793 for £23 - 10 - 0
William Gates & Nathl. Harrington Sureties   Interest paid up
John Goulds Bond dated January 24th 1791 for   33 - 6 - 8
John & Holloway Tayler Sureties   Interest paid up
William Gouldings Bond dated 4 march 1795 for   35 ———
Ignatius Goulding & John R Goulding Sureties Interest p^d. up
Zebulon Cuttings Bond dated 3^d. September 1790 for   50 ———
Peter Johnson & Jacob Holmes Sureties   Interest p^d. up
Samuel Flaggs Lease of Store Ground paid up

Levi Lincolns Bond dated 15th February 1785   51 - 10 —
Sureties Ignatius Goulding & Joseph Allen   Interest p^d. up

Joseph Allens Bond dated August 30th 1784   51 - 1 - 1
Sureties Elijah Dix & Saml. Allen   Interest p^d. up

Reuben Lambs Bond dated Sep^t. 1st. 1791   42 ,, 3 ,, 4
Sureties John Heart & Levy Eddy   Interest paid up

Jesse Tafts Bond dated July 21st. 1786   39 - 5 —
Sureties Josiah Lyon & Joseph Barber   Interest p^d. up

William Gates Dec^m. 1 1793   15 - 11 - 2
Sureties Thomas Wheeler & Nathaniel Harrington   Interest p^d. up

Oliver Watsons Jun^rs. Bond 28th march 1785   83 - 6 - 8
Sureties Oliver Watson & W^m. M^cfarland   Interest paid up

Daniel Heywoods Bond dated Dec^m. 1st. 1793   30 - 18 - 0
Sureties Ignatius Goulding & Daniel Goulding   Interest paid up

Eben^r. Hastings Bond 5 Jan^u. 1792   90 - 4 - 6
Sureties W^m. Gates & Samuel Gates   Interest p^d. up

John Chamberlains Bond dated 20th may 1790   101 ———
Sureties Ignatius Goulding & Daniel Goulding   Interest p^d.

Joseph Patch^s. Bond Sep^t. 11th. 1793   143 ———
Sureties Benj^a. Flagg & Aron Flagg   Interest p^d.

David Bigelows Bond No^v. 1st. 1782   £35 - 16 - 8
Surety John Green   Interest paid up

Leonard Worcesters Bond 13th. August 1793   33 ———
Sureties Nathan Patch Theop^s. Wheeler   Interest p^d.

Samuel Johnsons Bond No^v. 8th 1794   52 - 10 —
Sureties James Fisk Thomas Stowell   Interest p^d

Elijah Flagg Bond February 21st. 1795   48 - 9 - 6
Sureties Isaac Gleason & Edward Knight   Interest p^d

John Stantons Bond 10th march 1784   35 ———
Sureties Daniel Goulding & Palmer Goulding   Interest p^d.

Daniel Gouldings Bond Dec^m. 1st. 1793   29 - 8 —
Sureties Ignatius Goulding & Danl. Heywood   Interest p^d

John Stantons Bond 27 November 1786   19 - 10 —

Sureties Daniel Goulding & Palmer Goulding Interest p^d
Daniel Gouldings Bond 15 February 1785 48 - 10 —
  Sureties Palmer Goulding & Ignatius Goulding Interest p^d
Phineas Wards Bond dated No^v. 1 1773 22 - 15 —
  Sureties Samuel Curtis & David Ritchardson Interest p^d
Ignatius Gouldings Bond 1st. Dec^m. 1793 98 - 7 —
  Sureties Daniel Goulding & Jno. Chamberlain In^t. paid
William Gouldings Bond 7th. may 1792 14 - 10 —
  Sureties Ignatius Goulding & W^m. Johnson Inst. paid
Elias Manns Bond 1st No^v. 1792 20 ———
  Sureties Daniel Heywood & Jed^h Heley Int^r. paid
Saml. Browns Bond 21 July 1783 39 - 5 —
  Sureties Elijah Dix & Lemuel Rice Interest p^d. up to July 1793
Abel Stowels Bond 7 may 1792 26 - 14 - 7
  Sureties Cornelius & Thos Stowell Interest
Simeon Duncans Bond 15 Fe^b. 1785 40 ———
  Sureties Joseph Blair & Joseph Allen Int^r. paid
Jacob Millers Bond Dated 14 August 1794 18 - 15 —
  Sureties Jedediah Healey & Peter Stowell Intst. p^d.
    By Note Signed by y^e. Same Sureties for Interest from Sale
    of ye Land 12 - 2 - 8
David Stowells Bond dated march 23^d. 1795 26 ———
  Sureties Benj^a. & Nathl. Stowell Interest paid
Alpheus Eatons Bond dated 26 march 1795 10 - 10 —
  Sureties William Eaton & Simeon Duncan Inst. p^d

Amount of Interest money Rec^d. & paid
into the Treasury Sence last Report in- 202 - 8 - 1
cluding the Sum of thirty one pounds five
Shillings then in the hands of ye Selectmen is

              Samuel Flagg
Worcester April 6 1795   John Chamberlain } Selectmen of
              Nathl. Paine   Worcester
              Benj^a. Heywood

Voted that this meeting be dissolved and it was dissolved accordingly

            A True Entry   attest   Daniel Goulding Clerk

At a Town meeting held agreeable to the above Warrant on Monday the Sixth day of april A. D. 1795

Then the Following persons were Voted for & had the Number of Votes expressed against their Names

For Governor Samuel Adams 70 For Lieu[t]. Governor
    Samuel Phillips 1 Moses Gill 59
    William Cushing 1 Thomas Rusel 5
    Elbridge Gerry 4 Elbridge Gerry 2

For Senators & Counsellors David Bigelow 59, Levi Lincoln 20, Artimas Ward 29, Salem Town 34, Josiah Stearns 42, Jonathan Warner 34, Elijah Brigham 3, Samuel Flagg 21, Pliney Merrick 7, Martin Kinsley 11, Benj[a]. Reed 3, John Sprague 18, Nathaniel Paine 2, Samuel Baker 45,—

Town meeting held on Monday April 6th. 1795 to Vote for County Treasurer Samuel Flagg Chosen Moderator

    then M[r]. Samuel Allen had Ninety Votes for County Treasurer

    A True Entry   attest   Daniel Goulding Town Clerk

At a meeting of the Qualified Voters of the Town of Worcester at the meeting House of the first parish in S[d]. Town on Wednesday the Sixth day of may A D 1795 for the purpose of Collecting their Sentements on the Necessity or expediency of revising the Constitution in order to amendments agreeable to a Resolve of the General Court passed the Ninth of February last

Number taken for a Revision None, against a Revision Fifty Eight

On the Second meeting in the Warrant

Voted to Choose but one Representative the Current year

Then Chose Samuel Flagg Esq[r]. to Represent this Town in the Great & General Court the Current year to be convened at Boston on the last wednesday of may Instant

On the third meeting in the Warrant

Chose Samuel Flagg Esq[r]. Moderator

It was then moved & Seconded to See if the Town would Choose a Committee to meet a Committee Chose by the Town of Boylston to Settle the lines between the Towns of Worcester & Boylston, the motion being put passed in the Negative

Voted to Repair the Fence round the old Burying Ground & to build a Fence round the New burying Ground or the Land reserved for that purpose

Voted to Choose a Committee to repair the fence round the old burying ground & to Consult on a proper Time & measures for fencing the Land reserved for the New burying ground then Chose M^r. Samuel Brazer M^r. Charles Stearns & Capt. Joshua Whitney a Committee for Said purposes

Voted that the Selectmen Erect Guide posts in this Town agreeable to an act of the General Court at the expence of the Town

Voted to accept of a Road laid out by the Selectmen leading from Christopher Ranks^s. house to the Road near M^r. Asa Moors, the Same being no expence to the Town which report is as follows

The Selectmen Report (on the Petition of Christopher Ranks and others praying to have a Road Laid out from y^e. House of y^e. Said Ranks untill it meets a Road formerly laid out near Asa Moores) That they have laid out in the Town of Worcester a Town Road, as Follows vizt. Beginning at the Southwesterly Corner of the Said Chris^{tr}. Rank's House thence to a Corner of the wall near his well, thence as the wall now Stands by Deacon John Chamberlains land to his Southwest Corner being a Stake and Stones thence to a Small walnut tree and Stones the Southwest Corner of Willm. M^{c}farlands land by Saml. Kingstons land, thence about four Rods to a Chesnut tree by the East Side of the Road as now trod, thence Straight to the Said Kingstons House, thence on the Easterly Side of his house & Barn and Straight to a Chesnut tree in the line between Said Kingstons land and land lately owned by David Moore deceased, thence as the fence now Stands to ye Southwesterly Corner of Said Kingstons pasture thence as the Road is now trod untill it comes to an old cellar where Ruben Moore formerly built a house and Dwelt and where it meets the Road laid out from the County Road by Asa Moores to the Said Ruben Moores House, and the Said Road is laid two rods wide, and lies on the westerly Side of the afore described Courses which is Submitted

Worcester 20th April A D 1795
Samuel Flagg ⎫ Selectmen
John Chamberlain ⎬ of
Benj^a. Heywood ⎭ Worcester

Voted that this meeting be dissolved & it was dissolved accordingly

A True Entry   attest   Daniel Goulding Town Clerk

Worcester March y^e. 2^d. 1795

Then personally appeared Daniel Goulding & made Solemn Oath that he would diligently attend to & faithfully execute the office of Clerk of the Town of Worcester to which he is this day Choose accordingly to the best of his Judgment & Discretion

before me   W^m. Sever Justice Pacis

A True Entry   attest   Daniel Goulding Town Clerk

At a legal meeting of the Qualified Voters Inhabitants of the Town of Worcester on monday the Twenty fifth day of May A. D. 1795

Chose Benj^a. Heywood Moderator

Voted to Choose three agents to appear at the General Sessions of the Peace to oppose the laying out of a County road from Rutland to Worcester through Joseph Patches Land

Then Chose Nathaniel Paine Esqr. Benj^a. Heywood Esqr. & Deacon David Bigelow agents for Said Purpose

Voted that Samuel Flagg Esqr. be an agent to appear at the General Court to prevent the Northerly Part of Worcester being incorporated with the Easterly Part of Holden, Westerly part of

Boylston and the Southerly part of Sterling agreeable to a petetion Presented to the General Court by Ezra Beaman Esquire and Others for the purpose aforeSaid the Inhabitants of Worcester having been Notifyed to Shew cause if any they have why the prayer of Said Petition Should not be granted before the General Court of the Commonwealth on the third Wednesday of June Next

Voted to accept the Report of the Committee Chose to Settle accounts with the Town treasurer which report is as follows —

Dr   The Inhabitants of Worcester in acc^t. with Benj^a. Hey-   Cr.
       wood Treas^r.—
     to Cash paid Sundry Persons p^r. order of the Selectmen Viz^t.

1794 Dec^m. 1		£	s	d
N° 1	Paid Simeon Duncan	2	14	
2	M^r. Saml. Allen County Treasurer	45	8	
3	Deacon John Chamberlain	22	2	4
4	William Moore		6	
5	Ephraim Hemenway		1	
6	Increase Blake	1	16	
7	John Elder	13	13	
8	Capt Eli Chapen		1	
9	Benj^a. Heywood	1	12	6
1795 Fe^b. 23				
10	Daniel M^{c}farland		2	
March 2				
11	Capt. Samuel Brooks		6	
12	Capt. Daniel Goulding	19	10	6
13	Capt. Joseph Torrey	7	4	
14	John Gleason for Rebec^h. Duncan	3		
15	Rebeckah Duncan	3		
16	Samuel Brazer	31	13	5½
N°. 17	Paid Samuel Brazer	2		
18	Lot Hutchinson for Bricks	1	10	
19	Ditto for Ditto	3	6	
20	John Barnard	15		
21	Ditto	5	2	9
22	Ditto	4	4	

23	John Elder		2	7	8
24	Luther Mills		30		
25	William Knight			6	
26	David Curtis			15	1
27	Nathan White			17	4
28	Micah Johnson Ju[r].			2	10
29	Thomas Nickols		5	12	
30	Doct[r] Oliver Fisk		2	4	7
31	Micah Johnson Ju[r].		1	10	8
8th 32	Samuel Flagg Esq[r]. for Fire Engine		90		
23 33	John Gleason		3	5	9
34	Nath[l]. Paine Esq[r].		4	10	
35	Ditto		1	8	

April 6th

36	Elisha Smith		1	1	
37	Nathan Patch		8		
38	Deacon John Chamberlain for 2 Crows Heads		2		
39	Solomon Bixbee for 4 Ditto		4		
40	School Committee	1	70		
41	p[d]. 50 Minute men 6/ Each		15		

May 12

42	Joseph Kingsbury		16	10	
43	Samuel Curtis Esq[r].		2	4	
44	Martha Wiley		5	2	
45	Doct[r] Elijah Dix		5	10	
46	Daniel Baird Ju[r].		5	10	
47	Cap[t]. Sam[l]. Brooks		3	11	11½
48	Deacon John Chamberlain		2	12	6
49	Ditto		2	4	
50	Moses Miller		2	8	5
51	James Fisk		5	12	
52	Josiah Flagg			12	
53	Cap[t]. Nath[l]. Brooks			5	
54	Nathaniel Harrington			5	
55	Samuel Flagg Esq[r].		4	7	4
56	Ditto			5	

57	Samuel Brazer	1 8 7	
58	Jeremiah V. R. Stiles	5	
59	Harrington	1	
		£574 9 1	

1794
No^v. 3^d. By the Ballance due to the Town Brought From last account as Setled and allowed in Town meeting this day — £563 6 1¾

Dec^m. 3^d by Interest rec^d. of Joseph Patches Note for 1 year — 2,, 7,, 10

4 by the assessors Return of a Town Tax Committed to W^m. Mahan to Collect — 435,, 18,, 6½

9 by Interest on Henry Patches Note — 13,, 6

1795
Jan^u. 22 by Cash rec^d. of the Selectmen by Nathl. Paine Esqr. being Interest on Towns Bonds in their hands & gave a Rec^t. — 9,, 5,, 1

by Ditto rec^d. of Ditto by Deacon John Chamberlain for Ditto & gave a Rec^t. — 12,, 17,, 3

26 by Interest rec^d. of Eph^m. Mower on his Note of hand — 1,, 5

by Interest rec^d. on W^m. Youngs Note — 8

by Ditto rec^d. on Ignatius Gouldings Notes — 6,, 9

march 23 by Cash rec^d. of the Selectmen being reimbursement of expences in removing Mary Moore to Gloucester and a French Famely to Oxford Gave a Rec^t. — 8,, 1,, 10

Feb. 16 by Ditto rec^d. of Ditto by Nathl. Paine Esqr. being Interest on Towns Bonds in their hands gave a Rec^t. — 7 18,, 11

April 6 by Ditto rec^d. of Ditto by Nathl Paine Esqr. for Ditto & gave a Rec^t. — 66,, 9,, 4

by Ditto rec^d. by Deac^n. John Chamberlain for Ditto & gave a Rec^t. — 5,, 12,, 10¼

by the assessors Return of a further Sum Committed to William Mahan to Collect — 5

£1114,, 16,, 0½

By Interest on Nath^n. Patchs Note of 100£ — 16,, 16,, 6

£1131,, 12,, 6½

Amount paid out Brought
    Forward   £574 ,, 9 ,, 1
may To M^r. Saml. Chandler
Succeeding Treasurer his Rec^t.
for the following outstanding
Taxes Notes of hand &c. viz.—

Ballance of Taxes uncollected
in John Barnards hands   136 ,, 15 ,, 1½
Ditto in William Mahans hands 230 ,, 17 ,, 9
Saml. Fullertons Note dated
Dec^m. 12th. 1785 on Interest   12 ,, 16 ,, 6
Thomas Tracys Note dated
Dec^m. 12th. 1785 on Interest   4 ,, 10 ,, 7½
Uriah Wards Note dated Dec^m.
12th. 1785 on Interest   12 ,, 14 ,, 10¼
William Croxfords Note dated
Dec^m. 12th. 1785 on Interest   4 ,, 11 ,, 6¾
John Woodwards Note dated
May 29th. 1786 on Interest   6 ,, 8 ,, 7
William Taylors Note dated
April 4th. 1784 on Interest   13 ,, 5 ,, 6½
Joseph Patches & Others Note
dated Sep^t. 11th. 1793 on In-
terest 1 years Interest paid   17 ,, 0 ,, 0
                                £439 ,, 0 ,, 6½

Amount of 59 Vouchers for
moneys p^d. out Brought
Forward   £574 ,, 9 ,, 1
Amount p^r. Saml. Chandlers
Rec^t. brought Forward   £439 ,, 0 ,, 6½
Ballance of Joseph Patch and
others Note dated Sep^t. 11th.
1793 on Interest one years
Interest p^d.   19 ,, 0 ,, 0
Isaiah Thomas^s. Note dated
August 12th. 1794 on Interest   15 ,, 4 ,, 1
Deacon John Chamberlains
Note dated April 6th. 1795 on
Interest   0 ,, 19 ,, 10

Ballance of an Execution vs Nathan Patch	65 ,, 16 ,, 6	
Ballance of Nathan Patch[s] Recognizance dated Sep[t]. 11th. 1793 on Interest	11 ,, 14 ,, 3	551 ,, 15 ,, 2½
may 15th To my trouble Receiving in and paying out £574 ,, 9 ,, 1 @ 1 p[r]. Cent		5 ,, 14 ,, 10
		1131 ,, 19 ,, 1½
Amount of Credit		1131 ,, 12 ,, 6½
Ballance		,, 6 ,, 7

Errors Excepted   Benj[a]. Heywood Town Treasurer

Worcester May 16th. 1795 We the Subscribers a Committee for Settling with Benj[a]. Heywood Esquire late treassurer for the Inhabitants of Worcester have attended Said Service & report that the Said Heywood Charged himself with Eleven Hundred & thirty one pounds twelve Shillings and Six half penny that he has accounted for the Same in the following Manner viz[t]. by paying Sundry orders &c drawn on him to the amount of five Hundred & Seventy four pounds Nine Shillings and one penny And that he has delivered over to M[r]. Samuel Chandler his Successor in Office out Standing Taxes Notes Obligations &c to the amount of five Hundred and fifty one pounds fifteen Shillings & two pence half penny by which it appears there is a Ballance due to the Said Heywood of Six Shillings & Seven pence in Settling the Said Heywoods accounts there was a Charge of one per Centum on five Hundred & Seventy four pounds Nine Shillings & one penny amounting to five pounds fourteen Shillings & Ten pence the propriety of allowing which is Submitted by the Committee to the Inhabitants for their Consideration

Daniel Goulding)
John Chamberlain } Committee
Nath[l]. Paine)

Voted that this Meeting be dissolved & the meeting was Dissolved accordingly

    A True Entry   attest   Daniel Goulding Town Clerk

Worcester Town Records, 1795. 293

At a legal meeting of the Inhabitants of the Town of Worcester Qualified to Vote in Town affairs assembled on Monday the fifth day of October A. D. at the publick meeting house of the first Parish in Said Town after Choosing Samuel Flagg Esqr. Moderator the following Votes were passed vizt.—

Voted to Choose a Committee to examine the accounts brought in against the Inhabitants of this Town and make report at the adjournment of this meeting, then Chose Samuel Flagg Esqr. Benj^a Heywood Esqr. & Samuel Flagg [Curtis?] Esqr. a Committee for Said purpose

Voted that this meeting be adjourned to monday the Nineteenth day of this Instant October at three OClock in the afternoon then to meet at this Place and the meeting was accordingly adjourned

  A True Entry attest Daniel Goulding Town Clerk

At a meeting of the Qualified Voters of the Town of Worcester on Monday the Nineteenth day of October A, D, 1795 agreeable to an adjournment from the fifth day of the Same October the following Votes were passed — viz —

Voted to accept the report of the Committee Chose to examine divers accounts brought against the Town which is as follows

The Committee appointed by the Town of Worcester at their meeting on Monday the 5th. Instant to Examine accounts Exhibited against y^e. Town Report that they have examined y^e. following accounts due to y^e. following persons for y^e. Towns allowance & payment vizt.

N°. 1 To Capt. Joel How for putting one guide post on Tatnick Road	£0 ,, 7 ,, 0
2 To Thad^s. Chapen for Seven Sticks of Timber for a Bridge 16 feet each @ 2d	0 ,, 18 ,, 8
3 To Curtis & Lincoln for Iron Work for the Herse & House &c	1 ,, 8 ,, 0
4 To Deacon Eben^r. Read for Sundreys Supplyed John Willington & Famely from June 11th. to Octr. 14th. 1795 & House Room	4 ,, 10 ,, 10

5	To Increase Blair for 13 & ½ Cords of Wood dld Samuel Dennys Famely @ 6/	4 ,, 1 ,, 0
6	To Benj[a]. Heywood Esq[r]. for 1 bushel of Rye Supplied Simon Glasgow & for 5 guide posts dld & putting two of them up	0 ,, 18 ,, 6
7	To Charles Stearns for 2 hundred plank & 2 String pieces for a Bridge	0 ,, 16 ,, 0
8	To Thomas Nickols for Boarding & Cloathing Zack Johnson from 20th. October 1794 to 20th. Oct[r]. 1795 being 52 weeks @ 4/ is £10 ,, 8 ,, 0 deduct Cash in part 60/ leaves a Balance due	7 ,, 8 ,, 0
9	To Samuel Flagg for meet & grain Supplied State & Town poor from Jan[y]. last to this Time and Some assistance with men & Team in Building the Powder House	10 ,, 5 ,, 8
10	To Daniel Goulding for Sundries Supplyed in Building Powder House	8 ,, 0 ,, 2
11	To David Hersey for Building the Powder House	2 ,, 14 ,, 0
12	To Willard Morse for two Loads of Sand for D[o]	0 ,, 10 ,, 0
13	To Daniel Goulding for Supporting Widow Tracy & Children from 1st. No[v]. 1794 to 14th October 1795	23 ,, 4 ,, 9½
14	To William Goulding for Labour & Stuff for the Powder House & Boards for the Guide posts & putting up part of them	19 ,, 17 ,, 0
15	To Deacon John Chamberlain for Boarding & Clothing Nathan Houghton & Jenny Dyer from 15th. Oct[r]. 1794 to 15th. Oct[r]. 1795 being 52 weeks @ 10/ and Some provisions for Sam[l]. Dennys &c	27 ,, 7 ,, 7
16	To Moses Miller for Boarding Polly Blake and her Child from 20th august to 15th. Oct[r]. 1795 being 8 Weeks @ 7/	2 ,, 16 ,, 0
17	To John Elder for Boarding Clothing & Nursing John Spence from 3[d]. No[v]. 1794 to 19 Oct[r]. 1795 being 50 Weeks @ 6/ and other Extra expence	20 ,, 8 ,, 7

18	To James Fish for Wood Supplied Simon Glasgow the year past & 1 guide post 6/	3 ,, 0 ,, 0
19	To William Moore for Sundries Supplyed the Widow Blake in Sickness	1 ,, 3 ,, 0
20	To Daniel Goulding for Boarding & Clothing Charles Henery 20 weeks and James Roch 18 Weeks to this day	7 ,, 12 ,, 0
21	To the assessors for the year 1795	7 ,, 16 ,, 6
22	to David Andrews for Bridge plank	0 ,, 8 ,, 0
23	to Samuel Brazer for Sundries Supplied Sundrey State & Town poor	7 ,, 12 ,, 10
24	to Saml. Brooks for Supplies dld Simon Glasgow	0 ,, 3 ,, 9
25	to John Barnard for Supplies dld Simon Glasgow	1 ,, 13 ,, 6
26	to the Widow Mary Wheeler for Supporting Anna White from 6th April to the 19th. October 1795 being 28 Weeks @ 4/	5 ,, 12 ,, 0
27	to Jonathan Putman for Ringing the Bell y^e. year past in the evening Ending 10th. No^v. 1795	2 ,, 5 ,, 0
28	to Saml. Brazer for 10^{lb}. of Pork for Simon Glasgow dld this day	0 ,, 8 ,, 4

Worcester 19th Octr. 1795   £173 ,, 6 ,, 8½

Samuel Flagg } Committee
Samuel Curtis }

Voted that the Sum of three Hundred pounds be granted levied & assessed on the Polls & Estates in this Town & raised for the purpose of discharging the Bills against the Town & defraying the Expences of the Town

Voted to accept the report of Messrs Stearns & Brazer a Committee heretofore appointed for the purpose of Fencing the old burying ground and to view the New one & See what kind of Fence would be proper to build & when and that they be requested to perform the business agreeable to their report which is as follows viz—

The Committee appointed to fence the old burying ground and

to view the new one and report what kind of a fence will be proper and when to be built

Report 1st. That they have contracted for the Stone and work of the old ground the work of which is now performing and will be compleated Soon as possible also that at this meeting it will be Necessary to grant the Sum of four Hundred Dollars or upwards for the Said Expence

2dly they are of Opinion that the new ground Should have a good wall round it three Sides of Common Stone but the front Side of Stones from Mill Stone Hill that there be a Committee chosen to procure the Said Stones the ensuing winter and have the wall built as Soon as may be Next Spring also to grant money for the Said purpose

    Samuel Brazer Charles Stearns Committee

Worcester Octr. 19th. 1795

The meeting was then dissolved

 A True Entry attest Daniel Goulding Town Clerk

Worcester December 1795

Personally appeared M^r. Thomas Rice and made Oath before me the Subscriber that he would faithfully execute the duties of Collector of Taxes into which office he was chosen in April last

    Daniel Goulding Town Clerk

At a meeting of the Freeholders & other inhabitants of the Town of Worcester Qualified to Vote in Town affairs legally warned & assembled at the meeting House of the first Parish in Said Town on monday the Seventh day of march A. D. 1796 the following Persons were chosen into office and the following Votes passed vizt.

Samuel Flagg Esqr. Moderator

Daniel Goulding Town Clerk

Samuel Flagg Esqr. Nathaniel Paine Esqr. Benj^a. Heywood Esqr. Daniel Goulding Colo Phineas Jones Selectmen

Worcester Town Records, 1796.

Voted that the Selectmen be the overseers of the Poor the Current year

Samuel Chandler Town Treasurer

April 4th Sworn Samuel Flagg ⎫
April 4th Sworn John Chamberlain ⎬ Assessors
April 4th Sworn John Barnard ⎭

Nathan Heard Searcher & Sealer of leather

                  Ebenezer Mower ⎫
Sworn march 12th Henry Patch ⎬ Fence Viewers
Sworn April 4th. Phineas Jones ⎭

Sworn 19th April Charles Adams ⎫
Sworn 21st march Elijah Flagg ⎬ Field Drivers

April 4th Sworn Joshua Harrington ⎫
march 21 Sworn William Goulding ⎬ Tythingmen

Ignatius Goulding Simeon Duncan Viewers & Cullers of Staves & Hoops

                  Ephraim Mower ⎫ Clerk of the market
Sworn march 18th Samuel Bridge ⎭

Samuel Flagg John Stanton Joseph Allen Ephraim Mower Fire Wards

march 14th. Sworn Samuel Porter ⎫ Surveyors of Shingles
march 21st. Sworn William Goulding ⎬ & Clapbords

march 19th Sworn Joseph Mann ⎫ Deer Reeves
march 16th Sworn Nathaniel Harrington ⎭

Excused Ephraim Mower ⎫
march 12th Sworn John Barnard
march 14th Sworn Moses Perry
Sworn April 4th Joshua Whitney
                 Peter Slater
Sworn April 4th William Chamberlain
April 4th Sworn Isaac Willard
Sworn march 12th Frances Flagg ⎬ Highway Surveyors
Sworn march 19th Levy Flagg   & Collectors of
Sworn april 4 Ebenezer Reed   Highway Taxes
Sworn June 1st Ruben Gray
Sworn march 9th Daniel Baird
Sworn march 19th William Sever
Sworn may 16th Daniel Heywood 2d
Sworn may 27th Thomas Gates
                 William Trobridge
                 Jonathan Gates 2d. ⎭

Hog Reeves
 David Curtis Sworn Byfield Pierce march 28th Sworn
 John Tatman David Moore march 14th Sworn
 Edward Knight april 4th Frances Thaxter march 12th
  Sworn   Sworn
 David Willington march 14 Peter Slater april 4th Sworn
  Sworn
 asa Holbrook april 4th Sworn John Stow march 19th Sworn
 Isaac Willard Ju^r.

Voted that M^r. Henery Patch be Collector of Publick Taxes for this Town the Current year he giving Bonds with Suretys to the Satisfaction of the Selectmen for the faithfull performance of his trust and that he be allowed for Said Service Seven pence on the pound for the Sums he Shall Collect

Voted that the Sum of two Hundred & fifty pounds be assessed on the Polls & Estates in this Town & raised for the purpose of Supplying the Town with Schooling the Current year

Nathaniel Coolidge James Fisk David Bigelow William Trowbridge | Excused Noah Harris | Josiah Perry Nathl. Harrington Joseph Barber Eben^r. Reed Jonathan Gates 2^d. Benj^a. Flagg Ju^r. Committee to provide the Town with Schooling the Current year

Voted that the way & manner the School Shall be Kept be put by untill the adjournment of this meeting

Voted to Choose a Committee to See what Number of School Houses it is Necessary there Should be in this Town & Say where they Shall be placed & make an estimate of the Expence of building or Providing of them and make report at the adjournment of this meeting

Then Chose Benjamen Heywood Esqr. Samuel Curtis Esqr. & Daniel Goulding a Committee for Said purpose

Voted that this meeting be adjourned to monday the fourth day of april Next at Ten OClock in the forenoon then to meet at this Place & the meeting was accordingly adjourned

  A True Entry attest Danl. Goulding Town Clerk

Worcester ss march 7th. 1796 Personally appeared Danl. Goulding and was Sworn as the law directs to qualify him to act as Town Clerk for the Town of Worcester the ensuing year

      Before me Benja. Heywood Jus Peace
  A True Entry attest Daniel Goulding Town Clerk

At a meeting of the Inhabitants of the Town of Worcester Qualified by the Constitution to Vote for Representatives on monday march 7th. 1796 at the meeting house of the first parish in Said Town — for the purpose of Voting for a County Register & County Treasurer

Voted that the Selectmen be a Committee to count & Sort the votes given in for a County Register

Then the following persons were voted for as a County Register and had the Number of Votes expressed against their Names (viz)

Colo Danl. Clap 82 Colo Saml. Flagg 4 Capt. Joshua Whitney 1

Votes for County Treasurer 84 for Mr. Samuel Allen

then the meeting was Dissolved

  A True Entry attest Daniel Goulding Town Clerk

At a Town meeting held on Monday April 4th. A. D. 1796 by adjournment from a meeting held march ye. 7th 1796

Chose Deacon John Chamberlain Nathaniel Paine Esqr Benja. Heywood Esqr. Committee to Settle accounts with the Town Treasurer

April 4th Sworn Joseph Torry } Constables
    Sworn Alpheus Eaton

John Stanton David Andrews Highway Surveyors & Collectors of Highway Taxes

Excused Ephraim Mower from Serving Highway Surveyor & Collector of Highway Taxes the Current year

Voted that the Sum of three Hundred pounds be assessed on the Polls & Estates in this Town & Raised for the purpose of keeping the Publick Roads & Bridges in repair

Voted that the Same wages p^r. Day be allowed for a man Yoke of Oxen & Plow &c as was the last year

Voted that if there is any person or persons that have over worked their last year Highway Taxes that they be allowed for the Same towards this years Highway Taxes & if there is any person or persons that have not worked out their Highway Taxes that they have liberty to work out the Same provided they do it before the first of June Next

Voted that the Swine be under the Same restrictions the Current year that they have been this four years past

Chose Capt. Joseph Torry Hog Reeve   Sworn april 4th 1796

Chose M^r. Moses Perry School Committee man in the place of Noah Harris Excused

Chose Nathl. Paine Esqr. to Prosecute to final Judgment & Execution any Suit that it may be Necessary to bring in favour of the Town of Worcester & to defent any Suit that may be brought against the Said Town

Voted to discontinue the Bridle Road mentioned in the twelvth article in the Warrant for this meeting [1]

Voted that Nathl. Paine Esqr. be an agent to apply to the General Sessions of the Peace to have the County Road from Chapens Road So called by Henery Patches, & Peter Slaters discontinued

Voted that the Committee for Fencing the New Burying Ground be authorized & empowered, to purchase any lands which they may Suppose necessary for the purpose of accomodating the Same

---

[1] ARTICLE 12:—"to see if the Town will discontinue a bridle road originally laid out for the accomodation of a Farm formerly owned by John Kelso the present proprietor of Said farm having no wish to have the Same continued any longer"

and to exchange any part of the Same for any ground which they may Suppose proper and to make & Execute a Deed or Deeds thereof

Voted that the Same encouragement be given by the Town for Killing Crows within this Town the year ensuing that was the last year

Voted that the Selectmen be a Committee to Select out of the list Laid before the Town of persons liable to Serve as Jurors, a Number to Serve as Jurors at the Supreme Court

Voted that this meeting be adjourned to three OClock this afternoon then to meet at this place & the meeting was accordingly adjourned

  A True Entry attest Daniel Goulding Town Clerk

Met according to the above adjournment April 4th. 1796 three OClock afternoon

Voted to accept the list Laid before the Town by the Selectmen of persons lyable & Sutable to Serve as Jurors & the list they have Selected of persons Sutable to Serve as Jurors at the Supreme Judicial Court — See Files

Voted that the Sum of Forty five pounds be allowed by the Town to the Center School destrect for the purpose of keeping a Publick Latten and Greek Grammar School for the Town for the Term of one Year

Voted that the Sum of fifteen pounds be assessed on the Polls & Estates in this Town & Raised for the purpose of Supporting Schools in this Town in addition to the two Hundred & fifty pounds Granted in march last

Voted that the forty five pounds allowed to the Center School Quarter or destrect be paid out of the Sums granted for the Support of Schools & the remainder of Said Sums granted be divided or proportioned in the Same way and manner the money granted last year was for English Schools

Voted that this meeting be adjourned to monday the Second day of may Next at three OClock in the afternoon then to meet at this Place and the meeting was accordingly adjourned

 A True Entry attest Daniel Goulding Town Clerk

Worcester April 4th. Town meeting held agreeable to the above warrant to Vote for Governor Lieut. Governor & Senators & Counsellors then the following Persons were Voted for & had the Number of Votes Set against their Names

  For Governor his Excy Samuel Adams 42
     Honble Increase Sumner 102
     Honble William Cushing 3
     Honble Moses Gill 1
  For Lieut. Governor Honble Moses Gill 109 Votes
     Honble Increase Sumner 2
     Honble Jerathmeel Bowers 1
     Capt. Joshua Whitney 1
  For Senators and Counsellors

Salem Town	84	Pleney Merick	16
Daniel Bigelow	84	Jonathan Warner	31
Josiah Stearns	82	Barzaleel Taft	6
Samuel Flagg	42	Martin Kinsley	5
Benja. Reed	38	Edward Bangs	1
John Sprague	35	Nathl. Paine	1

  meeting Dissolved
 A True Entry Attest Daniel Goulding Town Clerk

At a Town meeting held at the publick meeting house of the first Parish in Worcester on monday may 2d. A. D. legally warned & assembled

Chose Samuel Flagg Esqr. moderator

Then Voted to abate the following persons Taxes in William Mahans Tax bills to Collect & that if he Should at any future Time Collect any part of them that he be accountable and pay the Same to the Town Treasurer Viz

William Brown	£0–5–0	Hezekiah Miller	0–5–0
William Heard	0–7–0	Lyman Peirce	0–5–0
Rufus Humes	0–5–0	Elijah Pike	0–4–6
Jabez Hibrows	0–5–0	Stephen Rawson	0–5–0
Silas How	0–5–8	Curtis Searl	0–5–0
Eben^r. Harwood	0–5–0	Henery Saunders	0–5–0
Daniel Grout	0–5–0	Eben^r. Willington ye 4th.	
Howland Kimbel	0–5–0		0–5–0
Alven Lamb	0–5–0	Eben^r. Whitmore	0–5–0

£4–7–2

Voted that John Barnard have liberty to lay before the Town a list of the Taxes that [he] wishes to have abated at Some future Town meeting

Voted that this meeting be dissolved and the meeting was dissolved accordingly

  A True Entry attest Daniel Goulding Town Clerk

At a meeting of the Qualified Voters for the Choice of Representatives legally assembled at the first Parish meeting House in Worcester on Monday may 2^d. 1796 agreeable to the warrant for Said purpose

Voted to Choose & Send two Representatives to the General Court to be convened at Boston on the last wednesday of this Instant may

Then Chose Samuel Flagg & Levi Lincoln Esq^{rs}. Representatives

Voted that this meeting be Dissolved and the meeting was dissolved accordingly

  A True Entry attest Daniel Goulding Town Clerk

At a Town meeting continued by adjournment from march meeting to this 2ᵈ. day of may A. D.

Voted to accept the report of the Committee Chose to Settle accounts with the Town Treasurer which report is as follows

Dʳ.   The Town of Worcester in accᵗ. Current with Samˡ.   Cʳ.
Chandler Town Treasurer

1795 may 16ᵗʰ

N								
1	paid Micah Johnson Jʳ.							
		5 Crows heads £0 ..			5 -	0		
2	Luther Blake	5	"	"	5	—		
3	Abel Heywood	5	"	"	5	—		
4	Danˡ. Mᶜfarland	5	"	"	5	—		
5	Joel Gates	4	"	"	4	—		
6	Jonᵃ. Rice	3	"	"	3	—		
7	Jonᵃ. Butler	5	"	"	5	—		
8	Levi Lincoln Juʳ.	4	"	"	4	—		
9	Josh Wheelock	3	"	"	3	—		
10	Thos Gates	1	"	"	1	—		
11	Josiah Perry	3	"	"	3	—		
12	James Baird	4	"	"	4	—		
13	Thomas Gray	20	"	"	1 ..	0 -	0	
14	Timᵒ. Merryfield	4	"	"	4	—		
15	Samˡ. Graves	8	"	"	8	—		
16	Wᵐ. Moore	3	"	"	3	—		
17	Abijah Peirce	4 Crows Heads			0 -	4 -	0	
18	Samˡ. Goddard Juʳ	5	Dᵒ		0 -	5 -	0	
19	Nathaniel Coolidge for a Trunk				1 -	2 -	0	
							1 - 11 - 0	
20	Isaac Green 4 Crows heads				0 -	4 -	0	
21	Abel Knight 1	Dᵒ			0 -	1 -	0	
22	C & S Chandler pʳ order Selectmen				2 -	12 -	9½	
23	Serval Moore				0 -	14 -	0	
24	Simeon Duncan				7 -	12 -	6	
25	Daniel Fenno				1 -	3 -	9	
26	James Quigley				6 -	10 -	0	
27	Micah Johnson Juʳ. 2 Crows heads				0 -	2 -	0	
28	Jer. Stiles pʳ. order Selectmen				3 -	3 -	0	

Worcester Town Records, 1796. 305

29	Henery Patch	1 - 2 - 0	
30	John Peirce	5 - 8 - 3	
31	Hezekiah Miller	1 - 1 - 0	
32	Amherst Childs by Danl. Baird	4 - 10 - 8	
33	Jon^a. Putman	2 - 5 - 0	
34	Penuel Merrefield 2 Crows heads	0 - 2 - 0	
35	John Elder p^r. order Selectmen	16 - 8 - 7	
36	Saml. Gould 1 Crows head	0 - 1 - 0	
37	John Chamberlain p^r. order Selectmen	27 - 7 - 7	
38	Jer^r. Stiles	0 - 7 - 11	
			80 - 17 - 0½
39	Daniel Goulding	8 - 0 - 2	
40	paid the assessors	7 - 16 - 6	
41	James Wilson	2 - 12 - 8	
42	Simeon Duncan	8 - 4 - 0	
43	John Stanton	1 - 4 - 0	
44	School Committee	220 - 0 - 0	
45	Increas Blair	4 - 1 - 0	
46	Willm. Goulding	19 - 17 - 0	
47	Jno. Atwood 1 Crows head	0 - 1 - 0	
48	W^m. Moore p^r. order Selectmen	0 - 3 - 0	
49	Simon Gates 4 Crows heads	0 - 4 - 0	
50	Thomas Nickols p^r. order Selectmen	7 - 8 - 0	
			280 - 11 - 4
51	Thadeus Bigelow p^r. order assessors	0 - 6 - 6	
52	Phineas Gleason	0 - 5 - 0	
53	Nathl. Grary	0 - 5 - 0	
54	Luke Brown	0 - 5 - 0	
55	Robert Peck	0 - 10 - 0	
56	Henery Patch	0 - 2 - 10	
	Esther Moore	0 - 5 - 0	1 - 19 - 4
58	John Tatman	£0 - 2 - 10	
59	James Bridge	0 - 5 - 0	
60	John Elder p^r. order Selectmen	4 - 0 - 0	

61	Tho[s]. Nichols	3 - 0 - 0		
62	Henery Patch	3 - 0 - 0		
63	Joseph Torry	0 - 6 - 0		
		————	10 - 13 - 10	
65	Daniel Goulding	7 - 12 - 0		
66	Daniel Goulding	4 - 14 - 6		
67	Joel How	0 - 7 - 0		
68	Simeon Duncan	6 - 0 - 0		
69	John Elder	4 - 0 - 0		
70	Mary Wheeler & Thomas W Millet	4 - 4 - 0		
71	Willard Morse	0 - 10 - 0		
72	David Andrews	3 - 9 - 0		
73	Simeon Duncan	2 - 10 - 0		
74	Abijah Peirce 1 Crows head	0 - 1 - 0		
75	Joseph Chadwick p[r]. order assessors	0 - 9 - 9		
76	Sam[l]. Flagg p[r]. order Selectmen	3 - 8 - 0		
77	Luther Mills	30 - 0 - 0		
		————	67 - 5 - 3	
78	Samuel Frink	3 - 12 - 0		
79	Daniel Fenno	2 - 9 - 1		
80	Eben[r]. Reed	4 - 10 - 10		
81	Elijah Harrington	0 - 5 - 10½		
82	Joseph Ball	0 - 9 - 0		
83	Daniel Baird	0 - 4 - 6		
84	Elias Stowell	0 - 5 - 0		
85	Thadeus Chapen	0 - 18 - 8		
86	Charles Stearns	5 - 0 - 0		
87	David Hersey	2 - 14 - 0		
88	Samuel Brazer & others	54 - 12 - 3½		
89	Daniel Clap	2 - 9 - 10		
90	David Andrews	5 - 0 - 0		
91	James Fisk	3 - 0 - 0		
92	Eben[r]. Reed	1 - 10 - 7		
93	Asa Ward	7 - 10 - 0		
94	Benj[a]. Thaxter	1 - 10 - 0		
95	Phin[s]. Jones	6 - 3 - 0		
96	Phin[s]. Gleason	0 - 5 - 10½		

Worcester Town Records, 1796.

97	Jon^a. Gleason	0 - 8 - 7½	
98	Jesse Sturtevant	0 - 5 - 10½	
99	Nathl. Harrington	0 - 5 - 10½	
			103 - 10 - 11
100	Samuel Brooks	£0 - 3 - 9	
101	Jonathan Holbrook	0 - 5 - 10½	
102	Josiah Peirce	13 - 10 - 0	
103	Curtis & Lincoln	1 - 8 - 0	
104	John Barnard	1 - 13 - 6	
105	Charles Stearns	0 - 16 - 0	
106	Laben Smith	0 - 15 - 0	
107	Saml. Flagg	10 - 5 - 8	
108	Saml. Brazer	7 - 12 - 10	
109	Simeon Duncan	5 - 3 - 0	
110	Amherst Child	8 - 10 - 11	
			50 - 4 - 6½
	To Ballance in y^e. Hands of the Treasurer		638 - 4 - 7½
			1238„19„10½

1795 May 15   By Ballance of Taxes in J^{no}. Barnards hands   £136..15..1½

By Ballance of D^o. in William Mahans D^o   230..17..9

———— 367„12„10½

Saml. Fullertons Note dated Dec^m. 13th. 1795 on Interest } 12 - 16 - 6

Thomas Tracys Note dated Dec^m. 12th. 1785 on Interest } 4 - 10 - 7½

Uriah Wards Note dated Dec^m. 12th. 1785 on Interest } 12 - 14 - 10¼

Wm Croxfords Note dated Dec^m. 12th. 1785 on Interest } 4 - 11 - 6¾

John Woodwards Note dated may 29th. 1786 on Interest } 6 - 8 - 7

Wm Taylors Note dated April 4th. 1794 on Interest } 13 - 5 - 6½

Joseph Patch & others Note dated Sep^t. 11th. 1793 on Interest 1 years Interest paid } 17 - ——

308 Worcester Town Records, 1796.

Ballance of Joseph Patch & Others Note dated Sept. 11th. 1793 on Interest 1 years Interest paid	19 -	
Isaiah Thomas Note dated August 12th. 1794 on Interest	15 - 4 - 1	
Deacon John Chamberlains Note dated April 6th. 1795 on Interest	19 - 10	
Ballance of an Execution vs Nath{n} Patch	65 - 16 - 6	
Ballance of Nathan Patchs Recognizance dated Sept. 11th. 1793 on Interest	11 - 14 - 3	184,, 2,, 4
June 30th. By Cash recd. of the Commonwealth by the hands of the Selectmen	14 - 17 - 6	
August 30th. By Cash Recd. of Saml. Denny Ju{r}.	1 ,, 10	
1796 Jany. 8 By Cash recd. of the Commonwealth by the hands of the Selectmen	40,, 18,, 1½	
Interest on Joseph Patch{s} Note for 1 year	2,, 3,, 2	
The assessors return of a Town Tax dld to Thos. Rice to Collect	550	609,, 8,, 9½
By Fractional part of ye State Tax	4,, 1,, 9	
By Cash recd. of ye. Selectmen for Interest	73,, 14,, 1½	77,, 15,, 10½
		£1238,, 19,, 10½

May 2d. 1796 We the Subscribers a Committee appointed to Settle with Saml. Chandler Town Treasurer have attended Said Service and report that the Said Saml. Chandler has Charged himself with Twelve hundred and thirty Eight pounds Nineteen Shillings and Tenpence ½ including the balance of the former Treasurers account that he has accounted for Six hundred pounds fifteen Shillings & three pence by producing Sufficient vouchers therefor—and that there remains the Sum of Six hundred and

thirty Eight pounds four Shillings and Seven pence half penny in his hands to be further accounted for
all which is Submitted
By Benj^a. Heywood ⎫
John Chamberlain ⎬ Committee
Nathl. Paine ⎭

For the Remainder of this meeting Look the fifth page forward

---

At a meeting of the Qualified Voters of the Town of Worcester, legally warned and assembled, at the meeting house of the first Parish in said Town, on Monday, the 26th. day of September, 1796.

Samuel Flagg, Esq. was chosen Moderator.

Voted, not to act upon the second article in the Warrant.[1]

Voted, That Abel Stowell have leave to erect a set of Scales, for the purpose of weighing Hay, on such part of the Common as the Selectmen shall direct.

Voted, That Benjamin Heywood, Esq. Nathaniel Paine Esq. and Dea. David Bigelow, be a Committee to examine and allow accounts, and report at the adjournment of this meeting.

Voted to adjourn this meeting to the first Monday in November next, at nine o'clock in the morning.

It was adjourned accordingly.

At a legal meeting of the Inhabitants of Worcester, November 7th, 1796, pursuant to adjournment from the 26th of Septr last.

It appearing that Daniel Goulding, Town Clerk being sick, was unable to attend the duties of his office, the Inhabitants proceeded

---

[1] "Secondly, To see if the Town will make any compensation to those persons of the Militia of said Town, who are ordered to Oxford for review, in October next, either by supplying them with ammunition, or in any other way which may appear proper."

to choose a Clerk pro. tem. and Leonard Worcester was chosen and Sworn.

Voted, That this meeting be adjourned until two o'clock in the afternoon. It was adjourned accordingly.

Met pursuant to adjournment, Novr. 7th, at Two o'clock in the afternoon.

Voted, To accept the Report of the Committee for fencing the Burying Ground.

Voted That the Standing School Committee be added to the Committee appointed in March last, upon the subject of School Houses; and that the Committee take up the subject again, and report at the adjournment of this Meeting.

Voted, To accept the report of the Committee appointed to examine and allow accounts, (except on the account of M^r. Daniel Waldo,) which report is as follows:

We, the Subscribers, having been appointed a Committee for the purpose of examining the accounts against the Town of Worcester, have attended to the same, and report that there appears to be due, Vizt.

N	1	To Samuel Brazer	£ 4,, 0,, 2
	2	To Saml. Flagg, John Barnard & John Chamberlain assessors	10,, 1,, 6
	3	To Samuel Flagg, for divers articles Supplied the Poor	8,, 2,, 9
	4	To John Stanton	2,, 17,, 5
	5	To Doctor John Green, for Medicine and attendance on the Poor of the Town of Worcester	9,, 19,, 9
	6	To Samuel Kingston	3,, 0,, 0
	7	To Joel How	0,, 9,, 0
	8	To James McFarland	4,, 18,, 0
	9	To Joel Bixby	3,, 17,, 0
	10	To Jonathan Gates and others	3,, 3,, 0
	11	To Daniel Waldo	10,, 0,, 0½
	12	To James McFarland	0,, 12,, 0

Worcester Town Records, 1796. 311

13	To Nathan Perry	0,,18,,	0
14	To Thomas Nichols	16,,15,,	0
15	To Ebenezer Mower	2,,14,,	5
16	To William Trowbridge	5,, 1,,	5
17	To Phineas Jones	6,, 7,,	2
18	To Judith Rice	19,,15,,	0
19	To Thomas Rice	2,, 2,,	0
20	To John Barnard	5,, 3,,	6
21	To John Chamberlain	22,,10,,	6
22	To John Nazro	0,,18,,	4
23	To Micah Johnson Ju^r.	0,,12,,	0
24	To Charles & Saml. Chandler	2,, 9,,	5½
25	To Asa Ward	4,,16,,	0
26	To John Elder	2,, 3,,	6
27	To Mary Wheeler	15,, 4,,	0
28	To David Griggs	1,,13,,	6
29	To Daniel Goulding	19,, 0,,	10
30	To Simeon Duncan	9,, 8,,	9
31	To Wm Trobridge for 125 feet Plank, @ 12/ per hundred	0,,15,,	0
	To James Fiske, for 8 Cords of Wood, dd S Glasco	3,, 4,,	0
		£194,, 7,,	0
	To Samuel Brooks for Sundries Supplied the Towns poor	1,,12,,	8
	All which is Submitted,	£195,,19,,	0

Nathl Paine } Committee
David Bigelow }

Voted, That one hundred pounds be granted to defray the incidental Expenses of the Town the current year; and that it be levied and assessed upon the Polls and Estates of the Inhabitants.

Voted, That this meeting be adjourned to the second Monday in December next, at two o'clock in the afternoon. And it was adjourned accordingly.

A True Entry,   Attest,   Leonard Worcester
Town Clerk, pro. tem.

Worcester Town Records, 1796.

At a Meeting of the Inhabitants of the Town of Worcester, qualified, to Vote for Representatives to the General Court, pursuant to the foregoing Warrant, on the Seventh day of November, 1796, for the purpose of giving in their votes for an Elector of President and Vice President of the United States, the following persons had the number of votes affixed to their names respectively, Viz.

    For Joseph Allen Esq. 72
    For His Honour Moses Gill 4
    For the Hon. Artemas Ward 2
    For the Hon. Levi Lincoln 1

The Meeting was then dissolved

A true Entry. Attest, Leonard Worcester Town Clerk, pro tem.

At a meeting of the Inhabitants of the Town of Worcester, qualified to vote for Representatives to the General Court, pursuant to the foregoing Warrant, on Monday, the seventh day of November, 1796, for the purpose of giving in their votes for a Representative in the Congress of the United States, for the Fourth Western District, the following persons were voted for, and had the number of votes affixed to their names respectively, viz.

    The Hon. Dwight Foster Esq. 66
    The Hon. Levi Lincoln Esq. 42
    His Honour Moses Gill Esq. 1

The Meeting was then dissolved

A True Entry. attest, Leonard Worcester, Town Clerk pro. tem.

Town meeting held May 2^d. 1796 by adjournment from march meeting

Voted that the Report of the Committee Chose to make an Estimate of School Houses be recommitted to them & that they further proced in the business and when compleated that they give information to the Selectmen that they may put an article in the Warrant to have the Town receive their report and act thereon

Voted to accept the Report of the Selectmen of the Situation of the Town Bonds in their hands which Report is as Follows

Report of the Selectmen respecting the Situation of the Towns Bonds in their hands

John Chamberlain Bond dated May 20th. 1790 £101— Interest pd
Alpheas Eaton   Do   Do march 26th. 1795   10-10 Interest pd
Jacob Millers   Do   Do August 14th 1794   18-15   Int. pd
Jacob Millers Note Do August 14th 1794   12-2-8   Int. pd
Ignatius Gouldings Bond Do Decm. 1st 1793   98-7-0   Int. pd
Saml Johnsons   Do   Do Nov. 8th 1794   52-10-0   Int. pd
Joseph Patch   Do   Do Sept. 11th 1793   143-0-0   Int. pd
Zebulon Cuttings   Do   Do Sept. 3d 1790   50-0-0   Int. pd
Ebenr. Hastings   Do   Do Janu. 5th 1792   90-4-6   Int. pd
Elijah Flaggs   Do   Do Feb. 21st 1795   48-9-6   Int. pd
John Stowers   Do   Do Sept. 12th 1795   20-16-0   Int. pd
David Stowell   Do   Do march 23 1795   26-0-0   Int. pd
Thomas Wheelers   Do   Do Decm. 1st. 1793   23-10-0
Abel Stowells   Do   Do May 7th 1792   26-14-0   Int. pd
Saml. Browns   Do   Do July 21st. 1783   39-5-0   Int. pd
Oliver Watson   Do   Do march 28th 1785   83-6-8   Int. pd
Daniel Heywoods   Do   Do Decm. 1st 1793   30-18-0   Int. pd
Simeon Duncans   Do   Do march 10th. 1786 40-0-0   Int. pd
William Gouldings   Do   Do may 7th 1792   14-10-0   Int. pd
John Goulds   Do   Do Jany. 24th 1791   33-6-8 Int. pd
John Stantons & Danl. Gouldings Do Do march 10th 1785
                                              35-0-0   Int. pd.
John Stantons & Danl Gouldings Do Nov. 26th 1786
                                              19-10-0 Int. pd
Daniel Gouldings   Do   Do Feb. 15th 1785 48-10-0   Int. pd
Joseph Allens   Do   Do august 30th 1784 51-1-1 Int. pd
Phins. Wards   Do   Do Nov. 1st. 1773   22-15-0 Int. pd
Levi Lincolns   Do   Do Feb. 15th. 1785 51-10-0   Int. pd
Leonard Worcester Do   Do august 13th. 1795 33-0-0 Int. pd
Jesse Tafts   Do   Do July 21st 1786   39-5-0   Int. pd

314   *Worcester Town Records, 1796.*

David Bigelow	Do	Do Nov. 1st. 1782	35 - 16 - 8	Int. pd
Willm. Gates	Do	Do Decm. 1st. 1793	15 - 11 - 2	Int. pd
Willm. Gouldings	Do	Do march 4th 1795	35 - 0 - 0	Int. pd
Ephraim Mowers Note		Do march 3d 1796	52 - 3 - 4	no Interest
Daniel Gouldings Bond	Do Decm. 1st. 1793	29 - 8 - 0	[Due

Samuel Flaggs Ground Rent is paid

 all the above Sums are well Secured by Sufficient Suretys and the Interest arising the last year amounting to £73 „ 14 „ 1½ has been paid into the Treasury

       Nathl. Paine
       B Heywood
       Saml. Flagg   } Selectmen
       Phineas Jones

meeting Dissolved
 A True Entry attest Danl. Goulding Town Clerk

Worcester Decm. 12th. 1796

 Henery Patch came before the Subscriber and was Sworn as a Collector of Taxes in the Town of Worcester agreeable to law in Such case made & provided

         Nathl. Paine Jus pacis
 To Capt Danl. Goulding Town Clerk
  A True Entry attest Daniel Goulding Town Clerk

 [The following entries were made upon the last leaves and insides of the covers of Volume IV.]

 We the Subscribers do hereby certify whom it may concern that Levi Bigelow Son of Mr. David Bigelow of this Town, & Deborah his wife, at the age of five years & ten months, by accident, on the fifteenth day of March, in the year 1779, was exposed, & within the reach of a horse that was then in the Said Davids Stable, & then & there, the margin of the Said Levi Bigelows right

Ear, was bitten & torn off by Said horse.—We also do hereby direct you to record this Certificate on the Town book that the misfortune abovesaid may not be any prejudice hereafter to the Said Levi

David Bigelow ⎫ Selectmen
John Green   ⎬   of
Jonathan Rice ⎭ Worcester

To M^r. Joseph Allen Town Clerk of Worcester

      A true Entry   att^s.   Jos. Allen Town Clerk

To Clark Chandler Town Clerk of Worcester

April 4th 1774

This is to give notice that Reuben Parmitter, his wife & Young Child have lately (viz) last Thursday [come] into Worcester from marlborough & now lives in my house near m^r. Nathan Perrys Said Parmitter having hired the place I desire you would give Notice to Selectmen & Enter this notice of record in the Town Book for which I will pay your fees   Your Sv^t

James Putman

Enterd from the Original ℔ C Chandler T Clerk

To the Selectmen of the Town of Worcester

    Gentlemen

The[se] are to advise you that I have taken Patte Right into my family to live with me she is about eight years of age and is the Daughter of John Right of Shrewsbury from whence she came to live with me last march

    I am Gen^t. your very humble Servt

Jonathan Rice

Worcester Dec^b. 10th 1774

Enterd from the Original ℔ C Chandler

Worcester Town Records, 1796.

To the Selectmen of Worcester Gentlemen. These are to inform you that I have taken from Boston Susana Mun a poor Girl about Eleven Years old to dwell with me untill she is eighteen Years old   I am Gentlemen your Humble Servt.

Wm Young

Worcester Augt. 30th 1775

To Either of the Selectmen of the Town of Worcester or the Town Clerk of Said Town

Benjamen Flagg of Worcester gives Information that Conrath alias Cornelius Schallhoss with his wife one Child by leave of Sundry of the Inhabitants belonging to the School Quarter in that Part of the Town he Lives in is admitted to reside and now Dwells in the School house in Said Quarter and have Dwelt their Sence the Twelvth of april currant   they are foreigners and Say they came last From North Carolina and their Circumstances are poor but they appear Industrious and are in good health

Benjamen Flagg

Worcester April 19th 1786

April 21st. 1786   Rec^d. Entered & Examined

Test   Daniel Goulding Town Clerk

To Daniel Goulding Town Clerk of Worcester in the County of Worcester

This is to give you Notice that I the Subscriber have taken up a mare Colt two Years old Dark Chesnut Colour a Small white Spot in her forehead & a Small Stripe down her Face and I Desire you to make an Entry of the Same according to the Law in Such Case made & Provided   Thadeas Bigelow

Worcester June 8th 1792

A True Entry   attest   Daniel Goulding

Broke into my enclosure on y^e. 26th. of Octr. 1793 a Fat Cow, Specked brown & White, both Ears Brown, face all white, the Right Ear Split the Left a half penny Cut out Supposed to be thirteen years old,   John Chamberlain

Worcester No^v. 6th. 1793

To Daniel Goulding Town Clerk   Pleas to Record the above as the Law prescribes in Such Case

Rec^d. No^v. 8th. 1793

    A True Entry   attest   Daniel Goulding Town Clerk

To Daniel Goulding Town Clerk of Worcester

June 11th. 1795

I hereby certify that on the fifth day of this present June that I the Subscriber found and took up a Stray Cow Supposed to be Nine years old a dark brown a hole bored in one horn   I desire you to make an Entry of the Same according to Law in Such made & provided   Joseph Patch

Received June 11th 1795

    A True Entry   attest   Daniel Goulding Town Clerk

To Daniel Goulding Town Clerk for Worcester

This is to give you Notice that I the Subscriber have taken up a mare Colt two years old a bay Colour the hind feet both white a white Spot on her forehead no artificial mark about her and I desire you to make an Entry of the Same according to Law in Such Case made & provided   Rhoda Flagg

Worcester July 20th 1795

    A True Entry   attest   Daniel Goulding Town Clerk

Received July 20th. 1795

Taken up by Micah Johnson of Worcester Six Sheep four of them has horns one a weather all white one yew has a Brown Face one has the Top of the Left Ear cut off & a Slit in the Top of the Right Ear

Worcester December 20th. 1784

Entered from the original   Daniel Goulding Town Cler

Taken up by the Subscriber a Red cow both Ears cropt high horns Some white on her Bag   Supposed to be Ten or Eleven Years old   Jonathan Lovell

Worcester December 29th 1785

S^d Cow was Prised this Day by M^r. David Bigelow & M^r. Nathl. Heywood to be worth £3„6..0

Dec^m. 31st. 1785   Rec^d. Entered & Examined

Daniel Goulding Town Clerk

Worcester 10th Septr 1787

Broke into the Inclosure of the Subscriber a Dark Sorell Horse Coalt Supposed to be two years old with a Blaze in his face and both hind feet White Trots all,   The owner of said Colt may have him paying reasonable Charges   Samuel Flagg

Octr. 2^d 1787 Rec^d and Entered by

Theophilus Wheeler Town Clerk

Worcester 3^d January 1788   We the Subscribers being this day appointed by Leu^t. Thomas Knight of Worcester to appraise two heifers, viz, one red & the other Dark brown as Directed in the advertizements, we adjudged the red heifer @ 1„12/ and the other @ 1„14/   As Witness our hands

Isaac Chadwick
Ely Flagg

Rec^d & Entered by Theoph^s Wheeler Town Clerk

To M^r. Theophilus Wheeler Town Clerk of Worcester

I hereby Certify that on the thirteenth day of Septr. last past five white Ewe Sheep with their right Ears cut off, and three white Weathers & one black weather with their right Ear cut off, broke into the Inclosure of the Subscriber and have remained there Since to this time, which I desire you to Enter in the Town Book
Robart Gray

Worcester Octr. 6th 1791

    A True Entry   att   Theo. Wheeler Town Clerk

To Daniel Goulding Town Clerk of Worcester in the County of Worcester

This is to give you Notice that I the Subscriber have taken up a Stray beast, a Steer, of a pale red Colour, white Rump three Years old and one peace of the left Ear cut of. and I desire you to make an Entry of the Same according to the Law in Such Case made & provided   Samuel Moore

June 2^d 1792

    A True Entry   attest   Daniel Goulding Town Clerk

Taken up and Strayed by Paul Kingston of Worcester a Small pale red Steer coming two Years old the owner is desired to take him away & pay the Costs

Worcester Decem^r. 15th. 1783

    Entered from the Original   Daniel Goulding T Clerk

Taken up in damage feasant impounded & Strayed by Nathan Patch of Worcester a dark brown mare four years old no Natural nor artificial mark about her

Worcester may 10th 1784

    Entered from the original   Daniel Goulding Town Clerk

[On the inside of cover.]

In Council June 19 1773 order that *Gershom Rice Israel Stephens David Bancroft Jonathan Stone Daniel Boyden Jacob Stephens Tho⁸. Drury Tho⁸. Drury Jun. Henry Gale Wᵐ Bancroft James Nichols Darius Boyden James Hart Thomas Baird James Hart Junʳ. Thomas Baird Jun. Oliver Curtis Comfort Rice Elizabeth Boyden Phe Bancroft John Boyden Daniel Bancroft Charles Hart James Nichols Peter Boyden* of Worcester *Benjᵃ Carter Charles Richardson Timothy Carter Phinias Rice Benjᵃ Carter Jun Rachel Buck Daniel Roper Gershom Bigelow Gershom Bigelow Jun Peter Hardy Daniel Comings Charles Richardson Jun* of Sutton *Samˡ Eddy Levi Eddy Peter Jenison Ruth Stone Jesse Stone Isaac Pratt Abraham Fitts Alexander Nichols David Gleason* of Oxford *John Crowle Jun Andrew Crowle Jonᵃ. Phillips John Hart Thoˢ. Scott William Yong Jonathan Stone* of Leicester, be & hereby are with their familys & Estates Erected into a Precinct & Shall Enjoy all the Powers & Previledges with Precincts in this Province by Law Enjoy and it is further ordered that all other persons (with their familys & Estates) liveing in the Towns of Worcester Leicester & oxford not further than three miles as the Roads are now trod from the Place hereinafter fixed for Building the meeting House upon together with all Such others in Sutton that live not further than one mile & an half from Said place who Shall Signify their desire to belong to Said Precinct by Lodging their names in the Secretarys office within Nine [   ] from this date be and hereby are Incorporated and made a part of the Precinct aforesaid

Ordered that the Spot for Erecting the meeting House upon be at the following place (Vizᵗ) at an oak Stump with Stones upon it Standing on the Westerly side of the County Road leading from Worcester to oxford near the Center of two acres of Land which Thomas Drury Conveyed to Jonathan Stone Daniel

Boyden & David Bancroft the Said two acres of Land Lieth in the Gore of Land that was annexed to the Town of Worcester

Sent down for Concurrance   Thos. Fluker Scy

In House of Representatives June 23: 1773 Read & Concured   Thos. Cushing Spk^r

Consented   T Hutchinson

A true Copy   Attest   John Cotton Dep S^y

A true Copy taken from the original

     Attest   Clark Chandler T Clerk

[End of the Fourth Volume.]

To the Gentlemen the Selectmen of the Town of Worcester

We the Subscribers Freeholders of the Said Town hereby request you to call a meeting of the Inhabitants of the Town of Worcester as Soon as may be that the Said Inhabitants may express their Sentiments & take Such measures as may appear to them expedient, respecting the Commercial Treaty entered into & ratified between the United States of America & Great Britain

And as in duty will pray

	John Stanton	William Caldwell
April 28th 1796	Daniel Clap	Jos Allen
	Eph^m. Mower	Leonard Worcester
	Saml. Chandler	Abraham Lincoln
	Thomas Rice	Jos Allen Ju^r.
	Nathl. Chandler	Stephen Salsbury
	Thos. Chandler	Edward Bangs
	John Nazro	Theoph^s. Wheeler
	Willm. M^{c}farland	Oliver Fisk
	Eben^r. Lovell	Daniel Waldo
	Asa Hambelton	Charles Chandler

At a legal meeting of the Inhabitants of the Town of Worcester in the County of Worcester and Commonwealth of Massachusetts on Monday the Second day of may in the Year of our Lord 1796 Chose Edward Bangs Esqr. Moderator

Voted to Send a memorial to the Honble house of Representatives of the United States praying that appropriation may be made for carrying the treaty into Effect — and that Edward Bangs, Isaiah Thomas, Samuel Chandler, Benjamen Heywood and William Caldwell be a Committee to draw a memorial for the purpose aforesaid — Whereupon the afore Named persons did present an address to the Honble the House of Representatives a True Copy of Which is hereunto annexed for the Consideration of the Inhabitants so assembled and which being read was unanimously accepted there being one hundred & Eighty qualified Voters present

Voted that a Copy of Said Memorial be transcribed by the Town Clerk and that he be directed to forward the Same to Dwight Foster Esquire their Representative in Congress to be by him presented to the house

To the Honorable the House of Representatives of the United States

The Inhabitants of the Town of Worcester in the County of Worcester & State of Massachusetts

Sensible that it is not wise in the people in their primary assemblies to decide confidently on important & difficult political questions or even to use their right of petitioning with design to impose their particular opinions. Yet on the present occasion when the voice of the people appears to be called for & is going forth to your Honorable body from all parts of the Union leaving all questions concerning the merits of the treaty with great Brittain take liberty to Suggest as our opinion that considering the present State of the treaty already ratified by the president & Senate. we believe from a Serious impression of Duty & considering the happy advantages of peace & neutrality now enjoyed by this country & the alarms the anxieties & interruptions to business if not war that may be the consequence of delaying to carry the treaty into effect it would be best & we therefore beg leave to express our wishes that your honourable house would not delay to make appropriations to carry the Same into effect

Voted that this meeting be dissolved & the meeting was dissolved accordingly

 A True Entry attest Daniel Goulding Town Clerk

At a legal meeting of the Inhabitants of the Town of Worcester December 12th. 1796 Pursuant to adjournment from November the 7th. Last

The Committee appointed upon the Subject of School Houses laid before the Town their report which was read it was then moved & Seconded to See if the Town would accept of Said report the motion was then put and passed in the affirmative — the report is as follows —

The Committee appointed to consider of the best manner of dividing the Town into School Destrects, Submit the following mode to the consideration of the Town (viz)

N° 1 Or the Center district to consist of all those Inhabitants which now compose that district except 'Doct'. John Green and on account of the great Number of minors within the Same to be considered as a double district and to be furnished with a School House calculated for keeping two Schools at the Same time

N° 2 The western or Tatnick district to remain as it now is

N° 3 Or Southwestern District to consist of those Inhabitants who now compose that district with the addition of Messrs. White, Tracy, Thadeus Chapen & Eli Chapen and to be furnished with a School house near the Bridge on the road leading to Oxford

N° 4 Or Southern District to be composed of the residue of the former one of that Name and all the district called Stowells district except the Estate late of Jon^a. Rice Elijah Harrington, Silas Harrington and Benjamen Heywood and will probably be best accomodated with a School House placed as near to the Bridge by M^r. Thomas^s. Mills as Shall be thought expedient

N°. 5 Or Southeastern district will be composed of the Said Estate Late of Jonathan Rice Elijah Harrington Silas Harrington

& Benj[a]. Heywood, the District called Bairds district and all the district called Gates district except Mess[rs]. Hastings and W[m]. Taylor in which a School house will best accommodate near the corner by Daniel Stearns old House

    N° 6 Or Northeastern district to be composed of Doct[r]. John Green Mess[rs]. Hasting William Taylor and the old district called Curtis[s]. district with the addition of Dan[l]. Chadwick Jon[a]. Gleason Cap[t]. Tho[s]. Stowell & Joseph Barber to have a School House at the corner of the road by M[r]. James Fisks —

    N°. 7 Or Northern district to consist of the present district in that part of the Town with the addition of Cap[t]. Nath[l]. Brooks M[r]. James Barber Cap[t]. John Gay & M[r]. Levi Flagg and to have a School House placed where the old one now is on burnt Coat plain

    N° 8 Or Northwestern district to remain as it now is with the addition of M[r]. Robert Smith

                  All which is Submitted
                            Benj[a]. Heywood p[r]. Order

Dec[m]. 12th. 1796

Voted to allow the following accounts against the Town viz[t].

To John Elder for Boarding & Nursing John Spence from 19th. Oct[r]. 1795 to 14th. Dec[m]. 1796 being 60 Weeks @ 8/	£24	0	0
Deduct Cash Rec[d]. 10 march last in part	4	0	0
Due	£20	0	0
To Jedediah Heley for a Coffin for Young Cary	0	12	0
To Jedediah Heley for 2 Coffins for Silas Hows Children	0	14	0
To Sam[l]. Flagg for Pork and Grain dld Sam[l] Denny	1	1	6
To William Goulding for repairs to the poor House & painting guide Posts	1	0	0
	23	7	6

Voted to abate to M^r. John Barnard
Sundrey Persons Taxes in his hands
to Collect vizt.

1792 Taxes Abner Childs	£0 ,,	3 ,, 9
Thomas Craige	0 ,,	3 ,, 9
Thomas Eayrs	0 ,,	10 ,, 5
Saml. Ethridge	0 ,,	11 ,, 9
Willm. Gilbert	0 ,,	3 ,, 9
Edward Hair	0 ,,	3 ,, 9
Thomas Knight	0 ,,	4 ,, 0
Jonathan Lynd	0 ,,	9 ,, 5
Barnard B McNutta	0 ,,	3 ,, 9
Joseph Miller	0 ,,	3 ,, 9
Israel Osburn	0 ,,	3 ,, 9
Elijah Pike	0 ,,	3 ,, 9
Willm. Wiley	0 ,,	3 ,, 9
David Wiley	0 ,,	3 ,, 9

1793 Taxes
State

Moses Adams	0 ,,	3 ,, 9
Increas Blake	0 ,,	1 ,, 9
Thomas Craige	0 ,,	1 ,, 4
John Childs Ju^r.	0 ,,	1 ,, 9
Edward Hair	0 ,,	1 ,, 4
Hale	0 ,,	1 ,, 4
Lymas Leonard	0 ,,	1 ,, 4
Jonathan Lynd	0 ,,	4 ,, 7
Barnard B McNutta	0 ,,	1 ,, 4
Josiah Sterne	0 ,,	1 ,, 4
William Treadwell	0 ,,	2 ,, 5
Caleb Weltch	0 ,,	1 ,, 4

Town

Moses Adams	0 ,,	1 ,, 6
Increas Blake	0 ,,	2 ,, 0
John Childs Jur	0 ,,	2 ,, 0
Hale	0 ,,	1 ,, 6
Edward Hair	0 ,,	1 ,, 6

Lymas Leonard	0 ,, 1 ,, 6
Jonathan Lynd	0 ,, 5 ,, 3
Bernard B McNutta	0 ,, 1 ,, 6
William Treadwell	0 ,, 2 ,, 9
Caleb Welch	0 ,, 1 ,, 6
	0 ,, 6 ,, 6
	£6 ,, 1 ,, 8

Voted that this meeting be Dissolved and the meeting was dissolved accordingly

A True Entry   attest   Danl. Goulding Town Clerk

At a meeting of the Qualified Voters of the Town of Worcester legally assembled, at the meeting house of the first parish in Said Town on Monday January the Ninth day A. D. 1797 [1]

The following Votes were passed vizt.

Chose Samuel Flagg Esqr. Moderator

A motion was made & Seconded to See if the Town would take any measures to build or provide publick School Houses in the Town the motion was put and passed in the affirmative

A motion was then made & Seconded to See if there Shall be any alteration in the School districts different from the report made by a Committee at the last meeting and accepted by the Town the motion was put and passed in the affirmative

Voted that M^r. Nathaniel Harringtons School district remain as it was before the proposed alteration made by the Committee

Voted that M^r. Benj^a. Stowells School district So called remain as it was before the proposed alteration

Voted that Notwithstanding the above Votes if any individual or individuals in Town find it for his or their Interest to leave his or their School district and Join any Other in Town that he or they may have leave provided he or they make known his or their

---

[1] ARTICLE 3:—"To See if the Town will cause the Bell in the first Parish meeting House to be rung at Nine OClock at Night the ensuing year"

Election before the first of march Next by giving information to the Town Clerk in writing mentioning the District that he or they have a Desire to belong to

Voted that Samuel Curtis Esq^{rs}. School destrict remain as it was before the proposed alteration

Voted to Choose a Committee to ascertain what bigness the School Houses Shall be in Each district the Expence of Each & the whole amount and where there is a dispute in any district where the School House Shall Stand they to determine on the place & make their report at the adjournment of this meeting

Then Chose John Nazro, James M^{c}farland, Willm. Trobridge, Samuel Curtis Esqr. Moses Perry, Saml. Harrington, Samuel Porter, James Fisk, Deacon David Bigelow & Deacon Eben^r. Reed a Committee for Said purpose

Voted that this meeting be adjourned to Monday the Sixth Day of march Next at two OClock in the afternoon then to meet at this Place & the meeting was accordingly adjourned

       attest Danl. Goulding T C

At a meeting of the Freeholders & Other inhabitants of the Town of Worcester qualified to Vote in Town affairs duly warned & assembled at the publick meeting House of the first parish in Said Town on Monday the Sixth day of March in the the Year of our Lord Seventeen hundred & Ninety Seven

Deacon John Chamberlain Chosen Moderator

Daniel Goulding Town Clerk

Samuel Flagg Esqr. Nathaniel Paine Esqr. Deacon John Chamberlain Colo Phineas Jones Benjn. Heywood Esqr. Selectmen

Voted that the Selectmen be overseers of the Poor the Current year

M^r. Samuel Chandler Town Treasurer

5th may	Sworn	Samuel Flagg Esqr.	⎫
5 may	Sworn	Collo Phineas Jones	⎬ assessors
		Doct^r. Oliver Fisk	⎭

16th march Sworn Thomas Johnson Searcher & Sealer of Leather

June 3d. Sworn Joshua Whitney ⎫
      Ebenezer Mower ⎬ Fence Viewers
      Ephraim Mower ⎭

      Ephraim Mower ⎫ Clerks of the market
20th of march Sworn Samuel Bridge ⎭

      Joshua Whitney Deer Reeve

June 3d. Sworn Joshua Whitney ⎫ Field Drivers
14 march Sworn Henery Patch ⎭

6th. march Sworn Asa Holbrook ⎫ Tythingmen
      Eli Gale ⎭

      Simeon Duncan ⎫ Viewers & Cullers of
17th march Sworn Frost Rockwood ⎭ Hoops & Staves

      William Goulding ⎫ Surveyors of Boards
      Samuel Porter ⎭ & Shingles

1798 Feb. 2d Swn Benjamen Andrews ⎫ Measurers of Wood
      Benjamen Butman ⎭ & Bark

15th march Sworn Samuel Johnson ⎫
24th march Sworn Thomas Sheperd
      Josiah Perry
      Jabez Stratton
15th march Sworn Ebenr. Willington 3d ⎬ Hog Reeves
      Thomas W Millet
      David Griggs
15th march Sworn John Ranks
      Elisha Smith
      Jonathan Gleazen Jur ⎭

      Capt. Daniel Heywood ⎫
15th march Sworn Samuel Jenison
      Paul Gates
      Joshua Whitney
14th march Sworn Henery Patch
15th march Sworn Nathl. Gates
5th may Sworn Benja. Heywood ⎬ Surveyors of High-
6th march Sworn Thadeas Chamberlain ways & Collectors of
      Ebenr. Reed   Highway Taxes
      Reuben Gray
      Benja. Flagg Jur.
6th march Sworn James Mcfarland
      Jonathan Lovell
      Isaac Putman
16 march Sworn Elias Stowell
5 march Sworn Jonathan Gleazen 1st ⎭

Benjamen Heywood Thomas Payson Phineas Jones Committee to Settle accounts with the Town Treasurer

John Nazro Daniel Clap Samuel Flagg Ephraim Mower Fire Wards

Sworn march 6th Ebenezer Reed } Constables
Sworn march 11th Peter Stowell

Sworn 6th march Chose Deacon Ebenezer Reed Collector of Publick Taxes for the Town the Current he giving Sufficient Bonds to the Satisfaction of the Selectmen for the faithfull performance of his Trust & Voted that he be allowed three pence three farthings for what moneys he Collects on the pound

Voted that the Sum of Four Hundred & fifty pounds be assessed and raised on the Polls & Estates in this Town for the purpose of keeping the Publick roads in repair the current Year

Voted that those that have a mind to work out their Highway Taxes that they be allowed at the rate of Six Shillings p^r. day for a man and for Oxen Carts Plows &c to be proportioned accordingly

Voted that if there is any person or persons that have not worked out their last year Highway Taxes that they have liberty to work out the Same provided they do it on or before the first of July Next at the rate of four Shillings a day for a man & Oxen Carts Plows &c in the Same proportion as the last year

Chose Nathaniel Paine Esqr. a Agent to prosecute or defend to final Judgment & Execution any Suit or Suits that may be brought for or against the Town

Voted that the Swine be under the Same restrictions the Current year they were the last year

Voted to abate to M^r. Thomas Rice Sundrey Persons Taxes in his Tax Bill which he Says he is not able to Collect but provided he at any future Time Collects any Part of them that he be accountable to the Town for the Same viz

	Town Tax	State Tax	Total D C
Benj^a French	0–66	0–32	0—98
Gideon Goold	0–66	0–32	0—98

Dan¹. Grant	0–66	0–32	0—98
Silas How	0–66	0–32	0—98
Jeremy Horton	0–66	0–32	0—98
Thomas Kelly	0–90	0–44	1—34
Thomas Linch	0–90	0–44	1—34
Isaac Livermore	0–66	0–32	0—98
William Maynard	0–66	0–32	0—98
Parker Parmer	0–66	0–32	0—98
Amasa Thomas	0–66	0–32	0—98
			11—48

Voted that this meeting be adjourned to monday the third day of April Next at two OClock in the afternoon then to meet at this Place and the meeting was accordingly adjourned,

   A True Entry Daniel Goulding T C

At a Town meeting held at the Publick meeting House of the first Parish in Worcester on Monday March the 6th. 1797 by adjournment from January the Ninth A D 1797

 Chose Deacon John Chamberlain Moderator Pro Tem

 Voted to Choose a Committee to See if the Remaining part of Samuel Curtis'ˢ Esqʳˢ. School destrect So Called cannot be accomodated or annexed to Other School destrects then Chose Deacon John Chamberlain Deacon David Bigelow & Mʳ. Nathan Heard a Committee for Said Purpose

 Voted that this meeting be adjourned to monday the third day of April Next at two OClock in the afternoon then to meet at this Place and the meeting was accordingly adjourned

  A True Entry attest Daniel Goulding Town Clerk

At a Town meeting held agreeable to the above adjournment on Monday April the third day A D 1797

 A motion being made & Seconded to See if the Town would reconsider a Vote passed at a Town meeting in January last giving any Person or Persons liberty of Joining any Other School destrect in Town than what he or they belonged to the motion being put passed in the Negative

A motion being made & Seconded to See if the Town would accept of the report of a Committee Chose to See if Saml. Curtis Esq^{rs}. School Quarter could not be accomodated the motion being put passed in the affirmative — the report is as follows viz

Your Committee appointed march last to view the Situation of Esqr. Curtis'^{s} School Quarter So Called have attended S^d. Service and beg leave to report as follows —

that we find the Situation of Said Quarter all together may be tolerably convened if they had a School house in the center and all in Said Quarter willing to remain their but as Several of S^d. Quarter wish to be taken into other Quarters it is our opinion that as is the wish of many to build publick School houses in Said Town that Said Quarter may as be accomodated for part to Join Colo Jones^s. Quarter where the School house is and the remainder to Join Benj^a. Stowells Quarter if the School House can be Set near the paper mill the North Side of the Bridge except Esqr. Curtis as it will make one School House less

all which is humbly Submitted

Worcester March 30th. 1797 John Chamberlain p^r. Order

Voted that the Sum of Seven hundred & fifty pounds be assessed on the polls and Estates in this Town & raised for the purpose of Building publick School Houses in Said Town

Voted to Choose a Committee to carry the building Publick School houses into effect — then Chose Saml. Brazer, Nathan Heard, Nathaniel Coolidge, Abraham Lincoln, William Goulding, Jedediah Heley, Capt. Holbrook, John Chamberlain, James M^{c}farland, William Trobridge, Phineas Jones, David Andrews, Joseph Kingsbury, Samuel Andrews, David Bigelow, Benj^a. Heywood, Saml. Harrington, Daniel Baird, James Fisk, Jonathan Gleason, Joseph Chadwick, Benj^a. Thaxster, Capt. Farror, Eben^r. Reed, Nathl. Stowell, Joshua Whitney, Samuel Goddard, Saml. Porter, Nathl. Harrington & Saml. Curtis Ju^r. a Committee for Said purpose

Voted that this meeting be dissolved & the meeting was dissolved accordingly

 A True Entry attest Daniel Goulding Town Clerk

At a Town meeting held on Monday April 3ᵈ. A D 1797 by adjournment from annual march meeting

Voted that the Sum of two hundred & Sixty five pounds be assessed on the polls & Estates in this Town & raised for the purpose of Supplying the Town with publick Schools the Current year

Voted that the Sum of Forty five pounds be allowed out of the above Sum to the Center School destrect for the purpose of keeping a Publick Grammar School for the Town the Current year and the remainder of Said Sum to be expended in the Same way and manner the money raised last year was for the Support of Schools

Then Chose the following persons a Committee to provide the Town publick Schools Nathˡ. Coolidge, Saml Andrews, Asa Hambelton, Samˡ. Curtis Juʳ. Nathˡ. Brooks, Phineas Bartlett, Joseph Holbrook, Samˡ. Harrington, Jonathan Grout, Samˡ. Goddard & Nathˡ. Flagg

Then Chose Jonathan Gates 2ᵈ. & Phineas Gleason Highway Surveyors and Collectors of Highway Taxes

Voted that this meeting be dissolved & the meeting was dissolved accordingly

 A True Entry attest Daniel Goulding Town Clerk

At a Town meeting held at the first parish meeting house in Worcester on Monday the third day of April A. D. 1797 the following Persons were voted for [for] Governor Lieuᵗ Governor & Senators & Counsellors & had the Number of Votes expressed against their respective Names—

For Governor
Honble Increase Sumner   88
Sulliven   37
Moses Gill   2
Elbridge Gerry   1

For Lieu^{t}. Governor
Honble Moses Gill   83
Sulliven   9

Senators & Counsellors

Levi Lincoln	76	Josiah Stearns	22
John Sprague	72	Benj^{a}. Reed	16
Danl. Bigelow	93	Saml. Flagg	13
Salem Town	94	Elijah Brigham	10
Barzale Taft	73	Pliny Merick	7
		Nathl. Paine	4
		Edward Bangs	1

The Meeting was then dissolved

  A True Entry attest Daniel Goulding T C

At a meeting of the Inhabitants of the Town of Worcester on Monday May 15th. A. D. 1797 For the purpose of Choosing one or more Representatives to represent the Said Inhabitants in the General Court to be convened at Boston on the last wednesday of May Instant

Then Chose Samuel Flagg & Levi Lincoln Esq^{rs}. for Said purpose

Then Voted that this meeting be dissolved and the meeting was accordingly Dissolved

  A True Entry attest Daniel Goulding Town Clerk

At a Legal meeting of the Qualified Voters of the Town of Worcester at the publick meeting house of the first parish in Said Town on Monday May 15th. 1797—

Chose Deacon David Bigelow Moderator

Voted to reconsider a Vote passed April last 3^d. Day for raising Seven hundred & fifty pounds for the purpose of Building Publick School Houses in Said Town—

Voted to accept the Following report of the Selectmen Shewing the Situation of the Town Bonds—

A list of the Town Bonds in y^e. hands of y^e. Selectmen

	Principle	Interest
Alp^a. Eaton W^m. Eaton & Simeon Duncan Sureties	£10 ,, 10 ,, 0	£0 ,, 12 ,, 7½
Jesse Taft Josiah Lyon & Joseph Barber Do	39 ,, 5 ,, 0	2 ,, 7 ,, 1¼
David Bigelow John Green Do	35 ,, 16 ,, 8	2 ,, 3 —
Joseph Patch Benj^a. Flagg & Aaron Flagg Do	143 ,, 0 ,, 0	8 ,, 11 ,, 7
Elijah Flagg Isaac Gleason & Edward Knight Sureties	£48 ,, 9 ,, 6	2 ,, 18 ,, 2
Thomas W Millet Eben^r. Williams & Isaac Putman Do	23 ,, 10 ,, 0	1 ,, 8 ,, 3
Jacob Miller Jed^h. Healy & Peter Stowell Do	18 ,, 15 ,, —	1 ,, 0 ,, 4
David Stowell Benj^a. Stowell & Nathl. Stowell Do	26 ———	1 ,, 11 ,, 2
Saml. Brown Elijah Dix Do	39 ,, 5 ,, —	2 ,, 7 ,, 1¼
Daniel Goulding Palmer Goulding & Igna^s. Goulding Do	48 ,, 10 ,, —	
Daniel Goulding Igna^s. Goulding & Danl. Heywood Do	29 ,, 8 ,, —	
John Stanton Palmer Goulding & Danl. Goulding Do	19 ,, 10 ,, —	
John Stanton Do & Do	35 ,, ———	
Daniel Heywood Ignatius Goulding & Danl Goulding Do	30 ,, 18 ,, —	1 ,, 17 ,, 0
Joseph Allen Elijah Dix Saml. Allen Do	34 ,, 11 ,, 1	2 ,, 1 ,, 5½
Eph^m. Mower Thomas Mower & Clark Chandler Do	42 ,, 3 ,, 4	2 ,, 10 ,, 6½
Isaac Jinks Benj^a. Drury given up Oliver Watsons Bond Do	83 ,, 6 ,, 8	5 ,, ———
John Gould John & Hol Taylor Do	33 ,, 6 ,, 8	2 ,, ———

Eben[r]. Hastings Will[m]. & Sam[l]. Gates Do	90 ,, 4 ,, 6	5 ,, 8 ,, 3½
John Chamberlain Ignatius & Daniel Goulding Do	101 ,, ——	6 ,, 1 ,, 2
Phin[s]. Ward Sam[l]. Curtis & David Ritchardson Do	22 ,, 15 ,, —	1 ,, 7 ,, 3½
Sim[n]. Duncan Joseph Blair & Joseph Allen Do	40 ,, ——	4 ,, 16 —
Abel Stowell Cornelius & Thomas Stowell Do	26 ,, 14 ,, 7	1 ,, 12 ,, 1
Will[m]. Gates Nath[l]. Harrington Do	15 ,, 11 ,, 2	- ,, 18 ,, 8
Zeb Cutting Peter Johnson & Jacob Holms Do	50 ,, ——	3 ,, ——
Sam[l]. Johnson James Fisk & Thos Stowell Do	52 ,, 10 ,, —	3 ,, 3 ,, -
Will[m]. Goulding Igna[s] & John R Goulding Do	35 ,, ——	2 ,, [r] 2 ,, -
Levi Lincoln Jos Allen & Igna[s]. Goulding Do	51 ,, 10 ,, —	3 ,, 1 ,, 9½
Will[m]. Goulding Igna[s]. Goulding & Will[m]. Johnson Do	14 ,, 10 ,, —	,, 17 ,, 5
Leonard Worcester Nathan Patch & Theo[s] Wheeler Do	33 ,, ——	1 ,, 19 ,, 7¼
Ignat[s]. Goulding Dan[l]. Goulding & John Chamberlain Do	98 ,, 7 ,, —	5 ,, 18 ,, -
Samuel Flaggs Lease of Shop Ground		3 ,, 12
		£80 ,, 5 ,, 8¾

The above Interest being Eighty Pounds five Shillings & Eight pence three farthings has been paid to M[r]. Sam[l]. Chandler Towns Treasurer as p[r]. his Receipt to Nath[l]. Paine Esq[r]. being the Interest arising on the above Bonds up to 1st. December 1796

N. B. Balance of Interest due on Dan[l]. Gouldings Bonds is £15 ,, 17 ,, 10½ to be accounted for on Settlement of y[e] Demands he has against the Town

£80 .. 5 .. 8¾
7 .. 18 .. 11¼
——————
£88 .. 4 .. 8

Samuel Flagg
Nath[l]. Paine   } Selectmen
Phineas Jones   of
Benj[a]. Heywood } Worcester

Voted to accept the following report of the Committee Chose to Settle accounts with the Town Treasurer

Town of Worcester in Acc^t. with Saml. Chandler Treasurer C^r

1796
May 2^d By Ballance due upon Settlement of accounts	£638 .. 4 ..	7½
By Cash received of the Commonwealth by the hands of the Selectmen	28 .. 2 ..	9
No^v. 7th. By Cash Received of Willm. Taylor for Interest due on his Note	2 .. 1 ..	1
Dec^m. 12th By assessors return of a Town Tax dld Henry Patch to Collect	440 .. 11 ..	9¼
1797 March 23^d. By Cash Rec^d. of the Commonwealth by the hands of the Selectmen	18 .. 7 ..	11¾
By Cash Rec^d. of the Selectmen for part of Interest money due to ye Town	69 .. 13 ..	10½
	£1197 .. 2 ..	1

D^r.

1	John Peirce p^r. Order of the Selectmen	£6 .. 2 .. 4	
2	Abel Heywood for 6 Crows Heads	6	—
3	Willard Johnson 5 Do Do	5	—
4	Danl. Flagg 5 Do Do	5	—
5	Jon^a. Butler 1 Do Do	1	—
6	Isaac Ball 4 Do Do	4	—
7	Caleb Johnson 4 Do Do	4	
8	Thomas Gray 16 Do Do	16	
9	Benj^a. Chapen 5 Do Do	5	
10	Senica Harrington 3 Do Do	3	
11	Henry Parker 1 Do Do	1	
12	Danl. Baird 5 Do Do	5	
13	Lawson Harrington 7 Do Do	7	
14	Mary Wheeler p^r. Order Selectmen	5 ,, 12 —	
15	Ezekiel Smith 5 Crows Heads	5	
16	Josiah Peirce 4 Do Do	4	

Worcester Town Records, 1797. 337

17	Josiah Peirce 5 Do Do	5
18	Micah Johnson Ju[r]. 5 Do Do	5
19	Tim°. Meryfield 4 Do Do	4
20	James Quigley p[r]. order Selectmen	6 ,, 12 —
21	Will[m]. Taylor p[r]. Do Do	2 ,, 11 ,, 3
22	Eben[r]. Lyon p[r]. Do Do	2 ,, 8 —
23	Abigail Ward p[r]. Do Do	12 —
24	John Stearns p[r]. Do Do	1 ,, 15
25	Abel Haywood 1 Crows Head	1
26	Will[m]. Mahan p[r]. Order Selectmen	4 ,, 7 ,, 2
27	Thomas Gray 3 Crows Heads	3 —
28	Abel Heywood 1 Do Do	1 —
29	William Mahan p[r]. Order Selectmen	24 ,, 10 ,, 5
30	Daniel Goulding p[r] order Selectmen	23 ,, 4 ,, 9½
31	Charles & S Chandler p[r]. Do	2 ,, 9 ,, 5½
32	John Chamberlain p[r]. Do	22 ,, 10 ,, 6
33	Amos Flagg 1 Crows Head	1 —
34	Dan[l]. Baird 1 Do Do	1
35	Sam[l]. Brazer & others p[r]. order Selectmen	139 ,, 6 ,, 1
36	Sim[n]. Coves 1 Crows Head	1
37	Daniel Baird 1 Do Do	1
38	School Committee p[r]. order Selectmen	220 ———
39	Assessors p[r]. order Selectmen	10 ,, 1 ,, 6
40	Jonathan Putman p[r]. Do	1 ,, 4 —
41	Sam[l]. Flagg "	12 —
42	Jed[h] Healy	1 ,, 6 —
43	Stephen Taylor	4 ,, 8 ,, 6
44	Amos Whitney 1 Crows Head	1 —
45	Micah Johnson p[r]. order Selectmen	12 —

43

46	Micah Johnson Ju^r.	5 ,, 10½
47	Abel Heywood	4 ,, 1 —
48	David Andrews	8 —
49	Thomas Rice	2 ,, 2 —
50	James M^{c}farland	5 ,, 10 —
51	John Elder	2 ,, 3 ,, 6
52	John Green Ju^r.	9 ,, 19 ,, 9
53	David Griggs	1 ,, 13 ,, 6
54	Amos Wheeler	5 ,, 10½
55	Jona Knight	2 ,, 10
56	Moses Miller	2 ,, 16 —
57	Saml. Kingston	3
58	Saml. Brazer	8 ,, 4
59	Sim^n. Duncan	9 ,, 8 ,, 9
60	Paul Goodale	12 —
61	Isaiah Thomas Ju^r	4 —
62	Danl. Goulding	19 ,, — ,, 10
63	John Chamberlain	6
64	Phin^s. Jones	1 ,, 8 ,, 8
65	Moses Miller	30
66	Saml. Brazer & others	12 ,, 2 ,, 9
67	Eliza Brown	18 ,, 4½
68	John Elder	20
69	Jesse Taft	5 ,, 10½
70	Mary Wheeler	15 ,, 4 —
71	Willm. Trobridge	18 ,, 6 ,, 4½
72	Eunice Rice	5 —
73	N Flagg & T Gleason	1 ,, 12 —
74	Willm. Trobridge	5 ,, 16 ,, 5
75	John Barnard	11 ,, 4 ,, 11
76	Miles Sprague	10 ,, 16
77	Saml. Moore	1 ,, 4 —
78	Eben^r. Mower	2 ,, 14 ,, 5
79	Daniel Baird Ju^r.	4 ,, 10
80	Jonathan Gates	3 ,, 3 —
81	John Nazro	2 ,, 1 —
82	John Stanton	2 ,, 17 ,, 5

83	Phineas Jones	6 ,, 7 ,, 2
84	Moses Miller	4 ,, 10 —
85	Nathan Perry	18 —
86	Nathl. Coolidge	45
87	Saml. Flagg	9 ,, 4 ,, 3
88	Saml. Brooks	1 ,, 12 —
89	Saml. Brazer	4 ——— 2
90	Amos Wheeler	4 ,, 10
91	Joel Bixby	3 ,, 17 —
92	Jos Morse	6 ,, 5 ,, 1
93	John Nazro	18 ,, 4
94	James Wilson	9 ,, 6
95	Jonathan Stearns	5 ,, 15 ,, 6
96	Willm. Goulding	1
	to Ballance carried to New account	424 ,, 0 – 5½

£ 1197 – 2 – 1

Worcester April 3^d. 1797

        Errors Excepted   Saml. Chandler Town Treasurer

Worcester April 3^d. 1797 We the Subscribers a Committee appointed to Settle with Saml. Chandler Town Treasurer have attended Said Service & report that the Said Saml. Chandler has Charged himself with Eleven hundred & Ninety Seven pounds two Shillings & one penny including the Ballance of his last account & that he has accounted for the Sum of Seven hundred & Seventy three pounds one Shilling & Seven pence half penny by producing of Sufficient vouchers therefor and that there remains Four Hundred & Twenty four pounds & five pence half penny to be further accounted for by him
      all which is Submitted by
                      Benj^a. Heywood } Committee
                      Thos. Payson   }

    Voted that this meeting be dissolved & the meeting was dissolved accordingly
        A True Entry   attest   Daniel Goulding Town Clerk

At a legal meeting of the Inhabitants of the Town of Worcester Qualified to Vote in Town affairs at the publick meeting House of the first Parish in Said Town on Monday the Twenty third day of October 1797

Chose Saml. Flagg Esqr. Moderator

Voted to Choose a Committee [to] examine the accounts that are brought against the Town at this meeting, then Chose Willm. Caldwell Esqr. M^r. Daniel Waldo Ju^r. & M^r. Samuel Brazer a Committee for Said Purpose

Voted to provide a pair of new wheels for the Hearse, then Chose M^r. Charles Stearns a Committee for to provide Said Wheels

Voted that this meeting be adjourned to monday the Sixth day of November Next at two OClock then to meet at this Place & the meeting was accordingly adjourned

  A True Entry attest Daniel Goulding Town Clerk

Met according to the above adjournment No^v. 6th. 1797

Voted to allow and accept the Report of the Committee Chose to examine the accounts brought against the Town which is as follows

The Subscribers a Committee appointed to examine the claims and demands exhibited against the Town of Worcester report as follows Viz^t. that there is due to

1	Daniel Waldo Ju^r.	D 36–72
2	Saml. & Charles Chandler & Co	8–24
3	John Elder in full for Supporting John Spence to No^v. 6	44–96
4	James M^{c}farland	17–34
5	Daniel Baird	6–33
6	Nathan Heard for mending Simon Glasgos Boots	–92
7	Daniel Fenno	6–76
8	Samuel Brazer	15–30

9	William Gates	47– 4
10	Thomas Nickels	53–28
11	Capt. Simeon Duncan	31–44
12	James Fisk	14–33
13	Doct^r. John Green Ju^r.	3–25
14	Deacon John Chamberlain	44–79
15	Asa Ward	32–99
16	Moses Miller	29–17
17	Capt. Samuel Brooks	15–13
18	William Goulding	8–13
19	Capt. Daniel Goulding	34–84
20	Samuel Flagg Esqr.	10–82
21	Assessors Bill	33–58

Worcester 6th. No^v. 1797   Daniel Waldo Ju^r. } Committee
                                  Samuel Brazer   }

Voted that the Sum of three Hundred Dollars be assessed on the Pools & Estates in this Town and raised for the purpose of defraying the demands against the Town

Voted that this meeting be dissolved and the meeting was dissolved accordingly

    A True Entry   attest   Daniel Goulding Town Clerk

At a Meeting of the Freeholders & Other Inhabitants of the Town of Worcester legally assembled at the meeting House of the first parish in Said Town on Monday the 18th day of December A. D. 1797 then the following Votes were passed Viz^t.

Chose Samuel Flagg Esqr. Moderator

A motion was then made & Seconded to See if the Town would reconsider any former Vote or Votes giving liberty for any person or persons to leave there School Quarter or Destrect & Join to any Other in Said Town the motion being put passed in the Negative [1]

---

[1] ARTICLE 2:—"To See if the Inhabitants will reconsider any Vote or Votes heretofore passed respecting the School quarter wherein Saml. God-

Then Voted that M^r. Samuel Goddard & M^r. Jon^a. Grout two School Committee men go on and provide a School master & have a School Kept as Near the Center of the remainder of there School Quarters as may be

Voted that this meeting be dissolved and the meeting was dissolved accordingly

  A True Entry attest Daniel Goulding Town Clerk

At a Legal meeting of the inhabitants of the Town of Worcester Qualified to Vote in Town affairs assembled at the meeting House of the first Parish in Said Town on monday the fifth Day of march A. D. 1798 then the following Votes were passed & the following Persons Chose into Office

 Nathaniel Paine Esqr. Chosen Moderator

 Daniel Goulding Town Clerk

 Samuel Flagg Esqr. Nathl. Paine Esqr. Deacon John Chamberlain Daniel Goulding M^r. David Andrews Selectmen

Voted that the Selectmen be overseers of the Poor the Current Year

 Sworn march 5th Doct^r. Oliver Fiske Town Treasurer

  Samuel Flagg Esqr ⎫
  Deacon John Chamberlain ⎬ Assessors all Sworn
  Doct^r. Oliver Fiske ⎭

 Sworn march 14th Ebenezer Reed ⎱ Constables
 Sworn   Peter Stowell ⎰

 Nathan Heard Sealer and Searcher of Leather

  Ephraim Mower ⎱ Clerks of the market
  Daniel Goulding ⎰

 Sw^n. march 5th Joshua Whitney ⎫
 Sworn May 23^d Moses Perry ⎬ Fence Viewers
 Sw^n. march 5th William Trowbridge ⎭

---

dard is a Committee man, which gave leave to any of the Said Inhabitants of the Said Quarter to remove to other Quarters — and to hear the Petition of Joshua Whitney and Others respecting Said Business"

David Moore Deer Reeve

Ebenezer Mower \} field Drivers
Samuel Gates

Moses Perry \} Tythingmen
Jedediah Healey

Simeon Duncan \} Viewers of Hoops & Staves
Frost Rockwood

William Goulding \} Surveyors of Boards & Shingles &c
Samuel Porter

Sw^n. march 5   William Eaton
Sw^n. march 17th Amherst Eaton
                     Samuel Goddard Ju^r.
                     Silas Bigelow
Sw^n. march 5th Walter Tufts   } Hog Reeves
Sw^n. may 17th William Taylor
Sw^n. June 11th William Parker Ju^r.
                     Willard Moore
Sworn april 2^d James Barrel
Sworn april 2^d Thomas Barber

Chose Deacon Ebenezer Read Collector of Publick Taxes for the Town of Worcester the Current year he giving Sufficient Bonds to the Satisfaction of the Selectmen for the faithfull performance of Said trust and Voted that he be allowed five pence on the pound for what money he Collects

Voted that this meeting be adjourned for One hour then to meet at this place & the meeting was accordingly adjourned

Met according to the above adjournment

Voted that the money granted for the Support of keeping publick English Schools in this Town the Current year be proportioned as it was the last year according to or by the Number of Minors in Each School Quarter or destrict

Voted that the Sum of two hundred & Twenty pounds be granted Raised and assessed on the Polls and Estates in this Town for the Support of Publick English Schools the Current year

Voted that the Sum of Forty five pounds be granted & assessed on the Polls and Estates in this Town and raised for the purpose of keeping a Grammar School the Current year

Then Chose Joseph Allen Esqr. Daniel Heywood 2^d. Nathl. Harrington, Joseph Barber, Benjamin Farrar, William Moore, Benjamin Heywood, John Tatman, Charles Stearns, & Joseph Chadwick a Committee to provide School Masters &c

Benjamin Heywood Phineas Jones Leonard Worcester Committee to Settle with the Town Treasurer

Samuel Flagg Esqr. Oliver Fiske Daniel Clap Ephraim Mower Fire Wards

	Daniel Clap	
	Joseph Chadwick	
Sworn May 23^d	Moses Perry	
Sworn april 2^d	Eli Chapen	
Sworn april 2^d	John Elder Ju^r	
	John Mower	
Sworn april 2^d	Nathl. Stowell	
Sworn	John Walker	
Sworn april 2^d	Benj^a. Thaxter	Highway Surveyors &
Sworn april 27th	Noah Harrington	Collectors of Highway
Sworn april 2^d	Joshua Harrington	Taxes
	Thomas Gray	
Sworn april 2^d	Jonathan Lovell Ju^r	
Sw^n. June 21st	Eben^r Williams	
	Asa Hambelton	
Sworn May 23^d	James Barber	
	Jonathan Gates 2^d	

Voted that the Sum of Four Hundred & fifty pounds be granted & assessed on the Polls & Estates in this Town & raised for the purpose of keeping the Publick roads in repair the Current year

Voted that the Same wages be allowed per day for a days work of men Oxen Carts plows &c as was the last year

Voted that those that did not work out their Highway Taxes last year have liberty to work them out provided they do it in the month of June Next

Chose Nathl. Paine Esqr. an agent to prosecute and defend any Suits that may be brought for or against the Town

Voted that the Swine be under the Same restrictions the Current year in this Town that they were the last year

Worcester Town Records, 1798.   345

Voted to abate to M^r. Thomas Rice Sundrey Persons Taxes in his Taxes to Collect vizt.

Otis Claflin Town & State	D 0 – 98
Ritchard Dodge	0 – 98
Joshua Johnson Ju^r.	0 – 98
Isaiah Thomas 3^d	0 – 98
Joshua Patch	7 – 10
John Noyce	2 – 13
	D 13 – 15

Voted to abate to M^r. Henery Patch Sundry Persons Taxes in his Taxes to Collect vizt.

Eben^r. Andrews	D 1 – 28
William Barber	0 – 83
Otis Claflin	0 – 83
Moses Coburn	0 – 83
Benj^a. Gowen	0 – 83
John How	2 – 33
Elisha Lavens	0 – 83
Willm Moore 2^d	0 – 83
John Noyce	1 – 43
Willard Parker	0 – 83
Joel Pratt	0 – 83
Tim^o Coney	0 – 83
John Coney	0 – 83
Calven Stone	0 – 83
Forbes Bond	0 – 83
	D 15 – 10

Voted that this meeting be adjourned to monday the Second day of april Next at two OClock in the afternoon then to meet at this place and the meeting was accordingly adjourned

    A True Entry   attest   Daniel Goulding Town Clerk

Worcester Town Records, 1798.

At a Town meeting held on Monday April 2ᵈ 1798 by adjournment from the annual march meeting the following Votes were passed viz

Voted to accept of the Report of the Committee Chose to Settle with the late Town Treasurer which is as follows —

Dʳ. The Town of Worcester in account with Samˡ Chandler Cʳ. Town Treasurer

N.					
1	Thomas Nichols pʳ. Order Selectmen	55	83⅓	16 15	—
2	Stephen Taylor	3	33½	1 -	—
3	Wᵐ. Moore	4	—	1 4	—
4	Jonᵃ. Putman	7	—	2 2	—
5	Nathˡ. Paine	18	—	5 8	—
6	Phillip Gross	12	—	3 12	—
7	James Trowbridge	1	75	— 10	6
8	John Elder	10	—	3 —	-
9	James Blak	14	—	4 4	—
10	Jonᵃ. Putman	28	33	8 10	—
11	Moses Miller	20	—	6 —	—
12	John Chamberlain	15	—	4 10	—
13	Wᵐ. Goulding	8	13	2 8	9¼
14	Benjᵃ. Heywood	3	8⅓	— 18	6
15	Thomas Rice	94	59⅔	28 7	7
16	Judith Rice	20	—	6 —	—
17	Judith Rice	65	83⅓	19 15	—
18	Thomas Rice	11	48	3 8	10½
19	Willᵐ. Brown	1	55	— 9	3½
20	John Chamberlain	44	79	13 8	9
21	Chaˢ. & Samˡ. Chandler	8	24	2 9	5¼
22	John Elder	44	96	13 9	9
23	Samˡ. Flagg	10	82	3 4	11
24	John Elder	10	—	3 —	—
25	Simeon Duncan	21	—	6 6	—
26	Asa Ward	16	—	4 16	—
27	Simeon Duncan	21	—	6 6	—
28	James Fiske	10	66⅔	3 4	—

29	Daniel Waldo Ju^r.	36	72	11 —	3¾
30	James Fiske	5	—	1 10	—
31	Asa Ward	10	—	3 —	—
32	Moses Miller	29	17	8 15	¼
33	Asa Ward	32	99	9 17	11¼
34	School Committee	733	33⅓	220 —	—
35	W^m. Gates	47	4	14 2	3
36	Thomas Rice	18	44	5 10	7¾
37	Frances Savage	2		— 12	—
38	James Quigley	26	—	7 16	—
39	Thomas Nichols	53	28	15 19	8¼
40	Nathl. Coolidge	150	—	45 —	—
41	Thad^s. & S Bigelow		80	4	9¾
42	Jos Morse	21	68	6 10	1
43	W^m. Chamberlain	11	33	3 7	11¾
44	Daniel Fenno	6	76	2 —	6¾
45	Nathan Heard		92	5	6¼
46	Simeon Duncan	13	44	4 —	7¾
47	Daniel Baird	6	33	1 17	11¾
48	James Fiske	14	33	4 5	11¾
49	James M^{c}farland	17	34	5 4	—½
50	Saml. Brooks	15	13	4 10	9¼
51	Assessors	33	58	10 1	5¾
52	Jno. Nazro	5	72⅓	1 14	4
53	Saml. Brazer	15	30	4 11	9½
	Amount of Debit Brought	1888	3⅓	566 8	2½
	To Ballance due upon Isaiah Thomas Note	23	68	7 2	1
	To Jo^s. Patches Note Sep^t. 11th 1793 2 years Interest paid	56	66⅔	17 —	—
	Ballance due upon W^m. Taylors Note april 4th. 1794 Interest paid to No^v. 1794	42	56⅓	12 15	4½
	John Chamberlains Note april 6 1795	3	30⅔	— 19	10
	Saml. Fullertons Note Dec^m. 13th. 1785 on Interest	42	75	12 16	6
	Thos. Tracy Note Dec^m. 12 1785 Do	15	10⅓	4 10	7½

Uriah Ward Do. Dec^m. 12 1785 Do	42	47⅔	12	14	10¼
W^m. Croxford Do. Dec^m. 12 1785 Do	15	26	4	11	6¾
Jno. Woodward Do May 29 1786 Do	21	43	6	8	7
Ballance Due upon Henery Patches Taxes	308	12⅓	92	8	9
Ballance Due upon Dea^n. Eben^r Reads Do	321	11⅓	96	6	8¼
To Error in Jon^a. Putmans order No. 10		15⅓		11	
To Cash paid over to Doct^r. Oliver Fisk	128	70⅔	38	12	3
	2909	36⅔	872	16	2¾
By Ballance Due upon Settlement of accounts	1413	41	424	0	5½
By Cash Rec^d. of Nathl. Paine Esqr	202	49⅓	60	14	11½
Interest Rec^d. upon Patches Recognizance	8	33⅓	2	10	—
Deacon Eben^r. Reads Taxes for 1797	1285	13	385	10	9¼
	2909	36⅓	872	16	2¼

The Committee appointed to Settle accounts with M^r. Saml. Chandler late Town Treasurer have attended that Service and report that the Said Treasurer has Charged himself with the Sum of two thousand Nine Hundred and Nine Dollars & thirty Six Cents & two third of a Cent including the Ballance of his last account—that he has paid out upon orders drawn on him by the Selectmen &c the Sum of One Thousand and Eight Hundred and Eighty Eight Dollars & Eighteen Cents and two thirds of a Cent and that he has delivered over to Doct^r. Oliver Fiske the present Treasurer in Cash Notes and arrears of Taxes in the hands of Collectors the Sum of One thousand and twenty one Dollars and Eighteen Cents making in the whole the above Sum with which he hath charged himself and his account is thereby ballanced in full   all which is Submitted

Worcester March 31st 1798
Benj^a. Heywood
Phineas Jones
Leonard Worcester

Voted that the Sum of Forty five pounds be allowed to the

Center School Destrect for the purpose of Supplying the Town with a Grammer School the Current year

Voted to Excuse Colo Daniel Clap from Serving Highway Surveyor the Current year

Chose Doct^r. Oliver Fiske Highway Surveyor & Collector of Highway Taxes in the room of Colo Daniel Clap Excused

Voted that the following Persons Taxes be abated to Henery Patch in his Tax Bill to Collect viz

Bill Blake	83
Solomon Bixbe	83
Elijah Warren	83
D	2–49

Voted that this meeting be Dissolved & the meeting was dessolved accordingly

A True Entry   attest   Daniel Goulding Town Clerk

At a meeting of the Inhabitants of the Town of Worcester of Twenty one years of age and upwards Qualified to Vote for Governor Lieu^t. Governor & Senators & Counsellors on Monday the Second day of April A. D. 1798 at the meeting House of the first parish in Worcester then the following persons were Voted for and had the Number of Votes expressed against their respective Names

For Governor		For Lieu^t. Governor	
Increase Sumner	81	Moses Gill	56
Moses Gill	1	Samuel Phillips	6
		Samuel Brazeer	1
Senators & Counsellors			
Salem Town	72	Nathl. Paine	3
Levi Lincoln	68	Benj^a. Heywood	1
Elijah Brigham	54	Jonas How	1
Josiah Stearns	66	Seth Hastings	2

Worcester Town Records, 1798.

John Sprague	56	Benj^a. Reed	1
Bez^l. Taft	33	Pliny Merick	3

Voted that this meeting be dissolved & the meeting was dissolved accordingly.

A True Entry   attest   Daniel Goulding Town Clerk

At a Meeting of the Freeholders and Other Inhabitants of the Town of Worcester Qualified to Vote in Town affairs legally assembled at the meeting House of the first parish in Said Town on Monday the Second day of april A. D. 1798

Samuel Flagg Esqr. Chose Moderator

Voted that the Selectmen be a Committee to agree with Some proper Person to take care of the burying Ground Toll the Bell & Dig Graves and that they Set or regulate the price of doing Said business

Voted that the Selectmen take care of the Powder House & the Stock therein or agree with Some proper person to take care of the Same

the Votes were then given in upon the expediency of dividing the County of Worcester into two Seperate and distinct Countys and there was one hundred and Forty against a Division and not one in favour of a Division

Voted that this meeting be dissolved and the meeting was dissolved accordingly

A True Entry   attest   Daniel Goulding Town Clerk

At a Town meeting held in Worcester on Monday the fourteenth day of May A. D. 1798 at the meeting house of the first parish in Said Town

Voted to Send one Representative to the General Court to be convened at Boston on the last wednesday of may Instant

Then Chose Nathaniel Paine Esqr. a Representative

Then Voted that this meeting be dissolved & the meeting was dissolved accordingly

A True Entry   attest   Daniel Goulding Town Clerk

At a meeting of the freeholders and other Inhabitants of the Town of Worcester Qualified to Vote in Town affairs legally Warned & assembled at the publick meeting House of the first parish in Said Town on monday the Twenty fourth day of September A. D. 1798

Samuel Flagg Esqr. Chosen Moderator

Voted to Choose a Committee to Examine accounts or Demands brought against the Town to make report at the adjournment of this meeting then Chose Benj^a. Heywood Esqr. Nathl. Paine Esqr. & M^r. Daniel Denny a Committee for Said Purpose

Voted to Choose a Committee to make a plan and an Estimate of Such a House as will be thought best to build for Samuel Denny to be the Towns property and that they lay the Same before the Town at the adjournment of this meeting, then Chose Samuel Flagg Esqr., Deacon John Chamberlain, and M^r. William Goulding, a Committee for Said Purpose [1]

Voted to Choose a Committee to Survey the New burying Ground and lay the Same out into proper Squares and Lots and Lay a plan before the Town at the adjournment of this meeting then Chose M^r. David Andrews M^r. William Trobridge & M^r. Samuel Brazer, a Committee for Said purpose

Voted that the following persons Taxes be abated or allowed to Deacon Ebenezer Reed the Towns present Collector provided that if he at any future time Collects all or any part of them that he be accountable to the Town for So much as he does Collect

---

[1] ARTICLE 6:—"To See if the Town will erect a house for Samuel Denny, on Condition that the Said Denny & his wife will convey a certain Tract of Land on which the Said Denny now lives for the use of the Town of Worcester—and to appoint Some person or persons to take a Deed of the Same"

		D C		D Cents
Silas Brooks^s	Town	0–62	State	0–44
Jon^a. Holbrook	Do	1– 2	Do	0–80
Rufus Flagg	Do	0–48	Do	0–32
John Flagg	Do	0–48	Do	0–32
Otis Claflin	Do	0–48	Do	0–32
Peter Goulding	Do	0–68	Do	0–50
Samuel Stone	Do	0–48	Do	0–32
Oliver Sibley	Do	0–48	Do	0–32
		4–72		3–34

D   C
3 — 34
4 — 72
─────
8 — 06

Voted that this meeting be adjourned to monday the Eighth day of October Next at two OClock in the afternoon then to meet at this Place and the meeting was accordingly adjourned

  A True Entry   attest   Daniel Goulding Town Clerk

At a meeting of the freeholders & Other Inhabitants of the Town of Worcester on the Eighth day of October 1798 by adjournment from September the Twenty fourth 1798

Voted to accept the Report of the Committee appointed to examine accounts & Demands against the Town which report is as follows

The Committee appointed to examine accounts brought against the Town have attended that Service and report as their Opinion that the following Contracts & accounts ought to be allowed vizt.

To the Selectmen to enable them to fulfil their contracts for the Support of Sundrey poor persons vizt.—

With Moses Miller for boarding & Clothing Nathan Houghton one year ending No^v. 20th. 1798 @ 4/9 p^r. Week   Dol^{rs} 41 – 17

Thomas Nichols for Zach^s. Johnson Same Time @ 5/   43 – 33

Worcester Town Records, 1798. 353

William Gates for Anna White Same Time @ 3/9	32 – 50
Jacob Smith for anna Tracy Same Time @ 4/6	39 ——
John Chamberlain for Jenny Dyer Same Time @ 4/4	37 – 55
Joshua Whitney for Benj^a. Randal one year Ending No^v. 14th. 1798 @ 5/8 p^r. Week	49 – 11
	241 – 66
Doct^r. John Green Ju^r. his acc^t. for doctering Rebeckah Duncan in her last Sickness	26 – 42
to Ditto his account for Doctering Simon Glasgow	29 – 76
to Ditto for Kezia Morse	10 – 75
Doct^r. Oliver Fisk for Doctering Edward Hair	7 – 54½
Saml. Brazer acc^t. for Supplies for Simon Glasgow & Saml. Denny	18 – 30
Nathl. Harrington boarding & Nursing Kezia Morse one year Ending Octr. 8th. 1798	32 – 50
William Chamberlain for Boarding Peter Willard from 10th march to 18th. August 1798	20 – 67
James Wiser further acc^t. for building Wall at the New burying ground	3 – 50
David Andrews for Clothing Supplied Peter Willard & Benj^a. Randal	7 – 1½
John Chamberlains acc^t. for Sundry Supplies &c	11 – 1
Walker & Shepard for repairing the Engine	9 ——
Samuel Flagg Esq^{rs}. acc^t. of Supplies for Peter Willard & M^{rs}. Conner	12 – 75
Eli Chapen for Timber & Plank for Bridges	2 – 55
Nathl. Paine Esqr. Supplies for Simon Glasgow	0 – 86
James M^{c}farland for Wood Supplied Saml. Denny	12 – 75
John Taft for Transporting Edward Hair from Boston to Worcester	3 ——
Jeremiah Stiles for painting 2 Guide Boards	1 – 25
Robert Gray for boarding Lucy Moore 6 & ½ Weeks	2 – 17
Isaac Gleason for 1 Barrel of Cyder delivered Simon	1 – 67
Elijah Flagg for Soap del^d. Simon Glasgow	0 – 42
John Elder ballance of his account for boarding John Spence 48 Weeks Ending Octr. 8th. 1798 & Clothing	37 – 40

Daniel Denny for Clothing for John Spence	1 – 26
Eben^r. Barber for boarding Danl. Gleason & wife 10 & ½ Weeks Ending Octr. 8th. 1798	21 ——
James Fisk for Wood Supplied Simon Glasgow	9 – 33
Benj^a. Andrews for making Clothes for James Thomas	1 – 11
Danl. Goulding his acc^t. for Sundry Supplies at the Poor House and Boarding & Clothing Jesse Tracy 65 Weeks	60 ——
all which is Submitted	585– 65

Worcester October 8th. 1798   Benj^a. Heywood
                                       Nathl. Paine
                                       Daniel Denny

Voted that the Sum of three Hundred Dollars be assessed & Raised on the Polls & Estates in this Town for the Purpose of defraying the Expences of the Town the Current Year

Voted to Choose a Committee to procure Stone & meterials for Building a Bridge over half way River near M^r. David Andrews then Chose M^r. David Andrews Deacon John Chamberlain & Capt. Joshua Whitney a Committee for Said Purpose [1]

Voted to accept the report of the Committee Chose to lay out the New burying ground into lots & that the Said Committee proceed and Stake out the Ground agreeable to their plan and that they lodge a Plan with the Town Clerk to be recorded in the Town Book [2] & that they leave another plan with the Saxton that he may dig the graves for the future agreeable to Said Plan

Voted to Choose a Committee to Consider the Expediency of Selling to Samuel Flagg Esqr. the Lot his Store Stands on and make an Estimate of the Value of Said Lot if they think it is best for the Town to Sell it, a[nd] make report at the next Town meeting then Chose Deacon John Chamberlain Deacon Leonard Worcester & Benj^a. Heywood Esqr. a Committee for Said Purpose

---

[1] ARTICLE 4:—"To See if the Town will take any measures for rebuilding the Bridge over half way river So called"

[2] This plan does not appear in the book. A copy is printed with the "Inscriptions from the Old Burial Grounds," in the first volume of the Collections of The Worcester Society of Antiquity.

Voted to accept the report of the Committee Chose to make an Estimate and a Plan for a House for Samuel Denny to live in to be the property of the Town   the report is as follows vizt.—

Worcester October 8th. 1798

The Committee appointed by y^e. Town at y^e. last meeting to view the House and Situation of Samuel Denny have attended that Service and report as their Oppinion that the Said Dennys House is not Tenantable it is very open and leakey and So rotten that it is more likely to fall before another Season than not—

The Committee are also of oppinion that it is necessary and expedient that the Town Should receive a Deed of the Said Denny & wife of their Land being about three acres, and to erect a Small House for their use where the old one now Stands of one Room 16 feet by 18 one Storey High with one Door 2 windows below of 15 Squares each and one in y^e. Chamber of 9 Squares a Brick Chimney with an Oven the Cellar will answer very well altering the Butment and raising one foot on the wall the Committee have estimated the expence of Such a House and find it may be Compleated for one hundred Dollars or not more than one hundred and Twenty Dollars   Which is Submitted

Samuel Flagg
John Chamberlain } Committee
Willm. Goulding

Voted to Choose a Committee to build a House for Saml. Denny or to agree with Some person or persons to build Said House agreeable to the above report on the best terms the[y] can and to take a Deed of Said Denny & his wife of their land for the use of the Town   Then Chose Benj^a. Heywood Esqr. Saml. Flagg Esqr. & Deacon John Chamberlain a Committee for the above Said purposes

Voted that this meeting be Dissolved & the meeting was Dissolved accordingly

A True Entry   attest   Daniel Goulding Town Clerk

Worcester Town Records, 1798.

At a meeting of the Inhabitants of the Town of Worcester Qualified to Vote for Representatives to the General Court on Monday the fifth day of November A. D. 1798 for the Purpose of given in their Votes for a Representative in the Congress of the United States for the fourth Western District they then gave in their Votes for the following Persons Viz

Dwight Foster 58   Levi Lincoln 69
Sam¹. Austin   1   Dan¹. Baird   1

The meeting was then Dissolved

   A True Entry   attest   Daniel Goulding Town Clerk

At a Meeting of the freeholders & Other Inhabitants of the Town of Worcester Qualified to Vote in Town affairs legally warned and assembled at the Publick meeting House of the first parish in Said Town on Monday the fifth day of November A. D. 1798 then the following Votes were passed Viz

Samuel Flagg Esq\ʳ. Chosen Moderator

Chose M\ʳ. Samuel Jeneson a School Committee man in the place of M\ʳ. Joseph Chadwick deceased

Voted that the Committe Chose Some time past to procure Stone & Other Meterials to build a Bridge over half way river proceed & procure Stone for Said Bridge Suitable for Arches

Voted to allow the following accounts viz—

to the Assessors for making Taxes for the year 1798	10 ,, 7 ,, 9
to Nath¹. Chandler for 125 Feet of Plank for Bridge	0 ,, 15 ,, 0
to Bridge & Wheeler for Sundrys Simon Glasgo	1 ,, 5 ,, 1
to Will\ᵐ. Gates for Extra Nursing Anna White	0 ,, 18 ,, 0
to Sam¹. Brooks for Supplies for Simon Glasgo	2 ,, 11 ,, 0½

Voted that this meeting be dissolved and the meeting was Dissolved accordingly

   A True Entry   attest   Dan¹. Goulding Town Clerk

At a meeting of the Inhabitants of the Town of Worcester Qualified to Vote in Town affairs legally warned and assembled at the meeting house of the first parish in Said Town on monday the fourth day of march A D 1799 then the following Persons were chosen into Office & the following votes were passed

Chose Samuel Flagg Esqr. Moderator

Chose Daniel Goulding Town Clerk

Samuel Flagg Esqr. Nathl. Paine Esqr. Benj^a. Heywood Esqr. M^r. David Andrews M^r. Ephraim Mower Selectmen

Voted that the Selectmen be overseers of the Poor the Current Year

Sworn march 11th M^r. Theopheus Wheeler Town Treasurer

Sworn march 7th. Samuel Flagg Esqr }
Sworn march 23^d. M^r. David Andrews } Assessors
Sworn march 7th. Benj^a. Heywood Esqr. }

Voted that M^r. Nathan White be Collector of Taxes he giving bonds to the Satisfaction of the Selectmen for the faithfull performance of his Trust and Voted that he be allowed five pence one farthing on the pound for what money he Shall Collect

Sworn march 4th Nathan White } Constables
Sworn march 4th William Eaton }

Nathan Heard Searcher & Sealer of Leather

Sworn march 9th Ephraim Mower } Clerks of the market
                      Oliver Fisk   }

Sworn march 7th Nathaniel Harrington }
                       Levi Flagg   } Fence Viewers
Sworn march 11th Ebenezer Mower   }

Sworn march 12th Paul Gates   } field Drivers
                        John Barnard }

                        Josiah Perry   } Tythingmen
Sworn march 7th   David Hersey }

Frost Rockwood   } Viewers and Cullers of Staves & Hoops
Ebenezer Hastings }

                        Samuel Porter   } Surveyors of Shingles
Sworn march 29th. William Goulding } Clapboards &c

David Bigelow Benj[a] Heywood John Chamberlain Committee to Settle accounts with the Town Treasurer

Chose Nathaniel Paine Esq[r]. Agent to prosecute or defend to final Judgment & Execution any Suit or Suits at Law that may be brought for or against the Town

Samuel Flagg Esq[r]. Oliver Fisk Daniel Denny Ephraim Mower Fire Wards

	Oliver Fisk	
	John Barnard	
	Samuel Curtis Esq[r]	
Sworn march 8th.	Josiah Perry	
	Nathan White	
Sworn march 11th.	Joseph Holbrook	
Sworn march 12th.	Paul Gates	
	Thomas Nickels	
Sworn march 14th.	Daniel Smith	Highway Surveyors &
Sworn march 7th.	Samuel Harrington	Collectors of High-
Sworn march 13th.	Stephen Heywood	way Taxes
Sworn May 26.	Moses Miller	
	Edward Knight	
	Daniel Rand	
Sworn June 16th.	Charles Stearns	
	Robert Smith	
Sworn march 8th.	Micah Johnson Ju[r]	
	Daniel Goulding	
	William Trow-bridge	

Voted that the Sum of Fifteen Hundred Dollars be granted & assessed on the Polls & Estates in this Town & Raised for the purpose of keeping the Publick Roads in repair the Current year

Voted that those that have a mind to work out their Highway Taxes be allowed Six Shillings p[r]. Day for a Man & Oxen Carts Plows &c in proportion as Usual

Sworn march 7th	William Walker	
Sworn march 8th	David Brown	
Sworn march 9th	Luther Moore	
	Jonathan Lovell Ju[r].	
Sworn march 4th	Isaac Gleason 2[d].	Hog Reeves
Sworn march 12th	William Gates Ju[r].	
Sworn march 11th	James Williams	
Sworn march 22[d]	Phineas Holbrook	
Sworn march 23[d]	Ezekiel Smith	
Sworn march 4th	Samuel Andrews	

Voted that the Swine be under the Same Restrictions the Current year they were last Year, in this Town

Voted that the Grammar School in future be kept as a moving School untill otherwise ordered by the Town to be kept three months in each district begining with the Center district and then to the other distrects in Rotation as the Selectmen Shall direct untill it Shall have gone through the Town

Voted that One Thousand Dollars be assessed & Raised on the Polls & Estates in this Town for the Purpose of keeping a Publick Grammar School & Englesh Schools agreeable to law and that in the first Instance the Grammar School be paid or a Sum taken out Sufficient to Support it & the Remainder be expended in keeping English Schools to be Divided or proportioned by the Number of Minors as Usual

Voted to Choose a Committee to See whether it is expedient to Divide the Center School Distrect So called and if thought best to Say where the division Shall be & make report at the adjournment of this meeting

Then Chose Samuel Flagg Esq[r]. Samuel Brazer, Daniel Goulding, Joseph Allen, & Oliver Fisk, a Committee for Said purpose

Voted that the Sum of Twenty five hundred Dollars be assessed on the Polls & Estates in this Town and Raised for the purpose of Building School Houses in the Several parts of this Town

Voted to Choose a Committee to Carry the Building Publick School Houses into Effect, Then Chose Daniel Denny, Samuel Brazer, Daniel Goulding, Nathan Heard, Oliver Fisk, Nathaniel Coolidge, Joseph Holbrook, James M[c]farland, William M[c]farland Ju[r]., Phineas Jones, Charles Stearns, David Andrews, David Bigelow, Samuel Andrews, Joseph Kingsbury, Benjamin Heywood, Daniel Baird, Samuel Harrington, David Flagg, James Fisk, Jonathan Gleason, Ebenezar Reed, Benjamen Thaxster, Benjamen Whitney Ju[r]. Elijah Burbank, Joshua Whitney, Nathaniel Stowell, Samuel Porter, Nathaniel Harrington & Samuel Curtis Ju[r]. For Said Committee & that where there is any dispute in any District as to the place where the School House Shall Stand this Committee to determine on the Place and

Voted that this Committee be considered as a Joint Committee

Voted that this meeting be adjourned to monday the first Day of April Next at three OClock in the afternoon then [to] meet at this Place & the meeting was accordingly adjourned

A True Entry   attest   Daniel Goulding Town Clerk

At a meeting of the Inhabitants of the Town of Worcester Qualified to Vote for Governor Lieu^t Governor Senators & Counsellors at the meeting house of the first Parish in Said Town on Monday the first day of april A. D. 1799 being legally warned & assembled

Voted that Samuel A Flagg be Town Clerk Pro Tem

Then the following Persons were Voted for & had the Number of Votes expressed against their respective Names—

For Governor

Increase Sumner
Elbridge Gerry
Eli Chapen

For Lieu^t. Governor

Moses Gill

For Senators & Counsellors

John Sprague	61	Bezaliel Taft	23
Levi Lincoln	25	Caleb Ammidown	27
Nathl. Paine	48	Thomas Denny	16
Elijah Brigham	66	Joseph Wood	21
Pliny Merrick	20	Daniel Baird	1
Samuel Flagg	24	Thomas Hale	1
Jabez Upham	6	Salem Town	41
Josiah Stearns			

Voted that this meeting be Dissolved and the meeting was Dissolved accordingly

A True Entry from M^r. Saml. Flaggs Minits Clerk Pro Tem

         attest   Daniel Goulding Town Clerk

Worcester Town Records, 1799.

At a meeting of the Inhabitants of the Town of Worcester Qualified to Vote for Representatives legally warned and assembled at the meeting house of the first parish in Said Town on Monday the first day of April A. D. 1799 then

Samuel Flagg Esqr. was Chosen Moderator

Then M^r. Samuel Allen had one hundred & twelve Votes for County Treasurer

Voted that this meeting be Dissolved & the meeting was Dissolved accordingly

A True Entry from M^r. Saml. Flaggs Minits Clerk Pro Tem

     attest Daniel Goulding Town Clerk

At a meeting of the Inhabitants of the Town of Worcester Qualified to Vote in Town affairs on Monday the first day of April A. D. 1799 by adjournment from last annual march meeting

Chose Theoph^{us}. Wheeler, Joseph Kingsbury, Samuel Gates, Benjamin Thaxster, Ebenezar Mower, Daniel Baird, Elijah Burbank, Phineas Jones & Nathaniel Flagg a Committee to Provide the Town with English Schools the Current year

D^r. The Town of Worcester in account Current with Oliver C^r.
  Fisk Town Treasurer

N^o.			
1	John Elder	20	—
2	William Knight	26	—
3	Jon^a. Stearns	23	83
4	Adam Quigley	30	33
5	John Chamberlain	4	—
6	Samuel Johnson	—	50
7	William Moore	5	25
8	Jacob Smith	8	—
9	Do	10	30
10	W^m. Mariam	7	50
11	Jon^a. Stearns	6	87
12	Asa Ward	1	50

13	Jacob Smith	40	—
14	Alpheus Eaton	6	33
15	Isaac Putman	6	55
16	John Farror	3	—
17	John Chamberlain	90	—
18	John Elder	42	57
19	Jeremiah Stiles	1	25
20	Joshua Whitney	50	78
21	Bridge & Wheeler	4	18
22	Henery Patch	92	45
23	Do	2	49
24	Flagg & Gleason	4	74
25	Moses Miller	43	17
26	Nathl. Paine	39	—
27	Daniel Goulding	60	—
28	John Chamberlain	11	1
29	Samuel Flagg	12	75
30	Daniel Goulding	34	84
31	Nathaniel Paine	—	86
32	Archibald McDonald	1	—
33	Benj^a. Andrews	1	11
34	James M^{c}farland	10	—
35	Robert Gray	2	17
36	Nathl. Harrington	32	50
37	Joseph Morse	22	42
38	Samuel Brazer	22	50
39	Robert Gray	4	41
40	David Andrews	11	14
41	D G Wheeler	1	53
42	Willm. M^{c}farland	6	36
43	Abel Whitton	—	80
44	James Fisk	10	—
45	Simeon Duncan	—	80
46	James M^{c}farland	—	80
47	Charles Stearns	9	67

48	Joseph Holbrook	5	83
49	John Elder	10	—
50	John Chamberlain	39	5
51	Daniel Fenno	12	56
52	Willm. Moore	8	67

53	Phineas Jones	8	—
54	James Wiser	3	50
55	Samuel Brazer	18	30
56	Walker & Shepard	9	—
57	John Green	3	25
58	Eben^r. Read	8	6
59	John Green	66	93
60	Stephen Salsbury	4	—
61	Oliver Fiske	7	54
62	Do	9	75
63	Joseph Allen	150	—
64	James M^cfarland	12	75
65	Daniel Goulding	15	—
66	John Elder	33	22
67	William Gates	3	—
68	Eli Chapen	2	55

To Sundrey demands delivered over to M^r. Theo^s. Wheeler viz

Ballance due on Isaiah Thomas Note	23	68
Joseph Patch^s. Note Sep^t. 11th. 1793 3 y^{rs}. In^t. p^d.	56	66⅔
Ballance due on W^m. Taylors Note Ap^l. 4 1794 Interest paid to No^v. 1796	42	56⅓
John Chamberlains Note April 6th. 1795	3	30⅔
Saml. Fullertons Note Dec^m. 13th. 1795	42	75
Thomas Tracys Note Dec^m. 12 1788	15	10⅓
Uriah Wards Note Dec^m. 12 1785	42	47⅔
W^m. Croxfords Note Dec^m. 12 1785	15	26
John Woodwards Note May 29th. 1786	21	43

Ballance due on Henery Patch
   Taxes for 1796   17 18⅓
Assessors Return of an addition to Do 13 23
Assessors Return of a Town Tax
   for 1798   1352 30
Cash p^d. M^r. Theo^{us}. Wheeler   34 66⅔
                                     1680 61⅔

                                     2938 83⅔

Dr The Town of Worcester in Account with Oliver Fiske   C^r
       Town Treasurer

By Cash Rec^d. of former Treasurer   128 70
By Do in part Ballance of Henery Patches Taxes   308 12⅓
By Ballance of D^n. Eben^r. Reads Taxes for 1797   321 11⅓
By Cash Rec^d. of the Selectmen   98 49
By Do. of N Paine Esqr. In^t. of Town Bonds   159 46
By Do. of Commonwealth by the hand of N Paine   300 —
By Do. of Jon^a. Gates for Highway Taxes   1 16⅔
By Do. Interest on Joseph Patches Note   10 20
By Sundrey Demands Rec^d. of former Treasurer   263 23⅓
By Assessors return of an addition to H Patch^s
    Taxes   13 23
By Assessors return of a Town Tax for 1798   1352 30
                                               2938 83⅔

The Committee appointed to Settle accounts with Doct^r. Oliver Fiske late Treasurer of the Town have attended that Service and report that the Said Treasurer has charged himself with the Sum of two thousand Nine hundred and thirty Eight Dollars & Eighty three Cents and two thirds of a Cent, that he has paid out upon orders drawn on him by the Selectmen &c the Sum of twelve hundred & Seventy one Dollars and forty five Cents for which Sufficient vouchers were produced and that he has delivered over to M^r. Theophilus Wheeler the present Treasurer in Cash Notes and arrears of Taxes in the hands of Collectors the Sum of Sixteen

hundred & Sixty Eight Cents and two thirds of a Cent and his account is thereby balanced in full
all which is Submitted

Benj^a. Heywood
Worcester April 1st. 1799   David Bigelow
John Chamberlain

Turn to the fourth Page forward for the Remainder of this meeting

---

At a Meeting of the Inhabitants of Worcester Quallified to Vote for Representatives, on the 13th Day of May A. D. 1799

Voted that Theophilus Wheeler be Clerk pro tem, of this meeting

Voted to Choose one Representative to the General Court the ensuing year

Voted that Nathaniel Paine Esqr. be the Representative of this Town to the General Court the ensuing year

Worcester ss. On the 14th Day of May A. D. 1799, Theophilus Wheeler was Sworn a Clerk, pro tem, to record the doings of the Town of Worcester in a Meeting, the Day aforesaid, of the Inhabitants of Said Town   Before Nathl Paine Jus^t. Pacis

A true Entry   Attest   Theoph^s. Wheeler Clerk pro tem

At the Same time and place

Voted that Samuel Flagg Esqr. be moderator of the meeting

Voted that the General School house Committee be authorized to enquire into the actual Situation of the Center district with respect to School accomodation, and to place the said Center Destrict on an equitable footing with the other Districts in the Town

Voted that the Selectmen or a major part of them be a Committee to meet any Committee which is or may be appointed by the Town of Boylston for the purpose of Settling any dispute relating to the Boundary line betwen Worcester & Boylston

Voted to dismiss the article that relates to the Suspension of the Grammar School[1]

Voted to accept the report of the Committee for laying out a Town Road betwen Capt. William Gates & Nathl. Harringtons

Voted to accept the report of the Committee for laying out the new Burying Ground into Lots

Voted that the Meeting be disolved—it was disolved accordingly

A true Entry   attest   Theoph^s. Wheeler Clerk pro tem

Committees reports

Laid out in the Town of Worcester a Town or private way Begining opposite Capt. William Gates House at a Stake and heap of Stones, and runing South twenty and an half degrees East Eighty seven rods to a Stake and Stones, meeting the old Town way leading from Nathaniel Harringtons, The aforesaid Town way to be two rods wide on the Easterly Side of the line afore discribed — Dated at Worcester April A D, 1799

Samuel Flagg
Nathl. Paine
David Andrews   Selectmen
Benjn. Heywood   of Worcester
Ephraim Mower

Your Committee chosen for the purpose of Surveying and laying out the new burying ground into Lots, have attended that service, and have numbered said Lots and entered the names of the heads of such families as have taken up any of said lots, on the plan in the hands of the Sexton and requested him to give the same to the Town Clerk that he may enter the same on the plan in his possession, and would recommend, that, when any Inhabitant has an occasion for taking a lot he may apply to the Town

---

[1] ARTICLE 4:—"To See if the Town will direct the Selectmen to Suspend the Grammar School untill it can be accomodated in the new School houses"

Clerk and whatever lot he chooses to take may be reserved for his family and entered on the aforesaid plans

David Andrews p^r. order

A true Entry   attest   Theoph^s. Wheeler Clerk pro tem

[Duplicate attested by Daniel Goulding Town Clerk.]

A Part of the Votes Passed at a Town meeting held by adjournment of march meeting held April 1st. 1799 The other Part recorded in the fourth Page back

Voted to acept the report of a Committee appointed to consider the expediency of dividing the Center School distrect which report is as follows

The Committee appointed by the Town at the annual meeting in march last to consider the expediency of dividing the Center School Distrect have attended that Service called the Destrect together who on mature deliberation and considering the Subject Voted almost unanimously that it was not expedient to divide y^e. Said Destrect   Samuel Flagg by order

Worcester 28th. march 1799

Chose Samuel Curtis Edward Bangs Stephen Salsbury Isaiah Thomas & Daniel Baird a Committee to Select one fourth part of the Persons Named in a list [of] Jurors presented by the Selectmen to Serve in the Supreme Court as Jurors

Voted to accept the report of the Committee chosen to Select one fourth part of the persons Named in a list of Jurors presented by the Selectmen to Serve in the Supreme Court as Jurors See the files for the Lists

it was motioned & Seconded to reconsider the Vote concerning building School Houses & Voted not to reconsider

Voted that this meeting be Dissolved and the meeting was Dissolved accordingly

a True Entry from M^r. Saml. Flaggs Minits Clerk Pro Tem
    attest   Daniel Goulding Town Clerk

In Obedience to a Warrant Derected to us the Subscribers we have met Samuel Hubbard & James Dodds of Holden at Leicester Line at the corner of Holden and Worcester thence Easterly on Holden & Worcester Line to a Black Oak Tree then to a Chesnut Tree west Side of Paxton Road then to a Chesnut on Major Davis^s. Land to a heap of Stones in Jonathan Moores Land with an apple Tree to an Oak Stump to a Hemlock to a Dry Chesnut to a Birch with Stones round to Oak Stump & Stones to Small Elm on Jon^a. Moores Land then to a white Oak & Stones west on the County [road] on Doct^r. Dixes Land to white Oak to heep of Stones on a Rock on Thad^s Chamberlains Land then to a Pitch Pine on Winter Hill on Eben^r. Barbers land then to a white Oak near Elisha Smiths to a Chesnut near Merryfields thence to Bended white Oak by Paul Goodales Land then to Boylston Line being the Corner of Worcester and Holden being a Small white Oak

      Samuel Hubbard
      James Dodds
      John Chamberlain
      Eben^r. Mower

Worcester April 15th. 1799 We the Subscribers have preambulated the Line between the Towns of Worcester & Ward and renewed the Bounds viz beginning at the Southwesterly Corner of Worcester at Lamper Hill So called & from thence to a heap of Stones in Joseph Clarks Land from thence to an apple Tree marked in S^d. Clarks Orchard from thence to a heap of Stones near the Road leading from Worcester to Ward from thence to a heap of Stones in the Road by Tho Tracys & from thence to a heap of Stones in Patch^s. land from thence to a heap of Stones in the Road near Timothy Tafts & from thence to the white Oak tree at the Southeasterly Corner of Worcester & the Easterly Corner of Ward

Eph^m. Mower } on the part   Jona Stone Ju^r. } on the part
David Andrews } of Worcester   James Eaton } of Ward

Worcester April 15th. 1799 The Subscribers met according to appointment at the N. W. Corner of Worcester to preambulate the Line between Worcester & Leicester proceded from S^d. Corner to a heap of Stones in Sylvesters land from thence to a heap of Stones in Nathan Greens Land from thence to a Chesnut tree Near the road by Greens from thence to an Oak tree in John Sargeants Land from thence a Birch tree between Sargeant and Putman from thence to an Oak between Putman & Sargeant & from thence to a heap of Stones at the S. W. Corner of Worcester & renewed Said Bounds

David Andrews } for Worcester Benj^a. Studley } for Leicester
Eph^m. Mower   John Sargeant

Agreeable to the within appointment we the Subscribers have met and Preambulated the Line and renewed the bounds between Worcester and Sutton   Tim^o. Taft
                                Moses Perry
Worcester April 15th. 1799 Ezra Lovel
                                David Dudley
See the appointment in files

Pursuant to the foregoing warrant we the Subscribers have preambulated the line therein mentioned begining at an heap of Stones being the South west corner of Boylston from thence to an heap of Stones in Jona Lovells Orchard Northerly of his house from thence the Line as formerly preambulated is disputed by the Town of Boylston untill it comes to an heap of Stones at the Northeast corner of L^t. Josiah Peirces land from thence the Line is agreed to by both Towns and runs to an White Oak tree being the Northeast corner of Worcester

April 15th. 1799
John Barnard } on the part   James Longley } on the part
Silas Bigelow } of Worcester   Jothum Bush   } of
                                 Oliver Sawyer } Boylston

Pursuant to the Within Warrant we the Subscribers have preambulated the line within mentioned begining at an heap of Stones near the remainder of an old Saw Mill belonging to Daniel Baird being the South west corner of Shrewsbury from thence to two Chesnut trees proceeding from one root on the westerly bank of the Long Pond So called from thence to a Black Oak tree at the Northerly End of Said Pond from thence to an heap of Stones between the land of Saml. Jenesons and Tyler Curtis from thence to a maple tree in Nathl. Heywoods meadow and from thence to an heap of Stones between Said Heywoods Land and Jona Lovells Land being the Northwest Corner of S^d. Shrewsbury

April 15th. 1799

John Barnard } on the part   Asa Rice } on the part of
Silas Bigelow } of Worcester   Jonah How } Shrewsbury

The above are a True Entry from the Returns
                attest   Daniel Goulding Town Clerk

At a Publick meeting of the Inhabitants of the Town of Worcester Qualified to Vote in Town affairs legally warned and assembled at the meeting house of the first Parish in Said Town on Monday the Twenty third day of September A D 1799 then the following Votes were passed vizt.

Samuel Flagg Esqr. Chosen Moderator

Voted to Choose a Committee to examine the accounts & Demands brought against the Town at this meeting and make report at the adjournment, then Chose Saml. Flagg Esqr. Nathl. Paine Esqr. & Doct^r. Oliver Fisk a Committee for Said purpose

A motion being made [and] Seconded to See if the Town would refer determining whether they would purchase for the use of the Center Quarter the building now improved as a School house the motion being put and passed in the affirmative[1]

---

[1] ARTICLE 4:—"To See if the Town will purchase for the use of the Center quarter the building now improved as a School House instead of building two New School houses in Said Quarter and in case the Town Should not agree to purchase Said Building to See if the Town will permit a School

A motion being made & Seconded to See if the Town would Discontinue a way leading from Daniel Stearns corner untill it meets the Road leading from Colo Benj[a]. Flagg[s] by Silas Harringtons the motion being put passed in the Negative

Voted that this meeting be adjourned to monday the Seventh day of October Next at two OClock in the afternoon then to meet at this Place & the meeting was accordingly adjourned

  A True Entry attest Daniel Goulding Town Clerk

At a meeting of the Inhabitants of the Town of Worcester Qualified to Vote in Town affairs at the meeting House of the first parish in Said Town on Monday the Seventh day of October A D 1799 by adjournment from the Twenty third day of September last past — then the following Votes were passed viz—

Voted that the Sum of Six hundred and Forty Dollars be assessed on the Polls & Estates in this Town and Raised for the purpose of defraying the Expences of the Town the Current Year

Voted to abate the following persons Taxes in Eben[r]. Reads Lists to Collect Viz

William Elder for 1797	$ 0 – 80
Same for 1798	0 – 82
Asa Estabrook for 1798	0 – 82
Joel Pratt for 1798	0 – 82
Robert Blair[s] Dog Tax	1 ——
Joseph Stickney[s] Dog Tax	1 ——
Lucy Newton[s] Dog Tax	1 ——
Isaac Stearns[s]. Dog Tax	1 ——
John Stearns[s]. Dog Tax	1 ——
William Stearns[s]. Dog Tax	1 ——
Phineas Gleason[s] Dog Tax	1 ——
	$10 – 26
John Gay[s]. Dog Tax	1 ——
	$11 – 26

house to be erected on the common for the use of the Said center Quarter Near Miss Waters[s]. To See if the Town will direct in what place a School House Shall be erected in the North part of the Center Quarter"

Voted to accept the Report of the Committee Chose to Examine the accounts brought against the Town which Report is as follows

The Committee appointed to Examine the accounts brought against the Town have attended that Service & report as their oppinion that the following accounts ought to be allowed vizt.

To William Gates for Supporting Anna White One Year (by Contract) Ending 20 No^v. Next at 3/6 by the Week £9 ,, 2 ,, 0	$30 ,, 33
to W^m. Gates for Nursing S^d Anna 19 & ½ Weeks at 50 Cents	9 ,, 75
To Thomas Nickels for Supporting Z Johnson One Year (by Contract) ending 20th. No^v. Next at 3/9 by the Week £9 ,, 15 ,, 0	32 ,, 50
Thomas Nickels for Extra Trouble in taking Care of the S^d. Z Johnson when Sick & Lame	2 ,, 66
John Chamberlain for Supporting Jenny Dyer one Year by Contract Ending 20 No^v. Next at 3/8 by the Week £9 ,, 10 ,, 8	31 ,, 78
To John Chamberlain for Sundries Supplyed Samuel Dennys Family to y^e. 4th. Instant	13 ,, 4
Eben^r. Barber for Boarding Daniel Gleason & his Wife one Year Ending 5th. No^v. Next at 9/5 by the Week £24 ,, 9 ,, 8	81 ,, 61
Luther Moore for Supporting Benj^a. Randall one year by Contract Ending 14th. No^v. Next at 4/10 by the Week £12 ,, 11 ,, 4	41 ,, 89
Luther Moore for Boarding Peter Willard 4 Weeks @ 5/6	3 ,, 67
Luther Moore for Boarding Edward Hair from 3^d. June last to 7th. Octr. Instant 18 Weeks @ 12/	36 ,,
Nathl. Harrington for Supporting Keziah Morse One Year Ending 5 No^v. Next at 2/9 by the Week £7 ,, 3 ,, 0	23 ,, 83
Moses Miller for Supporting Nathan Houghton one Year by Contract ending 20th No^v. Next @ 4/6 by the Week £11 ,, 14 –	39 ,,
Thomas Rice for Boarding Peter Willard 11 Weeks Ending 7th Octr. Instant @ 5/6 £3,,½	10 ,, 20

Paul Gates for Boarding Peter Willard 9

Weeks & three Days Ending 5th. July last @
5/6 Clothing 20/1 £3-10-4   11 „ 73

    Samuel Brazer for Sundries Supplyed the Poor   22 – 25

Willm. Trowbridge for Slit work and labour for the New burying Ground   5 – 66

    Asa Ward for 25 loads of Stones for Halfway River Bridge   8 – 33

    Micah Johnson Ju^r. for 305 feet of Bridge Plank   6 ——

    Phine^s. Jones for 20 Loads of Stones for Halfway River Bridge   6 – 66

    Thomas Gray for Boarding Lucy Moore 23 Weeks @ 1/6   2 & ¾ Yards Tow Cloth 5/6   6 – 50

    Abel Heywood for 13 Loads of Stones for Halfway River Bridge   4 – 33

    David Andrews for Sundries Supplies &c   20 – 6

    Charles Stearns for 45^{lb} Beef dld Samuel Denny   2 – 1

    Saml. Flagg for Sundries Supplied y^e. Poor   28 – 74

    The Assessors for making Taxes for 1799   35 ——

Daniel Goulding for Recording Births and Deaths & Sundries Supplied the Poor & New Books   28 – 83

    Henery Patch for 1 Load Wood for the Grammar School & Boarding 2 Poor Children   16 – 91

    John Farror for Sundries Supplied the Poor   1 – 57

Eben^r. Barber for Boarding Danl. Gleason and Wife 4 Weeks previous to his Contract @ 12/ and Extra Trouble in their Sickness the year Past 24/   12 ——

    Smith Butler for Sundries dld M^{rs}. Conner when Sick   1 – 75

    Oliver Fisk for Sundries to Cloth Lucy Moore   2 – 21

    John Green Ju^r. for Doctering the Poor from 30 June 1795 to Sep^t. 8 1799   51 – 12

Jedidiah Healey for making 2 Beers three Coffins Burying 3 Persons & Repairing the Herse House finding Lock &c   13 ——

Worcester Octr. 7th 1799

                               $640 – 92

All which is Submitted   Saml. Flagg ⎫
                          Nathl. Paine ⎬ Committee
                          Oliver Fiske ⎭

A motion being made to See if the Town would purchase the land & Building heretofore occupied as a School House in the Center Quarter in this Town for the purpose of accomodating the Center, School Destrect in lieu of Building two New School Houses as heretofore proposed, the motion being Seconded & put passed in the Negative

Voted that the Committee for Building Publick School Houses in this Town have Liberty to build a School House on the hill near M^{rs}. Waters^s. to accommodate the Center School Distrect

Voted that the Committee for building Publick School Houses in this Town meet and view the old School House Lot and agree where a School House Shall be built in the North part of the Center School Destrect

Voted that this meeting be adjourned to Monday the twenty Eighth day of this Instant October at two OClock in the afternoon then to meet at this Place And the meeting was accordingly adjourned

  A True Entry attest Daniel Goulding Town Clerk

At a meeting agreeable to the above adjournment October 28th. 1799

And Voted to accept the Report of the Great Committe for building Publick School Houses in the Town of Worcester which Report is as follows

The General School House Committee having Examined the Situation of the Center School distrect are of Opinion that it is expedient for the Town to grant the land belonging to the Town near the Court House to the Said distrect for the purpose of placing one of their School Houses on and if that district Should prefer any other Situation for a School House that they have the benefit of Said Land to purchase another place more to their Satisfaction

And the Committee are further of opinion that in order to accommodate the Said distrect it is expedient to build a third School house in the Same provide the Town Shall not be at any expence for land to Set it on or for underpining the Same

It is also the opinion of the Committee that one of Said Houses Shall be built Twenty five and the other two Twenty two feet Square   All which is Submitted

October 28th. 1799   Daniel Denny p^r. order

Then Voted that this meeting be dissolved and the meeting was dissolved accordingly

A True Entry   attest   Daniel Goulding Town Clerk

At the annual meeting of the Inhabitants of the Town of Worcester qualified to vote in Town affairs on Monday the third day of March A. D. 1800 at the publick meeting House of the first Parish of Said Town pursuant to the foregoing Warrant

Nathaniel Paine Esqr. Moderator of Said Meeting

Sworn   Oliver Fiske was chosen Town Clerk

Saml. Flagg Esqr. Nathl. Paine Esqr. Benj^a. Heywood Esqr. M^r. David Andrews Maj^r. Eph^m. Mower Selectmen and Overseers of the Poor

Sworn   Theophilus Wheeler Esqr. Town Treasurer

Sworn March 20   Saml. Flagg Esqr.
Sworn March 20   Benj^a. Heywood Esqr. } Assessors
Sworn March 20   M^r. David Andrews

Voted that M^r. Nathan White be Collector of Taxes he giving Sufficient bonds for the faithfull performance of his duty — and that he be allowed a Commission of five pence ¼ on the pound for what money he shall collect

Sworn   M^r. William Eaton
Sworn   M^r. Nathan White } Constables

Nathan Heard Searcher and Sealer of Leather

Sworn   Eph^m. Mower
Sworn   Ab^m. Lincoln } Clerks of the market

Joshua Whitney
John Barnard } Fence Viewers
Eben^r. Mower Sworn

Sworn Joseph Wheelock } Field Drivers
Sworn Henry Patch

Sworn Thomas Nichols } Tythingmen
Silas Bigelow

Simeon Duncan } Cullers of Staves and Hoops
Eben[r]. Hastings

William Goulding } Surveyors of Shingles
Daniel Denny   } & Clapboards

Sam[l]. Flagg Oliver Fiske Eph[m]. Mower Daniel Denny Fire Wards

	Isaiah Thomas	
Sworn	Tyler Curtis	
Sworn	Peter Slaytor	
Sworn	Elijah Burbank	
Sworn	Nathan White	
Sworn	Jesse Moore	
Sworn	Paul Gates	
Sworn	W[m]. Chamberlain	
Sworn	Eben[r]. Barber	Highway Surveyors and
Sworn	Reuben Gray	Collectors of Highway Taxes
Sworn	Aaron Flagg	
Sworn	Robert Blair	
Sworn	Elijah Flagg	
Sworn	Sam[l]. Porter	
	Charles Stearns	
	Jon[a]. Gleazen J[r].	
Sworn	Micah Johnson J[r].	
Sworn	Elias Stowell	

Voted to grant fifteen Hundred Dollars and to have the same assessed on the Polls & Estates of the Inhabitants for the purpose of keeping the highways in repair — also

Voted that those who choose to work out their highway Taxes shall be allowed 8[d] for each hours labour. Oxen Cart & Plow &c in the same proportion, as usual

Clark Whittemore Reuben Scott Moses Perry Dan[l] Heywood 2[d]. David Flagg Sam[l]. Gates James Williams Clark Goulding Benj[a]. Flagg 3[d]. Nath[l] Flagg jun[r] Hog-reeves [All sworn excepting Daniel Heywood 2d.]

Voted to allow the Swine to go at large they being yoked & ringed excepting in the Street

Voted to adopt the same methods as last year for carrying on the publick Schools

Theophilus Wheeler Silas Bigelow Nathl Harrington Benj^a Thaxter Joseph Patch Joshua Harrington Elijah Burbank Thad^s. Chapin Tyler Curtis School Committee

Voted to assess the Sum of $1000 on the Polls & estates of the Inhabitants of the Town for the purpose of keeping the publick Schools the current year

Nathl. Paine Esqr Benj^a Heywood Maj^r. Eph^m. Mower Committee for settling with the Town Treasurer

Voted to defer the consideration of the 8th [1] & 9th [2] articles to the adjournment of this meeting

Voted to annex Nathan Sever to Wm Gates School District

Voted to annex Robert Smith to the School District on Burn Coat Plain, so called

Voted that Theophilus Wheeler Esqr. Town Treasurer, be empowered to receive the Deeds of the Land on which the Publick School Houses are erected for the use of the Town So long as the Buildings are occupied for Town purposes

Voted to postpone the consideration of the 14th article [3] to the adjournment of this meeting

Meeting adjourned to the first Monday in april at 3 oClock P. M.

A true Entry   attest   Oliver Fiske Town Clerk

---

[1] In relation to Town Bonds.

[2] "To See what measures the Town will take for equally accommodating the Centre School District with School houses agreeably to the request of the Inhabitants of Said District."

[3] ARTICLE 14:—"To See if the Town will direct the Selectmen to draw orders on the Town Treasurer in favour of those persons who have claims against the Town for building the new School houses or to do any matter or thing respecting the same which they may think proper"

378   *Worcester Town Records, 1800.*

At the annual meeting of the Inhabitants of the Town of Worcester, qualified by the constitution to vote for Governor, Lieut. Governor Senators & Counsellors, convened agreeably to the foregoing Warrant on Monday Ap^l. 7 1800

The following persons were Voted for and had the number of Votes mentioned against their respective names Viz.

For Governor		Lieu^t. Governor	
Honble. Elbridge Gerry	140	His Honour Moses Gill	131
Honble. Caleb Strong	35	Honble. Caleb Strong	2
His Honour Moses Gill	1	Honble. Fisher Ames	3
Capt Joshua Whitney	1	Hon^l. Elbridge Gerry	1

Senators & Counsellors

Honble Salem Town	135	Nathl. Paine Esqr.	18
Hon^l. Levi Lincoln	104	Hon^l. Bezaliel Taft	25
Saml Flagg Esqr.	110	Col. Thos. Denny	8
John Whiting Esqr.	100	W^m. Henshaw Esq	1
Col. Saml. Jones	95	Saml. Curtis Esqr.	2
Hon^l. Elijah Brigham	41	Hon^l. Danl. Bigelow	7
Hon^l. John Sprague	35	Jabez Upham Esqr.	2
Hon^l. Josiah Stearns	24	Moses White Esqr.	3
Hon^l. Thomas Hale	14	Pliny Merrick Esqr.	1

Meeting dissolved

A true entry from the Minutes

                Attest   Oliver Fiske Town Clerk

―――

At a meeting of the Inhabitants of the Town of Worcester Qualified to Vote in Town affairs on Monday April 7th. by adjournment from the annual March Meeting Voted

To accept the report of the Com"tee for Settling accounts with the Town Treasurer

To accept the report of the School-House Com"tee

To direct the Selectmen to grant Orders to the Sub-Com"tees for payment of accounts exhibited for building schoolhouses in the several districts upon their procuring Deeds of the land on which they are erected for the use of the Town

Voted that the Town will not do anything further for the accommodation of the Center School district agreeably to their request (See article 9th)[1]

Oliver Fiske was chosen a School-Com"tee for the Center District in the room of Theop^s. Wheeler Esqr declined

D^r. The Town of Worcester in account current with T. Wheeler Town Treasurer
To Sundry Orders &c as pr Vouchers - Viz

N°				
1	Deacon Eben^r. Read		$11	26
2	Benj Heywood Esqr		56	52
3	James M^{c}farland			82
4	D^r. Oliver Fiske		97	99
5	Luther Moore		8	97
6	D^n. Eben^r. Read		37	12
7	Ezra Estabrook		—	83
8	David Andrews		4	33
9	Robert Blair		6	25
10	William Moore School Money		26	27
11	Elijah Flagg	Do	10	08
12	Charles Stearns	Do	88	55
13	Benj^a. Farrar	Do	39	48
14	David Andrews		7	02
15	Joel Bixbee		6	66
16	Eben^r. Williams School		9	87
17	James M^{c}farland		15	00
18	John Farror		2	54
19	Jonathan Gates 2^d		15	—
20	Assessors Order		34	63
21	Joseph Barbers School		28	27
22	Saml. Gates		—	80
23	W^m. Chamberlain		20	67

[1] ARTICLE 9:—"To See what measures the Town will take for equally accomodating the Center School District with School houses agreeably to the request of the Inhabitants of said District"

24	Jesse Craige	—	82
25	James Fisk	9	33
26	Asa Ward	6	66
27	Sam¹. Jennisons School	42	40
28	Ebenʳ. Barber	21	—
29	John Tatmans School	52	82
30	Thadˢ Chamberlain jʳ	42	67
31	Stephen Howard	—	82
32	Sam¹. Brooks	8	50
33	Thoˢ. Nichols	45	—
34	Daniel Denny	1	26
35	Abel Heywood	6	66
36	John Bairds — School	30	77
37	Walter Bigelow Do	40	00
38	Joseph Allen Esqʳ. Do	228	54
39	Danˡ Goulding	24	09
40	Joseph Morse	21	67
41	Charles Stearns	2	01
42	Paul Gates	11	73
43	Sam¹. Brazer	22	25
44	Luther Moore pᵈ John Read	27	63
45	Thomas Corbin	8	00
46	Revᵈ. Sam¹. Austin	31	17
47	William Gates	9	75
48	Nath¹. Harrington	23	83
49	Micah Johnson Jʳ.	6	00
50	Moses Miller	39	00
51	Paul Gates	1	82
Nº. 1	Wᵐ Gates	33	75
2	Wᵐ. Knight	20	00
3	Charles Stearns	6	66
4	Isaac Putman	15	92
5	Jack Melven	1	33
6	Calvin Park	40	00
7	James Quigley	50	00
8	Nath¹. Chandler	2	50
9	John Frink Jʳ.	8	82

10	John Frink	11	13
11	Rev^d. Saml Austin	21	00
12	W^m. Barker	1	33
N°. 1	Salem Town Esqr	15	00
2	Saml Flagg Esqr	15	30
3	John Chamberlain	44	82
4	Wm Gates	30	33
5	Joseph Patch	3	50
6	Adam Quigley	50	00
7	Calvin Park	96	59
		1763	41
	To Sundry Demands in the Treasury & carried to new a/c	4754	71
		$6518	12

By Sundry Obligations &c Rec^d of the late Treasurer as pr his a/c on record	1645	95
By Cash rec^d. of Do	34	66
Ap^l. 10 By Do Rec^d of N. Paine Esqr In^t	93	75
June 17 By Do Do Do	70	00
Decr. 24 Do Do Do	93	66
1800 } Feb. 28 } By In^t on J Patch's Note	3	38
By Tax Committed to Nathan White	4407	15
By Cash rec^d. of N. Paine Esqr	153	23
Ap^l. 5 By Do Do	16	34
	$6518	12

The Com"ttee appointed to Settle accounts with Theophilus Wheeler Esqr. Town Treasurer have attended that Service and report—that the Said Treasurer has charged himself with the Sum of six thousand five hundred and Eighteen Dollars 12/100 including the ballance of the former Treasurers account—That he has paid out in orders drawn by the Selectmen &c the Sum of Seventeen hundred & Sixty three Dollars 41/100 for which Sufficient vouchers were produced—which leaves a ballance of Four

Thousand Seven hundred & fifty four Dollars 71/100 for which he is further to account   all which is Submitted

Ap^l. 5 1800

Nathl Paine
Benj^a Heywood
Eph^m. Mower

Report of the Selectmen on the situation of the Town Bonds accepted

A List of Obligations belonging to the Town in the hands of y^e Selectmen

Principals	Sureties	Dates	Sums	Interest
Leonard Worcester	{ Nathan Patch { Theo^s Wheeler	Augt. 13 1793	$110.00	$6.60 paid
Alpheus Eaton	{ Wm Eaton { Simeon Duncan	march 25, 95	35.00	4.20 paid
Ignatius Goulding J^r.	{ Ignatius Goulding { W^m. Goulding	July 3^d, 99	305.33	7.48 p^d
Saml. Johnson	David Curtis Benj Butman	Feb 28. 1800	175.00	12.92 paid
Simeon Duncan	Joseph Blair Robt. Blair	Ap^l. 30 1798	133.33	8.00 paid
Joseph Patch	Benj. Flagg Aaron Flagg	Sep^t. 11. 93	476.66	28.60 paid
David Smith	Saml. Flagg Clark Chandler	Jany 17. 98	166.67	10.00 p^d
Phineas Ward	Saml. Curtis David Richardson	Novr. 1 1773	75.84	4.55 p^d
Eben^r. Hastings	Wm Gates Saml. Gates	Jany 5. 92	300.75	18.05 p^d
W^m. Gates	Thos. Wheeler Nathl Harrington	Decr. 1, 93	51.80	3.11 p^d
David Stowell	Benj. Stowell Nathl. Stowell	March 23, 95	86.67	5.20 paid
Ignatius Goulding	Ignatius Goulding J^r W^m. Goulding	March 12, 99	327.87	14.08 paid
Abel Goulding	Jno. Baker Jno. Goulding	Ap^l. 3. 99	135.99	5.54 paid
John Chamberlain	Ignatius Goulding Danl. Goulding	May 20, 90	336.80	22.20 paid
Abel Stowell	Cornelius Stowell Thos. Stowell	May 7, 92	89.10	

Worcester Town Records, 1800. 383

Danl. Heywood	Ignatius Goulding	Decr. 1, 93		
	Danl. Goulding		103.00	6.19 paid
Isaac Putman	Saml. Porter	Decr. 1, 97		
	Willard Morse		78.67	4.72 paid
John Noyes	Saml. Gates	Aug. 22, 97		
	David Stowell		133.87	8.00 paid
Jesse Taft	Josiah Lyon	July 21, 86		
	Joseph Barber		130.84	7.84 paid
Isaac Jenks	Benjamin Drury	Novr. 16, 96		
			277.77	16.67 paid
Saml. Brown	Elijah Dix	July 21. 83		
	Lem^l. Rice		130.84	7.84 paid
Eph^m. Mower	Thos Mower	March 3. 96		
	Clark Chandler		140.56	8.42 paid
Elijah Flagg	Isaac Gleason	Feb. 21, 95		
	Ed^d Knight		161.59	9.69 paid
Jacob Miller	Jed. Healy	Aug. 14. 94		
	Peter Stowell		62.50	3.75 paid
Jed^h. Healy	Jacob Miller	March 27, 97		
	Peter Stowell		69.33	4.25 paid
W^m. Goulding	Ignatius Goulding	May 7, 92		
	W^m. Johnson		48.33	2.90 paid
Levi Lincoln	Joseph Allen	Feb. 15, 85		
	Igna^s. Goulding		171.67	10.30 paid
David Bigelow	John Green	Nov. 1, 82	119.39	
Joseph Allen	Elijah Dix	Aug. 30, 84		
	Saml. Allen		115.18	6.90 paid
Samuel Flaggs	Ground Rent		12.00	12.00 paid
John Gould	Jno Taylor	Jany 24, 91		
	Holloway Taylor		111.11	13.33 paid

Worcester Ap^l. 7. 1800 $ 271.23

The above Sum of two Hundred & Seventy one Dollars and twenty three Cents Interest arising from the aforesaid obligations excepting eight Dollars has been paid to the Treas^r. by Nathl. Paine and by the Treasurer accounted for on the Settlement of his account

                         Saml. Flagg   ) Selectmen
                         Eph^m. Mower } of
                         David Andrews) Worcester

The Com"tee appointed to carry into effect the Votes of the Town for building School Houses beg leave to report, that they have so far executed their trust as that they have caused eight School Houses to be erected which are all nearly completed, except painting and for which they have agreed to pay the following sums which are to be considered as in full of all expences therefor—the Stoves and painting except Viz—

1st. In *Tatnick District* the Com"tee has erected one School House twenty five feet Square cost	$270,27
2^{d}. In *Col. Jones'* District near halfway River Bridge one of twenty four feet Square	270,27
3^{d}. At *Fisk's Corner* one of 22 feet Square	247,75
4th. On *Burncoat Plain* near Eben^r. Willington Jun^{rs}. one of twenty two feet Square	247,75
5th. On the *Sutton Road* near M^r. Burbank's Mills one of 22 feet Square	247,75
6th On the *Grafton Road* near M^r. Danl. Baird's one of 22 feet Square	247,75
7th Near *Capt William Gates'* one of 20 feet square	255,22
8th On *Holden Road* near M^r. B. Thaxters 18 feet square	202,70
	$1959,46

amounting in the whole to the Sum of nineteen Hundred & fifty nine Dollars & forty six Cents. Which sum taken from twenty five hundred Dollars granted by the Town, will leave a Ballance of Five Hundred & forty Dollars & fifty four Cents to be applied for building School Houses in the Centre District

The Com"tee further report that in order to enable them to pay for painting the aforesaid Houses together with the Stoves to be placed in them and to complete the building of three Houses in the Centre District, in addition to the aforesaid ballance of $540,64 the following sums will be necessary Viz

For building the third School House in the Centre	$236,49
For 11 Stoves @ $11,67	128,37
For Painting 11 Houses @ 24,00	264,00
Whole amount	$628,86

all which is submitted   Danl. Denny pr Order

At a Meeting of the Inhabitants of the Town of Worcester convened by the foregoing Warrant — Samuel Flagg Esqr. Moderator

Voted to raise the sum of six Hundred & twenty eight Dollars and 86/100 and to have the same assessed & levied upon the Polls and Estates of the Inhabitants, for the purpose of carrying into effect the report of the School Com"tee which has been accepted by the Town

Voted to allow the account of the Com"tee of arrangements for the 22^d. of Feb. last in Honour of Genl. Washington

Voted That the black Broad Cloth, which Shrouded the Desk, be presented to the two Clergymen of the Town — and that William Caldwell Esqr. be a Com"tee to present it

Voted that Horses and Mules shall not go at large the current year — also that all Neat cattle be prohibited, except Cows, which shall go at large only from the first of april to the first of November

Meeting dissolved

A true entry from the minutes

    attest Oliver Fiske Town Clerk

At a meeting of the Inhabitants of the Town of Worcester Quallified to Vote for Representatives, on Monday May 5 A. D. 1800

Voted to Send one Representative to the Genl. Court the ensuing Year

Voted that Nathl. Paine Esqr. be the Representative

Meeting dissolved A true entry from ye minutes

    attest Oliver Fiske Town Clerk

At a meeting of the Inhabitants of the Town of Worcester May 5th. agreeably to the foregoing Warrant, Saml. Flagg Esqr Moderator

Upon the 2ᵈ article Voted that the request of the Centre District be not granted [1]

Meeting dissolved   a true entry from the minutes

attest   Oliver Fiske Town Clerk

At a legal meeting of the Inhabitants of Worcester on Monday augᵗ. 25 1800 for the choice of a Representative to the Congress of the United States in the room of the Hon D Foster Esqʳ. resigned   The following persons were voted for & had the Nº. of Votes expressed against their respective names

Honˡ. Levi Lincoln Esqʳ.	127
Jabez Upham Esqʳ.	22
Seth Hastings Esqʳ.	5
Hon Salem Town Esqʳ.	2

Total: 156

A true entry   attest   Oliver Fiske Town Clerk

At a Meeting of the Inhabitants of the Town of Worcester in pursuance of the above warrant & for the purpose therein mentioned on Monday Octʳ. yᵉ twentieth A D. 1800

The following persons were voted for & had the number of votes expressed against their respective names

Viz Honˡ. Levi Lincoln Esqʳ	146
Jabez Upham Esqʳ	22
Seth Hastings Esqʳ	1
Capᵗ. J. Whitney	1

A true entry   attest   Oliver Fiske T. Clerk

---

[1] ARTICLE 2:—"To See if the Town will give leave to the Inhabitants of the Centre school district to lay out their Proportion of the Money heretofore granted and assessed for the purpose of building school Houses in Said Town in one or more School houses as to the said Inhabitants of the said Centre District may seem proper—or to do any other matter or thing which the Town may judge proper in and about the same"

At a Meeting of the Inhabitants of the Town of Worcester agreeably to the above Warrant on Monday Oct. 29. 1800

Saml. Flagg Esqr. Moderator

Voted to chose a Comtee on accounts consisting of three

Saml. Flagg Esqr ⎫
Nathl. Paine Esqr ⎬ Com"tee
Maj^r. Eph^m. Mower ⎭

Voted to postpone the consideration of the 3^d. article until after the above Com"tee have made their report[1]

Voted to discontinue the road from the great Post Road to Capt E. Wiswalls agreeably to his request (vide art. 4th)

Meeting adjourned to Monday Novr. 3^d. 3 °Clock P. M.

     Attest Oliver Fiske Town Clerk

At a Meeting of the Inhabitants of the Town of Worcester on Monday Novr. 3^d. A D. 1800 pursuant to the above Warrant — the following Gentlemen were voted for and had the number of Votes expressed against their respective names

Viz Hon^l. Levi Lincoln Esqr 194
    Jabez Upham Esqr 36
   Hon^l. Salem Town Esqr 1
    Seth Hastings Esqr 1

 A true entry attest Oliver Fiske Town Clerk

At a Meeting of the Inhabitants of the Town of Worcester on Monday Novr. 3^d. A. D. 1800 — By adjournment from Oct. 20th.

Voted to accept the report of the Com"tee on accounts which Report is as follows Viz — The Com"tee appointed to examine

---

[1] ARTICLE 3:—"To grant such sums of Money as may be necessary to defray the expences of the Current year and to receive the reports of any outstanding Com"tees"

accounts brought against the Town have attended that Service and Report as their opinion that the following accounts ought to be allowed — Viz —

To *Moses Miller* for Boarding & Cloathing Nathan Houghton ending y^e 20th. Novr. Instant 52 weeks @ 5/6 pr Week	$ 47,67
To *Thos. Nichols* for Boarding & Clothing Zach Johnson 52 Weeks ending 20 Novr. Instant @ 4/10	41,89
To *Deac. J. Chamberlain* for Boarding & Clothing Jane Dyer 52 Weeks ending 20 Novr. Instant @ 4/4	37,56
To *W^m. Gates* for Boarding & Clothing Anna White 52 Weeks ending Novr. 20 @ 4/	34,67
To *W^m. Gates* for Nursing S^d. anna when Sick	2,50
To *W^m. Parker Jr.* for Boarding & Clothing Benj^a. Randall 52 Weeks ending Novr. 14 @ 5/8	49,11
To *Eben^r. Barber* for Boarding & Clothing Danl. Gleazen & Wife 52 weeks ending Novr. 5 @ 8/4	72,23
To *Henry Patch* for Boarding & Clothing Edwd. Hair 56 weeks ending Novr. 6 @ 12/	112,00
To *Nathl Harrington* for Boarding & Clothing Kesiah Morse 52 Weeks ending Novr. 5 @ 3/10	33,22
To *Eph^m. Mower Jr.* & his Mother for Boarding & Clothing Nancy Conner 52 Weeks ending Novr. 17 @ 2/6	21,69
To *Saml. Brazer* for sundries supplied the Poor for one year last past	56,58
To *Saml. Flagg* for sundries d^d. Saml. Denny	1,34
To *John Farrar* for Sund. Supplied the Poor	1,50
To *Robert Blair* for Labour at ye Bridge by Judge Lincolns Mill	5,75
To *Saml. Flagg j^r* for a Journey to Walpole to notify that Town and a Journey to Mendon to procure a Grammar School Master & expences	12,35
To *Nathan White* for Labour & Materials for the New Bridge by Thos Mower's	89,67
To *Oliver Fiske* for sundries supplied the Poor	9,14
To *Nathan Heard* for Boarding a Prisoner in Goal 4 weeks @ 7/6 pr Week	5,00
To *Jacob Miller* for a Table at the Powder House	2,00

To *Jedediah Healy* for Coffins & Burying Sundry
Poor   12,17
To *David Andrews* for Timber & Railing the
Bridge at Halfway River   7,00
To *W^m. Chamberlain* for extra repairs on the
Road   1,00
To *Danl. Goulding* for divers supplies for the
Poor Recording Births & Deaths   23,23
To Thas^a. Chamberlain's extra Labour on the Road   1,68
To Benj^a. Butman for Boarding Ed^d. Hair 1 week &c   3,13

        All which is submitted $723,06

          Saml Flagg
          Nathl Paine } Com"tee
          Eph^m Mower

The Selectmen reported that they had drawn Sundry Orders Since the last Debt & Credit Meeting to the amount of four hundred thirty one Dollars 4/100 which has not been accepted

                                                Accepted

Voted to raise the sum of One Thousand Dollars for the purpose of defraying the expences of the current year and to have the same assessed upon the Polls & Estates of the Inhabitants of the Town

Voted to accept the further report of the School house Committee — Viz The Com"tee appointed to build School Houses beg leave further to report, that they have painted the Houses already built — the accounts, for which, amount to Two hundred & three Dollars 12½/100

                                  Danl. Denny P^r. Order

Meeting dissolved

        a true entry   attest   Oliver Fiske Town Clerk

At a meeting of the Inhabitants of the Town of Worcester on Monday Decr. 15. 1800 convened agreeably to the foregoing Warrant, the following Persons were voted for and had the number of votes expressed against their respective names

Viz Hon^l. Levi Lincoln Esqr.		142
Jabez Upham Esqr		8
Seth Hastings Esq		1

A true entry   attest   Oliver Fiske Town Clerk

At a meeting of the Inhabitants of the Town of Worcester on Monday Decr. 15. 1800 pursuant to the foregoing Warrant
Saml. Flagg Esqr. Moderator

Upon the Petition of Theophilus Wheeler Esqr. & Others (see next Page) Voted to reconsider a former vote of the Town so far as respects the large School House to be built in the centre District

Voted that there be granted to the Inhabitants of the centre School District their proportionate part of the Money heretofore granted & appropriated for the purpose of building School Houses on condition that the said Inhabitants erect & compleat two School houses — one in the South part of the District and the other in the North part of Said District — which Houses are to be not less than twenty two feet square

N. B. As the business of the third article was disposed of by the consideration of the second, it was not otherwise acted on [1]

Voted to abate the Taxes of the following persons borne on Nathan Whites list of Taxes for 1799   Viz

Benj^a. Newton	1 Poll under age	$ 1,83
Lucy Newton	1 Poll Do Do	1,83
Elisha Jacobs	not in Town	1,83
Abel How	Son a Soldier	1,83
John Tatman	overcharged	1,83
John Nazro	Do	1,83
W^m. Withington	not in Town	1,83
Nathl. Burges	Taxed in Brookfield	1,83
John Thayer	Taxed in Shrewsbury	1,83
Joshua Johnson	under age	1,83

---

[1] ARTICLE 3 :—"To See if the Town will direct the Com"tee for building School Houses to proceed & build a School House on the ground near Mrs Waters's agreeably to the request of Abel Stowell & others"

W^m. Town	not an Inhabitant May 1st. 1799	1,83
W^m. Young	very poor & out of Town	4,18
Joseph Bridge	out of Town	1,83
John Gay	poor & not an Inhabitant	3,31
		$ 29,45

To the Selectmen of Worcester Gentlemen Whereas the Inhabitants of this Town at their Meeting on the fourth day of March 1799 Voted to build School houses for the use of the several School districts — two of said Houses to be built in the Centre district — and on the twenty eighth day of Octr. 1799. at their meeting Voted, upon certain conditions, to be performed by the Centre District, to build within said district three School houses — all which Houses, except in the Centre District, have been built to the acceptance of the Town, and the Money therefor principally drawn — but the Houses in the Centre district are not built, nor contracted for.

And whereas the Inhabitants of s^d. Centre district, having deliberately considered their Situation and finding the number of the Minors to be nearly one third of the number of the Minors in the Town and those who would probably wish to attend the Schools so numerous that they cannot be accommodated with Houses built in the way and manner directed by the Town — They have therefore directed the Subscribers, their Com"tee, to request that the Town will reconsider their former Votes, which respect the building of Houses in the centre District and instead thereof, grant *that the said District draw from the Town Treasury the sum of Money heretofore appropriated for them, to be laid out in procuring such Houses as will best accommodate the District.*

We, therefore, in behalf, and by the direction of the said District, request you to insert an article in your Warrant for the next Town Meeting, touching the aforesaid premises

           Theoph^s Wheeler
Novr. 24. 1800   Isaiah Thomas
           Danl. Waldo j^r
Meeting dissolved
   A true entry attest Oliver Fiske Town Clerk

INDEX

General Index.

A

Academy, See Leicester Academy.
Accounts of Public moneys petitioned for, 25.
Adams, Charles, 128, 167, 199, 203, 209, 210, 229, 297.
  John, 18.
  Moses, 325.
  Newton, 254.
  Gov. Samuel, 75, 137, 147, 162, 182, 206, 239, 264, 285, 302.
Allen, Joseph, 9, 10, 14, 16, 18, 21, 25, 28, 30, 33, 34, 38, 43, 45, 51–55, 59, 61–63, 66, 70, 74, 83, 108, 109, 113, 118, 125, 127–129, 136, 139, 142, 167, 184, 185, 191, 194, 196, 204, 212, 214, 230, 231, 237, 248, 255, 256, 259, 280, 283, 284, 297, 312, 313, 315, 321, 334, 335, 344, 359, 363, 380, 383.
  Joseph, Jr., 321.
  Samuel, 27, 28, 38, 45, 83, 118, 128, 137, 148, 162, 167, 180, 185, 206, 231, 255, 264, 279, 281, 283, 285, 288, 299, 334, 361, 383.
Ames Fisher, 378.
Ammidown, Caleb, 18, 206, 360
Ammunition, Town stock of, petition to divide, 105 ; building for, 225 ; person to take care of, 350.
Andrews, Benjamin, 38, 42, 204, 237, 275, 328, 353, 362.
  David, 282, 295, 299, 306, 331, 338, 342, 351, 353, 354, 357, 359, 366–368, 369, 373, 375, 379, 383, 389.
  Ebenezer, 345.
  Samuel, 204, 331, 332, 358, 359.
Animals strayed, 316–319.
Anvil for Cato Walker, 26.
Arnold, Hannah, 19.
Assessors, See Town Officers.
Atwood. John, 305.
Austin, Rev. Samuel, 356, 380, 381.
Avery, John, 215, 216.
Ayres, See Eayas.

B

Bacon, John, 213, 214.
Baird, Daniel, 10, 24, 36, 42, 43, 48, 68, 71, 80, 85, 86, 88–90, 104, 107, 112, 113, 119, 120, 122, 127, 129, 131, 136, 138, 140, 144, 146, 151, 156, 159, 161, 166, 178, 179, 181, 190, 197, 205, 237, 244, 245, 248, 251, 260, 261, 280, 281, 297, 305, 306, 331, 336, 340, 347, 356, 359, 361, 367, 370.
  Daniel, Jr., 259, 261.
  John, 380.
  Thomas, 105, 320.
  Thomas, Jr., 320.
Baird's School Quarter, 324.
Baker Samuel, 18, 46, 75, 110, 137, 142, 148, 162, 183, 206, 214, 239, 264, 285.
  John, 382.
Baldwin, Nathan, 10, 14, 45.
Ball Isaac, 336
  Joseph, 10, 42, 75, 105, 107, 131, 178, 179, 182, 203, 238, 306.
Bancroft, Rev. Aaron, 29, 33, 35, 36, 38, 54, 55, 68, 75, 95, 98, 100, 143.
  David, 320, 321.
  Phe., 320.
  Timothy, 105.
  William, 320.
Bangs, Edward, 38, 83, 211, 212, 241, 264, 302, 321, 322, 333, 367.
Barber Dinah, 35.
  Ebenezer, 42, 70, 97, 160, 179, 354, 368, 372, 373, 376, 380, 388.
  James, 10, 29, 35, 109, 113, 160, 259, 261, 344.
  John, 75.
  Joseph, 11, 13, 20, 42, 57, 60, 66, 75, 76, 87, 114, 116, 118, 121, 129, 132, 144, 148, 152, 167–169, 176, 185, 188, 189, 191, 194, 195, 212, 231, 237, 255, 280, 283, 298, 324, 334, 344, 379, 383.

General Index.

Barber, Thomas, 343.
  William, 75, 192, 345.
Barber's School Quarter, 29.
Bardwell. Silas, 253.
Barker, William, 238, 381.
Barnard, John, 38, 42, 55, 58, 68, 144, 148, 159, 163, 169, 177, 181, 189, 194, 196, 203, 208, 212, 217, 219–121, 225, 226, 228, 229, 237, 240, 249, 250, 252, 253, 255, 256, 259, 260, 262, 263, 271, 272, 275, 280, 282, 288, 291, 295, 297, 303, 307, 210, 311, 325, 338, 357, 358, 369, 370, 375.
Barrell, James, 343.
Bartlett, Phineas, 332.
Barton, Jedediah, 151.
Beaman, Ezra, 149, 244, 271, 288.
Beef paid for, 60.
Bell, to be rung, 295, 326.
  Persons to ring, 79, 350.
  Repairs to the, 11, 23, 31, 32, 49, 65, 66, 91, 92, 126.
Bemis, Benjamin, 238.
Bigelow, Anna, 192.
  Daniel, 58-60, 302, 333, 378.
  David, 9, 10, 12-14, 39, 42-46, 48, 55, 58, 59, 65, 82, 85, 88-90, 114, 115, 117, 121, 130, 132–134, 140, 144, 148, 159, 162, 166, 168, 178–180, 185, 195, 197, 203, 231, 235, 237, 239, 244, 248, 256. 259, 280, 283, 285, 287, 298, 309, 314, 315, 318, 327, 330, 331, 333, 334, 358, 359. 365, 383.
  David, Jr., 135.
  Gershom and Gershom, Jr., 320.
  Jabez, 152.
  Joseph, 152, 259.
  John, 274.
  Joshua, 87.
  Levi, his ear bitten by a horse, 314.
  Mary, 31, 116.
  Samuel, 204, 238, 347.
  Silas, 279, 343, 369, 370, 376, 377.
  Thaddeus, 42, 69, 121, 131, 141, 160, 166, 238, 305, 316, 347.
  Timothy, 34, 38, 42, 43, 48, 72, 88, 128, 152, 172, 185, 232.
  Walter, 380.
Bill, Rebeckah, 251.
Billings, —— 177.
Birds, bounty for, 260, 280, 289, 301.
Births and Deaths recorded, 373, 389.
Bixby, Joel, 132, 246, 259, 261, 275, 310, 339, 379.
  Solomon, 35, 42, 58, 86, 116, 177, 204, 238, 289, 349.
Blackman, Nathan, 211, 238.
Blair, Increase, 144, 160, 237, 294, 305.
  Joseph, 10, 40, 42, 62, 69, 83, 119,

Blair, Joseph, 184, 195, 207, 230, 256, 284, 335, 382.
  Robert, 371, 376, 379, 382, 388.
Blake, Bill, 349.
  Ellis Gray, 152.
  Increase, 204, 270, 288, 325.
  James, 127, 165, 167, 346.
  Jason, 204, 235, 239, 279.
  Luther, 304.
  Polly, 294.
  Widow, 295.
Blakely, Abel, 254.
Blind Persons, 175
Bolton, 49, 65, 81, 91.
Bond, Forbes, 345.
Bonds, See Town Bonds, Pew Bonds.
Books for records paid for, 66, 173, 199, 373.
Boston, 49, 85, 353.
Boundary disputes, 286, 365.
Bounds perambulated, 149, 262, 368.
Bounty, for birds, 260, 280, 289, 301.
  to soldiers, 106, 128, 135, 267.
Bowdoin, Gov., 18, 46, 74, 110, 136, 147, 162.
  James, Jr., 137.
Bowers, Jerathmeel, 302.
Bowles, William, 40, 42, 43, 48, 70, 88, 97, 115, 165.
Bowman, Hepsebeth, 30-32, 116.
  Lydia. 31, 91.
Boyd, Mary, 65, 82, 91, 117, 127, 140, 155.)66, 190.
Boyden, Daniel, 320.
  Darius, 105, 320.
  Elizabeth, John, and Peter, 320.
Boylston, 149, 156, 174, 200, 217, 262, 286, 288, 365, 368, 369.
Boynton, Nathaniel, 160.
Bradish, Ebenezer, 266.
Bragg, John, 26. .
Braintree, 218.
Brazer, Samuel, 38, 42, 107, 113, 145, 159, 164, 165, 167, 178-180 193, 194, 204, 211, 228, 237, 243, 244, 255, 269, 275, 281, 286, 188, 290, 296, 306, 307, 310, 331, 337–341, 347, 349, 351, 353, 359, 362, 363, 373, 380, 388.
Bread, weight of, 13.
Brick, bought, 288.
Bridge, James, 305.
  Joseph, 390.
  Samuel, 10, 38, 42, 55, 74, 107, 128, 131, 167, 297, 328, 356.
Bridge at Lincoln Square, 172, 247.
Bridges, repaired, 160, 172–174, 201, 217, 218, 245–247.
  timber for, 49, 65, 127, 174, 293, 294, 353.
Brigham, Elijah, 239, 264, 285, 333, 349, 360, 378.

General Index. 397

Brigham, Samuel, 165-167.
Broadcloth presented to the ministers, 385.
Brooks, Agnes, 48, 81, 127, 175, 183.
    Betty and Nancy, 17.
    Elizabeth, 49, 81.
    Ephraim, 259.
    John, 253.
    Nathaniel, 9, 20, 31, 34, 42-44, 46, 48, 64, 68, 70, 72, 86, 97, 115, 116, 122, 136, 139, 141, 152, 159, 179, 191, 205, 236, 243, 244, 247, 248, 280, 282, 289, 324, 332.
    Samuel, 9, 11, 13, 20, 29, 31, 32, 34, 35, 39, 40, 42-44, 46, 48, 59, 65, 68, 70-72, 77, 78, 84, 90, 95, 97, 106-108, 112, 113, 115, 116, 119-121, 127, 128, 132-134, 138, 140, 144, 145, 149, 150, 153, 155-159, 163, 165, 167, 173, 178, 179, 183, 186, 190, 192, 202, 203, 217, 219-221, 228, 229, 235, 237, 244, 245, 250, 256, 271, 273, 275, 278, 280, 288, 289, 295, 307, 311, 339, 341, 347, 356, 380.
    Samuel, Jr., 27, 42.
    Silas, 352.
Brown, Eliza, 338.
    John, 75, 253.
    Luke, 305.
    Mary, 167.
    Samuel, 12, 14, 31, 45, 83, 118, 184, 231, 255, 284, 313, 334, 383.
    Thaddeus, 253.
    William, 115, 303, 346.
    William, Jr., 40, 140.
Browning, Joseph, 253.
Bruce, George, 84.
Buck, Rachel, 320.
Burbank, Elijah, 359, 361, 376, 377.
Burncoat Plain, 377, 384.
Burges, Nathaniel, 390.
Burying Ground, person to take care of, 350
    New, (Mechanic street) 29, 51, 269, 270, 300, 353, 373; committee to lay out lots, 351; report of with plan, 354, 366.
Burying Grounds, fences for, 286, 295, 296, 310.
Bush, Jotham, 369.
Butler, Jonathan, 304, 336.
    Smith, 373.
Butman, Benjamin, 153, 157, 163, 211, 238, 328, 382, 389.
Buxton, William, 99.

C

Caldwell, William, 321, 322, 340, 385.
Camp kettles, 270.
Campbell, Duncan, 152.
    James, 152, 253.

Candidate for the pulpit, 28.
Cannon, carriages, 114.
    loaned to Gloucester, 20.
Carter, Benjamin and Benjamin, Jr., 320.
    John, 177.
    Timothy, 320.
Case, Samuel, 280.
Case for Town Records, 208, 218.
Cary, ——, 324.
Center School Quarter or District, 53, 70, 323, 349, 365, 367.
    School Houses to be built in, 370, 374, 375, 377, 379, 386, 390, 391.
Chadwick, David, 13, 38, 40, 42, 105, 135, 236, 238, 260.
    Daniel, 72, 209, 238, 324.
    Isaac, 229, 245, 275, 318.
    John, 133, 134.
    Joseph, 204, 238, 306, 331, 344, 356.
    Jacob, 27, 43, 78, 95, 111, 122, 125, 140, 165.
Chamberlain, John, 32, 39, 40, 43, 58, 59, 64, 67, 68, 71, 77, 79, 84, 107, 109, 112, 113, 119, 120, 122, 125, 127-129, 131, 133, 138-141, 144, 146, 150, 153, 156-158, 166-169, 175, 178, 179, 185-187, 189-192, 195-198, 200, 201, 203-205, 208, 211, 214, 217, 218, 224, 226-232, 235-237, 241, 245, 249, 250, 256-259, 261-263, 265, 268, 270, 272, 273, 275, 278-281, 283, 284, 286, 288-291, 294, 297, 299, 305, 308, 310, 311, 313, 317, 327, 330, 331, 335, 337, 338, 341, 342, 346, 347, 351, 353, 354, 361-363, 365, 368, 372, 381, 382, 388.
    Thaddeus, 10, 43, 69, 70, 97, 133, 145, 160, 178, 179, 208, 238, 259, 328, 368, 380, 389.
    William, 178, 179, 212, 238, 260, 261, 297, 347, 376, 379, 389.
Chandler, Anna, 92, 117, 198.
    Charles, 13, 38, 42, 59, 173, 196, 200, 217, 229, 246, 271, 275, 304, 311, 321, 337, 340, 346.
    Clark, 16, 38, 42, 61, 66, 68, 83, 107, 118, 166, 167, 184, 315, 321, 334, 382, 383.
    Gardiner, L., 238, 247, 274.
    John, 134, 187.
    Nathaniel, 321, 356, 380.
    Rufus, 136, 196.
    Samuel, 13, 38, 39, 42, 69, 74, 128, 152, 173, 196, 200, 204, 207, 217, 220, 229, 237, 246, 260, 271, 275, 276, 281, 291, 292, 297, 304, 308, 311, 321, 322, 336, 337, 339, 340, 346.
    Thomas, 321.

Chandler, Winthrop, 253.
———, 161.
Chapin, Benjamin, 336.
  Eli, 38, 42, 86, 87, 144, 181, 184, 198, 209, 232, 235, 238, 257, 260, 288, 323, 344, 353, 360, 363.
  Thaddeus, 38, 43, 49, 65, 86, 87, 115, 116, 145, 151, 204, 209, 238, 264, 265, 293, 306, 323, 377.
Chapin's Road, 300.
Chenery, Dr., 183.
  Isaac, 194.
Child or Childs, Amherst, 305, 307.
  Benjamin, 43, 160, 178, 180.
  John, 157, 227, 249.
  John, Jr., 325.
  ———, 173.
Church difficulties, 36, 37.
Cider, price of, 353.
Circulating medium wanted, 23.
Claflin, Otis, 345, 352.
Clap, Daniel, 28, 45, 69, 128, 152, 180, 275, 299, 306, 321, 329, 344, 349.
Clark, Joseph, 368.
Clewes, Thomas, 58.
Cobb, David, 213, 215, 216.
Coburn, Moses, 345.
Coffins for paupers, 31, 49, 201, 324, 273, 389.
Collins, Lydia, 19.
Comins, or Comings, Daniel, 320.
  Temple, 249.
Commercial Treaty, memorial in favor of, 322
Committee of Correspondence and Safety, 10.
Coney, John and Timothy, 345.
Congress, Representatives in, voted for, 141, 142, 147, 233, 239, 279, 312.
Conner, Mrs. 353, 373, 388.
Constables, see Town Officers.
Constitution of Massachusetts, vote against revision, 285.
Constitutional Convention, delegates to, 130.
Continental money, 172, 189.
Convention, County, 12, 84–87, 104.
  to discuss grievances, 21.
Converse or Convers, Benjamin, 253, 267, 277.
Cook, Robert, 107, 131, 159.
Coolidge, Nathaniel, 43, 132, 238, 298, 304, 331, 332, 338, 347, 359.
Corbin, Thomas, 380.
Cotton, John, 321.
Cotton and Linen Manufactory, 152, 153.
Counterfeit Money, 116.
County, division of the, 48, 350.
County Officers voted for, 27, 44, 69, 148, 162, 180, 206, 285, 299, 361.
Courts to be annihilated, 90.
Coves, Simeon, 337.
Crafts, Ebenezer, 18.
  Edward, 111.
Craige, Jesse, 204, 211, 235, 238, 240, 250, 259, 261, 380.
  Thomas, 325.
Crawford, Robert, 116.
Crosby, Aɒiah, 81.
  Benjamin, 91, 92, 109, 155, 272.
  ——— ———, 51, 52, 56, 80, 127, 155.
Crowle, Archer, and John, Jr., 320.
Crowley, John, 274
Crows' heads, 337; bounty for, 260 274, 289, 301, 304–306, 336.
Croxford, William, 64, 67, 168, 173, 188, 291, 307, 348, 363.
Cummings, Temperance, 65, 80.
Cunningham, Clarissa, 153, 157.
Curtis, David, 289, 298, 382.
  John, 29, 32, 34, 69, 70, 86, 121, 122, 159, 165.
  Oliver, 320.
  Samuel, 19, 21, 38, 40, 42, 43, 46, 47, 64, 82, 109, 110, 117, 130, 131, 142–144, 148, 158, 162, 171, 176, 178–180, 183, 185, 186, 194, 203, 209, 211, 224, 229, 241, 251, 255, 258, 259, 261–265, 273, 274, 279– 281, 283, 289, 293, 295, 298, 327, 330, 335, 358, 367, 378, 382.
  Samuel, Jr. 238, 280, 331, 332, 359.
  Tyler, 42, 144, 235, 238, 240, 280, 370, 376, 377.
Curtis School District, 324, 327, 330, 331.
Cursing and swearing, see Swearing.
Cushing, Thomas, 18, 46, 74, 75, 110, 321.
  William, 264, 285, 302.
  ——— ———, 115.
Cutler, John, 170.
Cutting, Jonah, 105.
  Zebulon, 184, 231, 256, 282, 313, 335

D

Damages for alteration of road, 248, 271.
Damon, ———, 116.
Dana, Hon. Francis, 46, 182, 206.
  Samuel, 183.
  ———, 59, 60.
Davis, Ebenezer, 23.
  Jacob, 60.
  John, 150.
  Rev. Joseph, 59.
  Joshua, 253.

General Index. 399

Davis, ——, 368.
Dawes, William, 115.
Deer Reeves, see Town Officers.
Delegates to County Convention, 85-88; report of, 87.
Denny, Daniel, 351, 344, 358, 359, 375, 376, 380, 384, 389.
   Sally, 192.
   Samuel, 200, 217, 245, 246, 254, 270, 273, 294, 308, 324, 351, 353, 372.
   Samuel, Jr., 280.
   Thomas, 360, 378.
Desk for the Clerk, 246.
Dexter, Stephen, 13, 40, 43, 45, 70, 82, 97, 117; moved out of town, 95.
Dickinson, Richard, 161, 199.
Dingley, ——, 176.
Dix, Elijah, 12, 14, 29, 40, 45, 48, 56, 58, 66, 70, 72, 74, 77, 79, 82, 83, 87-89, 96, 99, 106, 108, 109, 113, 116-118, 128, 129, 132, 159, 163, 167, 168, 170, 172, 184, 185, 192, 204, 212, 228, 231, 234-236, 247, 250, 252, 255, 271, 275, 278, 283, 284, 289, 334, 368, 383.
Dodds, James, 368.
Dodge, Richard, 345.
Dog Tax, 371.
Dorr, Joseph, 105.
Douglas, Town of, 84.
Drury, Benjamin, 334, 383.
   Thomas, 105, 151, 320.
   Thomas, Jr., 320.
Dudley, David, 369.
Duffe, Luke, 253.
Duncan, Rebeckah, 288, 353.
   Simeon, 31, 38, 61-63, 73, 83, 99, 115, 117, 119, 144, 145, 148, 156, 163, 168, 174, 178, 184, 192, 200, 203, 204, 217, 228, 230, 235, 238, 252, 256, 259, 261, 274, 279, 280, 284, 288, 297, 304-307, 311, 313, 328, 334, 335, 338, 341, 343, 346, 347, 362, 376, 382.
Dunham, Elisha, 152, 253, 254.
Dwight, Elijah and Thomas, 214.
Dyer, Jenny, 91, 127, 175, 200, 217, 245, 270, 294, 353, 372, 388.

E

Eames, William, 262.
Ear bitten by a horse, 314.
Earthen-ware manufactory, 12.
Eaton, Alpheus, 231, 238, 256, 281, 284, 299, 313, 334, 382.
   James, 368.
   Reuben, 58.
   Samuel, 32, 50, 58, 64, 65, 91, 115, 116, 126, 140, 141, 156, 166, 191, 194, 195, 343.
   Sarah, 126, 156, 175.

Eaton, Thomas, 69.
   William, 231, 256, 275, 334, 343, 357, 375, 382.
Eayres, (or Ayres) Thomas S., 254, 272, 325.
Eddy, Levi, 231, 255, 283, 320.
   Samuel, 320.
Edward Benjamin, 161.
Elder, John, 40, 108, 113, 136, 140, 155, 166, 167, 173, 190, 192, 200, 209, 217, 228, 245, 246, 250, 251, 255, 270, 288, 293, 294, 305, 306, 311, 338, 340, 346, 353, 361-363.
   John, Jr., 144, 204, 280, 344.
   William, 17, 49, 58, 65, 80, 116, 117, 132, 159, 174, 228, 371.
Electors, Presidential, voted for, 142, 214.
Engine, see Fire Engine.
Engine House, 255, 269.
Engine repaired, 353.
Entrenching Tools, 12, 17.
Estabrook, Asa, 371.
   Ebenezer, 266.
   Ezra, 253, 379.
Etheridge, Samuel, 355.

F

Farrar, Benjamin, 344, 379.
   John, 362, 373, 379, 388.
   ——, 331.
Fences for Burying Grounds, 286, 295, 296, 300, 310.
Fence Viewers, see Town Officers.
Fenno, Daniel, 304, 306, 340, 347, 363.
Fessenden, John, 111, 137, 148, 162, 183, 206.
Field Drivers, see Town Officers.
Filmore, see Philmore.
Fire Engine, petition for a, 70, 72, 74; vote to purchase, 234; house for, 244; to be paid for, 248, 289; repaired, 353.
Fire Wards chosen, 163, 204, 259, 280, 358.
Fish, Simeon, 204, 205, 236, 238.
Fisk, James, 40, 105, 136, 139, 178, 179, 194, 212, 236, 238, 270, 283, 289, 295, 298, 306, 311, 324, 327, 331, 335, 341, 346, 347, 354, 362, 380.
   John, 58.
   Luther, 27.
   Oliver, (Town Clerk, 1800.) 212, 270, 289, 301, 327, 342, 344, 348, 349, 353, 357-359, 363, 364, 370, 373, 375, 376, 379, 388.
   Samuel, 105, 178.
Fisk's Corner, 384.
Fitts, Abraham, 320.
Flagg, Aaron, 257, 283, 334, 376, 382.

General Index.

Flagg, Amos, 337.
  Asa, 133, 134.
  Benjamin, 12, 15, 18, 36, 38, 39, 43, 48, 80, 88, 97, 257, 283, 316, 334, 371.
  Benjamin, Jr., 80, 108, 145, 158, 235, 238, 298, 328.
  Benjamin, 3d., 376.
  Daniel, 336.
  David, 105, 238, 359, 376.
  Eli, 318.
  Elijah, 43, 108, 238, 259, 261, 283, 297, 313, 334, 353, 376, 379, 383.
  Francis, 297.
  Isaac, 43, 69, 80.
  John, 352.
  Jonathan, 39, 43.
  Josiah, 10, 39, 40, 43, 115, 238, 269. 289.
  Joshua, 160.
  Levi, 80, 136, 166, 235, 247, 273, 297, 324, 357.
  Nathaniel, 105, 145, 172, 203, 205, 212, 235, 238, 259, 332, 338, 361,
  Nathaniel, Jr 376.
  Phineas, 39, 80, 109, 113, 127, 139, 146, 149, 166, 167, 179, 202.
  Rhoda, 317.
  Richard, 150.
  Rufus, 20, 72, 131, 145, 280, 352.
  Samuel, 13, 38, 39, 43, 46, 50, 57, 61, 69, 70, 72, 74, 79, 83, 111, 116, 118, 119, 128, 144, 148, 151, 158, 162–164, 167, 171, 174, 177, 178, 180, 182–184, 186, 187, 193, 198, 199, 201–204, 206, 207, 209, 211, 212, 214, 216, 220, 224–226, 228, 229, 231–235, 239, 243–247, 250, 255–265, 267, 268, 275, 276, 279, 280, 282, 284, 285, 289, 293–297, 299, 302, 303, 306, 307, 309, 310, 314, 318, 324, 326, 327, 329, 333, 337, 339–342, 344, 346, 350, 351, 353–362, 365–367, 370, 373, 375, 376, 378, 381–383, 385, 387–390; Land leased to, 16.
  Samuel, A. 360.
  Silas, 178, 179, 204.
  Stephen, 115, 199.
Fluker, Thomas, 321.
Follinsbee, Eunice, 201, 228.
Forbes, William, 58.
Foster, Dwight, 171, 183, 206, 213, 233, 239, 279, 312, 322, 356, 386.
Fowler, Ezekiel, 238.
  Samuel, 214.
Framingham, 31, 49.
Freeland, Dr. James, 84, 86.
French, Benjamin, 329.
  Cyrus, 57, 169.
Frink, John, 381.
  John, Jr., 380.
  Samuel, 306.
Fuller, Benjamin, 253.
Fullerton, Samuel, 64, 67, 108, 168, 188, 291, 307, 347, 363.

G

Gay, John, 324, 371, 390.
Gale Clarrissa, 156.
  Eli, 131, 132, 140, 145, 156, 163, 178, 190, 194, 251, 259, 274, 328.
  Henry. 320.
  Luther, 115.
  Noah, 58.
Gates, James, 222, 224.
  Joel, 304
  Jonathan, 99, 179, 212, 274, 277, 310, 338, 364.
  Jonathan, 2d, 69, 133, 235, 238. 241, 279, 280, 297, 298, 332, 344, 379.
  Nathaniel, 328.
  Paul, 61, 63, 119, 152, 185, 204, 231, 255, 328, 357, 358, 373, 376, 380.
  Samuel, 178, 207, 235, 238, 255, 260, 283, 334, 343, 361, 376, 379, 382, 383.
  Simon, 40, 132, 133, 217, 236, 237, 251, 305.
  Thomas, 132, 177, 297, 304,
  William, 38, 40, 42, 43, 61, 88, 105, 119, 184, 185, 205, 231, 233, 237, 255, 280, 282, 283, 314, 335, 341, 347, 353, 356, 363, 366, 372, 377, 380, 381, 382, 384, 388.
  William, Jr., 358.
Gates School District, 324.
General Court, to be removed to some country town, 25, 90.
  Representatives to, see Representatives.
Gerry, Elbridge, 136, 137, 206, 239, 285, 333, 360, 378.
Gilbert, William, 325.
Gill, Moses, 18, 46, 75, 110, 137, 142, 148, 162, 183, 206, 214, 239, 264 285, 302, 312, 333, 347, 360, 378.
Glasgow, Simon, 12, 19, 24, 31, 32, 48, 65, 80, 81, 91, 127, 149, 155, 173, 177, 201, 217, 234, 245, 246, 269–271, 294, 295, 311, 340, 353, 354, 356.
Glass for Meeting House, 31.
Gleason, Bezaleel, 133.
  Daniel, 354, 372, 373, 388.
  David, 320.
  Isaac, 87, 149, 201, 228, 283, 334, 353, 383.

General Index. 401

Gleason, Isaac Jr., 353.
  John, 10, 19, 42, 58, 59, 86, 288, 289.
  Jonathan, 20, 40, 42, 87, 178, 180, 238, 307, 324, 328, 331, 359, 376.
  Jonathan 2d, 280.
  Lydia, 201, 218.
  Phineas, 19, 115, 274, 305, 306, 332, 371.
  Silas, 247, 271, 275, 279.
  Solomon, 108.
  Thomas, 155, 156, 163, 173-175, 200, 217, 246, 338.
  ——, 163.
Gloucester, 21, 60.
Goddard, John, 48.
  Samuel, 19, 42, 58, 59, 106, 128, 133, 151, 158, 160, 166, 167, 173, 229, 238, 331, 332, 341.
  Samuel, Jr., 304, 343.
Goodale, Paul, 338, 368.
Goodell, Asa, 262.
Goodwin, John, 10, 31, 38, 49, 59, 60, 88, 91.
Gore, the, 321; petition for annexation, 36, 38, 47.
Gorham, Nathaniel, 75, 11c.
Gould, Gideon, 329.
  John, 177, 185, 232, 256, 282, 313, 334, 383.
  Samuel, 305.
Goulding, Abel, 382.
  Clark, 204, 376.
  Daniel, (Town Clerk, 1784-1786, 1792-1799.) 9, 10, 15, 19, 24, 27, 28, 39, 42-44, 46, 48, 49, 57, 61, 63, 68, 74, 76, 83, 117, 118, 155, 159, 163, 165, 168, 169, 184, 185, 188, 193, 195, 196, 201-204, 214, 217-219, 228, 231, 232, 234-237, 244, 246, 247, 250, 251, 256-258, 261, 270, 273, 277-281, 283, 284 287, 288, 292, 294-296, 298, 299, 305, 306, 309, 311, 313, 314, 327, 334, 337, 338, 341, 342, 354, 357-359, 362, 363, 373, 380, 383, 389.
  Ignatius, 10, 38, 39, 42, 49, 61, 62, 69, 83, 107, 118, 132, 144, 159, 178, 184, 185, 203, 219-221, 231, 235, 237, 256, 257, 259, 272, 277, 278, 282-284, 290, 313, 334, 335, 382, 383.
  Ignatius, Jr., 382.
  John, 382.
  John R., 282, 335.
  Millicent, 56, 92, 124-126.
  Palmer, 12, 13, 33, 38, 43, 45, 48, 51, 55, 61, 72, 83, 109, 117, 118, 155, 184, 193, 231, 232, 256, 257, 276, 277, 283, 334.
  Peter, 83, 118, 352.
  William, 238, 257, 277, 278, 282,

Goulding, William, 284, 294, 297, 305, 313, 314, 324, 328, 331, 339, 341, 343, 346, 351, 355, 357, 376, 382, 383.
Governor and State Officers voted for, 18, 46, 74, 110, 136, 147, 162, 182, 206, 239, 264, 285, 302, 333, 349, 360, 378.
Gowen, Benjamin, 345.
Grafton, 19, 65, 109, 174.
Grammar School, 26, 50, 52, 79, 81, 82, 90, 97, 108, 165, 172, 205, 225, 250, 332, 349, 359, 366, 373; Town presented for not keeping a, 135.
Grand Juror chosen, 107.
Grant, Daniel, 330.
Grant to the army and officers denounced, 22.
Grary, Nathaniel, 305.
Grave-digging, 31, 73, 350.
Graves, Samuel, 274, 304.
Gray, Jacob, 167.
  Reuben, 40, 42, 80, 87, 132, 145, 238, 275, 297, 328, 376.
  Robert, 17, 19, 87, 109, 113, 115, 274, 319, 353, 362.
  Thomas, 304, 336, 337, 344, 373.
Green, Benjamin, 42, 89.
  Isaac, 304.
  John, 70, 82, 91, 92, 117, 128, 165, 185, 196, 201, 212, 217, 256, 283, 310, 315, 323, 324, 334, 363.
  John, Jr., 166, 212, 246, 273, 275, 338, 341, 353, 373.
  Nathan, 369.
  Samuel, 150, 253.
  Timothy, 173, 193.
Grievances, Public, 88.
Griggs, David, 217, 252, 311, 328, 338.
  Samuel, 40, 159.
Gross, Philip, 346.
Grout, Abigail, 140, 155, 167, 175, 191, 195, 200, 228, 229.
  Benoni, 66.
  Daniel, 161, 303.
  Hon. Jonathan, M. C. etc., 46, 111, 137, 141, 142, 147, 171, 176, 183, 206, 213, 233, 239.
  Jonathan, of Worcester, 10, 42, 87, 178, 179, 238, 332, 342.
Guide Boards, 353.
Guide Posts, 286, 293, 294.
Gun House, 152, 255.

H

Hair, Edward, 235, 353, 372, 388, 389.
  Joseph, 254.
Hale, Thomas, 360, 378.
  ——, 325.
Halfway River, 209, 354, 356, 373.
Hambleton, or Hamilton, Asa, 238,

402   *General Index.*

Hambleton, Asa, 321, 332, 344.
  John, 116.
  Mary, 41, 92.
  Reubin, 42, 87, 99, 108, 109.
  Samuel, 40.
Hames for the Hearse, 271.
Hancock, Gov. John, 18, 46, 74, 110, 136, 147, 162, 182, 206, 215, 216, 239.
Hardy, Peter, 320.
Harrington, Elijah, 10, 42, 68, 86, 87, 144, 149, 205, 238, 248, 271, 274, 306, 323.
  Francis, 87.
  Isaac, 150.
  Joshua, 236, 344.
  Joshua, Jr., 80, 86, 178, 180, 203, 260, 274, 297, 377.
  Josiah, 10, 42.
  Lawson, 336.
  Nathan, 150.
  Nathaniel, 42, 87, 133, 159, 179, 184, 231, 236, 238. 256, 260, 261, 284, 283, 289, 297, 298, 307, 326, 331, 335, 344, 353, 357, 359, 362, 366, 372, 377, 380, 382, 388.
  Noah, 39, 47, 80, 178, 180, 344.
  Samuel, 327, 331, 332, 358, 359.
  Senica, 336.
  Silas, 42, 87, 153, 248, 260, 272, 273, 277, 323, 371.
Harris, Daniel, Jr., 58.
  Noah, 42, 69, 70, 97, 108, 109, 113, 158, 160, 163, 178, 179, 235, 237, 240, 259, 298, 300.
Hart, or Heart, Charles, 320.
  James, 265, 320.
  James, Jr., 105, 320.
  John, 231, 255, 283, 320.
Harwood, Ebenezer, 303.
  Nathaniel, 254.
Hasey, Benjamin, 192.
Hassum, Stephen, 152.
Hastings, Ebenezer, 178, 204, 219–221, 238, 255, 283, 313, 335, 357, 376, 388.
  Joseph, 42.
  Seth, 75, 349, 386, 387, 390.
Haven, Rev. Daniel, 28, 29, 33, 116.
Haverhill, 173, 175.
Hawes, Elijah, 70.
  Justice, 57.
  Stephen, 280.
  ——, 114.
Hawkins, Jeremiah, 238.
Hay Scales, 309.
Hayward, James, 39, 238.
  Stephen, 39, 160, 203, 238, 280, 282, 358.
  See Heywood.

Healey, Jedediah, 31, 38, 42, 49, 59, 107, 110, 112, 113, 116, 117, 201, 238, 251, 256, 260, 261, 277, 283, 324, 331, 334, 337, 343, 373, 383, 389.
Heard, Anthony, 176.
  John, 196, 200, 227.
  Nathan, 10, 38, 39, 42, 68, 88, 107, 128, 131, 144, 158, 178, 203, 212, 235, 238, 259, 260, 279, 297, 330, 331, 340, 342, 347, 357, 359, 375, 388.
  William, 303.
Hearse, repaired, 31, 50; house for, 244, 255, 269, 373; harness for, 271, 293; Wheels for, 340.
Heath, (town of,) 163, 191.
Hemenway, Ephraim, 288.
  Jacob, 41, 60, 87, 126, 139, 166, 168.
  Jeffrey, 59, 253.
  Samuel, 145.
  Scipio, 164.
Henry, Charles, 271, 295.
  Robert, 185.
  Silas, 132.
Henshaw, Daniel, 181.
  David, 150, 263.
  Samuel, 213, 214.
  William, 27, 28, 190, 378.
Hersey, David, 294, 306, 357.
Heywood, Abel, 19, 42, 59, 132, 163, 238, 304, 336-338, 373, 380.
  Benjamin, 27, 39, 42, 43, 69, 70, 74, 75, 108, 117, 132, 133, 136, 139, 141, 146, 148, 152, 155, 156, 158, 160, 161, 170, 171, 173, 176-183, 186, 187, 193, 194, 196-201, 203, 206, 207, 209, 214, 216-220, 224-226, 228, 230, 232, 235-237, 240, 243, 244, 247-249, 251, 252, 255, 256, 258-261, 264, 268, 271-273, 276, 279, 280, 287, 288, 292-294, 296, 298, 299, 309, 313, 314, 322-324, 328, 329, 331, 339, 344, 346, 348, 349, 351, 354, 355, 357-359, 365, 366, 375, 377, 379, 382.
  Daniel, 10, 42, 65, 69, 116, 133, 134, 160, 279, 283, 284, 328, 334, 383.
  Daniel, 2d, 87, 235, 238, 241, 282, 297, 343, 376.
  Nathaniel, 149, 150, 228, 262, 318, 370.
  Phineas, 38, 42, 115, 238, 274.
  See Hayward.
Hibrows, Jabez, 303.
Highways, labor on, price of, 11.
  damage, 248, 271.
Highway, Surveyors, see Town Officers.
  Tax, 11, 40, 69, 108, 132, 145, 160,

General Index. 403

Highway Tax, 235, 260, 280, 300, 329, 344, 358, 376.
Hinds, Nehemiah, 13.
Hog Reeves, see Town Officers.
Holbrook, Asa, 298, 328.
    Jonathan, 307, 331, 352.
    Joseph, 332, 358, 359, 363.
    Phineas, 358.
Holden, 19, 66, 71, 150, 265, 287, 368.
Holidays, to be paid for by those participating, 22.
Holland, James, 263.
Holmes, Jacob, 10, 39, 42, 184, 231, 248, 256, 274, 282, 335.
Horses and Mules regulated, 385.
Horse sheds on the Common, 225, 281.
Horton, Silas, 330.
Hosey, ——, 172.
Hospital for inoculation, 211, 212.
Houghton, Nathan, 156, 175, 200, 217, 245, 270, 294, 352, 372, 388.
——, 161
House for Samuel Denny, 355.
How, Abel, 390.
    Ezekiel, 13, 42, 43, 45, 82, 105, 118, 184, 231.
    Ezekiel, Jr., 82.
    Joel, 38, 55, 105, 106, 145, 159, 205, 208, 211, 212, 218, 244, 248, 252, 259, 261, 279, 293, 306, 310.
    John, 178, 345
    Jonas, 349.
    Silas, 303, 324, 330.
Howard, Stephen, 380.
——, 65.
Hoyt, Robert, 65, 66, 218.
Hubbard, Samuel, 266, 368.
Humes, Rufus, 303.
Hurd, see Heard.
Hutchinson, Aaron, 17.
    Barth, 253.
    Lot, 212, 288,

I

Impost, petition for repeal, 22.
Incorporation of Second Parish resisted, 95.
Indian child, 31, 156, 175.
Inoculation for Small-pox, 211, 212.
Interest on Town Bonds, 237, 242.
Interest to be divided between the two clergymen, 242.
Intrenching tools, 243, 272.
Ipswich, 200.

J

Jacobs, Elisha, 390.
Jail, new, stone given to build, 35, 42.
Jarvis, Charles, 213.
Jenison, Israel, 58, 73, 221.

Jenison, Josiah, 185.
    Peter, 320.
    Samuel, 10, 42, 99, 121, 204, 238, 328, 356, 370, 380.
    William, 38, 42, 73, 74, 115, 132, 166, 169, 177, 178, 188, 189, 226, 238.
Jenks, Isaac, 334, 383.
Jerome, or Jrom, Barnabas, 253.
Johnson, Abel, 245.
    Amos, 40,
    Ashbel, 155, 181, 183, 190.
    Caleb, 336
    Daniel, 91, 127, 165, 168.
    Ephraim, 183.
    Joshua, 65, 116, 390.
    Joshua, Jr., 345.
    Micah, 38, 42, 43, 55, 59, 95, 97, 144, 190, 195, 318, 337.
    Micah, Jr., 145, 173, 247, 289, 304, 311, 338, 358, 373, 376, 380.
    Mrs. 16.
    Nathan, 24, 222, 224.
    Peter, 42, 61, 83, 119, 184, 231, 256, 282, 335.
    Samuel, 58, 238, 283, 313, 328, 335, 361.
    Solomon, 152.
    Thomas, 328.
    Timothy, 235.
    Willard, 336,
    William, 42, 92, 187. 238, 257, 278, 284, 383.
    Zachariah, 91, 127, 155, 245, 269–271, 294, 352, 372, 388.
Jones, Asa, 58.
    Phineas, 10. 32, 42, 99, 106, 128, 145, 160, 163, 177, 179, 205, 235, 237, 241, 252, 263, 274, 296, 297, 306, 311, 314, 327, 329, 331, 335, 338, 339, 344, 348, 359, 361, 363, 373, 384.
    Samuel, 378.
    Sarah, 166.
    Timothy, 116.
    William, 10, 275.
Jordan, Edward, 152.
Jurors to be selected, 301, 367.
Jury lists, 42, 43, 237, 238.

K

Kelley, Thomas, 330.
Kelso, John, 41. 300.
Kendall, ——, 115.
Kendrick, John, 161.
Kimball, Howland, 303.
    Nathaniel, 173–175.
King, Hon. Mr., 88.
Kingsbury, Joseph, 40, 43, 88, 105, 144, 205, 229, 237, 244, 248, 255, 259, 261, 271, 289, 331, 359, 261.

General Index.

Kingston, Paul, 319.
  Samuel, 132, 159, 238, 280, 286, 310, 338.
Kinsley, Martin, 148, 183, 206, 214, 239, 264, 285, 302.
Knight, Abel, 304.
  Edward, 24, 32, 43, 65, 81, 86, 91, 116, 127, 140, 155, 166, 167, 177, 190, 193, 236, 238, 283, 298, 334, 358, 383.
  Jonathan, 338.
  Josiah, 42, 178, 179.
  Josiah, Jr., 280.
  Reuben, 70.
  Thomas, 10, 31, 42, 80, 86, 107, 109, 113, 116, 254, 318, 325.
  William, 43, 86, 149, 194, 238, 269, 289, 361, 380.
Knower, John, 69, 91.
Kyes, Danforth, 156.

L

Lamb, Alvin, 303.
  Reuben, 231, 255, 283.
Lamper Hill, 368.
Larned, Jeremiah, 162.
Lathe, Benjamin, 248, 274.
Latin Grammar School, 301.
Lavens Elisha, 345.
Leicester, 84, 86, 150, 174, 263, 320, 369.
Leicester Academy, inducement for removal to Worcester, 157.
Leonard, Lymas, 325, 326.
Lincoln, Abraham, 38, 43, 144, 148, 177, 211, 237, 259, 261, 321, 331, 375.
  Benjamin, 75, 110, 137, 147, 162.
  Levi, 19, 32, 38, 46, 52–55, 58–63, 66, 75, 83, 110, 118, 119, 128, 168, 169, 171, 184, 188, 205, 231, 256, 274, 279, 280, 283, 285, 303, 312, 313, 333, 335, 349, 356, 360, 378, 383, 386, 387, 390.
  Levi, Jr., 304.
Lincoln's Mill, 388.
Linen manufactory, 152, 153.
Livermore, Isaac, 330.
Longley, James, 369.
Long Pond, 150, 221, 370.
Lovell, Ebenezer, 9, 11, 12, 16, 20, 29, 32, 34, 43, 44, 46, 58, 59, 115, 160, 178, 201, 203, 204, 217, 237, 250, 275, 321.
  Ezra, 151, 369.
  Jonathan, 10, 43, 105, 149, 150, 196, 219, 228, 261, 279, 318, 328, 369, 370.
  Jonathan, Jr., 259, 344, 358.
  ——, 158.

Lydia, an Indian, 31, 156, 175.
Lyman, Samuel, 213, 214, 233, 239.
  William, 213, 214, 233.
Lynch, Thomas, 330.
Lynde, Jonathan, 325, 326.
  Thomas, 43, 99.
Lyon, Ebenezer, 337.
  Josiah, 43, 118, 132, 185, 231. 255, 283, 334, 383.

M

Maccarty, Betsey and Lucy, 31.
  Rev. Thaddeus, 14, 15, 21, 26, 60; funeral expenses, 31, 32, 60, 218.
  Dr. Thaddeus, 16, 38, 81, 115, 167, 168, 188, 191, 227, 229, 251.
  William, 167, 188, 191, 227, 229, 251.
Mahan, John, 65, 70.
  Samuel, 238.
  William, 10, 61, 86, 113, 119, 185, 231, 255, 260, 261, 290, 291, 307, 337.
  William, Jr., 219, 221, 280.
Malt House, 12, 15, 52.
Mann, Elias, 203, 235, 237, 240, 256, 259, 261, 279.
  Joseph, 297.
Mansey, or Melvin, Jack, 253, 380.
Manufactory, 152, 153.
Map of the Town, 268.
Marlborough, 49, 200, 230.
Maynard, Stephen, 111.
  William, 330.
McClellan, David, 59.
McCracken, Samuel, 14.
  Archibald, 362.
McDonald, Richard, 91, 127, 155.
McFarland, Daniel, 288, 304.
  Ephraim, 10.
  James, 10, 43, 49, 58, 59, 66, 87, 108, 167, 179, 191, 237, 260, 279, 310, 327, 328, 331, 338, 340, 347, 353, 359, 362, 363, 379.
  William, 30, 58, 83, 109, 113, 115, 117, 118, 145, 175, 228, 232, 238, 255, 283, 286, 321, 362.
  William, Jr., 159. 204, 208, 359.
McKelhony, Jane, 65.
Mc Neal, ——, 31.
McNutta, Bernard B., 325, 326.
McPine, Rosanna, 8.
McPune, Sarah, 91.
Meeting House, repairs, 20, 24, 29, 31; care of, 79, 80.
Mellen, or Melline, John, 253.
Melvin, see Mansey.
Mendon, 388.
Merriam, William, 361.
Merrick, Pliny, 264, 271, 285, 302,

General Index.   405

Merrick, Pliny 333, 350, 360, 378.
Merrifield, Penuel, 305.
    Timothy, 304, 337, 368.
Militia to be compensated, 309.
Mill Brook, 51, 109.
Miller, Ephraim, 31, 32, 42, 58, 64, 67, 115.
    Hezekiah, 303, 305.
    Jacob, 277, 284, 313, 334, 383, 388.
    Joseph, 32, 38, 39, 42, 115, 325.
    Moses, 40, 42, 59, 144, 155, 194, 218, 228, 235, 238, 241, 251, 269, 282, 289. 294, 338, 339, 341, 346, 347, 352, 358, 362, 372, 380, 388.
Millet, Thomas Wheeler, 247, 275, 306, 328, 334.
Milline, see Mellen.
Mills, Luther, 289, 306.
    Thomas, 323.
    ———, 116, 177,
Millstone Hill, 35, 42, 120, 133, 135, 181, 186, 209, 210, 236.
Minister chosen, 77.
Ministerial, Land sold, 61, 62.
    Money, 13, 45, 57, 104, 105, 114.
    Proceeds, 118.
    Property, division of, 77, 98, 99, 104, 105, 143.
    Taxes, exemption from asked, 51, 54.
    Tomb. vote not to build, 139.
Ministerial and School Land, authority to sell, 215; report of committee, 276; accounts, etc., 13, 29, 48, 183, 186, 198, 207, 219; plan, 221; committee to lay out lots, 29, 33, 51; report of, 60, 61; vote to sell, 34, 72; Resolves concerning, 208.
Minute Men, 289.
Moore, Asa, 10, 43, 88, 286.
    David, 10, 43, 107, 109, 113, 128, 159, 166, 229, 233, 265, 266, 286, 298, 343.
    Ebenezer, 235.
    Ephraim, 128.
    Esther, 305.
    James, 132.
    Jesse, 265, 376.
    John, 39, 43, 87, 144, 237.
    John, 2d, 43, 87, 235, 238, 240.
    Jonathan, 273, 368.
    Lucy, 353, 373.
    Luther, 274, 358, 372, 379, 380.
    Major, 160.
    Mary, 200, 290.
    Molly, 49
    Nathaniel, 88, 146, 156, 194, 245, 273.
    Reuben, 287.
    Richard, 65.

Moore, Samuel, 43, 109, 113, 132, 145, 150, 190, 204. 228, 235, 237, 241, 319, 338,
    Serval, 304.
    Thaddeus, 87.
    Willard, 343.
    William, 152, 204, 259, 274, 288, 295, 304, 305, 344, 346, 361, 363.
    William, 2d, 345.
    ☞ The spelling of this name may have been confused with that of Mower, (q. v.)
Morse Isaac, 47.
    Joseph, 339, 347, 362, 380.
    Keziah, 353, 372, 388.
    Lansing, 254.
    Richard, 82.
    Willard, 294, 306, 383.
Mossman, Oliver, 161
Moving school, 81, 359.
Mower, David, 195.
    Ebenezer, 132, 204, 238, 241, 266, 280, 297, 311, 328, 338, 343, 357, 361, 368, 375.
    Ephraim, 17, 38, 59, 68, 144, 193, 209, 210, 256, 259-261, 266, 273, 276, 280, 281, 290, 297, 300, 314, 321, 328, 329, 334, 342, 357, 358, 366, 368, 369, 375-377, 382, 383, 387, 389.
    Ephraim, Jr., 388.
    Esther, 165.
    John, 38, 42, 43, 69, 133, 145, 160, 178, 179, 237, 344.
    Samuel, 10, 38, 42, 69, 86, 87, 107, 109, 113, 127, 132, 133, 145, 178, 179, 196.
    Thomas, 209, 210, 238, 334, 383, 388.
    ☞ The spelling of this name may have been confused with that of Moore (q. v.)
Munn, Susanna, 316.
Munna, Susanna, 49.
Murray, Alexander, 194.

N

Nash, Jonathan, 41, 42
Nazro, John, 13, 17, 27, 31, 42, 43, 56, 64, 66, 68, 74, 79, 82, 94, 99, 108, 115, 128, 167, 218, 226, 235-237, 240, 250, 281, 311, 321, 327, 329, 338, 339, 347, 390.
Negroes: see Brooks (Agnes).
    Glasgow (Simon).
    Hemenway (Jeffery and Scipio)
    Mansey (Jack).
    Trueman (Prince).
    Walker (Cato).
    Willard (Peter).
    Worthington (Cato).

Newhall, Elisha, 174.
  Phineas, 263.
  Timothy, 183, 206, 239.
Newton, Abraham, 156.
  Benjamin, 80, 178, 390.
  Elijah, 39, 80, 159.
  Francis, 254.
  Lucy, 371, 390.
Nichols, Alexander, 320.
  Israel, 18, 46, 110, 148, 162.
  James, 320.
  John, 254.
  Jonas, 105.
  Thomas, 39, 69, 156, 203, 269, 289, 294, 305, 306, 341, 347, 352, 372, 376, 380, 388.
  Thomas, Jr, 42, 87, 235, 238, 241, 311, 358.
Northeastern School District, }
Northern   "   " } 324,
North western   "   " }
Northbridge, 84.
Noyes, Asa, 73.
  John, 345, 383.
Oath of Allegiance, 112, 137, 179.
Ordination, Committees, 68.
Osburn, Israel, 325.
  James, 254.
Osland, Jonathan, 68, 87.
Overseers of the Poor, see Town Officers.
Oxford, 290, 309, 320, 323.

P

Packard, Anna, 19.
Paine, John, 131, 191, 274.
  Nathaniel, 38, 128, 133, 166, 173, 182, 193, 194, 213, 234, 236, 258, 260-263, 265, 271, 273, 276, 279, 280, 282, 284, 285, 287, 289, 290, 292, 296, 299, 300, 302, 309, 314, 327, 329, 333, 335, 342, 344, 346, 348-350, 353, 354, 357, 358, 360, 362, 363, 365, 366, 370, 373, 375, 377, 378, 381, 382, 385, 387, 389.
  Samuel, 267.
  Sarah, 49, 267.
  Timothy, 10, 12, 13, 16, 19, 27-29, 32-34, 38-40, 42-44, 46-48, 51-55, 60, 62, 64, 66, 69, 70, 72, 74, 79, 81, 89, 91, 106, 108, 110, 111, 115, 117, 121, 125, 128, 129, 132, 137, 138, 141, 142, 147, 148, 151, 153, 157, 159, 161, 162, 171, 176, 177, 179, 182, 183, 186, 197, 199, 204, 206, 207, 209, 213, 225, 227, 246, 250, 266.
Pall to be purchased, 139, 140, 173.
Palmer, Parker, 330.
Paper Mill, 331.
Park, Calvin, 380, 381.

Park, William, 217.
  See Parks.
Parker, Henry, 336.
  Joanna and Lydia, 127,
  Willard, 345.
  William, Jr., 10, 68, 343, 388.
Parks, John, 192.
  Reuben, 173.
  See Park.
Parmenter, Reuben, 315.
Parochial accounts, 129.
Patch, Henry, 70, 115, 158, 184, 203, 232, 235, 236, 238, 240, 257, 272, 300, 305, 306, 314, 317, 328, 336, 348, 349, 362, 364, 373, 376, 388.
  Joseph, 197, 257, 283, 287, 290, 291, 307, 308, 313, 334, 347, 363, 377, 381, 382.
  Joshua, 345.
  Nathan, 10, 14, 24, 38, 40, 42, 45, 55, 57, 60, 66, 70, 71, 73, 74, 82, 83, 88, 107, 110, 112, 114, 118, 127-129, 132, 138-140, 144, 145, 156, 157, 165, 166, 168, 169, 172, 175, 177-179, 182, 190-192, 194, 195, 197, 202, 207, 210, 211, 218, 222, 224, 226, 228-230, 232, 234, 243, 247, 249, 256, 271-273, 277, 283, 289, 292, 297, 298, 308, 319, 335, 382.
Paupers, 49, 65, 66, 80, 81, 91, 126, 127, 146, 154, 155, 172, 174, 175, 200, 201, 217, 245, 246, 269, 310, 324, 340, 352, 354, 372, 373, 388, 389.
Paxton, 71, 85, 86.
Payson, Thomas, 235-237, 240, 252, 329, 339.
Peck, Robert, 305.
Peirce, Abijah. 235, 260, 261, 304, 306.
  Byfield, 238, 298.
  John, 36, 38, 40, 42, 43, 48, 64, 70, 88, 97, 105, 107, 113, 151, 166, 210, 220, 237, 244, 245, 248, 263, 266, 274, 276, 305, 336.
  Josiah, 10, 12, 17, 58, 59, 69, 70, 105, 108, 143, 144, 271, 307,336, 337, 369
  Levi, 58, 159.
  Lyman, 303.
  Oliver, 70.
  The spelling of this name confused with that of Pierce.
Peirce's School District, 11.
Penniman, Peter, 137, 148, 162.
Pension, for Simon Glasgow, 234.
Perambulation of Bounds, see Bounds.
Perry, Josiah, 10, 40, 42, 68, 108, 238, 298, 304, 328, 257, 358.
  Moses, 163, 181, 238, 297, 300, 327, 342-344, 369, 376.

General Index.   407

Perry, Nathan, 10, 13, 14, 27, 29, 35, 39, 40, 42, 43, 50, 56–60, 64, 66–69, 71, 73, 77, 79, 84, 91, 93–96, 104, 105, 107, 109, 111–114, 116, 119, 122, 124, 126, 129, 131, 137, 139–141, 143, 144, 146, 148, 151, 153, 155, 157, 159, 160, 162, 165–167, 173, 188–190, 194, 195, 204, 227–229, 250, 251, 311, 315, 338.
Peters, Andrew, 214.
Petition to General Court, 21, 22.
Pew Bonds, 45, 83, 118.
Pews, proceeds of sale of, 14.
Phelps, Abigail, 156.
Phillips, Jonathan, 58, 320.
   Samuel, 206, 215, 216, 239, 264, 285, 349.
Philmore, George, 173.
Pike, Elijah, 303, 325.
Piper, ——, 116.
Plan of the town to be made, 268.
Plans of land sold, 63, 221, 277.
Plank for bridges, 49, 65.
Poor House, 324, 354.
Poor persons, see paupers.
Porter, Samuel, 279, 297, 327, 328, 331, 343, 357, 359, 376, 383.
Post Road, 207, 387.
Pottery, 12, 15, 51.
Pound moved, 34, 64.
Powder House, 294, 350, 388.
Powder to be supplied soldiers, 107.
Powers, William, 200.
Pratt, Henry, 254.
   Isaac, 70, 131, 320.
   Joel, 345, 371.
Prayer, day of, for re-establishment of ministry, 28.
Precinct established, 320.
Prentice, Samuel, 38.
Presidential Electors voted for, 142, 214, 312.
Princeton, town of, 156.
Prisoner boarded, 388.
Proprietors' Records referred to, 133, 187.
Public Monies, inquiry concerning, 88
Pulpit, committee to supply, 32, 33, 56.
   Support of, 26.
Putman, Amos, 42.
   Isaac, 108, 121, 328, 334, 362, 380, 383.
   James, 315.
   Jonathan, 295, 305, 337, 346, 348.
   Rufus, 18, 46, 75, 110, 111.

Q

Quigley, Adam, 361, 381.
   James, 17, 48, 49, 59, 81, 116, 127, 139, 141, 165, 175, 183, 193, 209, 227, 228, 251, 274, 304, 337, 347, 380.
   John, 161.

R

Ramsey, William, 253.
Rand Daniel, 358.
Randall, Benjamin, 353, 372, 388.
Ranks, Christopher, 286,
   John, 328.
Rawson, Edward, 150.
   Stephen, 303.
Raymond, Daniel, 152.
Read, or Reed, Benjamin, 27, 28, 44, 206, 285, 302, 333, 350.
   Ebenezer, 293, 297, 298, 306, 327–329, 331, 342, 343, 348, 351, 359, 363, 364, 371, 379.
   John, 380.
Record Book paid for, 66.
Records case for, 208, 218.
Representatives to General Court chosen, 21, 47, 78, 111, 119, 138, 151, 164, 186, 209, 241, 265, 285, 303, 333, 351, 365, 385.
   Instructions to, 24, 25, 90.
Representatives in Congress voted for, 141, 142. 147, 171, 176, 213, 233, 239, 279, 312, 356, 386, 387, 390.
Repudiation advocated, 22.
Rice, Asa, 370.
   Comfort, 105, 320.
   Elijah, 83.
   Elizabeth, 175, 195.
   Eunice, 275, 338,
   Gershom, 320.
   Jonathan, 40, 88, 122, 145, 147, 160, 166, 167, 172, 179, 198, 304, 315, 323.
   Judah, 161.
   Judith, 194, 311, 346.
   Lemuel, 38, 42, 83, 88, 118, 184, 231, 255, 284, 383.
   Luke, 260, 261.
   Luther, 177.
   Phineas, 320.
   Reuben, 173, 177. 199.
   Samuel, 240.
   Thomas. 39, 87, 132, 178, 204, 218, 236, 251, 280–282, 296, 311, 321, 329, 336, 346, 347, 372.
   Zebediah, 71.
Richardson, Charles, and Charles Jr., 320.
   David, 82, 117, 185, 231, 255, 284, 335, 382.
   ——, 173.
Rider, Deborah, Philander, Rebeckah, Sarah, 19.
Roads, alteration in, 146, 236, 237, 244, 248.
   discontinued, 41, 300.
   laid out, 35, 44, 71, 109, 146, 209, 210, 244, 286, 366.

Robbins, Nathaniel, 59, 60.
Roch, James, 295.
Rock blasting, 271.
Rockwood, Frost, 328, 343, 357.
Rope for the Bell, 32.
Roper, Daniel, 320.
Ruggles, John, 66.
Russell. Thomas, 239, 285.
Rutland, 287.

S

Salaries of Public Officers, 88.
Salisbury, Samuel, 31, 58, 76, 190, 229.
Stephen, 18, 31, 42, 43, 56, 58, 128, 163, 165, 173, 176, 190, 196, 202, 204, 229, 237, 243, 247, 271, 321, 363.
Salt Rheum, charge for curing. 82.
Sand, price of, 294.
Sargent, John, 263, 369,
Saunders, Henry, 303.
Savage, Francis, 200, 228, 347.
Sawyer, Aaron, 263.
Oliver, 369.
Scales for weighing hay, 309.
Schallhoss, Conrath, or Cornelius, 316.
School, Committee, 10, 19, 70, 95, 108, 116, 132, 145, 167, 179, 190, 196, 198, 205, 228, 236, 251, 274, 282, 289, 298, 305, 332, 347, 351, 361, 377:
Districts or Quarters, 30, 53, 79, 80, 96, 280, 323, 326, 341, 342.
Land, see Ministerial and School Land.
Money, 45, 58, 60, 64, 96, 159, 258.
Tax, 10. 40, 53, 70, 108, 145, 179, 205, 260, 282, 298, 301, 332, 343, 359, 377.
School House to be moved, 152.
School Houses, 30, 35, 50, 52, 53, 310; to be built, 326, 327, 331; committee to build, 331, 359, 365, 367, 370, 377; tax to build, 359.
New, report of committee, 384; tax for, 385; houses painted, 389.
in Center District, 390, 391.
Schools, 11, 26, 50, 52, 79, 81, 82, 132, 164, 225, 251.
See Grammar School, Latin Grammar School.
Scott, Reuben, 276.
Thomas 320.
Searl, Curtis, 303.
Second Parish disputes concerning division, 96, 100-104; request to be incorporated, 119.
Second Congregational Society, incorporation resisted, 95, 120.

Sedgwick, Theodore, 213.
Selectmen, see Town Officers.
Sever, William, 177, 182, 197, 247, 273, 297.
Nathan, 377.
Severy, Jacob, 57, 169.
Shays's Rebellion, soldiers in, 106.
Shepard, Thomas. 211, 235, 240, 246, 275, 328.
William, 214.
———, 353.
Shrewsbury, 65, 81, 150, 156, 174, 217, 262, 370.
Shuttlesworth, ———, 65, 165.
Sibley, Oliver, 352.
Sikes, John, 253.
Singletary, Amos, 110, 137, 148, 162, 183, 239.
Skinner, Thompson T. 213, 214.
Slater, Peter, 86, 178, 179, 238, 297, 298, 300, 376.
Small-pox, hospital for inoculation, 211, 212.
Smead, David, 214.
Smith, Daniel, 358.
David, 382.
Dennis, 191.
Elisha, 42, 87. 133, 144, 242, 271, 289, 328, 368.
Ephraim, 127.
Ezekiel, 235, 240, 336, 358.
Gideon, 70, 97.
Ithamer, 254.
Jacob, 152, 156, 161, 353, 361, 362.
Jacob, Jr., 172, 194.
John, 38-40, 42.
Laben, 235, 240, 280, 307.
Lowis, 251, 252, 274, 275.
Robert, 12, 20, 29, 42, 43, 70, 72, 77, 88, 133, 152, 167, 235, 237, 244, 248, 324, 358, 377.
Simeon, 274.
Solomon, 253.
Susanna, 243.
Smith's School District or Row, 11, 20, 70, 72.
Soldiers' bounty, 267, 268.
wages, 57.
Sore leg, price for dressing, 175.
Southeastern, Southern, and Southwestern School Districts, 323.
Southgate, John, 150.
Spalding, Eliza, 174.
Reuben, 194.
Spence, John, 16, 17, 49, 50, 65, 66, 80, 91, 155, 174, 200, 217, 245, 246, 255, 270, 294, 324, 340, 353, 354.
Sprague, Jesse, 320.
John, 19, 46, 75, 111, 137, 142, 171, 239, 264, 285, 302, 333, 350, 360, 378.

General Index. 409

Sprague, Joseph, 24.
  Miles, 338.
Springfield, 71.
Stables on the common, 198.
Stanton, John, 10, 12, 15, 33, 38, 42, 45, 50, 51, 61, 63, 69, 74, 80, 83, 116–118, 145, 158, 163, 165, 178, 184, 190, 195, 202, 204, 228, 232, 235, 227, 246, 256, 257, 259, 273, 277, 280, 282, 283, 297, 299, 305, 310, 313, 321, 334, 338.
State House, site for offered, 234.
State Officers voted for, 18, 46, 74, 75, 110, 136, 137, 147, 162, 206, 239, 264, 285, 302, 333, 349, 360, 378.
Stearns, (sometimes spelled Sterne,) Bezaleel, 79, 80.
  Charles, 38, 40, 42, 109, 151, 237, 259, 261, 286, 294, 296, 306, 307, 340, 344, 358, 359, 362, 373, 376, 379, 380.
  Daniel, 80, 144, 160, 235, 238, 241, 271, 371.
  Isaac, 161, 371.
  John, 80, 139, 146–148, 272, 337, 371.
  Jonathan, 339, 361.
  Josiah, 239, 264, 285, 302, 325, 333, 349, 360, 378.
  William, 58, 59, 371.
  William Jennison, 87, 190.
Stephens, Israel, and Jacob, 105, 320.
Sterling, 288.
Stickney, Joseph, 371.
Stiles, Jeremiah, 290, 304, 305, 353, 362.
Stocks, new, 245.
Stone, Benjamin, 167, 229.
  Calvin, 345.
  Jesse, 320.
  Jonathan, 115, 151, 320.
  Jonathan, Jr., 105, 265, 368.
  Joseph, 27, 28, 151.
  Ruth, 320.
Stone given to build the Jail, 35, 42.
Story, Rev. Daniel, 77, 98, 99, 117, 129, 135, 166, 167, 192, 196, 227; proposals to, 78; preparation for ordination of, 93–95, 122; relinquishes right to ministerial property, 122; day for ordination, 122; answer, 123; ordination reconsidered, 124.
Stoves for new schoolhouses, 385.
Stow, John, 298.
  Samuel, 161.
Stowell, Abel, 38, 40, 42, 65, 81, 165, 200, 204, 211, 238, 240, 251, 257, 278, 284, 309, 313, 335, 382.
  Benjamin, 19, 38, 42, 43, 69, 86, 87, 159, 163, 172, 174, 178, 179, 193, 200, 201, 217, 218, 228, 237, 250, 256, 282, 326, 331, 382.

Stowell, Cornelius, 38, 42, 43, 55, 83, 118 121, 145, 155, 174, 185, 190, 195, 232, 257, 278, 284, 335, 382.
  David, 58, 59, 280, 284, 313, 334, 382, 383.
  Elias, 238, 275, 306, 328, 376.
  Nathaniel, 331, 334, 344, 359, 382.
  Peter, 238, 277, 329, 334, 342, 383.
  Thomas, 20, 38, 42, 69, 108, 121, 145, 166, 212, 235, 238, 241, 257, 278, 283, 324, 335.
  ——, 34.
Stowers, John, 31, 38–40, 42, 83, 115, 118, 128, 196, 211, 266, 313.
  Thomas, 61, 62.
Stratton, Jabez, 328.
  Josiah, 150.
Stratton, (Town of,) in Vermont, 197.
Strayed animals recorded, 316–319.
Strong, Caleb, 278.
  Simeon, 213, 214.
Studley, Benjamin, 369.
Sturtevant, Jesse, 306.
Sullivan, Gov. James, 333.
Sumner, Gov. Increase, 302, 333, 349, 360.
Supplementary fund, 90.
Sutton, 47, 48, 57, 84, 262, 320, 369.
Swearing, fines for, 190, 227, 249.
Swine regulated, 11, 41, 70, 108, 132, 144, 159, 179, 183, 204, 235, 259, 280, 300, 329, 344, 359, 377.
Sylvester, ——, 369.

T

Taft, Bezaleel, 111, 302, 333, 350, 360, 378.
  Henry, 81.
  Jesse, 39, 41, 43, 68, 76, 108, 109, 113, 114, 117, 118, 126, 132, 140, 145, 148, 152, 165–168, 185, 231, 246, 255, 273, 283, 313, 334, 338, 383.
  John, 353.
  Timothy, 132, 160, 238, 259, 261, 262, 280, 368, 369.
Tainter, Abijah, 262.
Tanner, Capt. 153.
  Hilyer, 80, 133, 145, 146, 156, 194, 204, 237.
Tatman, Jabez, 86, 87.
  John, 19, 42, 87, 160, 205, 238, 252, 262, 282, 298, 305, 344, 380, 390.
Tatnick, 293.
Tatnick Hill, 71.
Tatnick School District, 207, 323, 384.
Taxes abated, 67, 75, 114, 152, 161, 199, 253, 303, 329, 345, 352, 371, 390.
Taxes, see Highway Tax, School Tax, Dog Tax, etc.
Taylor, Abigail, 156.
  Abraham, 40.

Taylor, Anthony, 217.
  Hollaway, 232, 256, 282, 334, 383.
  John, 13, 43, 45, 61, 83, 117, 119, 137, 232, 256, 282, 334, 383.
  Lydia, 58.
  Othniel, 75, 76, 183, 221.
  Stephen, 337, 346.
  Timothy, 161.
  William, 40, 43, 87, 117, 121, 139, 143-145, 155, 159, 167, 168, 174, 188, 196, 200, 210, 217, 221, 228, 235, 238, 241, 246, 269, 273, 274, 307, 311, 324, 327, 336, 337, 343, 347, 358, 363.
Temple, Jonas, 149, 263.
Thaxter, Benjamin, 259-261, 280, 282, 306, 331, 344, 359, 361, 377, 384.
  Francis, 298.
Thayer, George, 161
  John, 390.
Thomas, Amasa, 330.
  Benjamin, 354.
  David, 82, 117, 168, 169.
  Isaiah, 10 14, 38, 42, 43, 55, 62, 79, 83, 88-90, 118, 128, 168, 199, 211, 212, 237, 250, 266, 291, 308, 322, 347, 363, 376, 391.
  Isaiah, Jr., 338.
  Isaiah 3d, 345.
Tomb, Ministerial, vote not to build, 139.
Tombs on the Common Burying Yard, 29.
Torrey, Joseph, 65, 116, 238, 288, 299, 300, 306.
Town, Salem, 264, 285, 302, 333, 349, 360, 378. 381, 386, 387.
  William, 390.
Town Bonds, 45, 82, 83, 114, 117, 184, 230, 255, 282, 313, 334, 377, 382.
Town Bounds perambulated, 149.
Town Officers elected, 9, 39, 40, 68, 107, 131, 143. 235, 258, 279, 296, 327, 342, 357, 375, 376.
Tracy, Anna, 353.
  George, 92.
  Jesse, 354.
  Mrs. 49, 199, 201, 217, 294.
  Thomas, 64, 67, 168, 188, 253, 254, 291, 307, 347, 363, 368.
  William, 161, 200, 246, 247, 270.
Treadwell, William, 38, 43, 61-63, 69, 83, 118, 218, 252, 325, 326,
Treaty, Commercial, 321, 322.
Trespass on Town property, 236.
Trowbridge, James, 41, 99, 346.
  William, 40, 43, 49, 69, 91, 108, 115, 144, 155, 158, 177, 194, 195, 235, 244, 245, 264, 265, 275, 280, 297, 298, 331, 338, 342, 351, 373.
Trueman, Prince, 254.

Tucker Benjamin, 201, 229.
Tufts, Andrew, 38, 70.
  Walter, 178, 343.
Tythingmen, see Town Officers.

U

Upham, Jabez, 360, 378, 386, 387, 390.
Uxbridge 149.

W

Wagoner, John Jacob, 277.
Wait, Hannah, 49.
Waite, Nathan, 263.
Waldo, Daniel, 43, 56, 70, 88, 99, 128, 155, 168, 194, 218 252, 274, 310, 321.
  Daniel, Jr., 204, 238, 340, 341, 347, 391.
Walker, Cato, 26, 31, 35, 64, 67, 222, 224.
  Christiana, 91, 165.
  Joseph, 272.
  John, 38, 115, 126, 166, 178, 179, 185, 209, 232, 238, 344.
  Mary, 126.
  Sally, 127, 155, 175, 200.
  William, 358.
  ———, 353.
Walpole, Town of, 388.
Ward, Abigail, 337.
  Artemas, 18, 46, 75, 110, 137, 141, 142, 147, 148, 152, 170, 176, 213, 285, 312.
  Asa, 10, 39, 43, 217, 238, 260, 275, 280, 306, 311, 341, 346, 347, 361, 373, 380.
  Luther, 161.
  Phineas, 13, 45, 82, 117, 174, 185, 193, 231, 255, 284, 313, 335, 382.
  Samuel, 116.
  Uriah, 64, 66, 152, 168, 177, 188, 291, 307, 348, 363.
Ward's Bridge, 173.
Ward's Mill, 160.
Ward, Town of, (now Auburn), 91, 151, 175, 264, 265, 368.
Warden, Samuel, 34.
Wardens, see Town Officers.
Warner, Jonathan, 18, 46, 75, 110, 148, 183, 206, 214, 239, 264, 285, 302.
Warnings for Town Meetings, 205.
Warren, Charles. 161.
  Elijah, 349.
  James, 18, 75, 137.
Washburn, Seth, 18, 46, 75, 110, 137, 148, 162, 183, 239.
Washington, General, funeral honors to, 385.
Waters, John, 23, 59, 80, 115, 152, 153, 166, 167, 194.

General Index. 411

Waters, John, Jr., 166.
  Mrs. 371, 374, 390.
Watson, Oliver, 83, 118, 184, 232, 255, 283, 313, 334.
  Oliver, Jr., 118, 184, 232, 255, 283.
Welch, Caleb, 325, 326.
  John, 59, 139, 161.
  ———, 31, 32.
Wesson, Joel, 42, 87, 132, 190.
Western School District, 323.
Whayland, Thomas, 127, 128, 227, 246, 249.
Wheeler, Amos, 43, 181, 212, 238, 280, 338, 339.
  D. G., 362.
  Joseph, 14, 16, 33, 38, 49, 55, 59, 65, 72, 77, 81, 107, 112, 113, 116, 117, 122, 125, 127-129, 131, 135, 138, 142, 144, 146, 149, 150, 156, 158, 164, 167, 171, 172, 175, 178, 186, 192, 194, 201, 229, 238.
  Joseph, Jr., 174.
  Mary, 295, 306, 311, 336, 338.
  Theophilus, 107, 112, 131, 138, 143, 158, 178, 179, 200, 203, 211, 256, 283, 318, 321, 335, 357, 361, 363-367, 375, 377, 379, 382, 390, 391.
  Thomas, 10, 32, 43, 69, 70, 77, 78, 88, 95, 97, 99, 108, 109, 113, 122, 138, 166, 181, 184, 209, 210, 231, 235, 237, 241, 247, 251, 256, 273, 282, 283, 313, 382.
Wheelock, Joseph, 253, 254, 376.
  Josh, 304.
  Willard, 253, 254.
White, Anna, 155, 200, 217, 246, 269, 270, 295, 353, 356, 372, 388.
  John, 65, 99, 115, 238.
  Moses, 378.
  Nancy, 174.
  Nathan, 43, 86, 87, 159, 203, 235, 238, 241, 254, 279, 289, 357, 358, 375, 376, 381, 388, 390.
Whiting, John, 378.
Whitmore, Ebenezer, 303.
  See Whittemore.
Whitney, Amos, 259, 261, 337.
  Benjamin, 10 40, 131, 159.
  Benjamin, Jr., 10, 43, 116, 145, 159, 238, 359.
  Capt. 135.
  Daniel, 152.
  Ebenezer, 144, 159.
  Israel, 274.
  Joshua, 10, 19, 24, 40, 59, 69, 83, 87, 88, 107, 113, 118, 122, 131, 133, 158-160, 178, 179, 181, 185, 198, 209, 210, 225, 232, 235, 237, 259, 279, 281, 282, 286, 297, 299, 302, 328, 331, 342, 353, 354 359,

Whitney, Joshua, 362, 375, 378, 386.
  Samuel, 40, 43, 59.
  Timothy, 149.
  ———, 58.
Whittemore, Clark, 376.
  See Whitmore.
Whitton, Abel, 362.
Wigwam Hill, 183, 186, 187, 199, 207, 219, 249.
Wilder, Abel, 46, 75, 110, 137, 141, 142, 148, 162, 183, 206.
Wiley, Martha, 127, 140, 156, 166, 190-192, 196, 229, 269, 289.
  William and David, 325.
Willard, Isaac, 39, 59, 107, 109, 113, 235, 240, 297, 298.
  Isaac, Jr., 144.
  John, 39, 80.
  Joseph, 167.
  Nahum, 65, 92, 116, 166.
  Peter, 271, 353, 372, 373.
Williams, Ebenezer, 247, 259, 275, 334, 344, 379.
  James, 358, 376.
Willington, Ebenezer, Jr., 43, 58, 86, 121, 132, 144, 260.
  Ebenezer, 3d, 328.
  Ebenezer, 4th, 303.
  Daniel 10, 87, 108, 121, 159, 178, 179, 271, 275.
  David, 40, 298.
  John, 293.
Wilson, Eliza, 175.
  James, 305, 339.
Winter Hill, 368.
Wiser, James, 353, 363.
Wiswell, Ebenezer, 31, 43, 71, 107, 115, 387.
  Ebenezer, Jr., 144, 178, 180, 210, 238.
Withington, William, 390.
Wood, Joseph, 148, 360.
Woodbury, Bartholomew, 151.
Woodward, John, 82, 168, 188, 291, 307, 348, 363.
  William, W., 254.
Worcester, Leonard, 237, 256, 283, 310, 313, 321, 335, 344, 348, 354, 382.
Worcester County, vote on dividing, 350.
Worcester Magazine, 104.
Worthington, Cato, 253.
Wright, John and Patty, 315.
Wyman, Ross, 150.

Y

Young, James, 108.
  William, 10, 11, 17, 20, 24, 25, 27, 43, 60-63, 83, 95, 99, 113, 117, 119, 185, 266, 272, 290, 316, 320, 390.
  William, Jr., 178, 185.

www.ingramcontent.com/pod-product-compliance
Lightning Source LLC
Chambersburg PA
CBHW050610300426
44112CB00012B/1444

The One Religion:

Truth, Holiness, and Peace desired by the Nations, and revealed by Jesus Christ.

EIGHT LECTURES

DELIVERED BEFORE

THE UNIVERSITY OF OXFORD,

IN THE YEAR 1881,

ON THE FOUNDATION OF

JOHN BAMPTON, M.A.

CANON OF SALISBURY.

BY

JOHN WORDSWORTH, M.A.

TUTOR OF BRASENOSE COLLEGE;
PREBENDARY OF THE CATHEDRAL CHURCH OF ST. MARY OF LINCOLN,
AND EXAMINING CHAPLAIN TO THE BISHOP OF LINCOLN.

WIPF & STOCK · Eugene, Oregon

Wipf and Stock Publishers
199 W 8th Ave, Suite 3
Eugene, OR 97401

The One Religion
Truth, Holiness, and Peace Desired by the Nations, and Revealed by Jesus Christ
Bampton Lectures 1881
By Wordsworth, John
Softcover ISBN-13: 978-1-6667-6187-0
Hardcover ISBN-13: 978-1-6667-6188-7
eBook ISBN-13: 978-1-6667-6189-4
Publication date 10/11/2022
Previously published by Parker and Co., 1881

This edition is a scanned facsimile of the original edition published in 1881.